Using Internet Primary Sources to Teach Critical Thinking Skills in the Sciences

Recent Titles in
Libraries Unlimited Professional Guides in School Librarianship

Teaching Electronic Literacy: A Concepts-Based Approach for School Library Media Specialists
Kathleen W. Craver

Block Scheduling and Its Impact on the School Library Media Center
Marie Keen Shaw

Using Internet Primary Sources to Teach Critical Thinking Skills in History
Kathleen W. Craver

100 More Research Topic Guides for Students
Dana McDougald

Curriculum Partner: Redefining the Role of the Library Media Specialist
Carol A. Kearney

Using Internet Primary Sources to Teach Critical Thinking Skills in Geography
Martha B. Sharma and Gary S. Elbow

Using Internet Primary Sources to Teach Critical Thinking Skills in World Languages
Grete Pasch and Kent Norsworthy

Leadership for Today's School Library: A Handbook for the Library Media Specialist and the School Principal
Patricia Potter Wilson and Josette Anne Lyders

Using Internet Primary Sources to Teach Critical Thinking Skills in Mathematics
Evan Glazer

Using Internet Primary Sources to Teach Critical Thinking Skills in Government, Economics, and Contemporary World Issues
James M. Shiveley and Phillip J. VanFossen

Creating Cyber Libraries: An Instructional Guide for School Library Media Specialist
Kathleen W. Craver

Collection Development for a New Century in the School Library Media Center
W. Bernard Lukenbill

Using Internet Primary Sources to Teach Critical Thinking Skills in the Sciences

CAROLYN JOHNSON

Libraries Unlimited Professional Guides in School Librarianship
Harriet Selverstone, Series Adviser

LIBRARIES
UNLIMITED
A Member of the Greenwood Publishing Group

Westport, Connecticut • London

Library of Congress Cataloging-in-Publication Data

Johnson, Carolyn, 1949–
    Using Internet primary sources to teach critical thinking skills in the sciences / Carolyn Johnson.
      p. cm.—(Libraries Unlimited professional guides in school librarianship, ISSN 1074–150X)
    Includes index.
    ISBN 0–313–31230–3 (alk. paper)
    1. Science—Study and teaching—Computer network resources. 2. Internet in education. 3. Critical thinking.
  I. Title. II. Series.
  Q182.7.J65 2003
  025.06′5—dc21   2001023302

British Library Cataloguing in Publication Data is available.

Library of Congress Catalog Card Number: 2001023302
ISBN: 0–313–31230–3
ISSN: 1074–150X

First published in 2003

Libraries Unlimited, Inc., 88 Post Road West, Westport, CT 06881
A Member of the Greenwood Publishing Group, Inc.
www.lu.com

Printed in the United States of America

The paper used in this book complies with the
Permanent Paper Standard issued by the National
Information Standards Organization (Z39.48–1984).

10 9 8 7 6 5 4 3 2 1

Contents

Acknowledgments, Permissions, and Dedications

~~Dedicated to all of the brave and courageous astronauts,
their scientific accomplishments and endeavors~~

Thanks to my Greenwood Press editor Debby Adams, series editor Harriet Selverstone, and Libraries Unlimited editors Sharon Coatney and Carmel Huestis, for their editorial guidance, helpful suggestions and comments.

Thanks also to my mother, Anona Johnson, a former legal secretary, for her editorial assistance, advice, and encouragement.

Those who gave approval for my featuring their documents or Web sites, and who offered comments on my manuscript, are gratefully acknowledged as well.

Special thanks to: Eric Apgar (grand nephew of Virginia Apgar); John Batchelor, Goddard Space Flight Center, NASA; Yinon Bentor, creator and manager, www.webelements.com; Lauretta Burke, World Resources Institute; Ian Cross, Faculty of Music, University of Cambridge, United Kingdom; Jane Dietrich, editor, *Engineering and Science Journal* (at Caltech); Ann Druyan Sagan (through her assistant, Vickii Barry); Brenda J. Dunne, Princeton University, education director for the Society for Scientific Exploration, Young Investigators Program; *Flora of North America* Editorial Committee members John McNeil and Nancy Morin; Carmen Giunta, creator and manager, Selected Classic Papers from the History of Chemistry Online; Jacqueline Havelka, Life Science Data Archive project manager at Lockheed Martin on behalf of Judith L. Robinson, LSDA project manager and NASA official; Lisa Heineking (for Tobias Bodine, manager), Department of Communications, Institute of Noetic Sciences; David Hershey, teacher and author; Alan B. Howard, director, American Studies Program, University of Virginia; Eric Jones, Los Alamos Research Laboratory, New Mexico; Carol Krause, director, Division of Communications, Office of Women's Health; Lawrence M. Krauss, professor of astronomy and physics, Case Western Reserve University, Cleveland, Ohio; Meave Leakey, doctor of paleoarchaeology, and head of the division of palaeontology, National Museum of Kenya, Nairobi, Africa; Karen Lentz, of *Science Magazine* Online; Liz Linton, director, Gifts of Speech Online; Eric v.d. Luft, curator, historical collections, Health Sciences Library, SUNY Upstate Medical University, Syracuse, New York; Kamlesh P. Lulla, NASA official; George Margolin, inventor; Jessica Mathewson, manager, Library Information Resources, Information Center, American Foundation for the Blind; Marissa Mills, Human Genome Management Information System, Oak Ridge Lab, Tennessee; John Mosley, executive editor, *Planetarian: Journal of the International Planetary Society*; Joseph Mussulman, producer and principle writer, Discovering Lewis and Clark Web site; Karl J. Niklas, editor in chief, *American Journal of Botany*, and professor of plant biology, Cornell University; Zisis Papandreou, Web site creator and manager, online excerpts from *The Physics of STAR TREK*; John Patrick, associate professor of Biochemistry and Pediatrics, University of Ottawa, Canada; Anusha

Perera, NASA Peer Review Services; Prentice Hall, Upper Saddle River, New Jersey, via Michelle Johnson, permissions administrator; Jay Rasmussen, Lewis and Clark Archives and Lewis and Clark on the Information Superhighway Web sites; Erin Marie Renfroe, creator and manager, Erin's Emily Dickinson Pages (with Fred D. White's article "Science in the Poetry of Emily Dickinson"); Peter Russell, with Alan Morgan, University of Waterloo, Ontario, Canada, for http://www.whatonearth.org; Judy Scotchmore, former science teacher, now Director of Museum Relations, Museum of Paleontology, University of California; Lorna Shaw, MuSICA coordinator; Judy Harrison Smith, the Apgar Family Association; Rob Smith, assistant to Michael E. Gorman, manager, Alexander Graham Bell Papers Project; Deborah Parrish Snyder, chief executive officer, Global Ecotechnics Corp, Santa Fe, New Mexico; Richard K. Stucky, chief curator, Denver Museum of Natural History; John Talbot, Research Associate, University of Ottawa, Canada; Phaedra Thomas, coordinator, Young Women's Resource Center, Center for Young Women's Health, Children's Hospital, Boston, Massachusetts; David and Laurie Trexler, dinosaur discoverers; Roger L. Vance, editor in chief, The History Net; Mark J. Winter, University of Sheffield, United Kingdom.

1
Introduction

Stewart Cheifet, host of PBS-TV's *Computer Chronicles* and *Internet Café*, said that every Saturday when he was a boy he looked forward to going to a planetarium. It would have been great if a computer had been around in those days, he added, because he would have been able to use the Internet to check NASA Web sites for daily updates on astronomical and astronautical discoveries and activities even throughout the day.

This book is a guide to and navigation tool for discovering the wonders of life featured in that cyber world of today, especially in the sciences, including the space sciences—one of the sciences that tends to spark and sustain interest in students and curious people of all ages.

The Web sites with primary documents and authoritative data reveal what this more-than-machine, the computer (one could say a type of brain), has to offer students. Students can explore the wide world of science by finding out about scientists' ideas and discoveries, experiencing virtual field trips, virtually meeting scientists of the past and present and virtually observing them as if in actual time as they think, work, and write. Many of these explorations and experiences would be lost to them or difficult opportunities to achieve without the Internet, and without this book's questions and activities that serve as guides.

This book presents a variety of primary documents and sources of authoritative information that are online, including current topics updated constantly and available in real time from noted authorities. This has not been possible in traditional library holdings except, to a degree, through newspapers and magazines, but is now available via computers and the Internet.

Through the Internet, primary documents are now readily available and enable students to learn first hand about scientific ideas and discoveries in scientists' own words or authoritative detailed renderings of those ideas, rather than from paraphrased information that often may not convey well the intent of the original documents. In addition, the lesson questions and activities are aimed at pinpointing the essence and particulars of what the documents' authors wanted to convey.

Due to the chaotic nature of the Internet and the incomplete nature of most search engines, it is essential that students be directed or guided to particular Web sites, special Web directories, or science areas of general Web directories, to research their assignments. They would otherwise be doing endless searches, presented with thousands of sites that are irrelevant, out of date, or not authoritative.

General educational search directories such as http://www.edinformatics.com, www. academicinfo.net, www.about.com, and www.studyweb.com (now for subscribers), plus science sections of general Web directories such as www.google.com and www.yahoo.com, are helpful Web guides, as are, but more so, particular online science search directories cited in this book, such as www.scientopica.com, AstroWeb, BioTech, and GeoGuide. It is essential to go to online areas such as these because the search will be guided, not haphazard, and yet provide opportunities for serendipitous discovery, itself an aspect of scientific activity.

PRIMARY DOCUMENTS IN THE SCIENCES

Primary documents in science are those written by scientists, or transcripts of exact words spoken by scientists. They can be detailed notes of step by step thought processes revealing and documenting observations, experiences, experiments, or discoveries, providing evidence or proofs of suggested theories. They may be in the form of field notes, professional diary or journal entries, records of field activities, records of case studies, records of laboratory experiments or tests, charts, tables, scales, or graphs, papers reporting discoveries and prepared for presentation at professional conferences or as speeches at academic or public gatherings or transcripts of those presentations or speeches, articles written for scientific publications (e.g., professional journals or magazines) or other noted periodical publications on the subject and including reports of discoveries or step by step explanations of scientists' conclusions or views of aspects of the sciences in which these scientists work, letters written to other scientists or scientific organizations or to students or friends or family members or to other people interested in the scientists' work, transcripts of interviews, transcripts of audiotaped field trip notes or case studies, memoirs or autobiographies.

Primary documentation is sometimes considered to be data or information provided by organizations set up by a scientist, the scientist's family, or someone with whom the scientist worked. The organization could also be one with which the scientist is or was involved, or an organization that supports, even has adopted as its main view, a scientist's claims, theories, discoveries, or conclusions, all fact supported by observation, experience, experimentation, and testing.

SCOPE OF THE BOOK—In General

The collection of documents represented in this book is a result of what could be found on the Internet, and working from what was available on reliable Web sites, with basics in mind including particular scientists, subjects, and documents, that tend to be studied by or taught to high school students.

This book's chapters that are based on those documents are organized chronologically by historical periods from early to recent times. Chronological arrangement is continued within these historical periods by particular years identified as the times of the documents' publications or, as in early writings, approximate times when the documents were written. When more than one document was published in a particular year, the group of documents for that year is arranged alphabetically by title.

This book's chapters can be accessed in three main ways. First, access is by the Contents pages with chronologically arranged documents and alphabetized documents by years. Next, access is by primary subjects in a subject guide that begins the Appendixes. Lastly, access is by particular subjects, authors, and titles, in an index.

An appendix with several sections is also provided. It features summaries of Web sites (some referred to in particular chapters) and arranged alphabetically in sections from A through J. Section topics, all science related, include biographies and career sources, databases, questions and answers or ask a question, magazines and newspapers, and organizations with activities for students, plus science in the news, Web sites with subjects connected to science, Science Web directories and Web directories with science subjects, additional primary science documents and sites with authoritative scientific data, and additional Web sites of interest and importance.

Related Internet Sites which are features of the last part of each chapter include site urls and summaries of Web sites that are related to the subject of a chapter's main document, may be part of a chapter's question or activity that connects something at a related site to the chapter's main document, and may provide information on the main document's author, or more data on the author's work, or more on the subject of the chapter's main document.

SCOPE OF THE BOOK—In Particular

The documents referred to in this book represent various aspects of science that range from the birth of scientific thinking to the progression of many particular aspects of science through time.

This book provides chapters on documents by classic or fundamental scientists that provide a basic knowledge of the sciences, by scientists who reveal aspects of scientific thinking (discovering, creating, logical step by step experimenting and experiencing processes), beginning with early documents emerging from or through philosophic and religious thought, by scientists who aim to benefit society through the sciences, by modern scientists who are forging the sciences of our own time, by scientists who present the sciences with relation to life (e.g., environmental concerns, outer space related and space program connections to people on the earth; young people's health, healthy eating, physical activity; advances in the medical sciences), by scientists who aim to make the sciences understandable and interesting to the average person, and by scientists who provide introductions to science via popular subjects (e.g., dinosaurs, zoos, bird watching, space exploration, inventing, mysteries of science), or popular media (e.g., television, movies, radio).

The most important early scientists whose works are featured in this book include Hippocrates (and his start of Western civilization's medical guidelines and ethics), then Leonardo da Vinci and Copernicus (both re-evaluating early aspects of science as they were related to religious doctrine), then Roger Bacon, Francis Bacon, and David Hume (who, although centuries apart, evaluated aspects of science with relation to philosophic thought, and began thinking based on experience, experiment, and society). At the beginning of the seventeenth century, Carl Von Linne provided a foundation for modern science with his meticulous classification of plants and animals.

During and since those early times, there has been a variety of scientific documentation and output. There have been scientific journal articles by scientists describing their discoveries and processes (pure scientific activities and documentation), or discoveries in their fields of specialty and their parts in them; special charts, scales, and tables that illustrate particular scientific discoveries; scientists' speeches describing what they have done or discovered; interviews with scientists to make their work understandable, interesting, and applicable; scientists' magazine articles describing their experiences in the field and the scientific conclusions plus insights they acquired through those experiences; scientists' essays suggesting applications of their fields of specialty (e.g., in education, and in the real world, with the sciences' importance to everyday life and to civilization); people educated in a science who then provide insights into that science's contributions to society, and its scientists' contributions to society; people who have experienced a science or something science related and ramifications of it in life and society (e.g., a person with a disability), then providing insights (in a speech, interview, or article) into those sciences as they deal with their situations; presentations, articles, or interviews, designed to make the sciences interesting, understandable to, and usable by, people in general, and adaptable to life and civilization; and precise descriptions of scientists' works, claims, and theories by people in organizations dedicated to the scientists' fields of research, sometimes in translation.

Topics and subjects of historic documents from the ancient and recent past referred to in this book cover a wide range, including the medical sciences; the birth of science as it emerged from religion and philosophy yet still included them; early sciences such as medical practices, botany, and ancient astronomy; pure scientific documentation; applied sciences (those that directly help society); and bringing the sciences to average people.

Documents represented by questions and activities in this book are directed primarily to high school students and beginning college students, but there are also some items that will also be interesting to and useful with younger students. Elementary through junior high school students will likely be drawn to the chapters referring to documents on living animals, extinct animals, outer space and space exploration, inventions, special health related topics such as physical activities and healthy snack foods, educational field trips, scientific anomalies, and science featured in the media. Also likely to draw younger students' attention are three or more chapters in particular. One chapter (see the Apgar chapter) features a scientist's document plus a related site with an award winning essay by a young student who conducted her own experiment based on that document's scientific conclusions. Other chapters (see the Keller chapters) feature documents detailing in her own words an experience by a well known person when she was young. Yet another chapter (see the Faraday chapter) features a scientist's museum talk designed especially for demonstrating a scientific process to young museum visitors. These documents, and others equally interesting, are presented in the forms of writings or transcripts of spoken words by scientists and others who have experienced an aspect of science or something science related, e.g., animal behaviorist Jane Goodall, doctor-writer Michael Crichton, Virginia Apgar (a doctor researching newborn babies), scientist astronauts Harrison Jack Schmitt, Kathryn Sullivan, and Peggy Whitson, astronomer Carl Sagan who popularized his field, inventor George Margolin who invented some movie technology, and Helen Keller. Other documents likely to be of special interest to younger as well as older students are those by Jane Goodall, oceanographer Sylvia Earle, paleoarcheologist Meave Leakey, and doctor Elizabeth Blackwell, in which first experiences in their professions are revealed, plus Margolin's document in which he claims "An Inventor Never Grows Up."

Also included in this book are chapters referring to documents by lesser known scientists or documents connected to organizations, but nonetheless of high interest, including for example, items by the United States Olympic Committee, the Society for Scientific Exploration and its Young Investigators Program (on unusual aspects of science), the Young Women's Health Resource Center, American Heart Association's Nutrition Committee and its scientific statement on nutrition and children (including adolescents), the U.S. Surgeon General's report on physical activity and health with reference to adolescents and young adults, and the U.S. Department of Agriculture and its Food Guide Pyramid, plus items by scientist writers on science in *Star Trek*, and a technology inventor who worked on the movie *2001: A Space Odyssey*.

Other documents represented in this book that make science fascinating to people in general are represented by the writings of, for example, planetarium expert James G. Manning, paleontology expert Richard Stucky, astronaut Edgar Mitchell, and astronomer Carolyn Shoemaker, plus databases such as NASA's Life Sciences Data Archive, "Scientific Anomalies" in *Science Frontiers Digest Online*, and MuSICA: Music and Science Information Computer Archive.

Equally of interest are women and science, represented in many of the documents to which this book's chapters refer. They include a variety of documents by women scientists, ranging from a letter by Elizabeth Blackwell (the first woman doctor of the United States) to laboratory notes written into an article for a scientific journal by Marie Curie (the chemist and physicist who was the first woman to win two Nobel Prizes in science), plus a chart by Annie J. Cannon (the astronomer who developed a system to analyze stars and was prolific in recording stars' "fingerprints"). There are the landmark article by Virginia Apgar (the doctor who created the Apgar tests for newborn babies), field notes published in books or articles by paleoarcheologist Meave Leakey, a research document on botany in the twenty first century by Christine Mlot, a book's overleaf introduction by Sylvia Earle on experiencing the oceans and studying environmental concerns with relation to them, an article by Jane Goodall on her studies of chimpanzees and what humans can learn from them, a journal article by astronaut Kathryn Sullivan who recreates her field trip experience in her own words, interviews with educator astronaut Barbara Morgan, a letter from space by the first NASA science officer

Peggy Whitson in the International Space Station, along with a letter from space by Columbia Shuttle astronaut doctor Laurel Clark, and an essay by Carolyn Shoemaker (an astronomer who is the co-discoverer of the comet Shoemaker-Levy) who suggests why space is important to the earth; and more.

Pure sciences are represented by chapters that refer to documents by Albert Einstein, Marie and Pierre Curie, Francis Crick, Stephen Hawking, and others.

Applied sciences are also represented by documents on, for example, a design for a biosphere, practical aspects of botany, medical advances, DNA and the human genome, and practical uses of discoveries made during space exploration expeditions.

Controversial aspects of particular sciences are also represented and include for example, scientific anomalies, mapping the human genome, cloning, evolution versus creationism, science and the Bible, particular medical practices, medical ethics, scientists' responsibility to society, who actually is responsible for certain scientific theories or discoveries (e.g., evolution, DNA), and who is correct when there are several theories on particular scientific subjects (e.g., dinosaur extinction, evolution and natural selection).

CRITICAL THINKING DOCUMENTS

Directly, and indirectly, critical thinking in science is represented in all of the documents that are featured in this book, and are referred to in the questions and activities that accompany chapters' references to those documents. Documents that may precisely or directly be called critical thinking documents include Roger Bacon's "On Experimental Science," Francis Bacon's "Preface" to *Novum Organum*, David Hume's "On the Rise and Progress of the Arts and Sciences," Excerpts from Carl Sagan's "Science as a Candle in the Dark," or "A Critical Thinking Kit," Richard Feynman's "The Role of Doubt in Science," astronaut Edgar Mitchell's Keynote Speech on his experience while in space, that caused him to think in a new way and develop a unique viewpoint; and the documents at the Web site of the Society for Scientific Exploration—Young Investigators Program, in which, and where, unusual aspects, or mysteries, of science are explored scientifically.

FUTHERMORE

There are documents that reveal the emergence of a changing world starting after World War II, in the middle of the twentieth century, such as those by Vannevar Bush, Richard Feynman, and Linus Pauling.

There are also documents that characterize the time in which we live, and documents that suggest the direction science is going, will go, or may go, in the near and distant future. Note looks at the scientific accomplishments of space exploration endeavors and tentative suggestions on where the U.S. space program might be redirected in space exploration endeavors after the Columbia Shuttle tragedy. Note in addition astronomer Carolyn Shoemaker's studies of near earth objects and their effects on our planet, Stephen Hawking's millennium lecture, astronomer Carl Sagan's critical thinking guidelines, astronaut Edgar Mitchell's keynote speech on how his experience in space expanded his consciousness and altered his way of thinking, Francis Crick's research that points to the brain as the new scientific frontier in the new millennium, various scientists' views of the importance of the computer, and many scientists' answers with views on which aspects of the various sciences are of utmost importance to the United States and the world as life on our planet continues into and evolves during the twenty-first century.

IN CONCLUSION

And so, aiming to add to, enhance, and enrich the already fascinating experience of using the marvelous machine known as a computer, the goal of this book is to get students caught up in the best of what this machine has to offer and is capable of. The computer provides the opportunity for students to experience, through reading or hearing, the exact words or precise authoritative data that a scientific discoverer has written or spoken, and reveals through the marvelous methods of communication (words and language) humankind's awesome creative activities and thought processes that involve science. By guiding students to the online locations of those particular documents, and offering questions and activities that aim to make those documents' words and data meaningful to students by striving to bring to life scientists' ideas, and something of their personalities, this book aims to show students the marvels of the world of science through time, and the scientific wonders of the world in which students live, discover, and experience, while becoming aware of the wondrous opportunities that beckon their participation and contributions.

II
Ancient, Medieval, and Renaissance Eras

"Hippocratic Oath" and "The Law of Hippocrates"
(Fifth Century B.C.)
URL: http://ftp.std.com/obi/Hippocrates/Hippocratic.Oath

SITE SUMMARY: This Oath was probably first written around the year 490 B.C., by the Greek physician Hippocrates, one of Western civilization's first physicians who is often called the Father of the Medical Profession. The translation here was first published in *Harvard Classics*, Vol. 38 (1910), and became a public domain document in 1993. From Hippocrates' time, it has been the creed of basic principles by which doctors guide the ways they do their work. Many still follow his guidelines. "The Law of Hippocrates" elaborates on the principles of the "Hippocratic Oath."

DISCUSSION QUESTIONS AND ACTIVITIES

1. By which two ways did Hippocrates declare he would keep this oath? What did he say he would follow for the benefit of patients? What are the four things he said he would avoid regarding patients? What did he say he would keep secret?
2. Which two methods of instruction did he use, and suggest, for teaching the skills of the medical profession?
3. What was Hippocrates' opinion regarding a particular "treatment" involving women? How has the medical profession's viewpoint and public opinion changed toward this now controversial subject? Keeping the oath in mind, how do you think Hippocrates might react to the conservative viewpoint on the subject? Choose another controversial subject concerning medical ethics, such as euthanasia, the death penalty, or cloning, and formulate an argument for or against it. Include in your answer a quote or citation from the "Hippocratic Oath" and another oath or principle to back up your decision. (For some help, see Web sites cited in the Related Internet Sites section below.)
4. Check these Web sites: Oaths, Quotes and Prayers for Physicians; Principles of Medical Ethics; and A Revised and Modernized "Hippocratic Oath." (Find their urls as cited in the Related Internet Sites section below.) Compare Hippocrates' oath's original tenets with a modern version, present-day medical principles, and medical-related or health-related prayer.
5. Regarding Hippocrates' Law: Who are people who may have a title but are not really what the title says they are? What should a person be who wants to learn medicine? What is bad about "inexperience" in the medical profession, and why and how might it be said of other professions in general, and another profession in particular? Study the Law's paragraph starting:

"Instruction in medicine is like the culture of the productions of the Earth. . . ." Think of other ways to apply this paragraph's metaphors. Consider the questions above (about what a person should be, and inexperience) with reference to a particular profession and the Web site on Professional Ethics. (Its url is cited in the Related Internet Sites section below.)

6. Look at medical ethics of the past and present, in general, and on one medical subject, at sites noted in Question/Activity no. 4 above and at sites such as "Hippocrates and Medicine in the Third Millennium"; Ethics Connection; and "Interlife Pro-Life Resources." (Find online as indicated in the Related Internet Sites section below.) Compare, contrast, and comment on what you find out.

7. Choose a particular medical situation, such as surgery, organ donations, disaster victims' treatments, special tests during pregnancy for conditions that endanger physical or mental health in a family's history, or an amniocentesis test during mid-life pregnancy. Imagine you are a doctor, a patient, or a patient's relative. Make a decision regarding the situation. Support your decision, quoting from a medical oath, principle, declaration, or prayer, found at sites cited in the Related Internet Sites section below.

8. Anthropologist Margaret Mead is quoted at the "Hippocrates and Medicine in the Third Millennium" Web site (its url is cited in the Related Internet Sites section below.) How did she refer to the medical profession and doctors with reference to the primitive world and the civilization of the ancient Greeks? What did she believe is the duty of society with respect to physicians? What did she say is a "priceless possession"?

9. Read articles by Abraham Lincoln, Carl Sagan, and Ann Druyan. (Find online via links at edinformatics.com as stated in the Related Internet Sites section below.) Noting complexities they saw with reference to the subject, comment on each well-known author's view on abortion, and provide quotations from what they wrote.

RELATED INTERNET SITE(S)

"Hippocrates and Medicine in the Third Millennium"

http://www.johnpatrick.ca/papers/jp_hippoc.htm

This article, by Dr. John Patrick, Associate Professor of Biochemistry and Paediatrics, University of Ottawa, offers pessimistic and optimistic views on Hippocrates' Oath and Law as they are or have been ignored or adapted and applied in modern times. Note the article's sections: Oaths versus Codes, Physician/Patient Relationships, Trust, The Sanctity of Life, and Transcendence. Note the quotation by U.S. anthropologist Margaret Mead, revealing her views of physicians with reference to the primitive world and ancient Greek civilization, society's duty to physicians, and a "priceless possession."

Principles of Medical Ethics (2001)

http://www.ama-assn.org/ama/pub/category/2512.html

Standards of conduct that define physicians' behavior toward patients. Established by the American Medical Association's Council on Ethical and Judicial Affairs.

Oaths, Quotes, and Prayers, for Physicians

http://members.aol.com/rnmlc/spiny.html

A doctor provides this collection of medical people's comments, quotations, and prayers related to health and medical conditions. Among the people are author-doctor William Carlos Williams. Included are the "Prayer of Maimonides" (by a twelfth century physician, translated 1917), and a 1983 version of the 1948 "Declaration of Geneva."

Biotechnology and Health Care Ethics at Ethics Connection

http://www.scu.edu/SCU/Centers/Ethics

This section of the Web site for the Markkula Center for Applied Ethics, at California's Santa Clara University, offers an articles database on health care ethics. Also note links to "browse related websites" and "practicing ethics."

Professional Ethics Links

http://www.chowan.edu/acadp/ethics/professional_ethics_links.htm

In this area of the Web site for the Center for Ethics at Chowan College, Murfreesboro, North Carolina, there are links to information on organizations, and standards of conduct or ethics, in various professions, such as environmental sciences, engineering, education.

A Revised and Modernized Version of the "Hippocratic Oath"

http://www.artsci.wustl.edu/~focus205/biomed/oath.htm

A version of the "Hippocratic Oath" approved by the American Medical Association.

Ancient Medicine/Medicina Antiqua

http://www.ea.pvt.k12.pa.us/medant

Note alphabet links to online documents, such as E for essays (including "Hippocrates: The Greek Miracle in Medicine"); R for resources online; and H for hypertexts of writings by Hippocrates and Galen (thought of as the physician who bridged the ancient and modern worlds of medicine while and after he lived during the first century A.D.).

Society: Issues: Abortion

http://www.edinformatics.com (type abortion in search box, click search button)

Click "Society: Issues: Abortion" link for links to pro-choice and pro-life views, the abortion issue as a dilemma, and alternatives to abortion. Note links to *Atlantic Monthly* magazine online items; articles online elsewhere (i.e., "Abortion in Law, History, and Religion"; "History of Abortion in the U.S."; Carl Sagan and Ann Druyan's "Is It Possible To Be Both Pro-life and Pro-Choice?"; "On Abortion: A Lincolnian Position"). See also links to InterLife Pro-Life Resources (with documents on the pro-life stance against abortion, euthanasia, and cloning); and Planned Parenthood of America Policy Statements (with pro-choice stances on abortion not known, thought of, or available in Hippocrates' time; and speeches such as "Responsible Choices").

"Women's Choices in the Western World: A Comparative Analysis" by Johanna Wilson

http://www.urop.uci.edu/Journal98/JohannaWilson/FramePage.html

Looks at various views of abortion, including, on page two, fourth paragraph, to the right, data on a long-held conservative viewpoint still advocated by some people.

Excerpt from Proclamation Three in "Is Abortion Really So Bad?" by Dr. J.P. Beeke

http://hometown.aol.com/twarren13/abort.html (scroll to last third of Web page)

See Proclamation's paragraphs six and seven. Note comment on "One way of catching class attention" to learn of a medical journal's classic case report (of medical students asked for recommendations on an abortion for parents with handicapped children, then discovering that an approval would have meant terminating the composer Beethoven).

"On Experimental Science"
Roger Bacon (1268)
URL: http://www.fordham.edu/halsall/source/bacon2.html

SITE SUMMARY: This translation of an excerpt from philosopher scientist Bacon's *Great Work*, also known as *Opus Maius*, reveals Bacon's logical reasoning that accompanied his experiments and experience. The work is considered to be a model that features the earliest appearance of steps and ways of thinking which have become fundamental and essential to scientific investigation and the thought processes involved. It is reproduced in the Fordham University Web site's *Medieval Source Book Online*.

DISCUSSION QUESTIONS AND ACTIVITIES

1. What, according to Bacon, does not happen without experiment? (Hint: Study the document's first paragraph.)
2. See the second paragraph. What, according to Bacon, are the two modes of acquiring knowledge? What does the first mode do, and not do, unless it does what? Tell what happens if the first mode, but not the second mode, is not pursued. Read Bacon's statement starting "Even if a man that has never seen fire, proves," then, keeping this comment in mind, think of another example in which "argument is not enough, but experience is."
3. What did Bacon "speak here of"? Did he agree or disagree with Aristotle? Explain.
4. See paragraph four, sentences one through seven, and nine through eleven. What do some authors do, according to Bacon, that cause readers to believe what is written? What is neglected and what happens then? Identify two examples that Bacon uses (e.g., one involving a diamond, or water freezing). What do these examples show? (Note: "a diamond" is misspelling "adamant.")
5. See paragraph five. What are two kinds of experience, according to Bacon? Explain. Note which kind of experience Pliny wrote about in his *Natural History*, and what example he gave. Which kind of experience did the people "who first gave science to the world" have? What is "in accordance with" what Ptolemy said? Why may one kind of experience conflict with generally accepted modern views, support what some people today think, and, in a particular way, show regained acceptance in some parts of today's scientific community? (Hint: See paragraphs six and seven. Consider one, two, and five of the "seven degrees of inner experience.")
6. See paragraph eight. What, did Bacon say, is "entirely unknown by the common people"? What can he not convince them of, unless he does what? Identify six things that will "enable . . . us to find out," according to Bacon, if he does what is referred to just above? What will happen then?
7. Some scholars' comments about this work suggest that a better translation of this work's title would be "On Experiential Science." Why?

RELATED INTERNET SITE(S)

Roger Bacon in Hyper History Online Timeline

http://www.hyperhistory.com

(Click Hyper History Online link.) Click the People link on the left, then select the years 1000 to 1500 on the right. Find and click Roger Bacon in a green science code name box in the timeline to get to a brief biographical sketch about Bacon, plus a link to another of his writings in translation ("Despair Over Thirteenth Century Learning" at the *Medieval Source Book Online*).

Roger Bacon, 1214 to 1294

http://www-history.mcs.st-and.ac.uk/Mathematicians/Bacon.html

The authors, J.J. O'Connor and E.F. Robertson of St. Andrews College in Scotland, feature biographical data on Bacon, with quotations, about the gradual growth of his interest in science. They comment on Bacon's writing something like a grant proposal (which a scientist might write today) to Pope Clement IV for "an encyclopedia of all sciences" that would be written by a group of scholars. A misunderstanding caused Bacon to do the work himself, which resulted in the *Opus Majus* and two other works: the *Opus Minus* ("Smaller Work") and the *Opus Tertium* ("Third Work").

Fourth Part of the *Opus Maius* by Roger Bacon

http://feature.geography.wisc.edu/woodward/bacon.html

In this 1996 rough translation by Herbert Howe of this part of the *Great Work* (with "sections of interest to geographical thought"), Bacon advocated gaining "factual knowledge of the phenomena of the heavens" while "considering the study of the heavens from the point of view of theology."

Manuscripts of Leonardo da Vinci
(1469–1518)
URL: http://www.museoscienza.org/english/leonardo/manoscritti.html

SITE SUMMARY: This site is provided by the National Museum of Science and Technology in Milan, Italy. It features a detailed history of the ten Leonardo da Vinci manuscripts, including for each one its name, current location, dates when written, and subjects. It contains links to Life of Leonardo, Leonardo on the Net, Leonardo's Machines, and Gallery with his drawings. The links next to the manuscripts' titles lead to the home pages of the institutions where the manuscripts are found.

DISCUSSION QUESTIONS AND ACTIVITIES

1. State the present title (and past title or titles, if any) for each of the ten manuscripts, the subjects (for text and illustrations) that each one features, dates for each, and names of owners (institutions or persons) of the present, and past.

2. Read, then provide, the precise description of Leonardo da Vinci's ideas on inventors and inventing, at the Inventors Workshop Web site. (Its url is cited in the Related Internet Sites section below.) Next, go to one of these invention Web sites: Medieval Technology Pages, National Invention Hall of Fame—Index to Inventions, Smithsonian Institution—Inventors and Inventions—Selected Links, International Federation of Invention Associations—Links to Articles, etc., Untimely Inventions, Community of Science, Inc.—U.S. Manual of Patent Classification, or Mothers of Invention. (Their urls are cited in the Related Internet Sites section that follow; in this book's chapter featuring George Margolin's "An Inventor Never Grows Up" which is an article in the Exploring the Inventor's Mind section of the *America's Inventor* online magazine; or in this book's Appendix B.) Choose an invention. Using da Vinci's basic ideas on inventing, describe the invention, and, if possible, a new yet related invention.

3. See the online news article "Manuscript Illuminates the Mind of a Genius" by journalist Regina Hackett. (Its url is cited in the Related Internet Sites section below.) To what is Hackett referring when she comments on the *Codex Leicester* and Leonardo, with the phrases "a magpie compilation" and "unique records of. . . ." Complete these comments by Bill Gates in Hackett's article, starting "The notebooks reflect. . . ." Cite two comments from the ones referred to just above; one by Gates, and one by Hackett. Apply each to something in the *Codex Leicester* manuscript or another da Vinci manuscript, translated or paraphrased. (Hint: See quotations/ paraphrases of Leonardo's words in Hackett's article, in areas of this chapter's main Web site: Manuscripts of Leonardo da Vinci, or at these Web sites whose urls are cited in the Related Internet Sites section below: *Leicester Codex*—A Masterpiece of Science—AMNH Exhibit Online, or Leonardo da Vinci (the *Codex Arundel*) at the British Library Online.)

4. See Hackett's article "Manuscript Illuminates the Mind of a Genius" found as cited in Question/Activity no. 3 above. According to Hackett, what is "essentially a medieval notion" and what did da Vinci do with it, with reference to sciences?

5. Visit the Leonardo Da Vinci Competition Web site. (Its url is cited in this book's Appendix G.) Read: Why Da Vinci? The Exam, How to Participate, Previous Year's Exams and Solutions, and a quotation by da Vinci. Think of something you could contribute to the competition. Describe it following Competition rules. (Tip: For help, see the Idea Finder—Contents Web site. Its url is cited in the Related Internet Sites section in this book's chapter featuring Margolin's article [found as stated in Question/Activity no. 2 above].)

RELATED INTERNET SITE(S)

Leonardo da Vinci Notebook (The *Codex Arundel* Manuscript) in British Library Online

http://www.bl.uk/collections/treasures/davinci.html

A virtual duplicate of two pages from *A Notebook of Leonardo da Vinci* (one of the manuscripts), plus data on subjects da Vinci wrote about on these pages, and information on the manuscript's odyssey.

Some Leonardo da Vinci Thoughts Translated and Quoted

http://www.cybernation.com/victory/quotations/authors/quotes_davinci_leonardo.html

This site features quotations on the subjects of genius, mind, rest, and understanding.

Leicester Codex—A Masterpiece of Science—AMNH Exhibit Online

http://www.amnh.org/exhibitions/Codex/topics.html

This site relates to an exhibit at the American Museum of Natural History featuring the only da Vinci manuscript part owned by an individual (Bill Gates) rather than a library or museum. It contains pages with reproductions of da Vinci's drawings, his original manuscript pages in Italian (written in his unique reverse mirror image style), and his words (in translation or paraphrased) on the moon and the sky page featuring his thoughts on the moon's light. See also other Web pages on the manuscript (e.g., on Nature and Movement of Water, From the Rivers to the Oceans, Measuring and Using Water, and Fossils and the Flood). Note also links to Codex Main and Science.

"Manuscript Illuminates the Mind of a Genius"

http://seattlep-i.nwsource.com/leonardo/genius.html

Journalist Regina Hackett, in a 1997 issue of the *Seattle Post-Intelligencer*, describes the Leonardo da Vinci manuscript known as the *Codex Leicester*, its travels through time, how Bill Gates acquired it, and where and how it has been exhibited since Gates bought it. She provides quotations in translation from the manuscript, a paraphrased translation of material discussed in the manuscript, and a quotation by Gates about da Vinci and the manuscript. Links lead to the Seattle Art Museum 1998 exhibit Leonardo Lives, plus Leonardo's Lab, Life and Legacy, Resources, and excerpts from the *Codex*.

Leonardo da Vinci at Inventors Workshop

http://www.mos.org/sln/Leonardo/InventorsWorkshop.html

Paragraph four of this site provides a succinct, clear description of da Vinci's "unique attitude about machines" (actually basic aspects of inventing and inventors). Paragraph one reveals his first involvement with machines. Paragraph five reveals what he was the first to write. Paragraph six reveals how his ideas are still of use five hundred years after they were put on paper. Note also links to Visions of the Future, Elements of Machines, and Leonardo's Mysterious Machinery.

Medieval Technology Pages

http://scholar.chem.nyu.edu/technology.html

Access to information on technology that existed, and was known, between 500 A.D. and 1500 A.D., is by clicking links to a timeline, a subject index, or references.

"Dedication" to *The Revolutions of the Heavenly Bodies*
Nicholaus Copernicus (1543)
URL: http://ragz-international.com/copernicus.htm

SITE SUMMARY: This document is a translation of Copernicus' "Dedication" essay that accompanies his treatise describing the scientific theory stating that the sun, not the earth, is the center of the solar system, an idea for which he has been remembered through time. The "Dedication" is like a letter in which Copernicus "talks" to the person to whom he chose to dedicate his publication. He reveals what his publication is about and his reasoning behind it. When he wrote "men of philosophy" or mathematicians, and philosophy, he was actually referring to scholars or other thinkers and thinking logically. This online translation is a reproduction of the one in the 1910 *Harvard Classics* print edition.

DISCUSSION QUESTIONS AND ACTIVITIES

1. Identify how long it was after Copernicus wrote "the commentaries in proof of [the earth's] motions" that he allowed his ideas to be published, and why? Tell reasons why he at last allowed his ideas to be published. Compare these situations (i.e., time between thinking of, then writing, then publishing, scientific ideas) with the way it happened in his day and the way it happens today. Consider the consequences of the way Copernicus handled the situation if he did it that way today.
2. In which metaphorical way did Copernicus refer to "drones among bees"? Apply this metaphor to something in your life, then to something around you, then to something in the present world, and then to something in the past. For each case, explain how this metaphor applies, and why to avoid it.
3. Why did Copernicus first decide to "look for another way of reckoning the movements of the heavenly bodies"? Elaborate on your statement, including his comments, and emphasizing his two main reasons.
4. Identify Copernicus' metaphor about a human body. Explain how he applied it to what is referred to in Question/Activity no. 3 above. What did he say about other people's "process of demonstration"? Describe what he said about and concluded from "fixed principles." Extra Activity: Think about what is referred to in the first parts of this Question/Activity just above. Apply each reference in a general way to something you know and to something in science in a successful way, and in an unsuccessful way. (Note: Support your choices with explanations.)
5. What disgusted Copernicus? What did it cause him to do? What did he discover? Provide quotations. Include references that he cited to two common things, then explain why and how he referred to them.
6. How did Copernicus include thinkers of the past in his study involving his idea? Why did he then decide to "postulate" something else? What did he postulate, how, and what did he discover as a result of his postulating? State what he "therefore" described in his first book, and in his other books. What did he not doubt with reference to other learned people? Why? (Note: See also the "Dedication" translation in the History Guide when answering. Its url is cited in the Related Internet Sites section below.)
7. Study the Dedication's last three paragraphs. What had Copernicus found "by many and long observations"? (Hint: Note the sentence with the phrases that follow "if," "not only," "but," and "that.") Extra Activity: Think of and describe a science related situation other than his example. Apply to that situation his way of thinking as these phrases show.
8. Study the Dedication, identify to whom Copernicus dedicated his work, and tell why. Next, see the Web site featuring the article "When the Earth Moved, Copernicus. . . ." (Its url is cited in the Related Internet Sites section below.) Tell what this article says about Copernicus and

his giving credit with reference to his treatise. Extra Activities: Imagine that you have made two discovery in science, and have written about what you discovered. Describe your "discoveries." (Note: One "discovery" should be in a science known during or just after Copernicus' time. The other "discovery" should be in a science of a time later than Copernicus' time [e.g., from the nineteenth, twentieth, or twenty-first century].) (Hint: Find information to help with your "discoveries" at the Web sites whose urls are cited in this book's Appendix B.) Choose someone of note to whom you would dedicate what you have written. Write a "dedication" in which you "talk" to that person as you explain why you chose her or him.

9. With the "When the Earth Moved . . ." article (cited in Question/Activity no. 8 above), the *Polish American Journal* honored Copernicus, a native of Poland. Choose a scientist from a nation that is a place of ethnic origin or heritage for you, your family, or your ancestors, or else a United States scientist who traces her or his ethnic origin or heritage to a nation to which your family traces its roots. Explain what this scientist has done for people in general, and for her or his nation of ethnic origin or heritage. (Hint: For information, see Web sites featuring scientists with ethnicity noted or searchable, such as Scientists at the Best Source for Canadian Science, and Eric Weisstein's World of Scientific Biography, whose urls are cited in this book's Appendix B.)

RELATED INTERNET SITE(S)

Nicholaus Copernicus

http://www-history.mcs.st-andrews.ac.uk/history/Mathematicians/Copernicus.html

Originating in Scotland at the School of Computational Science of the University of St. Andrews, this site has a 1995 biography of Copernicus by J.V. Field, president of the Da Vinci Society and research fellow at the Royal Institution. There are links to a list of books and articles on Copernicus, quotations, more information on related topics (e.g., Greek astronomy, a brief history of cosmology, orbits, and gravitation), other biography and encyclopedia Web pages.

The Copernican Revolution

http://phyun5.ucr.edu/~wudka/Physics7/Notes_www/node38.html

Click Copernican Revolution at the site From Middle Ages to Heliocentrism to find out how the publication of Copernicus' treatise "The Revolution of Celestial Spheres" ("De Revolutionibus Orbium Coelestium") caused the sixteenth century to be what Jose Wudka, a faculty member of the Physics Department of the University of California, Riverside, calls a "watershed in the development of Cosmology."

"When the Earth Moved, Nicholas Copernicus Changed the World"

http://www.polamjournal.com (click online library link)

Click the biographies link, then the Copernicus link, to find this article from the February 1993 *Polish American Journal* published on the occasion of the four hundred and fiftieth anniversary of the publication of "On the Revolution of the Heavenly Spheres" ("De Revolutionibus Orbium Coelestium"). It describes why Copernicus is thought of as the Father of Astronomy and a Sixteenth Century Renaissance Man and how he moved the earth and initiated great thinking.

Galileo's Considerations on the Copernican Opinion (1615)

http://home.mira.net/~gaffcam/phil/galileo.htm

In this detailed letter, meant for average people, Galileo offered support for the controversial Copernican viewpoint as he explained how the viewpoint is "indubitably certain" and is based on "the most correct judgment." He also commented on why ancient thinkers might have thought the other, long-held viewpoint, was true.

"Hamlet's Transformation"

http://www.jmucci.com/ER/articles/usher

This article, in the *Elizabethan Review Online*, is by Peter Usher, professor of astronomy and astrophysics at the Eberly College of Science, Pennsylvania State University. It is a look at the Copernican Revolution as reflected in Shakespeare's *Hamlet*. Usher claims that "*Hamlet* manifests an astronomical cosmology that is no less magnificent than its literary and philosophical counterparts." Footnote no. 5 refers to other articles about Hamlet and astronomy, including the article "Hamlet and the Infinite Universe," an excerpt from an article in *Bulletin of the American Astronomical Society*, 28, (1996), 1305, and now online in the Online Research/Penn State Journal, 18, no. 3, (September 1997), at http://www.rps.psu.edu/sep97/hamlet.html.

Excerpts of Copernicus' "Dedication" to *The Revolutions of the Heavenly Bodies*

http://www.historyguide.org/earlymod/dedication.html

This History Guide Web page features a 1972 translation, plus links to information on The Copernican Model, Copernican System, translations of *The Revolutions of the Heavenly Bodies*, and biographies of Copernicus.

III
Seventeenth Century

"Preface" to *Novum Organum*
Francis Bacon (1620)
URL: http://history.hanover.edu/texts/Bacon/novpref.html

SITE SUMMARY: This writing, translated by Basil Montagne in 1854, is the Preface to the second part of the three volumes of Bacon's work known as *Novum Organum*, or *The Works: True Suggestions for the Interpretation of Nature*. It is provided by the Hanover Internet Project and features Bacon's revealing new and basic scientific principles that are actually the foundation of scientific thinking. It is said that this work and its principles are a basic reason for the establishment of the Royal Society, the first scientific organization.

DISCUSSION QUESTIONS AND ACTIVITIES

1. See paragraph two, noting the last third of it as the main point. What did Bacon say about a process of the mind, and things on "matters intellectual"? To what did he compare logic, and how did he view this comparison? Do you agree with what he said on the subjects referred to in his comments on "matters intellectual" and logic? Why or why not? Provide your own example using his metaphor.

2. Read paragraphs five and six. What are the two things regarding science did Bacon say there should be? Which one did he prefer, and why?

3. Read paragraph five, noting sentence four as the main point. What did Bacon advocate as he opposed "specious opinions"? What, then, did he say, should one do, "as a true son of science," and what would happen if one did this, according to Bacon? What are the "names" he referred to, and, with you indicating two reasons, why did he say they are important?

4. See paragraph seven. Which three ways were used by people who, according to Bacon, wanted to form an opinion of his and other scientists' work? What should such people, according to Bacon, not hope they can do as they form an opinion? What are three other things that Bacon suggested these people should do or attempt instead? What, then, would be corrected, and how? What, finally, could happen to such people?

RELATED INTERNET SITE(S)

Francis Bacon, 1561 to 1626 at Hyper History Timeline

http://www.hyperhistory.com (click Hyper History Online link, then People link)

After selecting the years 1000 to 1500, find and click Francis Bacon in the blue name box in the timeline. Read the brief biography with the comment that he advocated "action science," and see the note on two of his writings, plus the link to his essays (e.g., "Of Gardens").

Sir Francis Bacon's New Advancement of Learning

http://www.sirbacon.org/toc.html

This site, dedicated to "exploring the many facets of Bacon," has a box of icons with a map of 1601 London in the background. Icon links include books that lead to a library that is an annotated bibliography of writings by and about Bacon, with links to many of them. Note, for example, his *The Advancement of Learning* (1605), identified as "the first description of science as a tool to improve the human condition"; and *The Sylva Sylvarum* or *A Natural History in Ten Centuries* (1627), plus essays (including "Of Gardens"), and *The New Atlantis* (which refers, as in paragraphs thirty-four and thirty-five, to a place called Solomon's House, now said to be a fictional representation of what would become the Royal Society). In the second part of the bibliography, see Henry Wheeler's 1999 work *Francis Bacon's "Verulamium": The Common Law Template of the Modern in English Science and Culture*; and, via a search for Royal Society in a search box below the map on the main page, find Noel Fermor's 1961 work *The Royal Society of London for Improving Natural Science* to find out about Bacon's influence on the organization. On the main page's map see also the icons for a newsletter, a forum, biographical data, and links.

Commentary on *Novum Organum*

http://www.sirbacon.org/novorgcom.html

Bacon, Francis, First Baron "Verulum"

http://www.xrefer.com/entry/251621

This site describes Bacon's writings and life. It refers to his theories of scientific method and classification, plus writings that anticipated a true science. (See more data at www.xrefer.com/entry/551377, e.g., on his inspiring the foundation of the Royal Society.)

Francis Bacon and the Royal Society

http://www.bac.edu/library/rarebooks/Royal.htm

This site's subject is "the foundation of the Philosophical Society in 1645 under the impetus of Francis Bacon, and its later development under the Royal Charter (1662) as the Royal Society" being "one of the most important developments in the history of science." There are illustrations of pages from the long published *Society Transactions* which, as the site writer claims, is evidence of the Royal Society's long time importance.

Francis Bacon—Life Outline

http://es.rice.edu/ES/humsoc/Galileo/Catalog/Files/bacon.html

This site was established by Richard S. Westfall, History Department, Indiana University. Note especially data on Bacon's education and scientific disciplines.

Lady Bacon

http://www.tir-nan.og.com/bristol/st-george/Characters/1999/lady_bacon_1999.htm

This site features data about, and quotations from the writings of, scholar Anne Cooke Bacon, Francis Bacon's mother. Quotes include advice she wrote to him in letters.

IV
Eighteenth Century

The Linnean Correspondence
(1735–78)
URL: http://www.c18.org/pr/lc/index.html

SITE SUMMARY: This Correspondence, the focal point of an ongoing electronic project titled Project Linnaeus, features letters (eventually 7,000) that Carolus Von Linnaeus (also known as Carl Von Linne) sent to, or received from, more than 500 people, including his students, other scientific thinkers, and organizations. The letters, arranged by date, are written in English and in other languages. They reveal Linne's thoughts (especially on botany) and his influence. There are summaries in English of some of the letters written in other languages. Links go to a guide (actually detailed information about the project), an introduction (to features of Linne's life), a bibliography, and biographical notes on the correspondents. The project is overseen by an Advisory Board headed by Bengt Jonsell (of the Bergius Foundation of the Royal Swedish Academy of Sciences).

DISCUSSION QUESTIONS AND ACTIVITIES

1. Find and read a letter written in English to Linne (e.g., by Peter Collinson). Identify at least one (if available, state two or three) science-related comment(s). Find Linne's letter written as a response. Tell what Linne answered. Indicate how Linne influenced the letter's writer. Provide the letter writer's profession and/or connection to Linne.

2. Find and read a summary/translation of a letter written to Linne in a language other than English (e.g., by Francois Boissier de La Croix de Sauvages). Apply activities in Question/Activity no. 1 above to the chosen letter and the letter's writer.

3. Find, and click link to, a detailed summary/translation of a letter, or detailed summaries/translations of letters, that Linne wrote to Christian Gottlieb Ludwig, a German physician; and one or more letters Ludwig wrote to Linne. Find also biographical data on Ludwig. After reading all, identify three science subjects written about in the letter or letters. (Note: Be sure at least one subject in each letter is a response to something said in the other letter.)

4. Find and read a translation/summary of a letter Linne wrote to an organization (e.g., the Royal Swedish Society, the Consistorium of Uppsala University, or the Kungliga Vetenstapssocieteten). Identify what he wrote about, and why.

5. Find and read references to some of Linne's thoughts at the Linnean Society of London Web site. (Its url is cited in the Related Internet Sites section below.) Explain why you think these thoughts cause scientists to claim that the book in which these thoughts are found marks the start of modern botanical nomenclature, as stated at the Society's Web site. (Note: As you read

these thoughts, note that nomenclature is defined at the Linnean System of Nomenclature Web site, found as cited in the Related Internet Sites section below.)

6. Write two letters. Write one to a scientist working in a science that interests you. Write the other letter to a science teacher in whose class you have been a student, and that class was interesting for you. State in each letter how this scientist/teacher inspires your interest; and perhaps has influenced you to consider pursuing a career in the science or some aspect of it. (Hint: For help, see any Web site on a scientist cited in this book.)

RELATED INTERNET SITE(S)

Of Project Linnaeus

http://www.linnean.org/html/collections/collections_project_linnaeus.htm

This Web page provides a detailed overview of Project Linnaeus; the focal point of it being the Linnean Correspondence Web site. This page reveals which texts will be featured, and how; plus what these texts show; and how the online project will utilize the Web. Note also when the Project was started, the collaborators who are responsible for the Project, and the reason for the Project.

Linnean Society of London

http://www.linnean.org/index.htm

Via the History link, visit the page with links (e.g., to a Linne biography featuring information on the floral clock Linne created, the plant Linnaea borealis [named after Linne], and a description of his classification of plants, based on what is in his book *Species Plantarum*, published 1735, with a 1758 tenth edition that is considered to be [as of 1910] the document starting modern botanical nomenclature, which Linne expanded on in his *Fundamenta Botanica* and *Classes Plantarum*). Note also links to Linnean Society publications with citations of articles for non-members, and full-text articles for society members, from *The Linnean Journal*, *Biological Journal*, and *Zoological Journal*, plus links to news and events, collections, library, search, and welcome.

The Linnean System

http://www.palaeos.com/Systematics/Linnean/Linnean.htm

This site features detailed information on the Linnean Taxonomic Hierarchy and What's in a Name? It also has links to the International Codes of Botanical and Zoological Nomenclature, Linne biographies, and Linnean Links (e.g., Taxonomy Methodology, and Taxonomy of Life; plus parts of the "Proceedings of a Mini-Symposium on Biological Nomenclature in the Twenty-First Century" which are opposing critical analyses and overviews of the Linnean System).

Linnaeus at History of Horticulture, Ohio State University Online

http://www.hco.ohio-state.edu/hort/history.html

Click link for, then browse, Archives—Eighteenth Century, then its name links, for link to a biography of Linnaeus, which cites his works, quotes about him by other scientists of his time, plus links (e.g., to biographical materials at the Department of Systematic Botany, University of Uppsala, Sweden).

Strandell Collection of Linne's Documents at Hunt Institute of Botanical Documentation

http://huntbot.andrew.cmu.edu/Departments/Collections/Strandell.shtml

This Institute, at Carnegie-Mellon University, Pittsburgh, PA, houses the Strandell Collection of Linnaean Documents, the largest collection outside of Linne's native Sweden, and donated in 1968 by Dr. Birger Strandell, a direct descendant of Linne. An online bibliographic catalog of these documents will be provided, and will have more than three thousand documents including Linne's writings, translations of them, his students' dissertations and other publications, plus clippings and secondary literature that reveal his impact on science.

Databases of Linne-Related Documents at Hunt Institute of Botanical Documentation

http://huntbot.andrew.cmu.edu/HIBD/Home/SiteIndex.shtml

Click links under databases area to Index to Binomials Cited in the First Edition of Linne's *Species Plantarum*, Index to Scientific Names of Organisms Cited in Linne Dissertations, and Original Linne Dissertations.

"Of the Rise and Progress of the Arts and Sciences"
David Hume (1742)
URL: http://www.infomotions.com/etexts/philosophy/1700–1799/hume-of-737.txt

SITE SUMMARY: This document is an excerpt from Volume Two of *Essays from The Writings of David Hume*, a British philosopher who thought and wrote about science and human nature, while being one of the first thinkers to develop scientific thinking that emerged beyond, yet utilized methods of, philosophical contemplation. The excerpt is reproduced here with modern spelling and pronunciation, and was edited and provided online, by James Fieser, from an 1875 translation of this work that was part of Hume's writings which were published during his lifetime from 1711 to 1776. (Note especially the parts of the document where Hume commented on the sciences.)

DISCUSSION QUESTIONS AND ACTIVITIES

1. See paragraph one, then identify what two things happen negatively, according to Hume, if someone says, "any event is derived from chance."

2. If, as Hume says, in paragraph one, "[an] event is supposed to proceed from certain and stable causes," then what happens, and what opportunity presents itself? Think of, and describe, an example.

3. See paragraph two and following paragraphs, then tell how, according to Hume, one can distinguish between chance and causes. What are two natural reasons?

4. In paragraph twenty-five, what did Hume say is "the only proper Nursery of these noble plants"? Tell what he actually meant by "nursery" and "plants" (i.e., what are they metaphors for?). Identify one group of "plants" and tell where they "take root" and "grow." How did he support his claims? Do you agree? Why or why not? Think of, and describe, examples to support what you think.

5. See paragraph forty-five in which Hume claimed, in a fourth observation, that once a society achieves perfection in one of the sciences, that particular science declines or does not flourish again. Do you agree? Why or why not? Think of, and describe, an example. Do you think scientists have, even today, achieved perfection in any of the sciences, or is there always room for improvement and new discoveries? Explain your viewpoint. Include examples.

6. Define emulation as Hume defined it in paragraph forty-eight. Note that Hume claimed that importing arts (including the "art" of scientific thinking) from one nation to another "in too great perfection . . . extinguishes emulation." Note also what he said the situation would do to youth. Do you agree? Why or why not? Think of, and describe, an example. (Note: See also paragraph forty-nine.)

7. "Mathematics and natural philosophy" are not, according to Hume, in paragraph thirty-one, "half so valuable as the most considerable branches of science." Consider his comment with reference to a science subject's merit and its existence in a monarchy. (Note: Among the disciplines he identified as sciences, Hume cited some of what is now thought of as science, yet he also cited metaphysics, religion, morals, and politics; so when you answer, be sure to choose a subject which is identified as a science today, and try to include a science that was known, possibly in an early form, during Hume's lifetime. For help, see the Web site Eighteenth Century—Resources—Science—Links, whose url is cited in the Related Internet Sites section below.)

8. Read paragraph fifty-one (the last paragraph) beginning with ". . . the sciences, like some plants, require a fresh soil. . . ." Do you agree with all, or part, of this statement? Support your comment with an example. (Note: Keep Question/Activity no. 4 in mind.)

9. Read Hume's comments related to science and/or learning in one of the following paragraphs: six, seven, eight, twenty, or twenty-four. Do you agree with what Hume claimed in the paragraph and comments you chose? Why or why not?

RELATED INTERNET SITE(S)

David Hume at Bjorn's Guide to Philosophers

http://www.knuten.liu.se/~bjoch509 (click Philosophers link, then Hume link)

Scroll to a biography, and information on his works (e.g., to "An Enquiry Concerning Human Understanding," with link to online text), papers (e.g., reviews of his writings), discussion lists, images, and a link to another Hume site.

On David Hume's Essays at *Internet Encyclopedia of Philosophy*

http://www.utm.edu/research/iep/h/humeessa.htm

This Web site's page notes the beginning of the essay as a form of writing, in formal and informal formats, and cites Hume as one of the first writers to write this way to express scientific thinking. An annotated list of his writings is provided, including "Of the Rise and Progress of the Arts and Sciences" (no. 14), "That Politics May Be Reduced to a Science" (no. 3), and "Of Simplicity and Refinement in Writing" (no. 20). See http://www. utm.edu/research/iep/ h/humeepis.htm also, for information on Hume being responsible for considering various ideas that are now thought of as aspects of science (e.g., causality).

David Hume Project at Leeds Electronic Text Centre

http://www.etext.leeds.ac.uk/hume

Click links or scroll to works, plus bibliography, secondary literature (i.e., critical analysis literature), and related sites, at this site which will be a free permanent resource to Hume's works in accurate and authoritative versions, plus constantly updated critical analyses of them by his contemporaries as well as by present-day scholars.

Eighteenth Century—Resources—Science—Links

http://newark.rutgers.edu/~jlynch/18th/science.html

See links to particular sciences (e.g., medicine, cognitive science's pre-history, and evolution), plus individual scientists (e.g., Galileo, Linnaeus, and Newton).

"Travels Through North and South Carolina, Georgia, East and West Florida . . . Containing An Account of the Soil and Natural Productions of Those Regions . . ."
William Bartram (1791)
URL: http://docsouth.unc.edu/nc/bartram/bartram.html

SITE SUMMARY: This text has been called the first natural history document by the first American naturalist, and the document that has the first scientific descriptions of birds based on personal observations in the United States. The Chapel Hill Libraries at the University of North Carolina provide this electronic version of Bartram's text whose full title is *Travels Through North and South Carolina, Georgia, East and West Florida, The Cherokee Country, The Extensive Territories of the Muscogulges, or Creek Confederacy, and the Country of the Chactaws, Containing An Account of the Soil and Natural Productions of Those Regions, Together With Observations on the Manners of the Indians*. Note also his descriptions based on observations of other animals, plants, and the land.

DISCUSSION QUESTIONS AND ACTIVITIES

1. Read the Introduction to Bartram's *Travels*. Identify what he wrote about birds that is said to be the first writing on these particular subjects. (Hint: See especially pages xxxi and xxxiii, also xxii and xxiii of the Introduction.)

2. See page fourteen of Bartram's *Travels*. Indicate how his description of a turkey provides a profile of the species, as suggested at www.bartramtrail.org.

3. Read Bartram's words in his *Travels* (e.g., on pages 284–285, and 384) on his observations of birds. How are his observations different from what other observers of his time and earlier observed? Why, do you think, as has recently been claimed, that Bartram's observations, but not other observers' observations, are considered to be scientific?

4. Provide brief phrases from some of Bartram's profiles of some birds other than the turkey (e.g., owls, a crane, vultures, "snake birds," "crying bird," and various "curious birds"). (Hint: For information, see, for example, Bartram's *Travels*, pages 49–51, 132, 135–136, 146–148, 150–152, and 284.) Extra Activity: Find a bird in your backyard, school yard, or a zoo aviary, and write a profile of it. Be guided by the way Bartram wrote his profiles of birds.

5. What did Bartram mean when he wrote "sylvan music"? (For help, see his *Travels*, page 154.) Extra Activity: Write about some sounds you hear that may be called yard music or aviary music.

6. Compare and contrast the features of a bird's profile by Bartram in his *Travels* with one by Alexander Wilson, another early American naturalist whom Bartram taught. (Find a bird profile by Wilson in the online excerpts from his *American Ornithology* [1840] whose url is in the Related Internet Sites section below.)

7. John James Audubon wrote a description based on his observation of birds in a particular situation, as can be seen in an excerpt from his writings cited in the Related Internet Sites section below. What was the special situation Audubon wrote about?

8. Keeping Question/Activity no. 6 above in mind, compare and contrast one of Bartram's bird profiles, including his way of writing about birds, with a bird profile written by one or more other naturalist ornithologists of the past (e.g., Mabel Osgood Wright, Olive Thorne Miller, John Burroughs, Roger Tory Peterson). Find urls to online texts of their writings in the Related Internet Sites section below.

9. Keeping Question/Activity no. 7 above in mind, think of, or find magazine articles on, two special situations, one from the past, and one from the present or recent past, that involve birds.

Write two essays of two hundred words each about those general situations but with different particular facts. (Hint: Special situations in general of the past or present may involve birds and hunting, pesticides, oil spills, urban habitats, the plight of a particular bird species [e.g., America's symbol: the Bald Eagle].) (Tips: Find early magazine articles at the Nutty Birdwatcher Web site as cited in the Related Internet Sites section below, and recent magazine articles at any Web site cited in this book's chapter featuring BirdNet—The Ornithological Information Source.)

RELATED INTERNET SITE(S)

The Official Site of the Bartram Trail Conference, Inc.

http://www.bartramtrail.org (click Sitemap link)

Note especially the links to detailed information on and about William Bartram's *Travels* (e.g., Organization, Impact of the Book, Bartram's Search for the Truth, Themes), William Bartram (e.g., Preface, Period of Exploration, as Naturalist and Spokesman for America, and Advisor to Naturalists), Discoveries (with his Species List), Bartram Trail, and Links.

Alexander Wilson, American Ornithologist

http://xroads.virginia.edu/~PUBLIC/wilson/front.html

The University of Virginia's American Studies Program provides a biography of Wilson, the noted self-taught bird aficionado, mentored by America's first naturalist William Bartram, consultant to Lewis and Clark, and known for writings that feature his sharp observations of birds. The biography page also contains a quoted note from Wilson to Bartram. In addition, there are links to birds' names, illustrations, and comments on what Wilson observed, from Wilson's *American Ornithology*, an eight volume series. Links to resources and other links are also provided.

Excerpts from Alexander Wilson's *American Ornithology* (1840)

http://www.ummz.lsa.umich.edu

At this University of Michigan Museum of Zoology Web site, click the Birds photo link, then click links to The Wilson Ornithological Society, The Wilson Society, Alexander Wilson, and *American Ornithology*, to get to the page featuring annotated links to the excerpts. Note the excerpts for the Carolina Parakeet with a text on Wilson's experiences, plus hand colored plates that illustrate birds.

"John James Audubon Wrote of the Passenger Pigeon . . ."

http://sun.science.wayne.edu/animals/bird/pigeon

Excerpt from Audubon's *Birds of America* (1844), in which he wrote about immense flocks of the passenger pigeon before this bird became rare, then extinct.

Pioneering Ornithologists Mabel Osgood Wright and Elliot Coues with Artist Louis Agassiz Fuertes Collaborated on *Citizen Bird* (1897)

http://memory.loc.gov/ammem/today/may04.html

Read quotations from *Citizen Bird* (a book for beginning bird watchers, including young people), then follow the title link for more links to, and information about, the full online text and a biography about Wright (one of the first women members of the American Ornithologists Union).

Olive Thorne Miller Articles on Cornell University's *Making of America* Web Pages

http://cdl.library.cornell.edu/moa/browse.author/m.132.htm

A bibliography of links go to online texts of Miller's published writings which are renowned for her keen observations of birds in their habitats, not from studies of dissected birds (as was done by many naturalists of her time and earlier). See articles that were published in the mid and later years of the 1800s in magazines of note including the *Atlantic Monthly*, *Scribner's Monthly*, and the *New Englander*.

John Burroughs Web Site

http://www.johnburroughs.org/index.html

At this in progress site, see links to writings about birds in the sections titled Food for Thought, Bird Index, and Writings By Burroughs (an American naturalist who wrote many nature essays, lived from 1837 to 1921, and was nicknamed "John o' Birds").

Birders Online Guide: North American Birds

http://www.a2z4birders.com/birds/index.html (click Enter)

Has information based on the field guides of Roger Tory Peterson, a naturalist who lived from 1908 to 1996 and popularized the study of birds and the hobby of birdwatching.

David Attenborough's *The Life of Birds* on PBS-TV

http://www.pbs.org/lifeofbirds

Note the link to About David Attenborough, the British naturalist who has brought the study of birds to television and made people's interest in birds a popular pastime. See also icon links to Bird Brains, Parenthood, Champion Birds, Bird Songs, Evolution, Classroom Resources, and The Making of *The Life of Birds*.

Birds and Nature at Nutty BirdWatcher

http://nathatch.birdnature.com/index.html

Features selected articles from this magazine that was published between 1897 and 1907.

Introduction to the Aves [the Birds]

http://www.ucmp.berkeley.edu/diopsids/birds/birdintro.html

Provides information about the unique features of the animal that is known as a bird, plus links to the fossil record, Life History and Ecology, Systematics, Morphology, Web Sites, Resources, images on How Birds Fly, and a reference book: *Birds of North America*.

V
Nineteenth Century

Journals of Meriwether Lewis and William Clark
(1804–6)
URL: http://xroads.virginia.edu/~HYPER/JOURNALS/toc.html

SITE SUMMARY: The University of Virginia's American Studies Department provides links to some reproduced chapters in the Journals Lewis and Clark wrote during their exploration of the Louisiana Territory, then a wilderness area, and today the U.S. states west of St. Louis, Missouri (except Alaska and Hawaii). Many Journal entries feature the explorers' observations of plants, animals, waterways, and geological and natural geographical features they discovered during their expedition, ordered by President Thomas Jefferson shortly after he bought the territory from France. (Click a chapter's link, and read, or click search and do an xroads search for expedition subjects.)

DISCUSSION QUESTIONS AND ACTIVITIES

1. What kinds of birds did Lewis and Clark discover according to the Journal entries for August 22 and July 20, 1805? How did they describe their discoveries? What names are these birds called today? (See also data at the Discovering Lewis and Clark, and Golden Gate California Audubon Society, Web sites; especially the Society's Early Birds—Lewis' Woodpecker, Other Expedition Birds, and Journals' Descriptions page. Then find data at the Journals site. [Find these sites as noted in the Related Internet Sites section below.])

2. What kinds of flowers did Lewis and Clark discover according to the Journal entries for August 21, 1805 and June 1, 1806? What names were given to these flowers? By whom? (See also the Lewis and Clark Herbarium site via the Natural History featured area at the Lewis and Clark Archive on the Information Superhighway Web site whose url is cited in the Related Internet Sites section below.)

3. Some animals and plants were not known until Lewis and Clark discovered them. Choose a Journal entry cited below. Name and briefly describe a previously unknown animal or plant. What was special about one group of animals? (May; June 4 and 11; July 1; September 11–22, 1805) (January–March; May–June, 1806). Option: Also cite comments from the Animals Lewis and Clark Discovered Web site whose url is cited in the Related Internet Sites section below.

4. Study Clark's definition of "sensible science," found in the Journal entry for January 21, 1804. (For help, see the Discovery Paths at the Discovering Lewis and Clark Web site.) Next, study timelines, or follow links, for information involving the rivers Lewis and Clark explored (via the American Rivers and Jefferson's West Web sites), then visit the University of Kentucky

Journals Project Web site found via the Lewis and Clark Archive on the Information Superhighway site, and search Clark's Journal. Choose descriptions of a plant and an animal he discovered. Describe how he applied "sensible science" in his descriptions. Visit a backyard, zoo,
botanical garden or park. Using Clark's criteria, describe an animal and a plant, at one or two
of these places. (Urls for sites referred to above are cited in the Related Internet Sites section
below.)

5. Look through Web site links at the Lewis and Clark Archive on the Information Superhighway, including the University of Kentucky Journals Project Web site, and visit the American
Rivers Web site. (Find sites' urls as cited in the Related Internet Sites section below.) Search
for information on a natural feature (e.g., river, mountain peak) that Lewis or Clark saw. Search
the Journals by dates. Describe the natural feature. Note "then" and "now" similarities and
differences where possible.

6. Find via the Lewis and Clark Archive on the Information Superhighway Web site: President
Jefferson's June 20, 1803 Letter to Lewis. (Its url is cited in the Related Internet Sites section
below.) Study the letter, then list the nature related studies Jefferson suggested that Lewis do
during the expedition. Next, imagine you are a president, suggest nature-related studies explorers should do when exploring new territory, today, first on Earth, in a particular natural
geographical area, and then on another planet. Describe how some views of exploration in the
past and present are similar, and different. (Note: See also Question/Activity no. 7 below.)

7. Find Web pages, noted in the Related Internet Sites section below, with documents by Presidents Thomas Jefferson, Bill Clinton, and George W. Bush; plus Congressman Rohrabacher
(via the Sciences at NASA Transcript of Request to Congress Web page); and historian Irving
Anderson (via the Lewis and Clark Heritage Trail Foundation Web site). Read each document.
Compare these men's thoughts on the Lewis and Clark Expedition. Identify their different
perspectives with relation to their times, positions, and points of view.

8. Besides writing descriptions of animals and plants, Lewis and Clark made illustrations of them.
Sometimes they picked and pressed plants, and killed then stuffed animals, to study them and
have evidence of them. Suggest other ways to study animals, especially ways available today
that are similar to, yet different from, the methods Lewis and Clark used. Do a "study an animal" project using one of today's ways, and one humane way used by Lewis or Clark.

9. Read President Jefferson's Letter to Lewis and Letter to Congress. (See urls for these sites cited
in the Related Internet Sites section below.) Jefferson thought there would be two great benefits that the United States would get from this area acquired in the Louisiana Purchase. What
are they? Do you agree, disagree, approve? Which of Jefferson's "benefits" was actually
"beneficial"? Which other things, not beneficial, have happened in parts or all of the original
territory? Which other benefits, especially nature related, have come from this area, especially
through time? (For information, see Web sites whose urls are cited in the Related Internet Sites
section below.)

RELATED INTERNET SITE(S)

National Park Service Lewis and Clark Heritage Trail Foundation

http://www.lewisandclark.org

Features links to Irving Anderson's "History of the Expedition" and a coming database at
www.lewishandclark.org/traildata.htm.

President Thomas Jefferson's Message to Congress, February 19, 1806

http://archives.gov/research_room/nail/search_nail.html (choose digital copies search)

Type "lewis clark" as keywords, select textual records from media menu, click search, get seven hits, then click display. Click thumbnail button under seventh item [no. NWL-233-PRESMESS9AD1-1]. Click page image links to get to digitized reproductions of Jefferson's three-page message telling Congress of the explorers' discoveries.

Discovering Lewis and Clark

http://www.lewis-clark.org (click Introduction link, then follow links)

This ongoing project has links to Journal excerpts by date, discovery paths (e.g., natural history and geography), quick trip suggestions, word search utility, an Expedition synopsis (with links to more data) by Harry W. Fritz (history professor at the University of Montana at Missoula), links to preparation, the Expedition, and the return trip, plus links to nineteen parts (e.g., A Critical Landmark, Majestically Grand Scenery, High on the Plains, Turning Point, and Down to the Sea, many with links to related data). See also a follow the map invitation and a suggestion to click links to progress through the site's documents. Note in addition a what's new at the site link, communications (e.g., links, and what's coming soon), links to other Lewis and Clark Web sites, special illustrations, and audio options. All features, very useful for aiding access to the Journals, are supported by the University of Montana's Technology Resource Center, and others, and is endorsed by the National Lewis and Clark Bicentennial Council. Some site areas require special software for access.

Lewis and Clark Archive on the Information Superhighway

http://www.lewisandclark.org/index.html

Links go to many informative sites. Access is via a main page with links to new sites just added to the archive, via a Featured Sites links page, and via a Full List links page. On the full list page note "President Jefferson's Letter to Lewis, June 20, 1803" (under J) (that instructs Lewis what to do on the trip), Birds and Mammals Observed by Lewis and Clark, Flora and Fauna found during the Expedition, and the University of Kentucky Lewis and Clark Journals Project (an online version of Journal parts, arranged, sometimes quoted or paraphrased, with access via dates, places noted, and data on botany, geology and zoology). On the Featured Sites links page note Natural History, Geography, Artifacts and Archaeology, Traveling the Lewis and Clark Trail, Lewis and Clark Education sites, plus general Lewis and Clark information sites. On the new sites' links page note the Academy of Natural Sciences Collections—Lewis and Clark Herbarium; and comments given in the Lewis and Clark Bicentennial Year by George W. Bush, then U.S. President.

Lewis and Clark at American Rivers—An Online Community of Activists and Friends

http://www.amrivers.org (click link to Find Out What Lewis and Clark Learned)

Learn about what Lewis and Clark encountered during their Expedition with relation to rivers, and what they might think if they returned today to retrace their journey. Find also, on bottom of a Discovering the Rivers page, a Rivers of Lewis and Clark link leading to information on the five rivers Lewis and Clark explored and efforts to restore them.

Sciences at NASA—Transcript of 1999 Budget Request to Congress

http://www.hq.nasa.gov/office/legaff/Calen98.html (click transcript link)

Data from a February 25, 1998 meeting notes ways NASA would use U.S. government money. See comments by Dana Rohrabacher (the head of the Congressional House of Representatives Committee on Sciences and Subcommittee on Space and Aeronautics) noting how he compared the Space Program to the Lewis and Clark Expedition.

Bill Clinton on the Lewis and Clark Expedition

http://www.smithsonianmag.si.edu/smithsonian/issues96/aug96/bill.html

On request of *Smithsonian Magazine* editors, Bill Clinton, then U.S. President, at the end of the twentieth century, chose a time in history he would most like to visit. This article explains his reasons for choosing this expedition and gives his evaluation of the trip.

Jefferson's West—Thomas Jefferson and the Lewis and Clark Expedition

http://www.monticello.org/jefferson/lewisandclark

See the statement on Jefferson's goals for the Expedition, a link to an Expedition timeline that features Jefferson sending Lewis to learn from scientists (named here), and nature discoveries. See also, under Preparations, link to instructions (in a June 20, 1803 letter to Lewis); and, under Origins—Library of America, link to scientific books brought on the expedition, and link to related links such as the Lewis and Clark National Forest.

Nature-Related Activities (no. 4, no. 5) in Lesson Plan on the Lewis and Clark Expedition

www.archives.gov/digital_classroom/lessons/lewis_and_clark/teaching_activities.html

Animals Discovered by Lewis and Clark

http://www.pbs.org/lewisandclark/living/idx_7.html

Expedition scholars and authors provide comments in print and via audioclips.

Early Birds—Lewis' Woodpecker, plus Other Expedition Birds, and Journal Descriptions

www.goldengateaudubon.org/Birding/Excursions/EarlyBirds/LewisWoodpecker.htm

This page has data on the only bird named for Lewis, the bird named for Clark, the bird sent alive to Jefferson, the number and kinds of birds found during the Expedition, the odyssey of the Journals' publication history, and early treatment of the Journals' scientific notes, including descriptions of birds and other animals.

"The Lewis and Clark Expedition's Ties to Pennsylvania" by Frank Muhly

http://www.lewisandclarkphila.org/philadelphiafrankmuhly.html

Has data on planning for the Expedition (e.g., Lewis' consultations with a naturalist, an ornithologist, a botanist, and other scientists who taught him basic health standards, how to look for fossils, how to navigate by the stars, survey land, and determine latitude and longitude), and post-Expedition aspects (e.g., a herbarium for discovered plants, and an artist who sketched discovered plants and birds). See links to more data and for educators.

Peter Custis, Naturalist on the Lewis and Clark Expedition

http://www.lewis-clark.org/FREEMANCUSTIS/ENGLISH/fr_floE9.htm

The Science of the Lewis and Clark Expedition

http://www.nps.gov/jeff/LewisClark2/CorpsOfDiscovery/preparing/science.htm

Paper Dinosaurs: A Hypertext Catalog of Rare Documents
(1824–1969)
URL: http://www.lhl.lib.mo.us/pubserv/hos/dino/welcome.htm

SITE SUMMARY: This is an online catalog of an actual exhibition that was held in the Linda Hall Library, Kansas City, Missouri, October 17, 1996 to April 30, 1997, and includes items from the History of Science Collection in this library that is "recognized as one of the world's leading collections of information on science, engineering, and technology." This catalog features rare books, journals, and articles in scientific journals, all illustrating the early history of dinosaur discovery and restoration. It contains excerpts (in actual words or precise data) and reproduced pages (including writings and illustrations), from noted primary documents featured in the exhibition, along with original documents' bibliographic citations. The site is accessible by scrolling down and clicking the Next box, Index box (with link to a bibliography featuring links to the documents), or Contents box (leading to the Contents links of exhibit items and other catalog items not in the exhibit).

DISCUSSION QUESTIONS AND ACTIVITIES

1. Go to the Paper Dinosaurs page with Richard Owen's document "Report on British Fossil Reptiles." (Find via the Contents Page, then the Main Exhibit Contents, then the link titled "The Word 'Dinosaur' Is Coined.") Identify the scientific name that Owen proposed for creatures now known as dinosaurs. Explain why he chose to distinguish these creatures from other animals. What did he suggest dinosaurs are "a distinct tribe of"? Identify "the principal and best established genera . . . of this tribe." Describe one of the genera in detail. (Hint: For more information, check a Web site cited in the Related Internet Sites section below.) Provide citations for Web sites used and Owen's document.

2. Read William Buckland's "Notice on the Megalosaurus or Great Fossil Lizard." (Find as suggested for the document in Question/Activity no. 1 above.) Describe his method of scientifically naming a particular dinosaur. Imagine a dinosaur you could name, then name it, using Buckland's method.

3. Choose a dinosaur person and citation listed in the Paper Dinosaurs Web site's index. Give the document's bibliographic citation and Web page url. Identify the discovery and idea that the document features, and provide quotations by the document's author, if available.

4. Provide a brief profile of Mary Anning (a noted early fossil finder who had one article published in a scientific journal). (Hint: Find information at Web sites cited in the Related Internet Sites section below, such as "Mary Anning, Fossil Finder." Note this biography, paragraph six, then tell who wrote a letter about Anning's skills, and when, then describe Anning's skills, quoting the letter writer. See the biography's paragraphs four and five. What did the biographer writer say are Anning's discoveries and claim is Anning's most important find from a scientific viewpoint? What did the letter writer or profile writer say about Anning and her work with reference to her social status? What are general features provided in this Anning's biographical profile?)

5. Keeping the Anning profile in Question/Activity no. 4 above in mind, provide two other profiles of paleontology people of the past. One person should be a scientist. The other person can be a self-taught dinosaur discoverer or fossil finder. (Suggestion: For the fossil finder be guided by the biographical profile of Mary Anning.) (Tip: For information on paleontology people of the past, see the Web sites on T.H. Huxley and the Huxley File, and Dr. Joseph Leidy 1823–91 Online Exhibit, plus The History of Paleontology, and Dinosaur Paleontology: An Overview, whose urls are cited in the Related Internet Sites section below. Note Web sites on paleontologists of the past and present cited in this book's chapter on "Paleobiology—In the News, Highlights, Subjects, and Links.")

6. Visit the Web sites Dinosaur Trace Fossils, and Dinosaur Tracks and Traces (noting its Overview of Dinosaur Tracking). (Find urls as cited in the Related Internet Sites section below.) Identify various items and ways of identifying dinosaur fossils. Explain one way of identification. Give an example of the identification method you chose. (Hint: Go to the Paper Dinosaurs Web site. Click the Contents link, then Table of Contents—Exhibited Items or Complete Index and Bibliography. Find a document about a head, footprint, or other identifying feature, then read about it, describe the feature and what it helps to identify about the creature with which it is connected.)

7. Check the Paper Dinosaurs Web site for locations of fossils. Find and describe something on a dinosaur that was discovered in an area near where you live. Extra Activity One: Find more information on this dinosaur and location at another Web site or area cited just below. Extra Activity Two: Find and describe something on a dinosaur in any location. Extra Activity Three: Identify three kinds of fossils as stated at the Weird Explorations in the History of Paleontology Web site. (Find information at one of these Web sites or areas titled Dinosauria—Translation and Pronunciation Guide, or Dinosauricon—Dinosaur Genus, or the Paleontology page at Neartica—Gateway to the Natural World of North America. [Urls for Web sites cited just above are cited in the Related Internet Sites section below, or in this book's Appendix B.])

8. See the documents "How to Create A Dinosaur Report" and "Basic Methods of Paleontology." (Find as cited below.) Imagine that you go searching for a fossil or discover a dinosaur either near where you live or at a place that you find interesting. What would you look for or find, and which things would you do? Write a report applying the guidelines in the documents cited above to information you find at the Paper Dinosaurs Web site, and at any of the Web sites or areas cited in Question/Activity no. 6 above. (Find "How to Create A Dinosaur Report" via the Dinosaurs area of the Zoom School Web site cited in the Related Internet Sites section of this book's chapter featuring "Paleontology: The Window to Science Education" by Richard Stucky, and note that document's section on "Basic Methods of Paleontology.") (Tip: Note Questions/Activities no. 1 and no. 2 in this book's chapter on Stucky's document to help you identify some of the guidelines for writing a report.)

RELATED INTERNET SITE(S)

"When Was the Dinosauria Named?" by Jeff Poling, 1996

http://www.dinosauria.com/jdp/dino/name.htm

In an interesting way, this essay reveals that Richard Owen named the dinosauria in an April 1842 paper that is a revision of a lecture given during July or August 1841 (the date usually, but in error, thought of as the date on which the word was first used).

Name That Dino: What Does the Word Dinosaur Mean and How Are Dinosaurs Named?

http://www.enchantedlearning.com/subjects/dinosaurs/allabout/Names.shtml

Classification—The Dinosauricon

http://dinosaur.umbc.edu/taxa/index.html

See the list of alphabetically arranged links of dinosaurs' scientific names by groups. Place a mouse arrow over a link s to see a common name. Click a link to see a ladder like scale of particular animals in a group and their placement in an evolutionary scheme. See for example Tyrannosauroidea.

Dinosauria Online—Translation and Pronunciation Guide, by Ben Creisler

http://www.dinosauria.com/dml/names/dinoa.htm or *http://www.dinosauria.com/dml/sitemap.html*

Alphabet letter links go to pages with data in abbreviated form on dinosaur names and their derivation, meaning, translation of, and the reason for them; plus the dinosaur's classification, the geological period when the dinosaur originated, the place where the dinosaur was first found, the last name of the person who gave the name, the date of the naming or the discovery, and the namer's comments quoted or paraphrased. See also the Dinosauria Online sitemap page with links to a Translation and Pronunciation Guide introduction page, and an instructional page with information on forming dinosaur names. In addition, note on the sitemap page links to an omnipedia, dispatches of scientific news on dinosaurs, a journal, hot links, and more.

Dinosauricon—Dinosaur Genus

http://dinosaur.umbc.edu/genera/index.html

This Web page provides detailed information on citing dinosaur's scientific names and their classifications. There is also a link to an alphabetic list of names. After clicking the alphabet list link, then a letter, a list of dinosaur names appears. Choose a name (e.g., maiasaura), then you will be taken to a page of information including names, size, species type, year of discovery, names of discoverers or experts involved with the discovered specimen, the time and place it existed, particular remains found, a brief essay including links, images, and links to information on particular dinosaurs who belong to the group and are known by both their general and a particular name (e.g., maisaura peeblesorum).

Dinosaur Tracks and Traces

http://www.isgs.uiuc.edu/dinos/dinotracks.html

This Web site, provided by the Illinois State Geological Survey Geoscience Education and Outreach Unit, has a link (with a summary) to an Overview of Dinosaur Tracking (with changing views of the importance of tracks and traces). It also features links, with summaries, to other sites on dinosaur tracks in various places.

Dinosaur Trace Fossils

http://www.emory.edu/COLLEGE/ENVS/research/ichnology/dinotraces.html

Anthony Martin, connected to the Environmental Studies Program at Emory University in Georgia, provides an introduction to and categories of trace fossils. See also, via links at http://www.emory.edu/COLLEGE/ENVS/research/ichnology, a Trace Fossils Image Database, a Trace Fossil Identification Guide, an Introduction to Ichnology (the study of plant and animal traces), a History of Ichnology, and an Ichnology newsletter.

The History of Paleontology

http://www.etsu.edu (do a search in the search box)

At this East Tennessee State University Institute of Mathematical and Physical Sciences Web site, see several pages of illustrations with brief information on paleontologists of note including Charles Lyell and his *Principles of Geology*, Baron Georges Cuvier who compared fossils with living animals, William Buckland, Gideon Mantell, Richard Owen, Charles Darwin, U.S. paleontologists Edward Cope and O. Charles Marsh, significant sites of the 1900s, some famous dinosaur species, and other significant finds of the 1900s.

Dinosaur Paleontology—Historical Overview

http://museum.montana.edu/www/paleocat/chriso/history

This Web page features a timeline on the study of fossils and people who found or studied them. Time periods, people, and studies include Ancient History (with its supposed dragons and griffins), Early History (with Jean Baptiste LaMarck and Charles Lyell), Recent History (with Mary Anning, William Buckland, Richard Owen, T.H. Huxley, and William Parker Foulke in New Jersey), the U.S. Wild West (with Edward Cope who found a kangeroo-like dinosaur, had a law named after him, and was part of a feud with O. Charles Marsh that sparked the U.S. interest in paleontology). Note also adventurers including Earl Douglas (who worked on what is now Dinosaur National Monument), Roy Chapman Andrews (said to be the model for Indiana Jones), field paleontologists who work for the Smithsonian Institution and the National Museum of Natural History, and the beginning of Modern Times with John Ostrom (supporter of Huxley's claim that birds are dinosaur descendants), and others (e.g., those who studied dinosaur physiology and ichnofossils).

Biographies at Strange Science: The Rocky Road to Modern Paleontology

http://www.strangescience.net (click links)

Biographies are of well known and lesser known fossil finders, paleontologists, and other scientists involved with some aspect of paleontology. Links are to women paleontologists or fossil finders, and individual paleontologists or discoverers of fossils.

T.H. Huxley File

http://aleph0.clarku.edu/huxley/toc.html or *http://babbage.clarku.edu/huxley/toc.html*

On this site for Thomas Henry Huxley, a nineteenth-century British biologist and natural history professor who studied fossils and influenced the teaching of science in schools, click the text index. See arranged by years the links to Huxley's paleontological and other science articles (e.g., 1856 "On the Method of Palaeontology"). On the Table of Contents page, also scroll to Guides, then click a link to the Frankensteinosaurus article on Huxley.

"On the Classification of the Dinosauria" 1870, by T.H. Huxley

http://aleph0.clarku.edu/huxley/SM3/ClDino.html

In this document that is part of the Scientific Memoirs at the Huxley Files Web site, Huxley, a doctor and biologist with an interest in natural history and paleontology, provided data identified as the "Classification and Affinities of the Dinosauria" and "The History and Definition of the Group." It includes Huxley's comment to a quotation by Richard Owen introduced here. There are also a discussion at the end of the document, and descriptions of dinosaurs found in particular places, including Britain, Central Europe and Germany, the Ural Mountains and India, and North America.

Doctor Joseph Leidy 1823–91 Online Exhibit

http://www.acnatsci.org/museum/leidy/index.html

This exhibit at the Web site for the Academy of Natural Science in Philadelphia, Pennsylvania, features data on this "father of American vertebrate paleontology," pioneer in the fields of protozoology and parasitology; expert in geology, entomology, and pathology; and natural history teacher. Links go to a biography, data on his work with fossils and his other studies. The fossils and other studies pages include precise references to his publications and what he wrote in them.

Mary Anning, Finder of Fossils, 1799–1847

http://www.sdsc.edu/ScienceWomen/anning.html

This biographical profile of a self-taught fossil discoverer features a quotation from a letter that points to Anning's knowledge and how she worked, and an annotation about Anning as cited in a 1995 issue of the *British Journal for the History of Science.*

Mary Anning in Weird Explorations into the History of Paleontology

http://www.dinosaur.org/dinotimemachine.htm

Notes that Anning had one publication in a paleontological magazine, describes Anning's first and more important discovery, and explains various kinds of fossils (e.g., type, holotype, genoholotype).

"The Chemical History of a Candle: Lecture One"
Michael Faraday (1827)
URL://www.fordham.edu/halsall/mod/1860Faraday-candle.html

SITE SUMMARY: This lecture, one of six referred to as the famous Christmas Lectures, was presented by Faraday to children at the Royal Institute of Great Britain during the 1827 Christmas season. It is provided online at the *Modern History Source Book* Web site with the five other "Chemical History of a Candle" lectures; all published as a group in 1860. These lectures have been referred to as "a classic of clear and fascinating scientific exposition." The reproduction of Lecture One, featured here, has nineteen paragraphs and six footnotes, and is accompanied, with the other lectures, by an Introductory Note on the work and life of Faraday, who lived from 1791 until 1867, was chemical assistant, then superintendent, at the Royal Institute; and professor of chemistry at the Royal Military Academy. He was also the scientific adviser to Trinity House, which was responsible for safe navigation around the shores of England and Wales especially by making sure that the lights in lighthouses stayed lit. While on this job he also took the initiative to make the lighthouse lights more efficient, which caused him to show how "scientific expertise can be used for practical purposes." Today he is considered to be, as he was during his lifetime, an "outstanding science lecturer of his time" who was gifted at explaining scientific concepts to popular audiences.

DISCUSSION QUESTIONS AND ACTIVITIES

1. See paragraph three. What, according to Faraday, does a natural candle do? Give an example of a natural candle. See paragraphs four through six, plus notes. Describe "candles . . . in commerce," tell what were they commonly called, then identify four types of manufactured candles, and reveal how wax candles were made.

2. See paragraphs eight through ten. What are three wonderful things about a burning candle? How does something natural "help" or "tease"? Explain each answer.

3. See paragraphs twelve and thirteen, plus footnotes no. 4 and no. 5. Explain "capillary attraction." Give examples. What do candles have to do with it?

4. See paragraph fourteen. What happens to a candle if it is turned upside down? Why?

5. See paragraph fifteen. What is another "condition" that should be learned about a candle? Why? What is a "pretty experiment" demonstrating it? What else is true about this experiment?

6. See paragraph sixteen. What are a candle flame's features? What are three things that cause them? Which two things don't rival a flame's brilliance? Why not? Why does a flame vary? (Hint: Hooker.) What happens when a candle is placed in sunlight or in bright electric lamp light, and what is curious about what happens?

7. See paragraph one. Complete Faraday's statement: "There is . . . , than by considering the physical phenomena of a candle." Why did he say this? Answer with quotes by Faraday.

8. See paragraph seven. What are luxuries in candles? What is nice about them, and what is not OK about them?

9. See paragraph ten. What did Faraday hope his young audience would see, what did he say "we come here to be . . . ," and what did he hope they would remember?

10. See paragraph nineteen. What did Faraday say about "the philosophy of the thing" and illustrations? Do you agree, or disagree, and why? Identify Faraday's concluding thought with reference to a candle and his young audience at the end of Lecture Six in the online Modern History Source Book's Faraday page, or at bottom of his On the Art of the Lecture at the Woodrow Wilson Leadership Program in Chemistry site featuring A Project on Faraday's 1827 Christmas Lectures. (See the Related Internet Sites section below for the Wilson

Program's url.) Apply to something you know around you, or in today's world, and science-related, each of Faraday's thoughts, which you stated to answer these questions.

RELATED INTERNET SITE(S)

Faraday at the Royal Institute of Great Britain Online

http://www.rigb.ac.uk/heritage/faradaypage.html

This page features details on Faraday's life and work. The Lecture page (found via a link) includes brief data about the annual science-related lectures for young people inspired by Faraday's lectures for young audiences, and annual discourses he also inspired. It includes, via a link, a list of Christmas Lectures from 1825, in PDF format. It also briefly describes other programs, including some especially for young scientists.

Michael Faraday Awards at the Royal Society Online

http://www.royalsoc.ac.uk (choose awards from pull-down menu)

Click search link, do search for Faraday, then see links to pages with information about Faraday awards which were set up and are still given in honor of the scientist, winners of the awards, and some lectures by award winners.

Faraday Project

http://www.users.bigpond.com/chergr/Faraday.htm

This site includes quotes from an 1870 biography about Faraday, plus links to data on his contributions to chemistry and physics. There is also a links page leading to sites with biographies featuring his perspectives on technology, chemistry and physics, and aspects of science arising from his work, e.g., the Faraday Effect.

The 1827 Christmas Lectures of Michael Faraday—A Project

http://www.woodrow.org/teachers/chemistry/institutes/faraday

This site (part of a project of the 1992 Summer Institute of the Woodrow Wilson Leadership Program in Chemistry), features links to Faraday's lecture On the Art of the Lecture, his lecture notes, and an introduction by Purdue University's Rita Biederstedt and Derek Davenport to a transcription of his notes for the lectures. This introduction features excerpts of letters by author-lecturer Charles Dickens urging Faraday to publish his scientific lectures for young audiences.

Life of Michael Faraday

http://www.top-biography.com/9093-Michael Faraday

Click Faraday's portrait, then see a page on Faraday at a Glance. Note also the links to Faraday's life, works, and contribution, plus quotations, and a chronology.

Faraday Christmas Lectures

http://www.xrefer.com (do subject search)

See two links. Click the link that leads to data on Faraday and the lectures. Click also the link leading to information on the lectures being continued today.

Alfred Russel Wallace Web Site
(1843–1913)
URL: http://www.wku.edu/~smithch

SITE SUMMARY: This site features documents by and information about the British naturalist known for thinking of the theories of evolution and natural selection at the same time Darwin thought of them (in ways similar and different), and for writing on several scientific subjects (e.g., natural science). Links go to full texts of Wallace's writings, quotations, interviews, most cited works, a biography including a list of his accomplishments, faqs, chronology, bibliography, misinformation alert, writings on Wallace and his works, Web site news, a list of archives containing Wallace papers, just for fun, a search box to works by or about Wallace, links to sites on subjects of interest to Wallace, and Smith on Wallace (writings by Charles H. Smith, Librarian, Western Kentucky University, and this Web site's creator and manager). Some faqs include: "Did Darwin steal from Wallace?" "Was Wallace forgotten when Darwin published his *The Origin of Species*?" "What were the subjects on which Wallace and Darwin disagreed?" and "Just how similar were Wallace's and Darwin's ideas on evolution as distinct from natural selection?" (Note frames version at www.wku.edu/~smithch/index1.htm.)

DISCUSSION QUESTIONS AND ACTIVITIES

1. Select from the Alfred Russel Wallace Web Site's Some Interesting Wallace Quotations page, a science related quotation. Identify Wallace's main point and what he used as a reason and an example to support it. Cite the work from which the quotation was taken, and, where necessary (i.e., for an example or reason), quote from this document, which can be found via the Wallace Web Site's Wallace Writings page.

2. Choose and read one or more of Wallace's articles from among the following: "On the Tendency of Varieties to Depart Indefinitely from the Original Type," "Contributions to the Theory of Natural Selection," "On the Limits of Natural Selection As Applied to Man," "Remarks on the Rev. S. Haughton's Paper on the Bee's Cell, and On the Origin of New Species," "On the Law Which Has Regulated the Introduction of New Species," and "The Advantages of Varied Knowledge." Find title links to these writings on the Wallace Web Site's Writings page, Biography page, or Most Cited Works page. Identify the main points that Wallace advocated in the article(s) that you chose, then what he cited as reasons and examples to support them.

3. Although Wallace advocated aspects of the theory of evolution that Darwin advocated, one aspect that Wallace questioned and had a different view of was evolution with reference to humankind's higher attributes. Identify Wallace's views of the development of humankind's higher attributes as related to Darwin's. Comment on whether or not you think Wallace's views are valid. Would you adopt these viewpoints, consider them as parts of an answer, adopt Darwin's or another evolutionist's or another scientist's viewpoints on the subject, or want to suggest something else? Tell your viewpoint(s) and reason(s). (Hint: For help to see how Wallace looked at this subject, read, for example, quotations on his thoughts regarding mind and matter, and the relation between spiritualism and evolution, on the Wallace Web Site's Some Interesting Wallace Quotations page, see his articles from which the quotations are taken [and found via the Wallace Web Site's Wallace Writings page]. See also via the Wallace Web Site's Wallace Interviews page his interview "New Thoughts on Evolution.")

4. Find some Wallace writings that the Wallace Web Site suggests are indications of Wallace's viewpoints on evolution that are different from Darwin's on a particular subject, other than the subject referred to in Question/Activity no. 3 above. Choose one of these writings and identify how Wallace's viewpoint differs from Darwin's.

5. At times during his life Wallace was known as Darwin's "right-hand man." Find some Wallace writings that the Wallace Web Site suggests support this claim. Identify the points that are said to, or seem to, support it.

6. Find writings by Wallace at the Wallace Web Site on one of the following subjects: mimicry, coloration in plants and animals (including four types), color patterns in animals, recognition marks, bird migration, and color vision. Identify his viewpoints on each subject and, where it applies, connections to aspects of evolution.

7. Wallace wrote on a variety of science or science-related subjects in addition to those related to evolution. Find and choose his writings on, and identify some things he wrote about regarding, one of these subjects: geographical distribution of animals and plants, geodesy, glaciology, age of the earth, the "flat earth" theory, types of islands, urban land use, and exobiology. Where applicable, reveal or suggest how the subject is related to evolution, or how his approach to the subject was ahead of his time.

8. Identify, with relation to Wallace, "Wallace's Line" and the "Anthropic Principle." (Note One: For help, browse the Wallace Web Site, especially the accomplishments cited on this site's Biography page. Note Two: See also the article "Design and the Anthropic Principle" at the Scholarly and Popular Sources Concerning Intelligent Design Web site whose url is cited in the Related Internet Sites section below.)

9. What is zoography, and why has Wallace been called "the father of zoography"? (Tip: Follow Note One in Question/Activity no. 8 above.)

10. Find one of the Wallace writings that the Wallace Web Site refers to as easy to read, or find one of Wallace's interviews or writings that interests you. Be sure it is a writing other than one of those you found for Questions/Activities no. 1 through no. 9 above. Identify what is easy to read or interesting, and provide the main points on the subject that Wallace wrote about, then comment on why you find the item interesting.

11. Keep Question/Activity no. 3 above in mind. Think about and compare Wallace's and other scientists' viewpoints on, or different theories of, evolution, and particular aspects of, or subjects related to, evolution (e.g., the beginning of life on the earth, natural selection, survival of the fittest, instinct, adaptation, variation, diversity within species [later called microevolution]), including views from scientists who lived before, at the same time as, and after, Wallace. Identify Wallace's views, reasons, and examples. Consider the following subjects with reference to Wallace and to scientists' concerns related to them, e.g., slow or sudden change, microevolution as opposed to macroevolution (the first referring to changes within species, the second to changes from one species to another), survival through competition (adversarial or friendly) or cooperation. (Hint: For help, follow Note One in Question/Activity no. 8 above, search the Wallace Web Site using the key words or phrases, go to the Wallace Web Site's Smith on Wallace page and find the Wallace Web Site creator's article "Alfred Russel Wallace on Spiritualism, Man, and Evolution: An Analytical Essay," then go to the Web sites whose urls are cited in the Related Internet Sites section below.)

12. Think about everyday life in a past time, life during a historical event, life in living history museums or outdoor places, or real situations that have required survival strategies. Next, think of a survival situation that might have happened during one of those times or in one of those places. Suggest how survival through the "survival of the fittest" or "natural selection" viewpoints could be applied, but with relation to cooperation rather than to adversarial competition. Suggest how a science (maybe an invention) of the time, or an available science (or invention), could be helpful. (Hint: For help, see the Web sites Living History Museums and Outdoor Areas, History of Science—Topics—Links to Sites, Scientists and Science at the HyperText History Timeline, History of Inventions—A Timeline, Lemelson—MIT Program Celebrating Invention and Innovation, other sites on inventions or science history. Find urls in this book's chapter on "An Inventor Never Grows Up," or parts B and I of the Appendix.)

RELATED INTERNET SITE(S)

A History of Evolutionary Thought

http://www.ucmp.berkeley.edu/history/evothought.html

Names links under the categories Founders of Natural Science, Great Naturalists of the Eighteenth Century, Preludes to Evolution, Natural Selection, and The Modern Synthesis go to Web sites with information on scientists and their contributions to evolution.

PBS-TV—Evolution

http://www.pbs.org/evolution

Main icon links go to areas on change, survival, extinction, humans, Darwin, religion, and more. See also links that go to faqs and a glossary with words and names of people involved with evolution. The site provides information on aspects of the theory of evolution that are generally accepted yet often questioned and re-examined.

History and Scientific Foundations of Evolution

http://www.newadvent.org/cathen/e.htm (scroll to subject's title link)

Features detailed and objective information on evolution theories. Evolutionists' various views on God with relation to their theories are provided. Introductory information reveals two main scientific theories of evolution. Note also "Evolution, Catholics and" on the letter "e" subject titles links page.

"Macro Versus Micro Evolution"

http://www.forerunner.com/forerunner/X0737_Macro_vs._Micro_Evol.html

An article by David Skjaerlund, a Michigan Department of Agriculture soil scientist.

Scholarly and Popular Sources Concerning Intelligent Design

http://www.origins.org/menus/design.html

See links to articles by or on well known and lesser known scientists and science writers. Note an article on Stephen Hawking, and other articles, e.g., "Design and the Anthropic Principle," "Darwin's Fine Feathered Friends: A Matter of Interpretation," "Small Scale Evidence of Grand Scale Design." See also links to other areas of the www.origins.com Web site (e.g., Debates, Darwinism and Evolution, Special Interest, Related Links).

Intelligent Design: Scientists' Observations

http://ic.net/~erasmus/RAZ537.HTM

Quotations (with print sources noted) on the intelligent design theory as applied to life's beginning on earth, and evolution, by well known and lesser known past and present scientists (e.g., Werner Von Braun, Robert Jastrow, Fred Hoyle, Charles Darwin, etc.).

"The Watch and the Watchmaker" in Excerpts from Paley's *Natural Theology* (1800)

http://courses.atb.rochester.edu/nobis/CAS105/Paley'sWatch

An example of the intelligent design theory described by William Paley, a philosopher and theologian. A *New York Times* April 8, 2001 article "New Theory of Life's Origin" refers to this idea (and is available online for a small price).

Excerpts from "Letter Concerning the Education of Women Physicians"
Elizabeth Blackwell (1851)
URL: http://memory.loc.gov/ammem/amtitle.html (search by title)

SITE SUMMARY: This letter, written by the first American woman to become a doctor, reveals Dr. Blackwell's viewpoint that human beings should be ranked by character rather than gender, and that women should be ranked not in second place or even in first place, but in their true places, in professions, especially in the medical profession. The letter was written in response to a comment made by Baroness Anne Isabella Milbank Byron that Blackwell objected to. Lady Byron had suggested that women doctors should assume a secondary position in the medical profession. Note also background information on Blackwell and the letter on the main Web page before search. Click letter page link for an online reproduction of the handwritten letter.

DISCUSSION QUESTIONS AND ACTIVITIES

1. Read the first and second paragraphs of the excerpts from Dr. Blackwell's letter to Baroness Byron. Explain her statements, applying them to her situation, then to women and the medical profession in general, women and a particular medical profession, and women and any science profession. (Tip: Give comments by, or about, other women, if possible.) (Hint: Check sites noted in Questions/Activities no. 4 and no. 6 below.)

2. Visit the Web sites or pages National Library of Medicine—Elizabeth Blackwell Exhibit Online, Creative Quotations from Elizabeth Blackwell, On One Hundred Fiftieth Anniversary of Blackwell's Graduation from Medical School, and Blackwell quotations at Quotations in Medicine Online. (Their urls are cited in the Related Internet Sites section below, or in this book's Appendix C.) Choose three quotations by Dr. Blackwell. Apply to these quotations parts of Question/Activity no. 1, specifically the part beginning "Explain her statements . . . ," then the tip and hint.

3. Keeping in mind that, and how, Dr. Blackwell struggled to obtain a medical education, then find patients and be a doctor, read student Sarah Sellers' 1998 article "The First Test! Through the Eyes of Dr. Virginia Apgar," especially paragraph four. (Its url is cited in the Related Internet Sites section of this book's chapter featuring "A Proposal For a New Method of Evaluation of the Newborn Infant" by Dr. Virginia Apgar, 1953.) What did Sellers write on Dr. Apgar's early professional life? (Hints: Note her choice of specialty within the medical profession, why she changed her mind, and how she fared in her new specialty.)

4. See "North American vs. European Attitudes Toward Advent of Women Physicians." (Its url is cited in the Related Internet Sites section below.) See also the Web sites Women in Science and Medical Fields; and Important Figures in Health Sciences, noting its links to Women in Health History, Distinguished Women of the Past and Present: Health and Medicine, and Real Women in Health Care. (Their urls are cited in the Related Internet Sites section below, or in this book's Appendix B.) Choose one of the first women who strove to become a doctor, and find out if she was successful or had a hard or a challenging time. Next, choose a woman of any time in a particular medical profession, then describe how she fared within it.

5. See the Web sites and pages Careers in Health and Medicine; Medical and Health Career Descriptions; Medical Doctor Occupational Profile; Physicians and Surgeons, and Related Occupations, in the Occupational Outlook Handbook. (Their urls are cited in this book's Appendix B.) See also to the Web sites cited in Question/Activity no. 4 above. Choose a medical profession you find interesting. Imagine you are thinking of pursuing this profession as a career. Note how people of your gender have fared in this profession or in one of its specialties, and if you would you still pursue it if it is considered an occupation for the gender opposite from

yours. Consider if you would choose to "swim against the tide" and try to make it in this controversial profession, or if you would choose a profession or a profession's specialty that has traditionally been a profession for your gender then "sail through the calm or navigable waters" or try to "surf the waves" (i.e., make inroads within that accepted profession)? Explain your decision, emphasizing why or why not.

6. Visit at least one Web site from each of the following groups. Group one: Women Physician Autobiographies; National Women's Health Information Center; Journal of American Medical Women's Association (JAMWA); Female Patient Magazine; Women's Health and Adolescent Health in Health Topics A–Z at Centers for Disease Control and Prevention Online; and Girl Power! in the News Index (with Research Studies and News); plus group two: Exploring the Relationship of Medicine and Literature; Roster of Physician Writers; the Literature, Arts and Medicine Database; and Reflections at the Medical College of Wisconsin—HealthLink. (Site urls are cited in the Related Internet Sites section below; or in this book's Appendix B, C, D, or F.) Choose from two sites (one each from the groups above) a woman physician and something she wrote; describe what she wrote about, quoting her when possible. Identify the format in which she wrote. (For help with identifying writing formats, see the Note in Question/Activity no. 7 below.)

7. Look at the various writing formats, at the sites in group two in Question/Activity no. 6 above, in which women physicians have written; then choose a format; next choose a subject that a particular woman physician has written about at one of the sites in group two; and write something of your own on the subject in general in the format you chose. (If possible, include in your writing something you, a family member, or friend, have experienced.) Next, look at the short writing formats at the sites cited below and in group one of Question/Activity no. 6 above; then choose one format; and write something on a medical subject in the chosen format. (Note: For help with identifying writing formats, visit the Web pages with Instructions to Authors in the Health Sciences; JAMWA instructions for contributors, and Journal of Adolescent Health author information. Their urls are cited in this book's Appendixes C and D.)

RELATED INTERNET SITE(S)

On One Hundred Fiftieth Anniversary of Blackwell's Graduation from Medical School

http://www.nlm.nih.gov/news/press_releases/blackwell.html

On January 28, 1999, the National Library of Medicine commemorated Blackwell's life accomplishments in an exhibit, with quotations from her diary and publications. This press release on the event provides a biography including quotations by Blackwell, and quotes about her by Tenley Albright, the chair of the library's board of regents; by Charles A. Lee, the library's director; and by Donald A.B. Lindberg, the dean of her medical school.

Elizabeth Blackwell, America's First Woman M.D., at NLM Exhibit Online

http://www.nlm.nih.gov/hmd/blackwell/index.html

An online version of the National Library of Medicine exhibit on Blackwell, this site features a biography with reproductions of pages from Blackwell's medical college notes, and her publication *Medicine as a Profession For Women*, plus her comment on how people reacted to her being a student in a medical school. Sections include Admission to Medical School, College Life, Graduation, and Career.

Elizabeth Blackwell on the Web

http://womenshistory.about.com/cs/blackwellelizabeth

This site features links to About Elizabeth Blackwell, some quotations, and an 1868 biography of her by a Rev. H.B. Elliott.

Creative Quotations from Elizabeth Blackwell

http://famouscreativewomen.com/one/1092.htm

Featured are some quotations from an 1848 letter and from her 1895 book *Pioneer Work for Women*.

"North American vs. Western European Attitudes Toward Advent of Women Physicians"

http://www.upstate.edu/library/advent.html

A speech presented April 9, 1999, by Eric v.d. Luft, collections curator, Health Sciences Library, SUNY Upstate Medical University, Syracuse, at the Fourteenth Annual Interdisciplinary Nineteenth Century Studies Conference "Transatlanticisms" at Ohio State University, Columbus. A featured part is "The Struggle of Elizabeth Blackwell."

National Women's Health Information Center

http://www.4.woman.gov

See links to Featured Health Articles with guest editors, News Archives, Press Releases, FAQs, Hot Topics, Women's Health News Today, Women's Health Time Capsule, Hot Topics in Congress, Information for Special Women's groups, Journals, and Young Women's Health Summit.

Women Physicians' Autobiographies

http://research.med.umkc.edu/teams/cml/womendrs.html

This bibliography has writings by women of the past and of recent times, from various areas of the world, and includes some annotations.

Excerpts from *On the Growth of Plants in Closely Glazed Cases*
Nathaniel B. Ward (1852)
URL: http://www.fortunecity.com/greenfield/clearstreets/84/ward/discover.htm

SITE SUMMARY: This document (an excerpt from a book with this title) provides Ward's detailed description of an incident that led to his accidental discovery in 1829 of what was first called a Wardian Case and is now known as a terrarium. Ward, a British medical doctor who had a lifelong avocational interest in plant biology, served as examiner of botany for the Society of Apothecaries and was involved with the Society's Chelsea Physic Garden of Medicinal Plants. Notes by David Hershey, that follow the excerpts, explain scientific words that Ward mentioned, Ward's continuing studies based on his discovery, the involvement of the Companion to the Botanical Magazine, the British Association for the Advancement of Science, the Linnean Society, the Royal Botanic Garden in Edinburgh, the Great Exhibition of 1851, the Royal Society, and the noted scientist Michael Faraday.

DISCUSSION QUESTIONS AND ACTIVITIES

1. "In consequence of" what, and whom, did "the science of botany" become Ward's "recreation from [his] youth up"? Explain and give examples of why you think Ward's interest was sparked by these influences. (For hints and data see these Web sites: Linnean Society of London, Project Linnaeus, Linnean System of Nomenclature and History of Horticulture. [Their urls are cited in the Related Internet Sites section of this book's chapter on The Linnean Correspondence.])

2. Which two botanical items or plants were major parts of Ward's "earliest ambition"? Why did all his attempts to keep these plants prove to be fruitless? (Hint: The cause still exists today, more intensely.) Describe how the problem referred to in above affects plants today.

3. What incident happened in the summer of 1829 that caused Ward to accidentally discover what became known as Ward's Case or a Wardian Case? Name three botanical items and one atmospheric feature involved.

4. How did Ward answer the following, his own, question, with reference to "that very tribe of plants" he had "for years fruitlessly attempted to cultivate"; and what were "the conditions necessary for its well-being"? Next, answer his question while applying it to a plant of your choice and while considering it as part of your own terrarium. Write on features of a terrarium, then make a terrarium of your choice. (For help with the second and third activities just above, see the Web sites: Plants and Youth—Designing and Building a Terrarium, Gardening Fact Sheets—Terrariums, Terrariums—Miniature Worlds in A Bottle, Terrariums—Landscapes in Miniature, and A Terrarium Resource Guide [especially its Magic Terrarium—Planting and Care, and Terrarium Q's and A's]. Their urls are cited in the Related Internet Sites section below.)

5. See Transporting Plants via the Nathaniel Ward's Terrarium Page. (Its url is in cited in the Related Internet Sites section below.) What was a special use that came about for Wardian Cases? What was Dr. Ward's part in it? Why is it not still used today?

6. See Ward's Biography via the Nathaniel Ward's Terrarium Page (whose url is cited as noted in Question/Activity no. 5 above.) Note, according to this biography, Ward's father, a doctor, sent the thirteen-year-old Nathaniel on a trip to deter him from his plan to become a sailor when he grew up. His father succeeded, with Ward agreeing to become his father's apprentice, then taking over his father's medical practice. On the trip, however, young Nathaniel became acquainted with some unusual plants, which led to his lifelong interest in botanical science; especially as an avocation (hobby) and as part of his profession. Think of a place where you might go and what you would experience there which might cause you to choose some-

thing related to it as your future profession, and/or avocation; especially one involving botany; or another natural science, or another science. Describe the place, noting something botanical, natural, or something else scientific. Give reasons for your choice.

7. See Ward's Biography (found as stated in Question/Activity no. 6 above). State the name of the plant that was named after Dr. Ward. Choose a plant. (Find plants, noting general names, at these Web sites: Terrariums—Miniature Worlds in a Bottle, or Plants and Youth: Designing and Building A Terrarium. [Their urls are cited in the Related Internet Sites section below.]) Give a name to a particular kind of your chosen plant. (For help naming the plant, see Rules for Naming Plants, at the Brooklyn Botanical Garden Online. [Its url is cited in the Related Internet Sites section of this book's chapter featuring the International Code of Botanical Nomenclature.])

RELATED INTERNET SITE(S)

Nathaniel Ward's Terrarium Page

http://www.fortunecity.com/greenfield/clearstreets/84/ward/dh321.html

See a portrait of Dr. Ward and an 1852 illustration of a Wardian Case. There are also links to a Biography of Nathaniel Bagshaw Ward (1791–1868), Transporting Plants, Other Uses, List of Literature Citations, 1970's Terrarium Craze, Accidental Discovery, Multiple Discovery, Important Botanists and Botanical Events of Ward's Era, and Teaching Suggestions.

Gardening Fact Sheets—Terrariums

http://www.civigardencentre.org/mg/terrariums.htm

At this site, the Ontario Gardening Education and Information Centre provides information on making terrariums with woodland, tropical, or desert plants and environments. It also notes how terrariums work, and their advantages.

Terrariums—Miniature Worlds in a Bottle

www.ville.montreal.qc.ca/jardin/en/info_verte/feuillet_terrarium/feuillet_terrarium.htm

This page is one of the Green Pages, a "virtual garden shed" that is "full of tools" and connects visitors to "an abundant harvest of information on many different aspects of horticulture and botany." It is provided by the Montreal, Canada, Botanical Garden, and has a detailed description of terrariums, and links to information on containers, materials, preparation, choosing plants, planting, maintenance, and additional information. It is also accessible by clicking Terrariums in the pull-down menu under "In the Green Pages" at http://www2.ville.montreal.qc.ca/jardin/en/biblio/carnet.htm.

Creating and Maintaining Terrariums—Landscapes in Miniature

http://www.thegardenhelper.com/terrarium.html

A Terrarium Resource Guide—from Terrarium Builders Guild

http://www.terrariums.org/terrariums

This guide provides suggestions on which plants to choose to make terrariums and how to set up, care for, and maintain terrariums. Click especially links to Terrarium Q's & A's; and Terrarium Care (also known as The Magic Terrarium—Planting and Care). See also the link to A Little Bit of History.

Terrariums—A "Get Growing Gardening Tip"

http://www.discoveredmonton.com/devonian/getgro95.html

The associate director of the Devonian Botanic Garden in Edmonton, Canada, Dr. Michael Hickman, provides this tip, one of the tips featured at the Garden's Web site. He introduces the tip with information about Dr. Ward and the Wardian Case.

Plants and Youth: Designing and Building a Terrarium

http://edis.ifas.ufl.edu/BODY_MG356

This fact sheet contains a chart of plants for terrariums, plus definitions of terms, a definition of a terrarium, and instructions for making a terrarium. It is provided by Kathleen C. Ruppert and Robert D. Black of the Florida Cooperative Extension Service, Institute of Food and Agricultural Sciences, University of Florida.

Alexander Graham Bell Notebooks Project
(1875–)
URL://jefferson.village.virginia.edu/~meg3c/id/AGB/index.html

SITE SUMMARY: The School of Engineering and Applied Science at the University of Virginia provides this in-progress online reproduction of the notebooks of inventor Alexander Graham Bell, who is best known for his invention of the telephone. It features notes on the process by which his invention was developed. The notebooks are accessible via a Table of Contents link. Included also, via a Bell Research Homepage link, are an Introduction by Professor Michael Gorman, and a bibliography titled "References for Technoscientific Thinking and the Telephone" which is a list of works by and about Bell. Via the Bell Research Homepage link, also find a Master Map with illustrations of Bell's inventions, and see links to search Bell's Path to the Telephone, plus a table of contents with information on the Map's features. An About the Project link on the Project site's main page leads to a page featuring links to Help Using the Notebooks, and Project History. Some pages found via the links in the Table of Contents also include notes via book icon links, and, via small book page icon links, there are reproductions of note pages in Bell's handwriting.

DISCUSSION QUESTIONS AND ACTIVITIES

1. Go to the link to Bell's March 10, 1876 Speech Transmission, found in the notebooks via the main Table of Contents link. See first page, then follow arrow link to the next page. State Bell's famous quotation which he said when he first tested his invention. What would you have said if you were Bell at that moment? Why?

2. Read the first section of Professor Gorman's Introduction (found as stated in this chapter's Site Summary above). Explain his description of Bell's invention process as compared with Thomas Edison's invention process. Indicate two methods of inventing. Explain how an inventor handles knowledge from other sources. Explain Bell's work with relation to a map and a flowchart.

3. Keeping in mind your answers to Question/Activity no. 2 above, think of your own invention idea, or choose an invention from one of these Web sites: Smithsonian Institution—Inventors and Inventions—Selected Sites, National Invention Hall of Fame—Inventions and Inventors Search, Community of Science, Inc.—U.S. Manual of Patent Classification, International Federation of Invention Associations—Articles, etc., Untimely Inventions, or Mothers of Invention. (Their urls, with site summaries, are cited in the Related Internet Sites section in this book's chapter featuring inventor George Margolin's article "An Inventor Never Grows Up"; or in this book's Appendix B.) Construct a map or flowchart of your idea. (Hint: For help, see the Flowcharting Help Page [Tutorial] Web site. Its url is cited in this book's Appendix F.)

4. Click the main Table of Contents link, then the link for March 15, 1876, and read a quotation by Bell. See also a Bell quotation at the end of paragraph six of the "Mental Models and Mechanical Representations" section of the Introduction. Read also Note no. 8 after the introduction. What are the titles of the Bell documents from which the quotes were taken? Identify the two styles of scientific reasoning referred to in the introduction; and tell which style Bell preferred. State the reason why Bell chose this style; why Bell's choice was good; and why the other style may also be good. Extra Activity: Apply one of the styles of scientific reasoning to an invention idea you have, or choose from the Web sites cited in Question/Activity no. 2 above.

5. Describe Bell's work involving Ohm's Law and Helmholtz. (For data, see March 20, 1876, entry via the Table of Contents; plus Professor Gorman's reference to Bell and "Helmholtz's scientific discoveries" in paragraph five of the first part of his Introduction.)

6. Professor Gorman, in his Introduction, states that Bell aimed toward "an analogy between technology and nature." See the Bell quotation in paragraph three before Note no. 18 in the

Introduction's "Ear Phonautograph" section. State the source of the Bell quote. What was the aspect of nature Bell aimed to duplicate? Did he succeed? Explain your answer.

7. Read paragraph six of the Introduction's "Harp Apparatus" section before Note no. 20. State the Bell quote and its source. Indicate what, according to Professor Gorman, became "the focus of Bell's successful telephone"; and how.

8. Go to Professor Gorman's table of contents page (not the main Table of Contents), via a link on his Introduction page. Find, read, and study, the reproductions of Bell's two patent documents, then go to the United States Patent and Trademark Office Homepage Web site (whose url is in this book's Appendix F), and study its features referred to in the Appendix's site summary for this Web site, especially with reference to patents. State the basic features of a patent document. Extra Activity: Following the format of Bell's patent papers, and what is provided for a patent document's format at the United States Patent and Trademark Office Web site (after a search), make and "fill out" a patent document to explain a new invention you have thought of, or one that is listed at a Web site cited in Question/Activity no. 2 above.

9. Go to the Introduction and read the section titled "Sound Into Current." Tell how Bell's understanding of music influenced his view of inventing something. Next, see the Bell quotation in paragraph three of the "Harp Apparatus" section of the Introduction, then state the quotation and its source, and tell what Bell said about a magnet and a musical sound. Next, go to the main Table of Contents via the link on the Project's main Web page. State a quotation from an entry (and give the date) on the subject featured in the first part of this Question/Activity, then explain the quotation's idea.

RELATED INTERNET SITE(S)

Alexander Graham Bell Family Papers at the Library of Congress, 1862–1939

http://memory.loc.gov/ammem/bellhtml/bellhome.html

This collection of digital replicas of Alexander Graham Bell's Papers is part of the Library of Congress' American Memory Project. It will have more than 4,500 items, including Bell's scientific notebooks, journals, articles, correspondence, blueprints, and photographs, that document his invention of the telephone, his aeronautical and other scientific research, his interest in the education of the deaf, and his family life. Links to information to aid access and understanding include: Collection Highlights, Timeline, Telephone and Multiple Telegraph, About the Collection, Collection Connections from the Learning Page, and Bell as Inventor and Scientist.

Turning Secondary Students into Inventors

http://jefferson.village.virginia.edu/~meg3c/id/id_sep/id_sep.html

At this site, which features information about an Invention and Design course for high school students, note, at the top of the page, a link to Modules (which features a Telephone Module link). In addition, see links to an introduction, resources, an index, and education. See also links to Suggestions for Using the Modules, References and Suggestions for Further Reading, and, based on an actual class which took the course, an Evaluation Report Submitted to the Dodge Foundation.

The Bible and Science
(1889)
URL: http://www.rae.org/b19th00.html

SITE SUMMARY: This book was written by Professor L.T. Townsend of Boston University, and was first presented, before publication, at a meeting in 1874, then again in 1883 under the title *The Bible in Light of Modern Science*, and then in lectures in 1884. It is provided online, introduced, and commented on by Doug Sharp, who declares: "although this volume is well over a hundred years old, the argument is timeless and still powerful." The book has nine parts sub-divided into various sub-topics; including: The Bible and the Exact Language of Science, Conflicts Between Science and the Bible, Author of Nature is Author of Bible, The Bible and Scientific Classification; The Art of Healing and the Bible; The Mind and the Bible; The Bible and Natural History, Geology, and Astronomy; plus Science Confirms Bible Theology.

DISCUSSION QUESTIONS AND ACTIVITIES

1. Choose one sub-topic from three of the nine parts featured in Townsend's book, then describe each topic as Townsend viewed it.
2. Visit at least two of the Web sites cited in the Related Internet Sites section below. Find something on the topic you chose from Townsend's book, or another topic. Describe similarities and/or differences between his views and what you find on the topic or subject at the Web sites. Include information on how the present time's views of the topic or subject reflect modern times or seem to stand beyond particular times (i.e., Townsend's), and therefore are relevant for any time (i.e., yours).
3. Choose a particular subject you can think of which is based on a topic Townsend mentioned (e.g., Plants in the Bible as a particular Bible and Natural History subject; Star of Bethlehem as a particular Bible and Astronomy subject). Describe its scientific and Biblical aspects; comparing and/or contrasting them. (Find information at the Web sites referred to in Question/Activity no. 2 above.)
4. Think of, and/or find, at one of the Web sites referred to in Question/Activity no. 2 above: a Bible-related science general topic or particular subject not mentioned by Townsend. Describe, with data from a suggested Web site, how the Bible seems to agree with the scientific view, or not. (Hints: Great Flood; dinosaurs and people living at same time.)

RELATED INTERNET SITE(S)

Bible Science Web Sites

http://www.pb.org/science.html

This site features links to sites on Biblical archeology and to Scientific Creationism (a view of creation opposite from evolution) and advocated by organizations linked here, such as the Biblical Creation Society.

The Bible and Science at the American Scientific Affiliation Online

http://www.asa3.org/topics/Bible-Science/index.htm

This page is part of the site for this organization of scientists interested in religion. The page features a series of papers on Biblical and scientific insights in dealing with questions about natural phenomena and the place of the Bible in stimulating modern science and scientific ideas.

Fitting the Bible to the Data

http://www.infidels.org/library/modern/vic_stenger/schrev.html

A review by Victor Stenger of the book *Convergence of Scientific and Biblical Wisdom*, 1998, by Israeli physicist Gerald Schroeder of the University of Hawaii.

Science and Christianity: Allies or Enemies?

http://homepages.tcp.co.uk/~carling/main_sci.html

This site features links to articles such as "God and the Big Bang" (with references to Bible verses), and organizations such as the Evangelical Environmental Network.

Center for Scientific Creationism

http://www.creationscience.com

See the online book *In the Beginning: Compelling Evidence for Creation and the Flood*; etc. Scroll to bottom left for "Questions Raised By the Bible's Book of Genesis, part 1:8a."

Supposed Bible/Science Conflicts

http://christiananswers.net/creation/menu-bible.html (click link)

Mysteries of the Bible—Science

http://www.biblemysteries.com/library/biblescience

This just started in-progress area features Bible verses seeming to refer to things scientific (e.g., the fossil bird/reptile: archaeopteryx).

The Qur'an and the Bible Foretelling Modern Science

http://www.answering-islam.org/Campbell/s4c1.html

"On a New Radioactive Substance Contained in Pitchblende"
Pierre Curie and Marie S. Curie (1898)
URL: http://webserver.lemoyne.edu/faculty/giunta/curiespo.html

SITE SUMMARY: This paper reveals the step by step research by the Curies that led to their discovery of radium and to their being awarded, with M. Becquerel, the 1903 Nobel Prize in Physics. This paper was published in the *Comptes Rendus*, no. 127. This translation was partly done by Carmen Giunta of the faculty of Lemoyne College, Syracuse University, New York, for this Web page (part of the Classic Papers in Chemistry Web site, whose url is cited in this book's Appendix B).

DISCUSSION QUESTIONS AND ACTIVITIES

1. Which minerals did the Curies say are very active, and from which point of view? What is probable if certain minerals are more active than uranium? (Hints: See the beginning of the Paper for the answer to the first question. Scroll down a bit for the answer to the second question.)
2. What does "the property of emitting rays" of uranium and thorium compounds do? What does it have to do with the active metal in each compound? What is of secondary importance?
3. What guided the Curies' research? How? What resulted?
4. What did the Curies discover when they analyzed some pitchblende and compared what they discovered to uranium? With what did they treat the pitchblende then? What main thing was verified? What was not found? What was accomplished but incomplete, and how did they judge it with some facts involving pitchblende?
5. By the Curies repeating different operations, what did they finally obtain, and what was its relation to uranium? What did they examine and seek, then what did they find out about uranium, thorium, and tantalum?
6. What did the Curies come to believe that involved pitchblende? What did they suggest if their belief was verified?
7. What were the two curious results of the examination of the spectrum of the substance that the Curies were investigating?
8. What did the Curies suggest that their discovery, if confirmed, be attributed to?
9. What was the Curies' research "guided constantly by"?
10. As the Curies did their research, they concluded that they had found a new substance. Why? What did they name it? Identify the two ways of naming a chemical substance. Extra Activity: Imagine you have discovered a new chemical substance. How would you name it, first if you followed the way the Curies named what they discovered, and then if you named it the way that their discovery was eventually named?

RELATED INTERNET SITE(S)

"Radioactive Substances, Especially Radium"—Nobel Lecture by Pierre Curie

http://www.nobel.se/physics/laureates/1903

On this Nobel Prize in Physics 1903 Recipients Page, click the Nobel Lecture link under Pierre Curie to get to this lecture, presented on June 6, 1905, available in PDF format.

"Marie Curie and Pierre Curie on the Discovery of Polonium and Uranium" (1996)

http://www.nobel.se/physics/laureates/1903

On this Nobel Prize in Physics 1903 Recipients Page, click the article link under Marie Curie or Pierre Curie for this lecture that was presented by Nanny Froman of the Royal Academy of

Sciences, Stockholm, Sweden, on February 28, 1996. See also links to biographies under Marie Curie and Pierre Curie, and other resources under Marie Curie.

The Curies: The Very Model of Modern Spousal Collaboration

http://www.almaz.com/nobel/physics/The_Curies.html

This newsletter item appeared in the American Physical Society's *APS News Online* (June 1996). It features comments on the collaboration of the Curies as a wife and husband research team.

Curie at the Exploratorium—A Museum of Science, Art and Human Perception

http://www.exploratorium.edu (do a search in the search box on upper right of page)

Do a search for Curie, then click Web page links that appear and feature the word Curie.

"Rays Emitted by Compounds of Uranium and of Thorium"
Marie Sklodowska Curie (1898)
URL: http://webserver.lemoyne.edu/faculty/giunta/curie98.html

SITE SUMMARY: This Paper provides data on Marie Curie's examination of substances to determine if they could make air a conductor of electricity. The Paper is based on research Curie conducted at the Municipal School of Industrial Physics and Chemistry, and was published in *Comptes Rendus*, no. 126. This translation has been provided online by Carmen Giunta of Lemoyne College, Syracuse, New York, as part of the Selected Classic Papers in Chemistry Web site. (Its url is in this book's Appendix B.) This paper was published just before the paper she wrote with her husband, Pierre (see this book's previous chapter on that Paper), which provided more information on their research involving the then newly discovered substance Radium.

DISCUSSION QUESTIONS AND ACTIVITIES

1. What did Curie study involving uranium rays and air?
2. When Curie examined substances other than uranium to determine if they would make air a conductor of electricity, which types of substances did she study? Which three things did she use, and how?
3. What did she discover with relation to uranium compounds she studied? What did she find remarkable about uranium and thorium?
4. What is pitchblende? What did she learn about it and how is that connected to uranium? Why is one fact "most remarkable"?
5. What increases with the thickness of sample layers of elements? To what extent does it involve compounds of uranium and of thorium oxide? Because of the way the thorium oxide reacts, what seems to be true regarding its relation to the rays it emits? What curious thing happens when rays from thorium oxide are emitted in a thick layer and in a thin layer?
6. What happens to rays emitted by uranium and thorium under action of Roentgen rays (x-rays)? To interpret the spontaneous radiation of uranium and thorium, what, did Curie say, one can imagine?
7. When describing her research, Curie wrote about absorption, transparence, photographic images of substances or their properties, and something that makes air a conductor of electricity. What did Curie observe that involved absorption? How, according to Curie, can one study transparence in various substances, and what always happens, yet what do the rays do anyway? What did she see in the photographs she took?
8. Keep Question/Activity no. 7 above in mind. Study the Web site on What Is Electricity? Identify which other things make air a conductor of electricity in the world around you, then give details about one. (The url of the Web site referred to is cited in the Related Internet Sites section below.)
9. Visit the Radioactivity—Science Radio Report—American Institute of Physics Web site area, then the Radio Reports area of the AIP Web site. (Both urls are cited in the Related Internet Sites section below.) Describe what is featured at the Radioactivity—Science Radio Report Web site area, noting Marie Curie, and radioactivity today.
10. Keep Question/Activity no. 9 above in mind. With help from the Radio Report Web site area, or another Web site featuring science and history data as noted anywhere in this book, imagine you are a radio news reporter or a scientist being interviewed by one. Think of "then" and "now" interview questions to ask or to be asked on any scientific discovery of today and its connection to a related scientific discovery one hundred, fifty, twenty-five, fifteen, ten, or five years ago. If a recent time is chosen, note how change occurs more rapidly (e.g., years ago one hundred or fifty years went by before changes, but less time goes by for changes in recent times).

RELATED INTERNET SITE(S)

Science in Poland: Maria Skłodowska-Curie

http://hum.amu.edu.pl/~zbzw/ph/sci/msc.htm

This site includes a biography, plus a list of "firsts" that Curie accomplished, a link to an exhibit: Marie Curie and the Science of Radioactivity, a definition of a "Curie unit," and what is considered as one of Curie's outstanding accomplishments. There are also quotations by Curie, with links to radium and polonium data at the WebElements Web site, and links to more sites about Curie. The quotations are undocumented.

Marie Curie—Chemist

http://www.astr.au.edu/4000ws/CURIE.html

The 4,000 Years of Women in Science Web site features a brief biography, plus Curie quotations without sources specified.

Marie Curie—A Nobel Prize Pioneer

http://www.france.diplomatie.fr/label_france/ENGLISH/SCIENCES/CURIE/marie.html

Note the introductory biography, then the sections From the Scientific Dream, and To the Humanitarian Dream, all including quotations by Curie and her husband, Pierre.

Nobel Prize Lecture (1911) by Marie S. Curie

http://gos.sbc.edu/c/curie1911.html

Curie gave this lecture on the occasion of her being the first woman to receive the Nobel Prize, for her discovery of radium, and for her being a second time Nobel prize recipient. In it she describes her experiments and discoveries, and explains the nature of the spectrum in the mineral radium.

Curie Articles in Archives and Timeline Archives at Science News Online

http://www.sciencenews.org (click Archives link)

Click Search Archives, then use the words Curie or Radium in the Archives search area. An article that this search leads to is "A Curie-ous Tale" (July 22, 2000) (of an American Institute of Physics exhibit). Also on the Archives page click the link to the Timeline, then scroll to November 1996, and find as part of this Seventy Years Ago Timeline Area "Radium Gift Useful to Marie Curie" (November 6, 1926).

American Institute of Physics

http://www.aip.org

Click the Center for History of Physics link and find a Marie Curie exhibit, plus selected Papers of Great American Physicists. See also the Media link that leads to Physics News Update, FYI, Press Releases, Inside Science TV News, and Science Radio Reports. Note, in addition, link to Education and Student Services.

Radioactivity—Science Radio Report—American Institute of Physics

http://www.aip.org/radio.html/radioactivity.html

Click a link to listen to a radio announcement of, or a link to read, a transcript on the one hundredth anniversary of the discovery of radioactivity (February 1996), for information on how this discovery has affected today's science.

"Radium and Radioactivity" by Marie S. Curie

http://www.physics.ucla.edu/~cwp/articles/curie.htm

This article was published in *Century Magazine*, January 1904. It features information on what the discovery of the phenomenon of radioactivity means.

What Is Electricity?

http://www.ktca.org/newtons/12/electric.html

Aspects of electricity are introduced here by an educational TV program team that is headed by Brian Hackney who is a physicist, electrical engineer, and meteorologist.

VI
Early Twentieth Century

"Star Spectral Classification Chart"
Annie Jump Cannon and Harvard University (1918–)
URL: http://www.wellesley.edu/Astronomy/annie/index.html

SITE SUMMARY: On the Annie Jump Cannon Homepage at the Wellesley College Web site, click the link with the phrase that begins "Oh, Be a . . ."; then scroll to see this reproduction of the "Star Spectral Classification Chart" (also known as the "Harvard Star Spectral Classification Chart") which was created by Annie Jump Cannon at the Harvard Observatory, while she worked on new additions to the *Henry Draper Catalogue* (a preliminary work published in 1890, and named to honor the astronomer-photographer Henry Draper who took the first photograph of a deep-space astronomical object and the first crude photograph of a star's spectra). Cannon expanded the Catalogue in several volumes, and published them between 1918 and 1924, with more material in 1949. The chart, primarily Cannon's work, remains a standard for identifying star types. (See also links to Career: Theorist of Stellar Spectra, and Understanding Her Work.)

DISCUSSION QUESTIONS AND ACTIVITIES

1. In the "Harvard Star Spectral Classification Chart" which letters are used to represent star types? What color is associated with each letter? What do the letters and the colors represent?
2. Mnemonics (a memory trick or game) has been used to help people remember the order of the star types of the "Harvard Star Spectral Classification Chart" by their letters. Think of a mnemonic example sentence to help you remember the order of the star types by their letters. (For information on mnemonics and the "Harvard Star Spectral Classification System," click mnemonics link to data at the NASA's Classification of Stellar Spectra—Explanation Web site. [Its url is cited in the Related Internet Sites section below.])
3. Identify what is said at the Sommers-Bausch Observatory Archives Web page about the importance and legacy of the *Henry Draper Catalogue*. (The Archives' url is cited in the Related Internet Sites section below.) Explain the ways that you think this importance and this legacy honor Cannon, and benefit astronomy.
4. What was important to Cannon's work in the work of Williamina Fleming, Antonia Maury, Henrietta Leavitt, Margaret Mayall, and Cecilia Payne-Gaposchkin? (For hints, see the Web sites: Powell's Reaching for the Stars; *Henry Draper Catalogue* with a Tribute to A.J. Cannon and the Women of Astronomy [at the Sommers-Bausch Observatory Archives Online]; Enchanted Learning Astronomy Glossary—Henry Draper and *Henry Draper Catalogue*; Cecilia

Payne-Gaposchkin at History of Women in Astronomy Online; Spectra of Stars—Lecture Notes; and Women in Astronomy—History. [Their urls are cited in the Related Internet Sites section below, or in this book's Appendix B.]) Which one of these women wrote a thesis, and on what?

5. What was the importance of Gustav Kirchoff's ideas and work with relation to Cannon's? (Hint: See data on Kirchoff's Laws in the Understanding Her Work area at the Annie Jump Cannon Home Page cited in the Site Summary above.)

6. What do scientists consider spectral lines to be, according to the author of the Web page Understanding Her Work (found as cited in Question/Activity no. 5 above)?

7. Identify and describe the features of the "MK System of Star Spectral Classification." (For help, visit the Web sites: NASA's Classification of Stellar Spectra—Explanation, and the National Academy of Sciences—Biographical Memoir—William W. Morgan. [Their urls are cited in the Related Internet Sites section below.]) Explain how the "MK System" differs from the "Harvard Star Spectral Classification Chart" system, and why the "MK System" is considered to be the successor to Cannon's "Harvard Star Chart," then provide examples. Identify the three people involved with the "MK System," and tell about each one's contribution.

8. The "Hertzsprung-Russell Diagram" is also important to star classification. Identify its connection to Cannon's "Harvard Star Chart." (For data, see the Web site: Stellar Evolution [plus Contributions to Analyses of Stars]. Its url is cited in the Related Internet Sites section below.)

9. Why is it important to know about star spectral classification, with relation to the sun, and to space travel?

RELATED INTERNET SITE(S)

Annie Jump Cannon in the National Women's Hall of Fame Online

http://www.greatwomen.org/women.php?action=viewone&id=33

Papers of Annie Jump Cannon—An Inventory at Harvard University Archives

http://oasis.harvard.edu/html/hua2001.html

Finding Aid to the Papers of Annie Jump Cannon

http://www.aip.org/history/ead/harvard_cannon/19990023_content.html

Henry Draper Catalogue and "Tribute to A.J. Cannon and the Women of Astronomy"

http://lyra.colorado.edu/sboinfo/readingroom/hd.html

This Web page provides information on parts of the *Henry Draper Catalogue* now in the collection of the University of Colorado's Sommers-Bausch Observatory Archive, plus the *Catalogue*'s importance and legacy. It also features a reproduction of one of Cannon's first photos of star spectra (1893) with data on how long it took to photograph it, and her first recorded observation of star spectra. Quotations by noted astronomers Edward C. Pickering and Harlow Shapely about Cannon and her work are also featured.

Cecilia Payne-Gaposchkin at History of Women in Astronomy Online

http://cannon.sfsu.edu/~gmarcy/cswa/history/cecilia.html

There is a brief but detailed biography of the first person to receive a Ph.D. degree in astronomy (in 1925) for research work done at Harvard College Observatory. This research "enabled her to assign a surface temperature to each type of star of Cannon's spectral classes." A 1960 quote about her thesis, stated by astronomer Otto Struve, is also given. The site also notes that Payne-Gaposchkin was the first person to receive the Annie J. Cannon Prize in 1934.

Reaching for the Stars—A Century Ago, Women Astronomers at Harvard Made Scientific History, by Jennifer H. Powell

http://www.hno.harvard.edu/gazette/1998/03.19/ReachingfortheS.html

Classification of Stellar Spectra—Explanation

http://lheawww.gsfc.nasa.gov/users/allen/spectral_classification.html

This site includes information on the first attempts to classify stars before Annie Jump Cannon's landmark work. It has the "Harvard Star Spectral Classification Chart" with descriptions of its aspects. Find the link to the mnemonics page which explains ways to remember Cannon's code. Note especially the mnemonics examples on Physics and Astronomy. Also provided is information on the "MK Star Classification Chart," named for its "authors" William W. Morgan, Philip C. Keenan, and Edith Kellman, called an addition or successor to Cannon's "Harvard Chart." The "MK Chart" includes luminosity, with measurements of the shape and nature of spectral lines to measure stars' surface gravity, in addition to Cannon's chart's surface temperature and spectral features of stars.

Stellar Evolution (Plus Contributions to Analyses of Stars)

http://www.astunit.com/tutorials/stellar.htm

This site defines stars, states how they can be analyzed, and notes Cannon's contribution to stars' analyses by classifications that emphasize star color and surface temperature, as shown by a chart that notes color, temperature, spectral characteristics, and letter designations. Also included is the "H-R Diagram" (the "Hertzsprung-Russell Diagram") which is another way to classify stars while including aspects of Cannon's "Harvard Chart." This Diagram, created by Ejnar Hertzsprung and Henry Norris Russell in the early twentieth century, emphasizes "a star's absolute luminosity . . . plotted against its surface temperature (or spectral type)." Data on stellar evolution notes nebular material, pulsars, quasars, novae, supernovas, binary stars, white dwarfs, and black holes.

National Academy of Sciences—Biographical Memoirs—William W. Morgan

http://www.nap.edu/readingroom/books/biomems/wmorgan.html

Based on Morgan's research notes, correspondence, and conversations with him, his colleagues, students, and wife, this memoir features information on his work on spectral classification known as the "MK System," and other astronomical areas; including notes.

Henry Draper—Biographical Details, Astronomical Contribution and Significance

http://www.ras.ucalgary.ca/~gibson/draper

Enchanted Learning Astronomy Glossary—Henry Draper and *Henry Draper Catalogue*

http://www.enchantedlearning.com/subjects/astronomy/glossary/indexd.shtml

Scroll to information boxes for a Draper biography, links to data on his star identification method, the work of Annie Jump Cannon and Margaret Mayall related to the *Catalogue*.

"What Is the Theory of Relativity?"
Albert Einstein (1919)
URL: http://www.basex-systems.com/emc2.htm

SITE SUMMARY: After the noted scientist Albert Einstein accepted an invitation to contribute something to the British scientific world, he sent this paper, in which he described a new theory. It was published in the *London Times* on November 28, 1919. In this paper, Einstein tells why he accepted the invitation, then explains his theory, sometimes using things familiar to average people as he attempted to clarify a point. He then places his theory in context within the history of physics. It is offered online by IBM business partner, Base X Systems, a researcher of futuristic technology and sciences.

DISCUSSION QUESTIONS AND ACTIVITIES

1. See paragraph one. What did physicists, astronomers, and other scientists do during wartime, and how did it reflect on their reputations? What do you think Einstein's statement means? Provide an example which you think is an illustration of what he said, and explain why you think so.

2. See paragraph two. What, according to Einstein, do various kinds of theories in physics do? What does it mean when one says one understands a group of natural processes? What does "the kinetic theory of gases" seek to do?

3. See paragraph three. What is a second set of important theories? What do they "employ"? Explain. (Hint: See sentence three.)

4. See paragraph four. What are the advantages of the "constructive theory" and the "principle theory"?

5. See paragraph five. Where does the "Theory of Relativity" belong? How does one grasp its nature? Identify what this theory resembles, and explain. Extra Activity: Explain further. (Hint: See paragraph eight.)

6. See paragraph six. What has been known since the days of the ancient Greeks with reference to the movement of something? Give Einstein's two examples. Provide two of your own examples based on Einstein's two types. Identify the phrase physicists use to refer to what is mentioned in the Question/Activity no. 5 above. What are the discoveries by Galileo and Newton with reference to the phrase physicists use? Extra Activity: Explain further. (Hint: See the first part of paragraph seven.)

7. See paragraphs nine and fifteen. What is kinematics? What does a clock have to do with it, and what relation is there to what is referred to in Question/Activity no. 6 above especially with reference to the phrase physicists use? How may one look at clocks with reference to the "general theory of relativity"?

8. See paragraph twelve, especially the last part. See also paragraphs thirteen and fourteen. What ought to be possible with reference to what is referred to in the part of Question/Activity no. 6 above that involves the phrase physicists use? What does this consideration suggest? What has "justified hopes," and what makes "the path thornier than one might suppose"? Explain. (Hint: What do Euclid, curvature of space, straight line, and plane, have to do with it?)

9. See paragraphs sixteen, seventeen, and eighteen. What does the new "theory of gravitation" diverge from yet agree with, and how? Identify three things that may be called criteria for distinguishing them, and that are "accessible to experience." What is the chief attraction of the theory, and why? What should "no one suppose"? Why not? Extra Activity: Explain an aspect of what is referred to just above. Provide an example. (For help, see any Web site referred to in this book.)

RELATED INTERNET SITE(S)

"Relativity—The Special and General Theory" by Albert Einstein

http://www.bartleby.com/173

This detailed work, the main subject of "What is the Theory of Relativity?" featured above, was published in 1920 by Henry Holt, and translated by Robert W. Lawson. This online version is arranged in four parts as "The Special Theory," "The General Theory," "Considerations on the Universe as a Whole," and Appendices. Each part features several chapters.

Albert Einstein Online

http://www.westegg.com/einstein

See the Einstein site links in the categories In His Own Words (e.g., an interview with the FBI, and an essay on science and religion), Quotable Einstein (e.g., Einstein's Wisdoms), Physics (with explanations of his work), Einstein Moments (with Einstein patents), Overviews (including a biography), Announcements, and Related Pages.

NOVA Online—Einstein Revealed

http://www.pbs.org/wgbh/nova/einstein or *http://www.pbs.org/wgbh/nova/prevsitesubj.html* (do search)

See the links to Timeline, Light Stuff, Genius Among Geniuses, Time Traveler, Relativity and the Cosmos, Einstein Links, and Teachers Guide. All are follow ups to the PBS-TV NOVA program on Einstein.

Albert Einstein Archives Online

http://www.albert-einstein.org or *http://sites/huji.ac.il/jnul/einstein/index.html*

Features include Literary Estate, with links to an Einstein Papers Project, and Einstein's Works; Einstein for Kids, with links to "Think Like Einstein," "How Smart Was He?" with a teachers guide; a mini exhibit; a book list; an Einstein biography via a portrait link; active holdings at the Jewish National and University Library; resources (e.g., lists of primary and secondary materials; and links to more Einstein sites), plus news (e.g., of new online texts and exhibits).

American Institute of Physics—A. Einstein—Image and Impact

http://www.aip.org/history/einstein

The American Institute of Physics' Center for the History of Physics provides Einstein photo links leading to Science and Philosophy (with Einstein quotations), $E = MC^2$ (with Einstein's voice), Quantum and Cosmos, an excerpt from Einstein's "The World As I See It" essay, The Great Works (with questions from and descriptions of his major theories, and where they were published), Formative Years, World Fame, Public Concerns, other links to Basic Einstein Facts, and more Einstein Web sites.

"A Simple Introduction to the Principle of Relativity"

http://www.phys.unsw.edu.au/~jw/relativity.html

This Web page provides a comparison of the ways the principle of relativity were viewed by Galileo, Newton, and Einstein. A clear example of Einstein's theory, plus links to more about his theory, are also provided.

How Einstein Arrived at E = MC², by Mort Orman, M.D., 1995

http://www.stresscure.com/hrn/einstein.html

This article is provided online by the Health Resource Network. It also has the title *Harness the Einstein Within You* and is online at http://www.changeforgood.com/fall2002.asp.

Albert Einstein Papers Project at the California Institute of Technology

http://einstein.caltech.edu

This site has some details on data in volumes that are being published in print and feature Einstein's scientific, professional and personal papers, manuscripts and correspondence. Some volumes' introductions are also online, as are some sample manuscript pages. A few quoted excerpts are in German. Called "the most ambitious documentation of the history of science ever undertaken," this project, so far including volumes one through eight of twenty-five that Princeton University Press is publishing, was started at Boston University and is being continued by CalTech, where Einstein was a visiting scientist.

Albert Einstein's Letters to Franklin Roosevelt

http://www.nuclearfiles.org/docs/1939/39082-einstein-roosevelt.html

Note the letter that Einstein wrote to Roosevelt on August 2, 1939, and see a brief explanation of the letter. Next, click the link to Einstein's letter of March 25, 1945.

"Physical Grounds for Einstein's Theory of Relativity: Roots of the Falsification of Twentieth Century Physics," by A.C.V. Ceapa, 1997

http://www.rnc.ro/book/titl4.html

"On the Discovery of Radium"
Marie Curie (1921)
URL: http://gos.sbc.edu/c/curie1921.html

SITE SUMMARY: Curie, a two-time Nobel Prize recipient and physics professor at the Sorbonne (a college of the University of Paris), presented this speech at Vassar College in Poughkeepsie, New York, on May 14, 1921. The speech, preserved in print as no. 2 of Vassar's Ellen S. Richards Monographs series, centers on what Curie called "the somewhat peculiar conditions of the discovery of radium" and her view that "the scientific history of radium is beautiful." The speech is provided online at the Gifts of Speech Web site, by Liz Linton, site director; and electronic resources and serials librarian in Cochran Library, Sweet Briar College, Virginia.

DISCUSSION QUESTIONS AND ACTIVITIES

1. Describe, in steps, the investigations leading up to the discovery of radium. Who were two other people associated with the work?
2. Why did she say "radium is no more a baby?" What, did she say, is the special interest of radium? What makes it important? In which ways? What is particularly important?
3. Name other elements sharing similar properties with radium.
4. What is compared to uranium and to gold?
5. To what does the "theory of transformation" refer? What is carnotite? Define emanations. What did she say about radioactivity?
6. What about radium has been studied closely, and has to do with light? How?
7. Curie mentioned her hope that her discovery would be used for medical purposes. Visit the Web sites: On the Positive Side of Uranium and Radioactivity (of the National Institute of Environmental Health Sciences), Uranium Information Centre—Resource Papers and Briefing Papers, Medical Physics Journal Online, Public Health Statement for Radium (from the Agency for Toxic Substances and Disease Registry), Radiation Information Resources, and Health Physics Society—Radiation Fact Sheets, Ask An Expert Questions and Answers, etc. (Their urls are in cited in the Related Internet Sites section below.) Find, state, and describe some of today's beneficial uses of radioactive substances. Cite and quote from scientific papers on the subject, found via these sites, to support your choices.
8. What did Curie say people must not forget? What is this proof of? State how she said it scientifically, and in a poetic way. Give two examples, one for the scientific, and one for the poetic, from the world you know or the world in general. State the connection between each example and what she said.
9. What is the "vast field" Curie mentioned? How did she connect it to her audience? How could you have a connection?
10. Choose a quotation by Curie from each of these Web sites: American Institute of Physics—Marie Curie, Marie Curie: Polish-French Chemist and Physicist, Science in Poland: Maria Sklodowska-Curie 1867–1934, Marie Curie—Chemist, and Nobel Prize Speech (1911) by Marie Curie. (Their urls are cited in the Related Internet Sites section below, or in this book's chapter featuring Curie's document: "Rays Emitted By Compounds of Uranium and of Thorium.") Cite the original sources of the quotes you chose, if possible, and/or the Web sites where you found the quotations. Apply the quotations to a science or sciences in today's society, showing how Curie's insight is relevant beyond her time.

RELATED INTERNET SITE(S)

American Institute of Physics—Marie Curie

http://www.aip.org/history/esva/exhibits/curie.htm

This site features the Curie quotations that begin "The life of a great scientist"; and "A great discovery." There is also a link to an AIP online exhibit: "Marie Curie and the Science of Radio-activity."

Marie Curie: Polish-French Chemist and Physicist

http://www.gale.com/free_resources/whm/bio/curie_m.htm

This biography, provided by a noted educational materials publisher, was written as an introduction for students, has a Curie quotation starting, "A scientist in his laboratory is not a mere technician" and features a metaphor that a young person can relate to.

Public Health Statement for Radium (1990)

http://www.atsdr.cdc.gov/ToxProfiles/phs9022.html

This statement is by the Agency for Toxic Substances and Disease Registry, Atlanta, Georgia. Eight contents parts include the questions: What is radium? How might I be exposed to radium? and How can radium affect my health?

Uranium Information Centre—Resource Papers and Briefing Papers

http://www.uic.com.au/index.htm

At this Australia-based site, click the link for Educational Resources with resource papers (in PDF format), including "What is Uranium?" and "The Physics of Uranium." Click also the link for Briefing Papers, with papers on Nuclear Power and Health, Nuclear Power for Electricity, Climate Change, General (e.g., the Nuclear Debate), etc.

On the Positive Side of Uranium and Radioactivity

http://www.niehs.nih.gov/kids/uranium.htm (or search for niehs logo via www.nih.gov)

The National Institute of Environmental Health Sciences cites some of the beneficial uses of radioactive substances today.

Medical Physics Journal Online

http://www.medphys.org

This site, for the journal of the American Association of Physicists in Medicine, has the current issue, archives, and a list of upcoming articles. Links are provided to summaries called abstracts, and sometimes full texts for non-subscribing visitors. Many are scholarly articles, but some are suitable to nonscientists (e.g., browse the archives for the 1999 volume 26, the September 15, 1999 issue, for "The Symposium Commemorating the Centennial of the Discovery of Radium by Marie Sklowdowska-Curie"; "Marie Curie and Nuclear Medicine"; "Marie and Pierre Curie and Radium: History, Mystery and Discovery"; and "A Simple Model For Examining Issues in Radiotherapy Optimization" (in the issue for July 15, 1999). (Some articles are in PDF format.)

Radiation Information and Resources

http://www.bios.niu.edu/sims/radium.html

Via one working link, the Biological Sciences Department of North Illinois University provides information on Radium (History and Basic Information), with a note on Curie.

Health Physics Society—Radiation Fact Sheets, Ask an Expert Q's and A's, etc.

http://www.aps.org (click links)

This organization, dedicated to promoting the practice of radiation safety, features fact sheets via a radiation facts link, with subjects including types of radiation, exposure, and risk. Also provided are a link to questions and answers on subjects including benefits of radiation, radiation basics, education, regulations, and standards.

"My Acquaintance with Zoological Park Animals"
Helen Keller (1923)
URL: http://www.afb.org (click Helen Keller link)

SITE SUMMARY: Scroll to the bottom of the page, click the "Helen Keller—Writings" link, then search for and click the "My Animal Friends" link to get to this essay which is part two of the article "My Animal Friends"; which was published in the *Zoological Society Bulletin*, September 1923. Keller describes her first experience at a zoo and another zoo experience. Both provide her unique perspectives because of her many disabilities. Featured here, courtesy of the American Foundation for the Blind and its Helen Keller Archives, this document is online on one of the Foundation's Web pages. Go directly to the article at http://www.afb.org/htm_asp/DocumentID=1220/info_document_view.htm.

DISCUSSION QUESTIONS AND ACTIVITIES

1. Name the three types of animals Keller was "formally introduced to." Describe her "meeting" with each animal. Describe experiences she had with some of the same zoo animals and another zoo animal, both years later, noting how her later experience was similar to, and different from, her earlier experiences. (Hints: In your answer, include a comment on her age, or time in her life, at the time of each visit, and when the article was published. After checking the Helen Keller pages at the American Foundation for the Blind Web site, or one of the Web sites: Tragedy to Triumph, and The Life of Helen Keller [their urls are cited in the Related Internet Sites section below], note which "sense experiences" she was not able to have, then include and identify one or more of the "sense experiences" she was able to have with each zoo animal.)

2. Which zoological park did Helen Keller visit, and which one did she probably visit? (Hints: Note cities where the zoos she mentioned are located; then search the Web sites: Worldwide Links to Zoos and Aquariums, and Zoos Worldwide. [Their urls are cited in the Related Internet Sites section below.]) Find and describe information about each of these parks, and a zoological park near where you live. (For your answer to the second part of this activity, be sure to include similarities and differences between "your" local park and the parks Keller visited.)

3. Visit a local zoological park. (It can be the one found for Question/Activity no. 2 above, but if possible, choose another one.) Note also the At the Zoo Web pages in *ZooGoer Magazine*—Online Archives. (Its url is cited in the Related Internet Sites section below.) Think about Keller's zoo visits. Write about your own observations of zoo animals which you experience while using the senses Keller could use, and then while using the senses she could not use, then state why you think she missed something, or maybe not, and instead had a unique, enriching experience.

4. Referring to what you did for Question/Activity no. 3 above, compare and contrast your experiences and Keller's experiences with some young people's experiences, including those of children who visited zoos as stated in the report "Children, Animals, and Leisure Settings" more than seventy years after Keller's visits. (Its url is cited in the Related Internet Sites section below.)

5. When she described one of the zoo animals she visited, Keller used a simile. After your zoo visit suggested in Question/Activity no. 3 above, think of your own simile to describe something about one of the zoo animals you "met." (Hint: For a definition of simile, see the Web site: Glossary of Rhetorical Terms. [Its url is cited in this book's Appendix F.]) Explain why it is worthwhile to describe something with a simile, and support your answer with science-related comments.

RELATED INTERNET SITE(S)

The Life of Helen Keller—Royal National Institute for the Blind—FactSheet

http://www.rnib.org.uk/wesupply/fctsheet/keller.htm

Sections of this fact sheet include an introduction, Helen Falls Ill, Anne Sullivan, Helen Meets Anne, The Frost King, Helen Enters Radcliffe College, Helen Tours the World, The Miracle Worker, Helen Retires from Public Life, Helen's Legacy (with quotations), and Further Information.

Tragedy to Triumph—The Life of Helen Keller

http://www.graceproducts.com/keller/life.html

Part of the In Search of Heroes series, this Web site sample features an outline of Helen Keller's life, including excerpts from her writings and speeches, as they appear in Joseph P. Lash's definitive book *Helen and Teacher*.

World Wide Link to Zoos and Aquariums

http://www.zooweb.com

This site features live animal cameras also known as zoocams from zoos around the world. There are also links to zoos and aquariums (with links to those most visited) in North America and other areas of the world, conservation, education, and forum. In a Zoo Guide, there are Zooper sites (the best zoo Web sites), Top Sites (the most viewed Web sites), Zoo Groups (Who's Who in Zoos) of people and organizations.

Zoos Worldwide

http://www.zoos-worldwide.com

Zoo News, Zoo Site of the Day, Animal of the Month, and Zoo Info (also called Links Galore), are among the features of this site. There are also links to zoo Web sites in North America and other parts of the world, with each site featuring information in the native language of the zoo's nation.

"Children, Animals, and Leisure Settings"

http://www.psyeta.org/sa/sa3.2/birney.html

This report, by Barbara Ann Birney, was published in the *Society and Animals Journal of Humane Studies* 3 (1995), a publication of the Psychologists for the Ethical Treatment of Animals organization. Based on interviews with children revealing their reactions to animals they saw during visits to zoos and museums, the report contains introductory information, research methods and questions, and results, plus various sources on where the children got their information.

ZooGoer Magazine—Online Archives

http://www.fonz.org/zoogoer/zg-archives.htm

Note especially each issue's At the Zoo page, and BioAlmanac, plus other features. See also "My Vision for the Future" (an article in the January–February 2002 issue) about the Smithsonian National Zoological Park by the park's former chief veterinarian, Lucy H. Spelman.

Fiona Sunquist's "End of the Ark"

http://www.nwf.org/internationalwildlife/zoos.html

This article first appeared in print in *International Wildlife* (November–December 1995). It is provided here online by the National Wildlife Federation Web site. Journalist Sunquist provides a historical overview of the changing purpose of zoos since the first one appeared, and the status of zoos during the early 1990s.

"June Skies"
Helen Keller (1932)
URL: http://www.afb.org (click Helen Keller link)

SITE SUMMARY: Scroll to the bottom of the page, click the "Helen Keller—Writings" link, then search for and click the "June Skies" link, to see this article, published in the June 1932 issue of *Home Magazine*. Provided online by the American Foundation for the Blind, this article features Keller's comments, thoughts, and feelings, on what she could experience of nature, especially of the sky during the month when the spring season ends and the summer season begins in the Northern Hemisphere, during the daytime and at night, including the night sky as presented in a planetarium. It reveals Keller's unique ways of "observing" physically and with an "inner sight." It also includes what she thought and what she learned that people on the earth could experience of the sky. Find the document directly at http://www.afb.org/info_document_view.asp?documentid=1202.

DISCUSSION QUESTIONS AND ACTIVITIES

1. See paragraph one. What did Helen Keller imagine experiencing as she thought about the sky in the month of June and about a bird who flies there? Which bird did she talk about? Write a brief portrait of this bird. (Hint: To find information about the bird that Keller wrote about, go to the Bird of the Week area [via its alphabetical list] of the Cornell Laboratory of Ornithology Web site. Its url is cited in the Related Internet Sites section of this book's chapter featuring BirdNet—The Ornithological Information Source Web site.)

2. Keeping Keller's experience of a bird in mind, as indicated in Question/Activity no. 1 above, choose and describe a bird known to be around during the month of June, or about that time of year in the Northern Hemisphere (late Spring, early Summer), in the area where you live. Describe this bird in the ways that Keller imagined the bird she experienced, then in other ways that you have experienced or can experience a bird. (Note: To help you find and describe a bird that is around in the month of June, or thereabout, go to this book's chapter on the BirdNet Web site referred to in Question/Activity no. 1 above, then visit these Web sites cited in that chapter's Related Internet Sites area: "What is Migration?" Cornell Laboratory of Ornithology, "Excerpts from the Life Histories" in the *Birds of North America*, the Nutty Birdwatcher, and other Web sites referred to in that chapter's Question/Activity no. 10.)

3. See paragraphs four through seven. Quoting phrases or words (especially those that are metaphors or poetic) that Keller used, briefly describe her descriptions of what she knew is in the night sky and how the night sky must be. Also briefly describe what she said a planetarium represents, a special machine in it and what that machine is for, and what a planetarium show shows of the night sky as people of the earth experience it (in general, but also especially as experienced at the time Keller wrote this article).

4. Keeping in mind what you did with Question/Activity no. 3, choose three places on different parts of the earth that Keller mentioned (such as a city, state, nation, or region). Cite something astronomical (such as a planet or a constellation) that can be found in the night sky in each of these particular places, especially some time during the month of June (either in late Spring or early Summer), and during three other months, one each in Winter, Autumn, and early Spring or late Summer. (For data, check the Web sites for the Skywatching Center, Star Journey, StarGazer, The Sky This Month, Space—In the Spotlight, Space Calendar, *Astronomy Now* Magazine's Breaking News or The Night Sky, *Astronomy* Magazine's Calendar of Events, and *Sky and Telescope* Magazine's Sky At A Glance. [Their urls are cited in the Related Internet Sites section below, or in this book's Appendix D.])

5. See paragraph eight. What did Keller say about a planetarium with reference to people on the earth in the past, and of the future? Do you agree or disagree with what she said? Explain her point of view, and yours. Check the Web sites This Month in the History of Astronomy, Some Favorite Links—Astronomy—History of Astronomy, Space Calendar, History of Astronomy—Links, and Space—In the Spotlight. (Their urls are cited in the Related Internet Sites section below.) Describe something astronomical that people of the past experienced, and that people of the future, on the earth, may experience. (Hint: For the second part of the activity just above, consider what can or will be experienced with help from space exploration aids similar to what exists now, such as space telescopes, modern earth based observatories, artificial satellites, the space station, a space shuttle, and probes.) (Option: Try using the Solar System Live Web site if your computer can accept special software. Its url is cited in the Related Internet Sites section below.)

6. In paragraph nine, how did did Keller define a planetarium? Referring to planetarium visits, she urged parents and teachers to "avail themselves of this opportunity to acquaint children with the wonders of the universe and to cultivate their inner vision." Choose a planetarium at one of these online areas: the Planetarium Reference Library's Planetarium Web Sites or Planetarium Compendium, or *Sky and Telescope* Magazine's Resources—Organizations, Planetariums, etc., or one you can find via the science areas of general Web directories. (Their urls are cited in the Related Internet Sites section in this book's chapter featuring "The Role of Planetariums in Astronomy Education," or in this book's Appendix D or Appendix E.) If possible, visit a planetarium. Choose one thing that happens at your chosen planetarium or something that can be experienced there. Describe it and explain how it could "cultivate [your] inner vision." (Hint: For help, and insight, note Keller's comments referred to in Question/Activity no. 7 below.)

7. Keller aimed to express to readers her unique ways of experiencing. Read paragraphs two, three, and ten to discover what she said on this subject. What did she say readers can see, and in which way that is different but similar could she experience? What did she say would happen "if we would look into our own minds"? What, according to her, does the imagination do, and which two things did she attribute to the imagination? Note the vivid phrase she used to describe what readers see (which she said, maybe ironically, she could not see). Apply your imagination in the way she described, and think of, then describe, three other vivid phrases to describe astronomical objects or phenomena.

RELATED INTERNET SITE(S)

Skywatching Center

http://www.earthsky.com/Features/skywatching

This site features links to data on Tonight's Sky (for every day of the current month), About Tonight's Sky, Skywatching Forecast, Star Pronunciation Guide, and Skywatchers Toolbox (Internet sources). There are also links to science subjects, including many sky-related items in: News Bulletins, Science FAQs, Articles, and Cool Site Reviews.

StarGazer: The International Edition

http://www.netside.net/starhustler

This site provides the scripts of the latest one-minute and five-minute episodes, plus past shows' scripts, including the first one of November 4, 1976, that are vignettes of current astronomical features presented by "Star Hustler" astronomer Jack Hornheimer, on PBS-TV stations in cooperation with the Miami Museum of Science and Space Transit Planetarium. Note also the

Star Hustler's favorite phrase, links to the episodes in online video versions requiring special software, and links to FAQs, Questions and Answers, a Star Hustler biography, listings of planetariums and museums, and favorite links.

Space Calendar at NASA's Jet Propulsion Laboratory, California Institute of Technology

http://www.jpl.nasa.gov/calendar

Links by month (including current month) for a full year feature descriptions and links to more data on space related activities and anniversaries. This is information on astronomical occurrences, manned and unmanned space exploration, and other happenings. An archives covers the past two years.

Star Journey

http://www.nationalgeographic.com/features/97/stars/chart/index.html

Clicking on a part of a star chart or map of the Northern or Southern Hemisphere brings up illustrations of astronomical features in that part of the sky. Note also on the page for each sky part: a list that indicates particular features on the chart, a link to images from the Hubble Space Telescope, and a link to Star Chart Notes for more information. On the main page, see also links to the Hubble Telescope, for details about this "eye on the universe," and Star Attractions, for interesting features of constellations, star clusters, nebulae, our Milky Way Galaxy, and other galaxies.

Space—In the Spotlight

http://space.about.com/education/space

Note the link to About Space Daily News for information on subjects including space's teenage stars, and what the students of the NASA Student Involvement Program are doing. See also many other links to information on natural happenings in space, current unmanned probe missions, and current humans-in-space happenings. See also highlighted news items of the present and from the past, and This Date in Space History.

The Sky This Month

http://www.wokr13.tv/astro.main.asp

On this Web page, provided by a TV station in Rochester, New York, find out about the astronomical events of the current month, and featuring something about the moon, the planets, the constellations, space missions, and special astronomical events.

Solar System Live ["An Interactive Orrery"]

http://www.fourmilab.to/solar

Select time, date, viewpoint, observing location, orbital elements, and something to track in the solar system. To use this site downloading special software is required.

Some Favorite Links—Astronomy—History of Astronomy

http://www.phys-astro.sonoma.edu/index.html

Scroll to Favorite Links, click Astronomy link, then History of Astronomy link, then note links with subjects including Ancient Astronomy, Greek Astronomy, The Art of Renaissance Science, Cosmology since 1900, and people including Copernicus, Galileo, Brahe, and Newton.

This Month in the History of Astronomy

http://astro.martianbachelor.com

Originally connected with the Astronomical Society of the Pacific and the Colorado Springs Astronomical Society, this periodically updated Web site by an astronomer features links by month to astronomers' biographies, plus astronomical discoveries and events that occurred on particular days and years in history during a particular month.

History of Astronomy—Links

http://www.astro.uni-bonn.de/~pbrosche/hist_astr

This links page was set up by Wolfgang Dick who has university degrees in physics and astronomy, has worked at the Main Astronomical Observatory of the Academy of Sciences in the Ukraine, and has done research for the International Earth Rotation Service. The page features links to general information (e.g., overview, brief history, from ancient through twentieth-century astronomy); museums, observatories and other places; topics (e.g., anniversaries, calendars, solar system, constellations, nebulae, star clusters, and more), historians, persons, other information sources, and more links.

VII
Later Twentieth Century and
Early Twenty-First Century

"As We May Think"
Vannevar Bush (1945)
URL: http://theatlantic.com/unbound/flashbks/computer/bushf.htm

SITE SUMMARY: This landmark article was published in the July 1945 issue of the *Atlantic Monthly* magazine. Bush, an electrical engineer and director of the U.S. Office of Scientific Research and Development from 1945 to 1947, proposed a challenge to scientists as the world emerged from World War Two into an era of peace. In this challenge, as the magazine editor stated, Bush urged scientists who were turning away from "the application of science to warfare" to "turn to the massive task of making more accessible our bewildering store of knowledge." He also examined what science is and what it means to civilization and people; noted some postwar sciences and then projected something about them into the future; and then suggested something that turned out to be foresight regarding computer language and the Internet.

DISCUSSION QUESTIONS AND ACTIVITIES

1. According to Bush, what are four things that war causes scientists to do, in general, within their professions? Which two types of scientists have the same objectives during times of war and peace? Identify which type of scientist is most challenged by the change from war to peace, and suggest why, then give Bush's example, and think of another. (Hint: See introductory paragraphs.)

2. See Part One of Bush's article. What, according to him, has been of "lasting benefit" regarding people's "use of science" and "the new instruments" which "research brought into existence"? In your answer, state what Bush said, and give his examples, then give particular examples based on his general ones. What endures as a result of communications made possible by science?

3. See Part One, paragraphs four through eight. What happened in Gregor Mendel's time with reference to his publication, and why? Identify a similar yet different thing Bush said happened in the post–World War II era and may still be happening, then give an example. Identify what Bush said with reference to the postwar world and "the days of square rigged ships," and tell if this is true today, then suggest why or why not. What are some "signs of change" that Bush mentioned? Choose one and explain its presence in today's world. Identify things that Gottfried Wilhelm von Leibnitz and Charles Babbage invented, and when, then tell why their inventions could not fit into their times and societies. Read what Bush said about a Pharoah, then choose an invention invented during modern times, and choose a time from

the past. As you choose, think why that invention could not fit in that time in history. After choosing, explain why the invention would not fit in that past time. (Tip: For help see the Smithsonian Institution: Inventors and Inventions—Selected Links, and the National Inventors Hall of Fame—Inventions and Inventors Search Web sites. Their urls are cited in the Related Internet Sites section of this book's chapter on the document "An Inventor Never Grows Up.")

4. See Part One, paragraph nine, Part Eight, paragraphs four through six. How did Bush refer metaphorically to a spider web and its "gossamer parts"? What analogy did he draw between an eye and a cable of a TV set? Note also Part Two, paragraph eight, and what he said about TV. Apply the metaphor and the analogy using your own examples in a way similar to Bush's, or think of two science-related examples, keeping in mind the following activities when choosing: describe two science subjects using an analogy for one, a metaphor for another. (For help defining metaphor and analogy, search in the online Dictionary and Encyclopedia at http://www.infoplease.com.)

5. Read Part Two, paragraph one. What are three things that must be so if a record is to be useful to science? Which six things were available at the time, according to Bush, to make these three things so? Are any of the six things still used today? Do you know of some other new thing in use for this purpose at the present time?

6. See Part Two, especially paragraphs two and three, the last sentences of paragraphs two through four, sentence five of paragraph three, paragraph five of Part Three, all of Part Two, paragraphs ten through twelve and five through six. Think on what Bush envisioned about photography, then tell if anything he said in 1945 about photography in the future happened in the way he said, or differently, including in your answer his references to a walnut. State briefly what he said on different types of photography, then include for one type, as he noted, what he said on photography during the U.S. Civil War, the way it was different from the way it was in 1945 (and is today also). Choose one type of photography noted and describe with details, including his comments, and data from modern times. (Note: To find more information on the photography Bush wrote about, see the Web sites or pages "Micro and Scientific" at What Kinds of Photography Are There?, Photography in Your Science Fair Project, Stereoscopy: Where Did It Come From? Where Will It Lead? Invention of the Fax Machine, Instant Photography and Edwin Herbert Land in the Invention Dimension, Photography—Advice and Techniques—Technique—[specific science photography type] via particular Web directories [e.g., www.msn.com and www.looksmart.com], plus Learn Photography at www.photo.net, and Photographic Resource, or photography magazines with science subjects [e.g., *Outdoor Photographer*]. Their specific urls and Web site description are in the Related Internet Sites section below, or in this book's Appendix B, Appendix D, Appendix E, or Appendix F.)

7. Keeping in mind what Bush wrote in the paragraphs cited in Question/Activity no. 6 above, identify what was important, and still is, about a type of photography and libraries? Read paragraph three, then identify two places that scientists use photography. Give two examples, with details, of a scientific use of photography in each place. (Tip: For more information, see the Web sites and pages cited in Question/Activity no. 6 above.)

8. See Part Three, paragraphs six, seven, and ten. What did Bush say involves mature creative thought? Keeping in mind that Bush said that for repetitive thought there can be mechanical aids, give an example of a repetitive thought and a mechanical aid with relation to that thought, then apply that example to something in particular with relation to physicists as indicated by Bush.

9. Read Part Five, noting paragraphs one, three, and four; Part Six, noting paragraph four; Part Seven, noting paragraphs one through three and the last sentence of four; plus Part Eight, noting paragraphs one, two, and four. What is something scientists do and what types of pro-

cesses are involved, then what happens when these processes are employed, and what is there an opportunity for then? Considering it another way, what is "a keen instrument" in the hands of a teacher, and what is then "readily possible"? Consider further what special application Bush noted, then, in connection with it, what, according to him, may people do "some day" and which three-word phrase did he use to describe something that will help them do this? What did he say about scientific research and what is "a much larger matter"? Identify the essential feature of a "memex." Provide, in general, steps for "building of a trail," then apply it to a science subject you choose, being sure to keep in mind Bush's example as a guide. What did Bush say about trail blazers, physicians, and chemists, then how, did he say, science may help them? (Tip: For help, see the Web sites or pages "Memex" at the Electronic Labyrinth and "As We Are Thinking." Their urls are cited in the Related Internet Sites section below.)

10. Read Part Eight, paragraphs ten and three. According to Bush, what may the "applications of science" allow people to do in a positive sense? Think about his "Prophesy based on extension of the known has substance" and apply it to a science subject you choose.

RELATED INTERNET SITE(S)

As We Are Thinking—A Review of Vannevar Bush's "As We May Think"

http://www.rpi.edu/dept/llc/webclass/web/project1/group6/contents.html or search at *http://www.rpi.edu*

Created by Rensselaer Polytechnic Institute students in 1996, this Web page has links to the various parts of a detailed review of Bush's article. There are an Introduction, Historical Perspectives of the article, Philosophical Perspectives, Bush's Technological Predictions, and a Hypertexting link going to Raising the Issue "What is Hypertexting?"

"Memex" at the Electronic Labyrinth

http://jefferson.village.virginia.edu/elab (Click the Index link, then the M link)

Scroll to the Memex links group and click the memex link for a page with a definition of memex and information about it in Vannevar Bush's "As We May Think" article. On this page, see also links to data on Bush's involvement with memex, and explanations of special words related to memex (e.g., nodes, path, and link).

"Micro and Scientific" at What Kinds of Photography Are There?

http://www.azuswebworks.com/photography/ph_home.html

Among the nine kinds of photography for which information is provided here, note especially "Micro and Scientific," one of the kinds of photography that Bush mentioned in his article "As We May Think." See other information on photography, such as basics, composition, and history, in the Focus on Photography area found via a link at the bottom of the page and at http://azuswebworks.com/photography/index.html.

Photography in Your Science Fair Project

http://www.kodak.com/global/en/service/education/scienceFair/sect1Summary.shtml

Click links to the article "How Photographs Help Your Science Fair Presentation," Introduction; Special Techniques (such as photomicrophotography), General Picture Taking Techniques, Photography Guidelines with Considerations and Questions, and a Science Fair Main Page with information on ways that photography can be useful in the study of, and research in, the sciences (as referred to in Bush's "As We May Think").

"Stereoscopy: Where Did It Come From? Where Will It Lead?"

http://userwww.sfsu.edu/~hl/stereo.html

This article by Harold Layer was published in *Exposure* magazine, Fall 1979. It provides information on Galileo and Newton and other scientists, revealing connections between science and photography, binocular vision, the evolution of basic stereo concepts, and the events leading to the discovery of stereoscopy (one of the types of photography that Vannevar Bush mentioned in his article "As We May Think"). Related links are included.

Events in the Life of Vannevar Bush

http://www.cs.brown.edu/research/graphics/html/info/timeline.html

This Web site provides a timeline of Bush's accomplishments and publications, plus quotations by him and others, including Franklin Roosevelt who was the U.S. President at the time that Bush's article "As We May Think" was written.

"A Proposal for a New Method of Evaluation of the Newborn Infant"
Virginia Apgar (1953)
URL: http://www.apgarfamily.com/Apgar_Paper.html

SITE SUMMARY: First presented at the joint meeting of the International Anesthesia Research Society and the International College of Anesthetists in September 1952, and then published in *Current Researches in Anesthesia and Analgesia* (July–August 1953), this paper proposes a multi-part method of determining a baby's state of health as soon as possible after birth to quickly detect life-threatening problems and avoid complications. This method, know as the Apgar Score, after the Columbia University Presbyterian Hospital doctor who proposed it, has become a standard test procedure for newborn babies. (The paper is a highlight of the official Dr. Virginia Apgar Web page, a feature of the Apgar Family Web site.)

DISCUSSION QUESTIONS AND ACTIVITIES

1. Identify the five tests Apgar suggested for "simple, clear classification" or "grading" of newborn infants. Explain Score ratings in Dr. Apgar's Paper in connection with fair, good, and poor conditions.

2. If a newborn baby has a no. 2 rating for test no. 1, and a no. 1 rating for test no. 2, what is the baby's condition?

3. How are test descriptions and timing somewhat different on the Apgar Score Chart (1995–1998) from what Apgar stated in her paper? (The url for the Neonatology on the Web site, where this chart is found, is cited in the Related Internet Sites section below.)

4. Today, besides the Apgar Tests, other tests are given to newborns. (See data at the Web sites for the American Academy of Pediatrics' Newborn Screening—Fact Sheets, and Table of Newborn Screening by State; the March of Dimes and American Academy of Pediatrics' Public Health Information Sheet; the Newborn Screening Practitioners Manual; plus Resources and Literature Citation of the Month at Neonatology on the Web. [Their urls are cited in the Related Internet Sites section below.]) Should any tests be given? Which tests do you think are essential, or may not be necessary, and why or why not? Some tests require a baby's heel to be pricked to obtain blood. Another test requires a suction device to be used in a baby's nose. Should these invasive procedures, usually stressful and painful, be done? Why or why not?

5. Should special tests automatically be given if there is a family history of a medical condition? Should parents' religious beliefs be followed always or sometimes, even if a baby's condition seems to require medical attention? Who should judge these situations, and how?

6. Visit the Official Dr. Virginia Apgar Web Page. (Its url is cited in the Related Internet Sites section below.) Note the acronym developed to help people remember Apgar test types at a glance. How does the acronym help one remember? Extra Activity: Make an acronym for someone and something else medical- or health-related. Describe the value of the acronym. Option: Choose a woman and what she has accomplished. (For ideas, see the Web sites: Important Figures in the Health Sciences—Their Lives and Works; Women in the Sciences and Women in Medical Fields; plus other Web sites which have some medical-related entries, such as Astronaut Biographies. These sites' urls are in this book's Appendix B: Science Biographies and Career Sources.)

7. Read the 1998 essay "The First Test! Through the Eyes of Dr. Virginia Apgar," by student Sarah Sellers. (Its url is cited in the Related Internet Sites section below.) See information before paragraph one, then paragraphs eleven and eighteen, and identify what qualifies the comments of young Sellers as worth noting, then suggest what she meant when she wrote

"Thank you, Dr. Apgar, for seeing them through your eyes . . . ?" See paragraphs eight, nine, ten, thirteen, and fifteen, then tell how the Apgar Score is similar to, yet different from, early assessments of infants at birth. Why is the Apgar Score better? How is the Score slightly different today?

8. Read paragraphs seven and eight of Seller's article (found as cited in Question/Activity no. 8 above). Why was it especially important, according to Sellers, that Dr. Apgar created the Score, then published it, in the late 1940s and early 1950s? What were the steps Apgar used to create the Score?

9. See paragraphs one and twelve in Seller's article (found as cited in Question/Activity no. 8 above). What, in general, and what exactly, did Sellers write about the word "yardstick" as stated by a Dr. James Nelson, and then about the phrase "a common language"? With your answer to the Question/Activity no. 9 above in mind, apply that word and that phrase to two other things; one each in another area of a medical- or health-related science, such as pediatrics. Explain how your choices fit this word and this phrase. (For help, see Web sites such as the ones for the journal *Pediatrics*, the Archives of *The Future of Children—The Journal*, and the Archives for *Pediatric and Adolescent Medicine*. [Their urls are in the Related Internet Sites section below.])

10. See Question/Activity no. 3 in this book's chapter on the Web site with Excerpts from a *Letter on the Education of Women Physicians*, 1851, by Dr. Elizabeth Blackwell.

11. Read "Apgar: A Commentary" (found as cited in the Related Internet Sites section below.) Why, does Dr. Fox say, the Apgar Score should never be abandoned or revised? Do you agree or disagree? Why or why not? Explain how Apgar's Score is vital today; then how and why it might be expanded to include problems that may arise in today's newborns and are unique to today's generation of infants.

12. Compare or contrast some of Dr. Fox's claims as stated in his article that is referred to in Question/Activity no. 12 above, with some claims by Dr. Selma Harrison Calmes as stated in her articles "Development of the Apgar Score" and "Virginia Apgar and the Apgar Score." (See their urls in the Related Internet Sites section below.)

13. In Dr. Calmes articles (found online as stated in Question/Activity no. 13 above), note the notes on Dr. Apgar's 1958 and 1966 papers that are research follow-ups to the research and Score of her 1953 paper. Identify how the later research is connected to the earlier research, and how the early and later research are important to each other.

14. Study Dr. Apgar's writing style, as cited at Neonatology on the Web, then study a recently published health- or medical-related article that you find at any Web site cited in this book (e.g., in the journal *Pediatrics*, the Archives of *The Future of Children—The Journal*, and the Archives of *Pediatrics and Adolescent Medicine*). Compare Dr. Apgar's style with the style of a medical writer of today. (Find urls for some Web sites referred to just above in the Related Internet Sites section below.)

RELATED INTERNET SITE(S)

Official Dr. Virginia Apgar Web Page

http://www.apgarfamily.com/virginia.htm

This site features biographical data on Dr. Apgar, information on the acronym suggested by Dr. Joseph Butterfield and based on her name to help one remember the features of the Apgar Score. A link leads to a speech by Eric Apgar (her grand nephew and the site's creator) accepting her induction into National Women's Hall of Fame. Other links lead to sites in the medical areas in which Dr. Apgar worked. (This page is a featured link at the Apgar Family Web site http://www.apgarfamily.com.)

"The First Test! Through the Eyes of Dr. Virginia Apgar"

http://apgar.net/virginia/SELLER_PAPER.html

This award-winning essay was written in 1998 by Sarah Sellers, a middle school student.

"Apgar: A Commentary"

http://cpmcnet.columbia.edu/news/review/archives/medrev_v1n2_0006.html

This article is an affirmation of the Apgar Score. It focuses on what the Score is, and is not, tells why it should not be revised or abandoned, and reveals why it is universally accepted and applied. Written by Dr. Harold E. Fox, of the Department of Obstetrics and Gynecology, Columbia University, College of Physicians and Surgeons, New York, the article was published in the *Physicians and Surgeons Medical Review* (also called the *P and S Medical Review*), March 1994.

"Development of the Apgar Score" and "Virginia Apgar and the Apgar Score"

http://apgar.net/virginia/Selma2.html and *http://apgar.net/virginia/Selma4.html*

These articles, by Dr. Selma Harrison Calmes, were published, respectively, in a 1985 publication published by Springer-Verlag, in Berlin; and in the *American Society of Anesthesiologists (ASA) Newsletter*, September 1997. The articles provide information on what led Apgar to develop the Score, how she went about it, and what resulted during the time shortly, and a few years after, its publication. There is data from later papers Apgar published in 1958 and 1966 as follow-ups on the research that led to the 1953 paper, and there are interviews with her colleagues.

Neonatology on the Web

http://www.neonatology.org (scroll to, and click, index link)

Links to note go to articles under Apgar, and the Apgar Scores. These articles include "Evaluation of Newborn—Apgar—Title Page" (a reproduction, with a note on Apgar's writing style and how it is different from today's medical writing style); "D.R. (Delivery Room) Exam" and "Apgar Scores (1995–1998)" which show what is being tested, the Score number, what is observed and done to determine the Score, and what condition each Score represents. There are also links to Classic Papers [in Neonatology], Literature Citation [of the Month] (with a brief description), and Resources, plus Resources Elsewhere [on the Web] that lead to writings by pediatric professionals and some articles that first appeared in medical journals, and other publications.

Newborn Screening Fact Sheets, and Table of Newborn Screening by State

http://www.aap.org/policy/01565.html

These Fact Sheets, published in the journal *Pediatrics* (September 1996), by the American Academy of Pediatrics, describes eleven tests now given to newborn infants in the United States, and provides a link to a table showing which states give particular tests, since no national standard requirements exist.

Newborn Screening Tests—Public Health Information Sheet

http://www.noah-health.org/pregnancy/march_of_dimes/testing/newborn.html

New York Online Access to Health (NOAH) provides this sheet as part of its mission to make available reliable consumer health information on the Web. In this sheet the March of Dimes, for the American Association of Pediatrics, describes disorders that tests detect, which tests are usually given, how soon after birth tests are done, how tests are done, and what parents should do if their babies are diagnosed with a condition.

Newborn Screening Practitioner's Manual (2002)

http://www.mostgene.edu/pract/praclist.htm (click link)

This manual, developed by members of the Newborn Screening Committee of the MoSt GeNe, and published by the Mountain States Regional Genetic Services Network emphasizes, in PDF format, guidelines in the U.S. Mountain States Region, but follows general national procedures. It describes the tests given, indicates inheritance issues, and "assists practitioners in understanding the components of newborn screening and their importance in ensuring that children affected with these conditions are able to achieve their highest potential." Before clicking the link to the manual, scroll to the bottom of the page for a link to the Network's *Genetic Drift* periodical online, and note especially its links to articles in the *Genetic Drift* Winter 1998 issue on "Issues In Newborn Screening."

Archives of *Pediatrics and Adolescent Medicine*

http://archpedi.ama-assn.org

See articles on medical conditions that occur in babies just days after their birth, and medical situations in pre-school-age children, plus childhood occurrences that lead to particular behavior in adolescents.

Archives of *The Future of Children—The Journal*

http://www.futureofchildren.org/homepage2824/archive.htm

Aiming to provide timely objective information based on the best available research, this site offers links to journal articles which feature subjects such as low birth weight, drug-exposed infants, and critical health issues for children and youth (e.g., post-9/11 stress). See also the links to the latest journal (in PDF format) with an annotated contents page, future highlights in upcoming issues, recent research, conversations with questions and answers (e.g., on early childhood development), and the Media/Press Room.

Pediatrics

http://www.pediatrics.org

At this Web site for this journal which features data on medical conditions in infants, in children during early and later childhood, and during adolescent and young adult years, see the link to the current issue's contents page, with full access to electronic articles, but access to the print issue's articles by subscription only. See also the link for browsing previous issues' contents pages and accessing those issues' electronic articles. Note the link to the contents page for the journal's upcoming issue. Article subjects range from the technical reports to scientific viewpoints of commonly-known conditions. Subjects of articles have included medical conditions related to birth rate, risk factors for the early onset of illnesses, children's injuries from community sports, cholesterol and children, and more.

"A Structure for Deoxyribose Nucleic Acid"
J.D. Watson and F.H.C. Crick (1953)
URL: http://www.nature.com/genomics/human/watson-crick

SITE SUMMARY: This paper, published in the scientific journal *Nature*, on April 2, 1953, describes conclusions that James Watson and Francis Crick made based on their research involving the structure of deoxyribose nucleic acid (DNA). As a result of this work, Watson and Crick won the Nobel Prize in Chemistry. In this paper they reveal novel features of the structure.

DISCUSSION QUESTIONS AND ACTIVITIES

1. Read Watson and Crick's paper, then identify the names of the parts or components of DNA, scientifically called deoxyribose nucleic acid. Extra Activity: Give more details about the features of DNA. (Tip: For data, visit the Web sites the DNA Learning Center—Genes in Education [with its "DNA Beginnings" feature], the "Structure of DNA" in the *Molecular Biology Notebook Online*, DNA Files, and DNA Sciences. [Their urls are cited in the Related Internet Sites section below.])

2. Study Watson and Crick's paper. What are the features of the "radically different structure" involving DNA components that Watson and Crick suggested? (Hints: Note the diagram; paragraph four, sentences two, four, and five, the second part of six, plus eight and nine, and references to common, plus some metaphoric, words connected to scientific ones.)

3. See Watson and Crick's paper, paragraph six (sentence one), paragraph seven (the second part of the first sentence), and paragraph eight (the last sentence). What is "a novel feature of the structure," and what was found? Study the statement with this sentence structure: "if only _____, it follows that _____, then _____," and note that this statement includes examples of a hypothesis and a syllogism. Visit another Web site and find definitions for hypothesis and syllogism, then think of another science related hypothesis and syllogism. (Hint no. 1: Visit the Web sites with Logic in the Work of Aristotle, Logic at the Science-Humanities Education Service, and Syllogism at bartleby.com, for definitions and explanations of hypothesis and syllogism. Their precise urls are cited in this book's Appendix F. Hint no. 2: To find a science subject and data so that you can form a hypothesis and a syllogism, visit any science related Web site cited in this book.)

4. See Watson and Crick's paper, paragraphs two through four, and thirteen. Identify, with names and examples, six influences on Watson and Crick's claims. Include how scientists' ideas were different from their ideas, similar to their ideas, not helpful to them and why not, plus helpful with what they concluded. Provide some details on DNA related ideas of some of these other scientists who influenced Watson and Crick, including quotations if possible. Extra Activity: Identify two reasons why Franklin was not given the full credit due for her contribution until nearly fifty years after the publication of Watson and Crick's paper. (Hints: For more details, visit the Web sites or pages for Rosalind Franklin at Contributions of Twentieth Century Women in Physics; Photograph of X-Ray of DNA Molecule at the Book That Sheds Light on a Scientific Landmark Web page; Historic Figures: Rosalind Elsie Franklin, 1920 to 1958; A Science Odyssey: People and Discoveries: Rosalind Franklin; A Science Odyssey: People and Discoveries: Watson and Crick, Wilkins, and Franklin; the Nobel Prize E-Museum—Biography of Maurice Hugh Frederick Wilkins [1962], with Nobel Lecture; and the 1962 Physiology/Medicine Nobel Prize Presentation Speech. Their urls are cited in the Related Internet Sites section below.)

5. Identify "the celebrated understatement" near the end of the Watson and Crick paper, and suggest why is it said to be an understatement. Write, then explain, another science-related under-

statement, then, basing your answer on an actual science field's happening that is mentioned in any Web site cited in this book, choose an understatement that you find, or create one.

6. At the beginning of their paper, Watson and Crick claimed that the features they had discovered "are of considerable biological interest." Explain why.

7. Why is it important that the structure of DNA was discovered?

8. It has been said that the Watson and Crick paper is a model of scientific writing. Identify some features you think indicate that this comment may be true, then explain your reason for thinking that.

RELATED INTERNET SITE(S)

DNA Learning Center—Genes in Education

http://www.dnalc.org

At this Web site for the Dolan DNA Learning Center in the Cold Spring Harbor Laboratory in New York, see the link to the award winning "DNA From the Beginning," plus links to Gene News, Genetic Origins, features, resources, and more links, as well as a search in archives option (e.g., for the structure of DNA).

"Structure of DNA" in the *Molecular Biology Notebook Online*

http://www.iacr.ac.uk/notebook/courses/guide/dnast.htm

This colorfully illustrated Web site by Nathalie Castells-Brooke, Ph.D., features Components of DNA and a Few Principles, DNA: Some Facts, What's in a Name?, and Further Information.

DNA Files: Genetic Science Documentaries on National Public Radio (NPR)

http://www.dna.org

At this Web site which aims to "unravel the mysteries of genetic science" through radio programs, see links to information about the programs, behind the scenes, search, and interact. See also the link for information on learning more (with more links to online information on DNA basics that started just after Watson and Crick's discovery, and DNA today, e.g., on subjects including Basic Genetics, Genes and Identity, Genes and Behavior, Genes and Medicine, plus Gene Testing, Genes and Cloning, Genes and Longevity, Genes and Stem Cells, Genetics and Applied Ecology, Genetics and Infectious Diseases, Genetics and Astrobiology, and DNA Marketplace including resources, genes and food, and patenting DNA).

DNA Sciences

http://dna.com

At this Web site for DNA Sciences, Inc., a company dedicated to applied genetics, read about the four methods of application this company uses, then see links for Family Genetics (with its DNA Basics, and Special Report), and Science and Discovery (with its data on genetics transforming health care).

DNA Pioneer Dr. James D. Watson—*Time* Yahoo Chat Transcript from March 24, 1999

http://www.yahoo.com (search for "Online Chat with Dr. James Watson 1999")

This chat, sponsored by *Time* magazine and Yahoo.com, features Watson as one of the twentieth century's one hundred noteworthy scientists and thinkers, and a "discoverer of the secret of life."

James Dewey Watson—Nobel Lecture

http://www.nobel.se/medicine/laureates/1962/watson-lecture.html

Click the link for "The Involvement of RNA in the Synthesis of Proteins," the lecture presented December 11, 1961, available here in PDF format. See also a biography link.

Francis Harry Compton Crick—Nobel Lecture

http://www.nobel.se/medicine/laureates/1962/crick-lecture.html

Click the link for "On the Genetic Code," the lecture presented on December 11, 1962, available online here. Note also a biography link.

Nobel E-Museum Biography of Maurice Hugh Frederick Wilkins, 1962

http://www.nobel.se/medicine/laureates/1962/wilkins-bio.html

This page provides biographical information on the third scientist (of King's College, London, England) who, together with Watson and Crick (of Cambridge University in England), was given the Nobel Prize in Chemistry for discovering DNA while collaborating with their research. Click also the link to Wilkins' Nobel lecture "The Molecular Configuration of Nucleic Acids" presented December 11, 1961 and online in PDF format.

Rosalind Franklin at Contributions of Twentieth Century Women to Physics

http://www.physics.ucla.edu/~cwp

Click the "Eighty-Six Eminent Physicists" link, then choose and click Crystallography in the pull-down menu, and then Franklin's name for links to a biography, a list of her publications, and information on her contributions and honors, including data that indicate she should be given equal credit for the discovery of DNA. Find here quotations by colleagues, historians, and others, and, via links, "A Tribute to Dr. Franklin" by W.M. Stanley, and a biography "Light on a Dark Lady" by Anne Piper (her lifelong friend) who provides details on how Franklin's research was important to the discovery of DNA, and quotes Watson's 1998 comment that acknowledges Franklin's contribution to the discovery after years during which her part in the discovery was ignored. Piper also notes Franklin's science related influence on Piper's children.

Historic Figures—Rosalind Elsie Franklin, 1920 to 1958

http://www.bbc.co.uk/history/historic_figures/franklin_rosalind_elsie.shtml

This biography of Franklin features detailed data on the x-ray photograph of the DNA molecule that she took, her research related to it, and how Watson and Crick came to know about it then use it as part of their work. Note also the information on a paper that Franklin wrote on the subject before the paper written by Watson and Crick, although their paper was published before she got the chance to publish hers. See links to other sites with more biographical information on Franklin.

Photograph of X-Ray of DNA Molecule in Book Sheds Light on a Scientific Landmark

http://www.npr.org/programs/atc/features/2002/oct/darklady

Along with information on the book *Rosalind Franklin: Dark Lady of DNA* and a link to an audio version of an interview with the author Barbara Maddox, this Web page features a reproduction of the photograph of the x-ray of the DNA molecule that was photographed by Franklin and "sparked a scientific revolution." It also has a quote by Watson on his reaction when he first saw the photograph, and information that aims to explain Franklin's true role in the discovery of DNA. There are, in addition, links to sites with more data and information (e.g., Watson speaking on *Talk of the Nation* in 2000).

A Science Odyssey: People and Discoveries: Rosalind Franklin

http://www.pbs.org/wgbh/aso/databank/entries/bofran.html

Read a biography on Franklin and her contribution to the discovery of DNA, and her connection with Watson, Crick, and Wilkins. See also a link to "You Try It: DNA Workshop." Do a search at www.pbs.org and see annotated links to more than fifteen pages of information that include facts on Franklin and her DNA research.

A Science Odyssey: People and Discoveries—Watson and Crick, Wilkins, and Franklin

http://www.pbs.org/wgbh/aso/databank

Type Watson and Crick in the search box. Click Enter. See three links that go to information on the contributions of Watson, Crick, Wilkins, and Franklin to the discovery and description of the DNA structure. A photo of a DNA model is on one page.

1962 Physiology/Medicine Nobel Prize Presentation Speech

http://www.nobel.se/medicine/laureates/1962/press.html

This speech was presented by A. Engstrom, of the Royal Caroline Institute, when the Nobel Prize was awarded to Watson, Crick, and Wilkins, who were credited with the discovery of DNA.

Life Sciences in the Twentieth Century (1988) by Garland E. Allen

http://depts.washington.edu/hssexec/newsletter/1997/allen.html

This article reveals what occurred before, after, and during, the discovery of DNA. Learn about Watson, Crick, Wilkins, and Franklin in "Biochemistry and Molecular Biology."

"There's Plenty of Room at the Bottom"
Richard P. Feynman (1959)
URL: http://www.zyvex.com/nanotech/feynman.html

SITE SUMMARY: This transcript of a classic talk presented on December 29, 1959, at the annual meeting of the American Physical Society at Caltech (the California Institute of Technology), was first published in the February 1960 issue of Caltech's *Engineering and Science Journal* and was described by the editor of the time as "an invitation to enter a new field of physics." In this talk, Feynman, a physicist at Caltech, drew attention to the subject by commenting that in the year 2000 people would look back and wonder why no one "seriously moved in this direction" toward "a staggeringly small world that is below" until the time this article was written, presented, and published. Introducing the subject further, he identified that new field of physics as "the problem of manipulating and controlling things on a small scale," a concept now known as the science of nanotechnology.

DISCUSSION QUESTIONS AND ACTIVITIES

1. What did Feynman say people talked about as soon as he mentioned the subject? Describe one of the examples they gave, and tell how he objected. Identify his example and give details.
2. Read the sections "Information on a Small Scale" and "How Do We Write Small?" Identify and describe how, according to Feynman, all of the information people have accumulated in all the world's books can be written, and identify instead of which other way. In what thing did he say this can be done? (Hint: Identify shape, size, and composition.) To what common thing you know did he compare this thing? (Hint: It can barely be seen by human eyes.)
3. How is Feynman's theory related to biology? Give one of his examples, and one of yours. State some fundamental problems in biology of the time, and identify how, he said, answers to these problems can be found, then tell what is one easy answer to the problem, and two particulars, to this answer. How did he suggest many problems of biology would be made easier to solve? What, did he say, is marvelous about a "biological system"?
4. What is important about Feynman's talking of looking at someone's face? How did he involve computers? What else did he think about computers, microfilm, and the electron microscope of the time when he wrote this article?
5. What did Albert R. Hibbs suggest to Feynman regarding uses of nanotechnology? Have these suggestions become useful today? Include in your answer information at the Web sites Nanotechnology, and Nanotechnology in the News (with links to articles on Nanotechnology and NASA Applications, Medicine, Recent News, and Prospects). (Urls of the sites noted are cited in the Related Internet Sites section below.)
6. As one goes down in size, what problems arise, according to Feynman? Give Feynman's example (hint: Van der Waals), and your own example. Explain your choice; including a connection between it and Feynman's theory.
7. "When we have some control of the arrangement of things on a small scale" what, did Feynman claim, will be true? What new opportunities would there be when atoms are dealt with on a small rather than a large scale?
8. Why did Feynman mention "If only I could train an ant to do this"? What did he leave to the imagination? Why, according to him, should anyone do any of this? Why and how should high schools get involved?

RELATED INTERNET SITE(S)

Links to Feynman's Theory, Lectures, etc., at Richard Feynman Dedicated Site

http://www.geocities.com/CapeCanaveral/Launchpad/7045 (click Hot Links link)

Scroll to Feynman: Theory, then click on Feynman's Diagrams, and then Theory, at the bottom of the page, to find out about "the fundamental (smallest) building blocks from which all matter is made."

Nanotechnology in the News

http://abcnews.go.com/sections/scitech

Type nanotechnology in the search box at the right, and choose ABC News, then search to find current news articles on the subject, such as "Science of the Very Small," "Smaller Magnets for Bigger Hard Drives," and "Mirror Hair Thin Fibers May Create Novel Cloth." (More information may also be available via a section search by choosing ABC News on TV, Health, or all sections, at the bottom of the search results page.)

Foresight Institute Update 7 (December 15, 1989)

http://www.foresight.org/Updates/update07/index.html

This Web page provides scientists' information on nanotechnology, including "Recent Progress: Steps Toward Nanotechnology," "The National Science Foundation Looks At Nanotechnology," plus a note about it and *Star Trek*. See also the sitemap link that leads to other updates, and see the nanotechnology link that leads to a page of information for the general reader, FAQs, special topics such as the history of nanotechnology, studying nanotechnology, projected applications of technology, and sources of further information.

Nanotechnology

http://nano.zyvex.com/nano

Ralph C. Merkle, a former executive editor of *Nanotechnology Journal*, and 1998 winner of the Feynman Nanotechnology Prize, provides information on core concepts of molecular technology, plus links to recent news, and other information, such as articles on the Web, the sci.nanotech newsgroup, journals (e.g., *Nanotechnology*), sites with links (e.g., Foresight Institute, NanoLink List, National Federation of Science Nanotechnology Database), related groups (e.g., Center for Nanoscale Science at Rice University, sections of NASA and the National Space Society), FAQs, and unusual images.

Richard P. Feynman—Nobel Lecture, 1965

http://www.nobel.se/physics/laureates/1995/feynman-lecture.html

Access Feynman's lecture "The Development of the Space Time View of Quantum Electrodynamics" in PDF format, and see the link to a biography about him.

NASA Life Science Data Archive
(1961–)
URL: http://lsda.jsc.nasa.gov/index.cfm

SITE SUMMARY: The National Aeronautics and Space Administration at the Lyndon B. Johnson Space Center features here a database of documents on life science experiments involving humans, animals, and plants, in manned and unmanned space missions, conducted from 1961 to the present, and including some missions and experiments now considered historic. Note the Search Database link that leads to a page for searching Experiments, Missions, and Documents; plus Data Sets (from Life Science Experiments), Sessions (on experiments' what, where, and when), Bio-specimens (human parts that have been the subjects of research), Hardware used during experiments, and particular Personnel. Note also the Overviews link that leads to Life Sciences Research Interests links, and Historic Missions. See more links, e.g., for the Reading Room (with online documents), What's New, Photo Gallery, and Just for Fun. In the Related Internet Sites section below, see this site's Biosatellite Missions and Sitemap pages' descriptions.

DISCUSSION QUESTIONS AND ACTIVITIES

1. Click the LSDA's Search Database link, then click the Documents or Experiments link. Choose one of the Payload/Mission photo links, then search for, and choose, three particular space flights of recent times. Be sure to choose different types of flight, such as a particular shuttle flight mission, and a particular international space station mission. As you choose, select flights with different life science experiments, so one experiment involves a plant or plants, another involves an animal or animals, and the next involves a human or humans. After choosing, give the experiment's title, and some data from the experiment's description, research area, species studied, spaceflight mission name and number, scientific results, a principle investigator, and something from additional information (e.g., parameters measured, hardware items, experiment type), plus an alternate name for the experiment, and a related experiment. If possible, give a citation from a publications list, and cite one document from the Documents area after searching there. If available, also include an experiment's proposal source and date, plus sponsoring and managing institutions. (Tip: You may choose Scientific Results in the Document Type menu on the Documents page to find some data.)

2. Click the LSDA's Search Database link, then go to the Documents page, select an experiment from the Experiment Title menu, or select an experiment from the Document Type menu; then search for, and choose, three different experiments. As you make your choices for this activity, and as you provide information for your choices, follow the "as you choose" and "after choosing" directions in Question/Activity no. 1 above. (Help hint: You may choose experiments with words including "Effect of," "Influence of," "Investigation of," or "During spaceflight.") Extra Activity: Select one thing on the Life Sciences Interests pages in the LSDA's Overviews area, and one in the Life Sciences in the NASA Subjects Index links list. (Its site url is cited in the Related Internet Sites section below.) Give information for both as directed above.

3. Click the Search LSDA Database link, then click the Missions link. Choose the unmanned Biosatellites link. Select an experiment from the pull-down menu, then tell about the experiment's purpose, how it was to be carried out, if what was planned was achieved, and if the animals included survived. Next, go back to the Missions area and click the Cosmos-Bion Satellite link, select an experiment, and apply the activities suggested just above to it. Extra Activity One: Go to the Web sites Pioneering Efforts in Space, Space Today Online—Dogs [and Other Animals] in Space, and Animal Astronauts. (Their urls are cited in the Related Internet Sites section below). Choose one animal from each Web site, tell which spaceflight

it was put on during the very early days of the space program, and describe the experiment this animal was part of. Tell if the experiment was a success, and if the animal survived. Extra Activity Two: Read the article "Laboratory Animals in Space" whose url is cited in the Related Internet Sites section below. Choose one subject the authors write about, then search for information on it at the LSDA. Compare what you find at each site, and tell how each helps you to understand the subject.

4. Click the LSDA's Search Database link, then the link to the Hardware page. Search for and select one specially named mission from each of the following pull-down menus: Payload/ Mission Participation (e.g., Spacelab Life Sciences One), Hardware Type (e.g., Test Equipment, Circadian Rhythm; Habitat Facility, Plants; Sample Collection Devices, Air/Gas), Hardware Item (e.g., Aquatic Animal Experiment Unit, Gravitational Plant Physiology Facility), and Research Area (e.g., Behavior and Performance, Chronobiology, Plant Biology, Muscle Physiology). As you make your choices, then provide information for what you chose, follow the "as you choose" and "after choosing" directions in Question/Activity no. 2 above.

5. Click the LSDA's Search Database link, then the link to the Sessions page. Choose a Session name from the pull-down menu (e.g., Inflight Analysis of Ground-Prepared Test Samples, Internal Space Exposures, Rotating Chair), and Experiment Type. When you make your choices, then provide information for what you chose, follow the directions in Question/ Activity no. 2 above for "as you choose" and "after choosing."

6. Go to the LSDA's Historic Missions page, found as cited in the Related Internet Sites section below. Choose and describe three experiments that are now considered to be part of an historic manned mission (e.g., from one of the Mercury, Gemini, Skylab, Apollo, Apollo-Soyuz, or NASA-Mir programs). Apply the "as you choose" and "after choosing" directions from Question/Activity no. 2 above.

7. Click the LSDA's What's New link. Choose and click a link to an experiment recently done. Explain it. Include what you find in the "after choosing" directions in Question/Activity no. 2 above. Option: Try finding something on this experiment that has been reported by the news media at these Web sites: CNN—Sci/Tech, PBS Online News and Views (on Science and Technology, Earth and Space), Science News Online, New York Times on the Web (its Science and Technology sections), Time.com—Newsfiles—Science, "Spaceflight Now" at Astronomy Now Online; Sky and Telescope (its news and archives); and the NASA Goddard Space Flight Center Science Question of the Week. (Their urls are cited in this book's Appendix B, D, or H.)

8. Click the LSDA's Search Database link, then the Hardware link, and select a Shuttle Student Involvement Program from the Payload/Mission Participation menu. Next, click the Experiments link, then do a Student Experiments search in the search box, and choose one experiment found during the search. For both findings, follow the "after choosing" directions in Question/Activity no. 2 above.

9. Visit the NASA Student Flight Opportunity Web page, with information on the NASA Student Involvement Program (NSIP), the NASA Shuttle Small Payload Project, and other programs and projects. (Note: the NSIP is today's version of the Shuttle Student Involvement Program referred to in Question/Activity no. 8 above.) (This Web site's url is cited in this book's Appendix G.) Imagine you have decided to think of and contribute ideas for an experiment to the NSIP or the SSPP for possible selection and inclusion in a space shuttle mission or a space station mission. Think of an idea, being sure it is a life science idea in one of the three topic areas the NASA Life Science Database Archive features. Following the NSIP or SSPP Web site's guidelines (e.g., the NSIP's Learning Goals, Designing An Experiment, Research Project Components, Judging Criteria), and the format indicated in the "after

choosing" directions in Question/Activity no. 2 above for documents in the LSDA, provide details of your idea. (Suggestion: Contribute your idea as the NSIP or the SSPP instructions indicate via the Student Flight Opportunity Web site.)

10. Visit the Astronauts Biographies Web site. (Its url is cited in the Related Internet Sites section below.) Search for, then choose, a current astronaut. Read her or his biography, noting under Spaceflight Experience a shuttle mission or a space station mission in which this astronaut has participated. Next, click the LSDA Search Database link, then the Experiments link, and select the program (e.g., shuttle or space station) in which this astronaut was involved, then find this astronaut's mission in the Mission (Payload) Menu. Choose any experiment done during that mission, and describe the experiment with details as indicated in the "after choosing" directions in Question/Activity no. 2 above. Note the featured astronaut as well as the other crew members with whom she or he worked on the mission.

11. Find a current astronaut's biography at the Astronaut Biographies Web site referred to in Question/Activity no. 10 above. When searching, find an astronaut who has another profession. Is this other profession vital to an experiment conducted during a shuttle flight or space station mission in which this astronaut was a crew member? (Hint: mission specialists and payload specialists usually have other professions, often scientific.) Extra Activity: Find a payload specialist astronaut from a nation you claim as a place of ethnic origin. Apply instructions from Question/Activity no. 10 above to the astronaut.

12. If possible for your computer, access the Astronaut Fact Book at the Astronaut Biographies Web site, then adapt and apply to this astronaut from the past the two activities suggested in Question/Activity no. 10 above, and while using instructions from Question/Activity no. 6 above for the LSDA's manned Historic Missions pages.

RELATED INTERNET SITE(S)

NASA—LSDA—Sitemap

http://lsda.jsc.nasa.gov/sitemap.html

Links go to Search Database; Overviews with Research Overview, Historic Missions, Space Shuttle Missions, NASA-Mir Program, and Unmanned Missions; plus Related Links (e.g., online books, educational and research resources), What's New, Glossary, Photo Gallery, Just for Fun, and Site Tour.

Unmanned Biosatellite Programs

http://lsda.nasa.gov (click Search Database link, then Missions link)

Click the link for the Cosmos-Bion Satellite Project, or the Biosatellite Program. The Cosmos-Bion Project, which lasted for nearly two decades, from 1975 through 1992, was a multinational program that was headed by the Russian Space Agency, and included the U.S., the European Space Agency, and other nations among the participants who sent animals into space as parts of experiments. The Biosatellite Program, by the United States, from 1967 through 1970, included four satellites with experimental animals.

Historic Missions at the NASA Life Sciences Data Archive

http://lsda.jsc.nasa.gov/historic.cfm

Links go to experiments on the flights for Project Mercury, 1961–1963; Project Gemini, 1964–1966; Apollo, 1967–1972; Skylab, 1973; and the Apollo-Soyuz Test Project, 1975.

Astronaut Biographies at the Lyndon B. Johnson Space Center

http://www.jsc.nasa.gov/Bios/index.html

This site includes information about types of astronauts, and links to biographies of them (e.g., career astronauts, payload specialists, active astronauts, management astronauts, and former astronauts). See the Astronaut Fact Book (in PDF format) with former astronauts' biographies. Flags of payload specialists' nations are featured beside name links.

NASA Subject Index

http://www.nasa.gov/nasaorgs/subject_index.html

This access point for NASA's Internet information provides links under subjects such as Life Sciences, plus Aeronautics, Astronautics, Chemistry and Materials, Engineering, Geosciences, Mathematics and Computer Sciences, Microgravitiy, Physics, Social Sciences, Space Sciences, Standards, and General Information.

Pioneering Efforts in Space

http://www.redstone.army.mil/history/pioneer/welcome.html

Scroll to information on early unmanned space flights conducted by the United States Army before the formation of NASA. Note the section on "Monkey Flights."

Space Today Online—Dogs [and Other Animals] in Space

http://www.spacetoday.org/Astronauts/Animals/Dogs.html

This site provide brief information on space flights by the United States, Russia, and other nations, from the 1950s through the 1998 Columbia shuttle Neurolab mission, which included dogs and other animals. There are some links to news articles, photos, and sound files.

Animal Astronauts

http://ham.spa.umn.edu/kris/animals.html

This site, set up by a research associate at the NASA Goddard Space Flight Center, provides information about dogs, monkeys, and chimps, who were sent on spaceflights during the early years of the space program. The links pages features links to the U.S. Biomedical Space Research Timeline on the NASA Neurolab Web site, the *New York Times* newspaper articles from the early days of space exploration, Soviet Dogs in Space: Their Stories on Stamps, and books and magazines related to animals in space.

"Laboratory Animals in Space" in the Animal Welfare Information Center Newsletter

http://www.nal.usda.gov/awic/newsletter/v6n2 (click 6n2borko.htm link)

Published in the Center's November 17, 1997 newsletter, this article, written by Gary L. Borkowski of Pennsylvania State University, and others, features information on ways animals have demonstrated that living organisms can survive in space. It has information on the space shuttle's, the international space station's, and ground control's involvement.

NASA Projects

http://spacelink.nasa.gov/NASA.Projects

Featuring information on NASA's programs and activities, this site has a popular projects pull-down menu, and a browse area with annotated topics links. Both lead to pages or sites with documents on the projects. Popular projects include Human Space Flight, the International Space Station, the Hubble Telescope, the Mars Pathfinder Mission, the Chandra X-Ray Observatory, the Cassini Mission to Saturn, Microgravity Science and Research, Ozone Research, and the TOPEX/Poseidon Ocean Mapping. Browsing topics include Earth and Space Sciences, Biological and Physical Research, Human Exploration and Development of Space, and Aerospace Technology. See also a search box, annotated links under Related Materials on Spacelink, and Related NASA Internet Sites, and more.

National Space Science Data Center—NASA's Goddard Space Flight Center

http://nssdc.gsfc.nasa.gov

This site provides information from spaceflights on topics other than the life sciences. Note topics such as Astrophysics, Earth Science, Space and Solar Physics, Planetary and Lunar Data from Space Flight Missions. There are an archive and a data and documents dissemination area, with links to Web pages or other Web sites featuring data on science experiments in which spaceflight missions have been involved.

"The Social Responsibilities of Scientists and Science"
Linus Pauling (1966)
URL: http://www.nsta.org/pubs/tst/feature0001pauling.asp or www.nsta.org (click high school, Science Teacher, and archives links, then search)

SITE SUMMARY: Written by Pauling when he was a Research Professor of Physical and Biological Sciences at the Center for Study of Democratic Institutions in California, this article is based on an address he gave at the annual convention of the National Science Teachers Association (NSTA), April 3, 1966. It first appeared in print in the May 1966 issue of the *Science Teacher*, was reprinted in the January 2000 issue, excerpted, and then reproduced online, by the NSTA. In this article, Pauling points out situations unique to the modern world and obligations involving those situations that scientists have because of their actions and knowledge. (Once freely accessible, this article is now accessible to students only if their educators are NSTA members.)

DISCUSSION QUESTIONS AND ACTIVITIES

1. Read paragraph one. Name two things that Pauling said about "a special responsibility" that scientists have in the modern world.
2. Read paragraph two. What in general, and in particular (i.e., six things), changed because of scientists' discoveries, and why? Provide two examples (one each from the past and the present), from one of the first five answers you provided when identifying six things in particular. Tell what special part scientists must now play because of their discoveries, and give an example from the world you know about.
3. Read paragraph three. What is known by scientists, and by non-scientists? Give an example other than the one Pauling mentioned.
4. See paragraph five. What did Pauling believe everyone will have? How long will it take, if what doesn't happen? What did he believe will win, and will happen?
5. See paragraph twelve, the first and last sentences. What, according to Pauling, must scientists learn to do, and what is the question they must ask themselves?
6. See paragraph thirteen. According to Pauling, scientists have general responsibilities resulting from what, and in relation to what? Identify their duty (including three aspects) because of these responsibilities.
7. Identify eleven problems with which scientists may be concerned, then choose one problem. How has human civilization fared in solving this problem, and how, in general, have scientists helped, or tried helping? Identify and describe a way that Pauling has helped. Quote him if possible. (Tip: For some help, especially with regard to human civilization, and Pauling's helping, see the Web sites for the Pauling Virtual Exhibition, Nobel Prize in Chemistry—1954— Presentation Speech, Linus Pauling and the Peace Movement—A Conversation with the Nobel Laureate, and Scientists for Global Responsibility. Their urls are cited in the Related Internet Sites section below.)

RELATED INTERNET SITE(S)

Linus Pauling Research Notebooks

http://www.osulibrary.orst.edu/specialcollections/rnb/index.html

Links go to digital reproductions of Pauling's handwritten notebooks one to forty-six in his cryptic handwriting, an extensive alphabetical subject index, and selected highlights. Among the highlighted items note Early Books One Through Thirteen on the Structure of Crystals which eventually led to his publication *The Nature of the Chemical Bond* (one of the "seminal texts of modern science"), notes on writing and editing his "influential text" *College Chemistry*, and an open letter to George H.W. Bush in 1991 that begins with a statement on duty with reference to scientists and rulers. In the highlights area see also notes on Pauling's work on protein structure, superconductivity, bond lengths, atomic nuclei, anesthesia, and more.

Ava Helen and Linus Pauling Papers at Oregon State University

http://osu.orst.edu/dept/spc/subpages/ahp/index2.html

This site has a detailed bibliographical listing that is "considered to be one of the more important scientific archives of an individual" of the twentieth century. There are also some links to articles and Web sites about Pauling. Features include links to a new "Overview 'The Science and Humanism of Linus Pauling, 1901–1994' by Stephen F. Mason," "Special Collections Reading Curriculum," "1995 Pauling Symposium Papers Online," and a "Pauling Centenary Celebration." Pull-down menus lead to a catalogue with links to citations of correspondence, publications, manuscripts and typescripts of articles, speeches, and books, research notebooks, newspaper clippings, biographical items, science, peace, and more, plus other Pauling information (e.g., a timeline of his life, and a Linus Pauling Exhibit).

Linus Pauling, Scientist and Humanitarian—Virtual Exhibition

http://www.paulingexhibit.org/exhibit/index.html

This exhibit and its Web site (established primarily by the Pauling Family and Oregon State University), features information on The Scientist, Early and College Years, Pauling Speaks Out, a Table of Contents with Pauling's Process of Discovery, What Do We Mean By Structure? "What is a Molecule?" "What is a Chemical Bond?" "What is a Protein?" plus a Biography (with The Chemistry of Life—Introduction, Vitamin C and Orthomolecular Medicine, An Exciting Detour Into Quantum Physics, The Science of Peace), etc.

"The Nature of the Chemical Bond—IV—The Energy of Single Bonds and the Relative Electromagnetivity of Atoms" by Linus Pauling (1932)

http://dbhs.wvusd.k12.ca.us/Chem-History/Pauling-1932/Pauling-electroneg-1932.html or *http://dbhs.wvusd.k12.ca.us/Chem-History/Pauling-1932* (click link)

This article was first published in the *Journal of the American Chemical Society*, September 1932, and is considered a landmark paper in the history of chemistry. Pauling, a winner of the 1954 Nobel Chemistry Prize, may be best known for the "landmark research on the nature of the chemical bond" as revealed in this article, and for that research's "application to understanding the structure of complex substances such as protein molecules and antibodies" (as stated at the Pauling Virtual Exhibit Web site). It is provided by the Chem Team and has a link at Carmen Giunta's Selected Classic Papers in Chemistry Web site. It is also a "Contribution from the Gates Chemical Laboratory, California Institute of Technology, no. 326."

Nobel Prize in Chemistry 1954—Presentation Speech by Professor G. Haag

http://www.nobel.se/chemistry/laureates/1954/press.html

Haag, a member of the Nobel Committee for Chemistry at the Royal Swedish Academy of Science, presented this speech to Pauling, an honored guest on receiving the Nobel Prize in Chemistry, and provided information on Dr. Pauling's work that led to his being awarded the prize. There are also a link to a biography of Pauling, and a link to Pauling's Nobel lecture "Modern Structural Chemistry" given on December 11, 1954, and available here in PDF format.

Excerpts from a Last Interview with Linus Pauling—Institute of Optimum Nutrition

http://www.internetwks.com/pauling/last/pinv.html

On how Pauling thought he would be remembered, and his view of Vitamin C's value. From April 9, 1994 talks with QED BBC-TV's Tony Edwards and Patrick Holford during a Power of Prevention Conference.

"Linus Pauling" in *Biographical Memoirs* (Volume 71, 1997)—National Academy Press

http://www.nap.edu/books/0309057388/html/221.html#pagetop or *http://www.nap.edu* (search in the Search All Text box)

If trouble accessing, go to www.nap.edu, do a search for, and follow the links to, *Biographical Memoirs* (volume 71, 1997), then find and click their "Read Online" link.

Linus Pauling and the Peace Movement—A Conversation with the Nobel Laureate

http://globetrotter.berkeley.edu/convervations/Pauling/pauling1.html

The first of an eight-page typed transcript (all provided here) of a conversation with Pauling as winner of the Nobel Peace Prize in 1963. This conversation occurred at the Institute of International Studies in 1983.

On Being a Scientist: Responsible Conduct in Research

http://www.nap.edu/books/0309051967/html/index.html

The National Academy Press provides this online book which was issued in 1995 by the Committee on Science, Engineering, and Public Policy. See contents page links to The Social Foundations of Science, Values in Science, The Scientists in Society, Responding to Violations of Ethical Standards, Misconduct in Science, Error and Negligence in Science, Conflicts of Interest, Experimental Techniques and the Treatment of Data, The Allocation of Credit, and Discussion of Case Studies.

Apollo Lunar Surface Journal
(1969–72)
URL: http://www.hq.nasa.gov/office/pao/History/alsj (click Apollo logo patch link)

SITE SUMMARY: Using transcripts and audio recordings of the air-to-ground transmissions of the Apollo lunar missions 11, 12, and 14 through 17, Eric Jones, an astronomer who works at the Los Alamos New Mexico National Research Laboratory, has provided a document of the activities of each Apollo lunar mission. The astronauts' words of their experiences as they did these activities are featured, as are their follow up comments provided later. The Apollo 17 Journal was done in conjunction with geologist astronaut Harrison Jack Schmitt. Each mission's Journal features background information, plus links to particular word-for-word parts of the mission. See links in the left column that lead to summaries, overviews, preliminary science reports, tech debriefs, mission reports, and more. Note also a Bibliography and WWW Link, plus links to a prologue, a foreword, and astronaut information. Some pages are accessible only in PDF format, and video entries are available with special software.

DISCUSSION QUESTIONS AND ACTIVITIES

1. Find information on Apollo 15 as suggested in the hints that follow. What was the unusual rock that was discovered on the moon? What are its features? Why is it important? What Biblical name has it been given? Who are the astronauts discovered it? Is the rock really what it appears to be or what some people think it is? Support your claim either way with astronauts' and/or scientists' statements. (Hints: Look for information on Apollo 15 at the Apollo Missions Science Experiments Web site [whose url is cited in the Related Internet Sites section below]. Next, find excerpts from Apollo 15 with quotations in the *Apollo Lunar Surface Journal* by clicking the link for this particular mission's summary, then by clicking the link for this particular mission's journal, and then browsing the links of the daily day to day activities. Also note the Apollo 15 preliminary science briefs at the *Journal's* Web site.)

2. Find information on Apollo 17 as suggested just below. What was the soil with the unusual color that was found on the moon? Who discovered it, and how? What is important about the soil? (Hints: Look for information on Apollo 17 at the Web sites with Apollo Missions Science Experiments and an Interview with Harrison Schmitt. See the Related Internet Sites section below for these Web sites' urls.)

3. Find information on the Apollo 12 mission, following the suggestions in the hints in Question/Activity no. 1 above, but applying them to Apollo 12. What is a lunar KREEP rock? How are some Apollo 12 and Apollo 11 rocks similar to, yet different from, rocks in Hawaii? Which two geological things are different about the Apollo 11 and Apollo 12 lunar landing sites, and what did these things seem to indicate? What types of lunar material did Apollo 12 bring back to Earth, and what did the material indicate with reference to pre-mission expectations? What did the Copernicus Crater have to do with Apollo 12?

4. Keeping Question/Activity no. 3 above in mind, see the Web site for the Lunar Sample Laboratory Facility (with online tour), found as cited in the Related Internet Sites section below, then identify two new methods of analysis which have been developed to study lunar geological samples.

5. Visit the Apollo Missions Science Experiments Web site (whose url is cited in the Related Internet Sites section below). Choose any Apollo mission. Describe its science related mission. Select and describe a surface experiment, and an orbital one, conducted during this mission. Add details from the *Apollo Lunar Surface Journal*. (Tip: Browse through the *Journal* as suggested in the Hints for Question/Activity no. 1 above, but apply it to your chosen Apollo mission.)

6. Often the Apollo astronauts used special phrases to describe vividly (e.g., poetically, metaphorically) something they saw or did, or they used special words (i.e., acronyms, initialisms) to refer to a piece of equipment, an instrument, or scientific activity. Select an example in Hint no. 1, then explain how the special words, types of words, or phrases made the experience uniquely interesting. In the *Journal*, find the Apollo 17 mission, and another Apollo mission, or a mission chosen for Question/Activity no. 5 above, and give an example, with description, of each of the types of special phrases or special types of words noted above, in the missions referred to just above; then tell how these special words made the experiences interesting. (Hint no. 1: See example words and phrases in the Station Eight entries of the Apollo 17 part of the *Journal*, with numbered journal locations noted, e.g., "instant rock" no. 166:43:34; "kangaroo hop" no. 167:10:01; "a hundred million years of play" no. 167:27:00; "I'm looking at the Sculptured Hills, and . . ." no. 166:35:02; "Tracy's Rock" in the Station Six areas; and LM and EVA, no. 166:36:05.) (Hint no. 2: See definitions for the special types of words and special types of phrases referred to above at the Web sites for Glossary of Rhetorical Terms With Examples, and the ISO Glossary of Terms and Definitions. [Their urls are cited in this book's Appendix F.])

7. Keeping Question/Activity no. 6 above in mind, think of an experience that you have had, or imagine having, in a natural place, describe it using a special type of phrase and a special type of word indicated above, and tell how this phrase and this word made the experience extra interesting. (Hint: For information, go to any Web site cited in the Related Internet Sites section below, or to any Web site on the subject cited anywhere in this book.)

8. Imagine you are a geologist exploring the moon. What would be interesting to find, and important to find? Consider importance with relation to the Earth, the moon, and space exploration. Include what would have been known during the time the Apollo missions occurred; what was known at the time of the 1994 document "Toward A World Strategy and Utilization of Our Natural Satellite: A Report," and what is known today. (For information, see the *Apollo Lunar Surface Journal*, Exploring the Moon [found via links at the Exploring the Moon: Apollo Missions Web site pages cited in the Related Internet Sites section below], and go to the Web site of "Toward A World Strategy and Utilization of Our Natural Satellite: A Report" that is featured in another part of this book.)

9. Find and read the *Apollo Lunar Surface Journal*'s entry for Apollo 17, no. 140:45:08. What did Gene Cernan, the last Apollo astronaut to walk on the lunar surface, say about his experience on the first day, then the second day, of the mission? Give or suggest specific examples that illustrate what he referred to in his comment. (Hint: For information, read the parts of the *Journal* involving his experiences, and see Web sites in the Related Internet Sites section below that refer to the Apollo 17 mission.)

10. Keeping Question/Activity no. 9 above in mind, write a two hundred word essay applying Cernan's comments to an experience that you imagine having, either on the moon or some place on the earth. Be sure to feature a science subject (e.g., something geological, or something about another earth or lunar science). (Hint: Adapt and apply the hint in Question/Activity no. 7 above to this Question/Activity.)

RELATED INTERNET SITE(S)

Top Ten Scientific Discoveries from Apollo

http://cass.jsc.nasa.gov/pub/expmoon/science/lunar10.html

Apollo Missions Science Experiments

http://cass.jsc.nasa.gov/expmoon/Apollo_Experiments.html

Note the Apollo 11 and Apollo 12 surface experiments, and the Apollo 14 through 17 surface and orbital experiments. See also the link to Lunar Science Results.

Exploring the Moon: Apollo Missions

http://cass.jsc.nasa.gov/pub/expmoon/apollo_landings.html

This site, from the NASA funded Lunar and Planetary Institute, provides links to data on and analyses of lunar science experiments conducted by the Apollo 8, the Apollo 10, and the Apollo 11 through Apollo 17 missions, including orbital experiments and surface experiments. Click on an Apollo mission number link, then note especially links to Science Experiments and Lunar Samples. See also the links to each mission's overview, landing site, surface operations, and mission photography, plus links to more information on all Apollo missions (e.g., index, appendix, and additional resources). The overview page has information on experiments involving the lunar surface, craters, basin, interior structure, gamma-rays, and x-rays. The Additional Resources page includes a link to the Lunar Sample Laboratory Facility (with tour) Web page (whose url is http://www.curator.jsc.nasa.gov/curator/lunar/lun-fac.htm). The Index page includes a link to other Exploring the Moon Web pages that feature information on unmanned lunar probes.

Interview with Harrison Schmitt at the Exploration Network

http://.exn.ca/Stories/1999/07/07/54.asp

The Web site of Discovery Channel Canada features this transcript of a July 7, 1999 interview with geologist astronaut Schmitt. This interview included Schmitt's comments on how he got into the Space Program, helped Apollo 11 astronauts discover geological specimens on the first moon landing, helped plan science activities for other Apollo moon missions, then what he as a geologist did himself on the moon during the Apollo 17 mission. His unusual geological discovery and the features of the landing site he helped to select for the mission are featured, as are his scientific reasons for why there should be a return to the moon.

"Saffir–Simpson Hurricane Damage Intensity Scale"
Herbert S. Saffir and Robert H. Simpson (1971)
URL: http://www.weatherwise.org/qr/qry.scale.html

SITE SUMMARY: This Scale was invented by Saffir, an engineer and expert in storm damage to buildings, and by Simpson, a weather expert and Director of the National Hurricane Center. The Scale's purpose is to characterize hurricanes' intensity by using as criteria the amount of observable damage done to buildings of different sizes and to parts of nature such as shrubs and trees, both with relation to a storm's pressure, and wind speed, plus the surge of coastal waters in a storm's path; all on a numbered scale ranging from minor to catastrophic. This Web page, part of the Web site for *Weather Wise: The Magazine About Weather*, provides the Saffir–Simpson Scale data as it first appeared in print, and as it has appeared yearly since then. It also features the scale's history as explained by the National Oceanographic and Atmospheric Association (NOAA) meteorologist Thomas Schlatter who consulted with Saffir in the year 2000 to provide an answer to a question sent to *Weather Wise*.

DISCUSSION QUESTIONS AND ACTIVITIES

1. How many categories of hurricanes did Saffir and Simpson suggest?
2. What are three natural features that hurricanes in every category share, but each in its own way, as bases for determining hurricane categories? State specifically how these natural features are different for each category.
3. Describe some "effects" or "damages observed" that Saffir and Simpson identified with each hurricane category which the natural features noted in Question/Activity no. 2 above influenced.
4. Identify each hurricane category and each key word that identifies each type of damage a hurricane in each category causes. (Hint: See also the Web page NOAA's About the Saffir–Simpson Scale at the Hurricanes: Nature's Greatest Storms Web site whose url is cited in the Related Internet Sites section below.)
5. If a current hurricane does the following, which rating should it have? Its winds are one hundred twenty-five miles per hour, the ocean's surge is ten feet, the sea floods inland eight miles, and large buildings are damaged by floating debris. (Hint: See also the Web page with NOAA's About the Saffir–Simpson Scale; found as cited in the Hint for Question/Activity no. 4 above.)
6. Visit the weather news areas of the Web sites Disaster Center—Hurricane Index Page, Center, NOAA—Hurricanes: Nature's Greatest Storms, the Weather Channel Web Site, CNN Storm Center—Hurricane Tip Center, and the National Hurricane Center of the National Weather Service. (Their urls are cited in the Related Internet Sites section below.) Follow the Saffir–Simpson Scale and give details of a current hurricane, and one of the recent past.
7. Go to the Web sites for the NHC/TPC Archive of Past Hurricane Seasons, and Five Hundred Years of Hurricane History at the *Sun–Sentinel: Hurricane*. (Their urls are cited in the Related Internet Sites section below.) Choose a historic hurricane. Following the Saffir–Simpson Scale, give details of your chosen hurricane, and if possible, give a quotation about the storm by a historic person who was an eyewitness. Imagine you were an eyewitness to a storm noted at a Web site cited in Question/Activity no. 6 above, or in Question/Activity no. 7, then write a one hundred-to two hundred-word "eyewitness account."
8. What should you do if a hurricane comes to the place where you live? (For help, see the following Web sites, and especially some of their special areas. Disaster Center—Hurricane Index Page [noting its "Standard Family Disaster Plan" and "Prevention Guide to Promote Safety

and Health"]; the Hurricane Tip Center at the CNN Storm Center [particularly its "Is Your Home Ready For A Natural Disaster?"]; and Q and A with Herbert Saffir. [Their urls are cited in the Related Internet Sites section below.])

9. See the Web site with the *Weather Wise* meteorologist's answer to a question someone asked about the Saffir–Simpson scale. When and where did Saffir first suggest aspects of what would become main parts of the hurricane scale, what were these parts, and what was the type of document in which he presented his ideas? Which part of the scale did Simpson suggest? Which publication provided the scale's first appearance in print, and when? Which way was the scale first used, and when? What existed before the scale to describe a hurricane, and what was its feature?

RELATED INTERNET SITE(S)

Disaster Center—Hurricane Index Page

http://www.disastercenter.com/hurricane

This site provides links to data on recent previous hurricanes; plus, via its Weather Sites link, data on current hurricanes. Other links go to "Why Talk About Hurricanes?" "The Standard Family Disaster Plan," "Prevention Guide to Promote Your Personal Health and Safety," and Hurricane Science for Kids, Hurricane Hunters, Education Hurricanes, Hurricane FAQs plus Hurricane Q and A, FEMA—Fact Sheet: Hurricane, Hurricane: The Basics, a version of the Saffir–Simpson Hurricane Scale, Hurricane Watch Net, the National Hurricane Center, and more. The Weather Sites link leads to a page on forecasts, with links to sites with current or recent weather information for each U.S. state.

NOAA—Hurricanes: Nature's Greatest Storms

http://hurricanes.noaa.gov

This Web page, provided by the National Oceanographic and Atmospheric Association online features links to Hurricane News, and Hot Topics. Other links go to NOAA pages such as the National Hurricane Center, the Atlantic Oceanographic and Meteorological Lab, the Pacific Hurricane Center, satellite images, weather-related organizations, and products such as Hurricane Basics, and FAQs. Under products, see also the links to About the National Hurricane Center/Tropical Prediction Center, interesting fact-based NOAA's Hurricane Story Ideas, and another version of the Saffir–Simpson Hurricane Scale (found at http://www.srh.noaa.gov/FTPROOT/EWX/html/saffir.htm with each damage category's key word, plus storm surge identified).

Hurricanes—Online Meteorology Guide

http://ww2010.atmos.uiuc.edu/(GH)/guides/mtr/hurr/home.rxml

This site includes a video of an aerial view of a hurricane and links to information such as hurricane definition and growth, stages of development, structure, movement, damage and destruction, plus hurricane tracks, hurricane hunters, satellites and hurricanes, and hurricane preparation. The ability to fly through a hurricane or interact with a hurricane via special software, downloadable here or at other sites with links here, are provided. See also a version of the Saffir–Simpson scale on the hurricane information page at http://ww2010.atmos.uiuc.edu/(Gh)/guides/mtr/hurr/stages/cane/home.rxml provided by the Department of Atmospheric Science, University of Chicago, Urbana–Champaign.

Hurricanes: How They Work, What They Do

http://kids.earth.nasa.gov/archive/hurricane/saffir-simpson.html

This site provides a version of the Saffir–Simpson Scale, and Did You Know? facts, plus questions and answers, and a link to Find Out More About Hurricanes.

CNN Storm Center—Hurricane Tip Center

http://www.cnn.com/WEATHER/storm.center/index.html#hurricane

See: Hurricane Tips, Hurricane Terms (e.g., Hurricane Watch, Hurricane Warning), Timeline of Deadly U.S. Hurricanes, Is Your Home Ready for a Natural Disaster? Top Weather Stories (at far right), Storm Watch e-mail, the Hurricane Intensity box (with Saffir–Simpson Scale features), a recent year's hurricanes, and related sites.

National Weather Service—National Hurricane Center

http://www.nhc.noaa.gov

Note the links to Top News of the Day, Latest Information, Active Tropical Systems (of the storms that often become hurricanes), Tropical Weather Outlooks, Marine Forecasts, Sea Surface Temperature Analyses, News and Information, Current Season Summaries and Reports, Tropical Weather Discussions, and additional resources. See also the links under "Get Storm Info," "Learn About Hurricanes," and "Hurricane History."

Weather Channel Web Site

http://www.weather.com

Note the Weather Center's Top Stories with the next day's national weather forecast, News Links, and Seasonal Links (e.g., Storm Watch), plus What's on the Weather Channel, Connect with Your Weather (e.g., with regard to your health, recreation, home and garden), and, available via special download, Getting Weather Reports Sent to You.

NHC/TPC Archive of Past Hurricane Seasons

http://www.nhc.noaa.gov/pastall.shtml

The National Hurricane Center and the Tropical Prediction Center, with Todd Spindler of the NHC and the National Oceanographic and Atmospheric Association, provide this site which includes links to information on Atlantic, Caribbean, and the Gulf of Mexico Hurricanes from 1958 to the present; Eastern Pacific Hurricanes from 1988 to the present; Hurricane History in the Atlantic; Some Infamous Atlantic Storms; the Deadliest, Costliest and Most Intense U.S. Hurricanes of the Twentieth Century; Deadliest Atlantic Hurricanes, 1492 to the Present; Central North Pacific Hurricanes from the 1880s to 1999; Hurricane Tracks, Hurricane Season Forecast Verification Reports from 1995 to the present; and Hurricane Season Climatology.

Sun–Sentinel: Hurricane

http://www.sun-sentinel.com/news/weather/hurricane

This Web page that is part of a southern Florida newspaper's Web site, features the latest news and information about hurricanes, a meteorologist answering questions, storm survival, and stormtracking. A Learn More area features links to Hurricane Science, Hurricane Science News (e.g., "Hurricanes Have Followed the Career of the Scale Inventor"), and Five Hundred Years of Hurricane History (e.g., the 1800s, when scientists began to understand hurricanes; 1495–1800s, when Christopher Columbus and Benjamin Franklin recorded their observations of storms, including some quotations here; then the 1950s to the present, and new ways of predicting hurricanes).

Beaufort Wind Force, Saffir–Simpson Hurricane, and Fujita Tornado Intensity Scales

http://www.friesian.com/wind.htm

A detailed outline of scales relating to winds from calm to devastating, based on and comparing the Beaufort Wind Force Scale developed in 1806 by Admiral Sir Francis Beaufort, the Fujita–Pearson Scale for Tornado Wind Intensity proposed in 1971 by T. Theodore Fujita and Allen Pearson, and the Saffir–Simpson Hurricane Scale.

Saffir–Simpson Page with the "Saffir–Simpson Hurricane Intensity Scale"

http://www.cit-net.com/george/ss-scale.html

The scale as adapted from the undated *The Hurricane and Its Impact* by R.H. Simpson and H. Riehl (LSU Press).

Miami Museum of Science—Hurricane: Storm Science

http://www.miamisci.org/hurricane/hurricane0.html

At this Web site for young people, which features information about hurricanes, see the icon links to "Inside A Hurricane," "Killer Storms," "Survivors," and "Weather Instruments," plus Current Weather Data, and a Hurricane Hotlist. Note also a teacher's guide and a "healing quilt."

Risk Frontiers—The Saffir–Simpson Damage Potential Scale

http://www.es.mq.edu.au/nhrc/web/scales/scalespage7.htm

A version of the scale, plus background notes on the contributions of Herbert Saffir, Robert Simpson, and H. Riehl, including something not in the *Weather Wise* 1974 paper.

An Interview with Dr. Robert Simpson in the *Mariners Weather Log*, April 1999

www.nws.noaa.gov/om/mwl/apr1999.pdf

(html version via title search at google.com)

Q and A with Herbert Saffir

http://www.sunspot.net/news/weather/hurricane/sns-hc-saffirqanda.story and at
http://www.newsday.com/news/weather/hurricane/sns-hc-saffirqanda.story

A June 24, 2001 interview of Saffir by the *Sun–Sentinel*, a Southern Florida newspaper. Features Saffir's comments on how some work he did for the United Nations, and his being a structural engineer, led to his inventing a part of the hurricane scale, plus how he and Simpson started working together. Other comments are on recent hurricanes, and what people should do if this type of storm comes to where they live.

Sport Science Resources
(1971–)
URL: http://www.sportquest.com/resources/sportscience.cfm

SITE SUMMARY: On this page of the SportQuest Web site that is a source for sport information, note the Sports Science link leading to links to sites such as Andrew's Sport Science for Beginners, and Healthy Athlete. Note also the links to information on a variety of science-related sports topics, including techniques and skills, mental training, physiology, kinesiology, nutrition, psychology, medicine, physical therapy, injury, drugs, and biomechanics. See in addition the Sports link to links for individual sports, and the Topics link that leads to other links under a Sports Science section (e.g., Sports Sciences and Physical Education Programs, General Fitness, and more). Links to other special categories include youth, the disabled, women, associations (national and international), magazines and e-zines, a directory of newsgroups and listservs (leading to a sports medicine listserv link), a bibliography, philosophy, and humanities.

DISCUSSION QUESTIONS AND ACTIVITIES

1. There are a variety of science-related aspects to sports, as revealed in the documents at the Sport Science Resources area of the SportQuest Web site; and at the Web sites The Physics of . . . , Sports at BioMedNet, Gatorade Sport Science Institute, *Sport Science—A Peer Reviewed Journal Site for Sport Research* (whose urls are cited in the Related Internet Sites section below). Visit the Sport Sciences Resources area of SportQuest and one or more of the Web sites cited above. Choose and read about two aspects of science; one that can be applied to sports in general, and one to a particular sport. Write two essays of one hundred to two hundred words on how these aspects of science apply to sports in general, and a sport that you choose, whether it is one that you play, one that you as a spectator like to follow via the media (e.g., TV, radio, newspapers, magazines, or news at Web sites), or one that you choose at random. (Note: If possible, quote a scientist.)

2. Optional Activity: Chose a sport you like as a player or as a spectator, or one you select at random, and different from the ones you chose for Question/Activity no. 1 above. Think of and find something on your own about this sport that can be interpreted from a scientific point of view. Explain this aspect and its science connection. (Tip: To help support your idea, you can cite information and quotations by scientists that you find at any Web site cited in this book.)

3. Click the Other Directories link in the general area of the Sport Science Resources Index of the SportQuest Web site. (Find as cited in the Related Internet Sites section below.) Select "all sports" from the pull-down menu, then type the word Science in one search box, and the word News in the other search box. Click go, then choose and click the link for an item that appears, then describe a sports science subject in the News. (Note: If possible, quote a scientist.) Extra Activities 1 and 2: Try to find and describe a science-related news item on a particular sport, then a news item on a particular science (e.g., sports medicine or sport nutrition). Extra Activity 3: Try to find and describe a science-related news item in the News areas of *Sports Science—A Peer Reviewed Journal Site for Sport Research* Web site. (Find as cited in the Related Internet Sites section below.)

4. Click the Magazines and E-Zines link in the Sport Sciences Resources area of the SportQuest Web site. Choose a journal's link (e.g., to *Science and Sports, Journal of Exercise Physiology, The American Journal of Sports Medicine, Athlete Insight: The Online Journal of Sport Psychology,* and *The Journal of Excellence*). Select an article from one of the chosen journal's issues, then state and describe the article's main point. Next, choose a general topic featured in a journal issue's article. Think of and write about something on a particular subject related to this general

topic. (Note: If possible, quote a scientist.) Extra Activity: Look for articles at the *Sport Science—A Peer Reviewed Site for Sport Research* Web site. (Find as cited in the Related Internet Sites section below.) Apply the activities just above to these articles.

RELATED INTERNET SITE(S)

SportQuest Resources Index

http://www.sportquest.com/resources/index.html

Note links under General (e.g., to International Sport Information Centres, Other Directories), links under Special Interest (e.g., Olympics, women, the disabled, Sport Information Research Centre [SIRC] Highlights), the Search Your Way link (e.g., in the database or texts) for a particular sport, the link to a List of Sports (with links), and the link to Canadian Sports Categories.

Sport Science at the Exploratorium

http://www.exploratorium.edu/sports

This site has Questions and Answers, Ask Us Archives, and articles on sports, such as baseball, skateboarding, cycling, and hockey, with titles such as "That's the Way the Ball Bounces," "Hands Up" by a rock-climbing physicist, and "Going Up? Get Fit."

Sport Science: A Peer Reviewed Journal Site for Sport Research

http://www.sportsci.org/index.html

This site takes a practical approach to the science of sports, featuring items from the current issue and issues of the recent past. Note links to News and Comment, Perspectives, Original Research, and Reviews. See also Tests/Technology, Train/Perform, and Statistics, plus Sports Medicine, Sports Nutrition, Research Resources, and Contents by Issue.

The Physics of . . .

http://www.k12.wa.us/staff/trobinso/physicspages/PhysicsOf.html

Select the link for the first letter of a sport. Search the links under that letter to physics information on that sport, e.g., the Physics of Tennis and the Physics of Swimming.

Sports at BioMedNet

http://journals.biomednet.com/search

After free registration by educators, access is available to articles or abstracts of articles. A "quick site search" done by selecting Journals, BioMedNet, Research, Reviews, or Web sites from the pull-down menu, then by typing in the search box: Sports, Adolescent Sports, or Children's Sports (which includes adolescents), and clicking Go, brings links to article titles. Clicking a title link brings the article's full text or an abstract of the article. Research articles have included "Physiological Issues Surrounding the Performance of Adolescent Athletes" and "Sports Participation and Health Related Behaviors Among U.S. Youth." Some articles have only their abstracts online, but online purchase of articles is available.

Gatorade Sport Science Institute

http://www.gssiweb.com/sportsciencecenter/topic.cfm?id=88

Site visitors who are professionals in the areas of science, medicine, nutrition, and sports can find out information on sports science topics (e.g., young athletes, sports psychology, sports nutrition, sports medical conditions, environmental conditions and training, dietary supplements, and more). See also the links to the Science of Gatorade Tour, Sports Science Exchange, and Gatorade Research with questions and answers.

SportQuest Recognized as the Best Sport Information Web Site

http://www.sirc.ca/pressreleases/pr971022.html

In this press release of October 27, 1997, features of the SportQuest database are provided, three Web-based recommendations of the SportQuest Web site are cited, and the existence of the database for more than twenty-five years is noted.

"Scientific Anomalies"
in the *Science Frontiers Digest Online* (1976–99)
URL: http://www.science-frontiers.com/sfonline.htm

SITE SUMMARY: This site, put online by Knowledge Computing, provides news items, reports, and articles on unusual scientific phenomena drawn from scientific journals, including the *New Scientist*, *Scientific American*, and *Nature*. It has "reports of observations and facts that challenge prevailing scientific paradigms" and things anomalous, even bizarre, in astronomy, biology, geology, geophysics, physics, archaeology, psychology, and mathematics. Browse by issue month and year, or use the search area. Digest reports beginning in the year 2000 are available only by subscription, although Contents pages can be viewed without subscribing.

DISCUSSION QUESTIONS AND ACTIVITIES

1. Think of an unusual science subject and find an item about it in the "Scientific Anomalies" in the *Science Frontiers Digest Online, 1976–99*; or choose a subject and item from the "Scientific Anomalies" in the *Digest Online*. Describe information on your subject as presented in your chosen item in the *Digest*. Emphasize the subject's scientific aspects while noting unusual, anomalous, aspects. Give your viewpoint, noting why or why not the subject is plausible.

2. See the Web sites: MSNBC News—Mysteries of the Universe; National Health Museum—Mystery Spot; then the Biggest Mysteries Megasite On Planet Earth; Planetary Mysteries, and Mysterious Places. (All urls are cited in the Related Internet Sites section below.) Choose a science-related general topic, then a particular subject of that topic, from one site each from the two groups of Web sites cited above. Describe the subject's features, emphasizing its scientific aspects while noting its unusual or anomalous aspects. Option: Give your own example, noting and emphasizing what is suggested just above.

3. Visit the media Web sites: PBS-TV Science Mysteries; PBS-TV Mysteries of Deep Space; then Unsolved Mysteries, With Robert Stack, On Lifetime TV; or Encounters with the Unexplained on PAX-TV. (All urls are cited in the Related Internet Sites section below.) Choose two science mysteries, one each from a media Web site program's Web page, from the two groups cited above. Read about, and describe in two essays, what you discover, emphasizing unusual or anomalous aspects. Search for, and add to your descriptions, information on your chosen subjects from what you find at any Web site cited in the Related Internet Sites section below. Include your viewpoint. (Note: For the second essay other "mysterious" TV programs' or movies' Web sites that you find may be chosen, if they feature what the Society For Scientific Exploration would consider acceptable subjects of investigation: meeting its unusual "scientific aspects" criteria (as stated in its Mission Statement found via a link on the main SSE Web page cited in the Related Internet Sites section of this book's chapter featuring the "Recommended Reading: Online Articles" for the Society For Scientific Exploration Young Investigators Program.)

4. Find Questions/Activities no. 6 and no. 7 in this book's chapter that features "Recommended Reading: Online Articles" for the Society For Scientific Exploration Young Investigators Program. Adapt these Questions/Activities to something you discover via the Web sites featured in this chapter on "Scientific Anomalies" in the *Science Frontiers Digest Online* as noted in the main url and Site Summary above.

RELATED INTERNET SITE(S)

Biggest Mysteries Megasite on Planet Earth

http://www.mysteries-megasite.com/home.html

A list of subject links leads to links with information on science-related subjects and subjects with features interpreted scientifically. See the links to, for example, Astronomy, Aurora Borealis, Ball Lightning, Bermuda Triangle, Vortices, Crop Circles, Nazca Lines, Ley Lines, Mysterious Places, Waterfalls, National Parks, National Monuments, Bible Mysteries.

Mysterious Places

http://www.mysteriousplaces.com/index2.htm

Cited by PBS-TV's NOVA program as a valuable Internet source, this site features links to data on Stonehenge (which some people think is an ancient astronomical observatory), the Bermuda Triangle, Easter Island, and other mysterious places (e.g., the face on Mars, sacred landscapes). At this site, "learn how scientists and anthropologist are piecing together the mysteries of these 'power places' and find out how the lessons learned can have an impact on our world today." See also the links to In the News, Virtual Tours, Educator Link, Related Sites, and Talk on the Message Board.

Planetary Mysteries

http://www.planetarymysteries.com

See the moving, alternately appearing, links to New Frontiers in Science, New Mars Face Information, and more, plus other links under Science to information on mysteries involving Energy, the Earth, the Moon, Planetary Systems, and more. A search area, ways to send comments or suggestions, and links are also featured.

PBS-TV Science Mysteries

http://www.pbs.org/neighborhoods/science/#mysteries

This site includes features of programs on subjects such as Faith and Reason, Evolution, and investigations on the NOVA program (e.g., the Beast of Loch Ness, Hunt for Alien Worlds), and the Scientific American Frontiers program (e.g., on "Life's Little Questions" and "Life's Really Big Questions").

PBS-TV Mysteries of Deep Space

http://www.pbs.org/deepspace

Included are features found by the Hubble Telescope, experts' answers to viewers' questions, and classroom activities, all based on the PBS program.

National Health Museum—Mystery Spot

http://www.accessexcellence.org/AE/mspot

See Teacher Developed Mysteries such as a microscope mystery. See also other mystery activities based on real or imagined science-related incidents or happenings.

MSNBC News—Mysteries of the Universe, via the Technology and Science Front Page

http://www.msnbc.com/news/TECH_Front.asp

Scroll to Special Reports, then click the subject's link, to find out about news on unusual science phenomena, including Mysteries of Your Health, Mysteries Great and Small, and more.

Unsolved Mysteries, with Robert Stack, on Lifetime TV

http://www.unsolved.com/home.html

Note, for example, information on episodes based on especially unusual true mysteries with science connections found via the Miscellaneous link. Stories have included subjects such as a Bioenergy Healer, Canadian Crop Circles, a Real Life Dr. Doolittle, Twin Connections, and more.

Encounters with the Unexplained on PAX-TV

http://www.pax.tv/shows/encounte

Click on the next episode link, or the message board link, or the cast bios link, to find out more about renowned scientists and others as they "explore puzzles that have baffled" humankind for generations.

"Interview with Charles F. Richter"
at the National Earthquake Information Center,
U.S. Geological Survey, Web Site (1980)
URL: http://wwwneic.cr.usgs.gov/neis/seismology/people/int_richter.html

SITE SUMMARY: First published in the *Earthquake Information Bulletin*, January–February 1980, this transcript is a shortened version of an interview with the inventor of the first modern and most well-known earthquake scale that was developed in 1935 and then named after him. The scale is still used today in an adapted form (to extend its capabilities beyond a local location) to detect the epicenters of earthquakes. In this interview, Richter revealed how he became interested in seismology (the study of earthquakes), provided explanations of the earthquake scale and the versions used today, and suggested what should be investigated and done regarding earthquakes.

DISCUSSION QUESTIONS AND ACTIVITIES

1. Read the *Earthquake Information Bulletin* Interview with Charles Richter. Describe what Richter said about the origins of the instrumental magnitude scale, the commonly held idea that magnitude is based on a scale of ten, then the difference between magnitude and density and what it has to do with radio transmissions.

2. What, according to Richter, is meant by the size of an earthquake? What does it mean in general scientific terms, and in specific seismological terms?

3. What, did Richter say, is remarkable about the scale and about the modifications involved in applying the scale to worldwide earthquakes?

4. What did Richter say about "assessing seismic risk" and of putting effort into measures that reduce earthquake hazards?

5. What did Richter comment about a Dr. Beno Gutenberg (who explored scales other than the Richter Scale) and about a Dr. Hiroo Kanamori (the developer of a detailed perspective of an individual earthquake, which is related to something in astronomy)? Keeping in mind your answer to Richter's comment about Kanamori, think of or find any subject in an earth science or another science (with information available via any Web sites cited in this book.) Describe this subject in a way that compares it to something else which has to do with a science, to make clearer what the subject is about.

6. How did Richter respond when asked to predict what he saw for seismology in the decade following the time of the interview? Include a Richter quotation and apply it to earthquakes. Next, think about, then adapt and apply, his quotation to any earth science area or another science field and something particular in it. Give your own ideas, although you may support them with data at a Web site cited anywhere in this book.

7. Study the Modified Mercalli Intensity Scale (1998) with descriptions provided by Richter, and used to analyze earthquakes today. (Find it online as stated in the Related Internet Sites section below.) How many levels are used to analyze earthquakes' status from light to very violent? What are the number, and "shaking severity" word, that indicate the levels of different earthquakes you would experience if people cannot walk steadily, people cannot steer cars, liquids are disturbed, large bells ring, and sand shifts horizontally on beaches?

8. Find, identify, and state a difference and a similarity between the Mercalli Scale with Richter's descriptions, and other earthquake detection/analysis scales. For example, compare aspects of this Scale with features of earlier scales, another scale used today, e.g., the Rossi–Forel Scale, and the Macroseismic Intensity Scale (found as noted in the Related Internet Sites section below), then with a feature of the Richter 1935 Scale which is described at the National Earthquake Center Web site (as cited in the Related Internet Sites section below).

9. Visit the Web pages or sites for New Scientist—Disasters—Earthquakes, New Scientist—News—Earthquakes, and the National Earthquake Information Center. (Their urls are cited in the Related Internet Sites section below.) Find information on a recent earthquake, a well-known earthquake of the twentieth century or the twenty-first century, and an earthquake that occurred before the twentieth century. Apply an earthquake scale's features (e.g., the Mercalli Scale's features, then, optional, another scale's features) to each of the earthquakes on which you find information.

10. Look again at the interview with Richter. At the time of the interview, with what was Richter involved? What was a key factor in what he was doing?

11. Check the interview with Richter again. How did Richter first become interested in seismology? Think of something you like to do now, or would like to do, and suggest which occupation you think you could pursue to include this interest. Option: Keeping in mind how Richter came into the career field with which he is now identified, think of an unusual way you might get to pursue a career you like.

RELATED INTERNET SITE(S)

New Scientist—Disasters—Earthquakes, and New Scientist—News—Earthquakes

http://www.newscientist.com/hottopics/disaster and *http://www.newscientist.com/news*

On the Disasters page, click an earthquake link, e.g., "Killer Quake" (about one that occurred three hundred years ago). On the News page, type the word "earthquakes" in the search box, then click the go button, and wait to see a page appear that has annotated links to information about research on earthquakes or information on recent earthquakes.

National Earthquake Information Center

http://wwwneic.cr.usgs.gov

This site contains links to areas such as a Current Earthquakes bulletin, Current Earthquake Information, General Earthquake Information, Earthquake Information Sources, Today in Earthquake History, Seismograph Station Codes, and the U.S. National Seismographic Network. Also included are a "report an earthquake" area, a site index with alphabetically arranged links to many earthquake subjects such as "Richter, Charles" and the "Richter Scale" (on the original modern scale first created in 1935), plus a pull-down menu with links leading to other earthquake Web sites.

Modified Mercalli Intensity Scale (1998), with Descriptions by C.F. Richter

http://www.abag.ca.gov/bayarea/eqmaps/doc/mmi.html

The Modified Mercalli Intensity Scale, provided by the Association of the Bay Area (California) Government, is one of several earthquake detection scales, and a favored one. "Full Descriptions" explaining features of earthquakes represented in the scale are excerpted from Charles Richter's *Elementary Seismology* (1958). There are Roman numbers indicating levels of intensity of earthquakes from mild to severe; full descriptions of earthquakes' influence on people, objects, and structures. Summary Damage descriptions and Shaking Severity indications are also provided. Under the scale, descriptions of masonry durability levels mentioned in the scale's descriptions are given.

European Macroseismic Intensity Scale (1998) (EMS-98) (Educational Version)

http://www.gfz-potsdam.de/pb5/pb53/projekt/ems/index.html

Click the Contents link, then note the links to an introduction and the complete version of the EMS-98 Scale (an earthquake analysis scale developed by the European Seismological Commission, Working Group Seismic Scales). Scroll past the introduction link and the EMS-98 link to the many Guidelines and Background Materials links (e.g., The Nature of Intensity, The Structure of the EMS-98 Scale), and find the last link that leads to the scale's short version which was made especially for educational purposes.

Rossi–Forel Scale, 1873 (Short Version)

http://www.sfmuseum.org/hist1/rf.html

The Museum of the City of San Francisco provides this nineteenth-century version of an earthquake damage and intensity scale with ten features, from Herbert Tiedemann's *Earthquakes and Volcanic Eruptions: A Handbook on Risk Assessment* (1992).

Invention Online Museum Presents Charles Richter, Measuring Earthquakes

http://www.inventorsmuseum.com/richter.htm

Introduction to the Earthquake Intensity Database—1638–1985

http://www.ngdc.noaa.gov/seg/hazard/intintro.shtml

This is managed by the National Oceanographic and Atmospheric Association, National Geophysical Data Center, and features information on the History of Earthquake Intensity Scales, Collecting Data On Earthquake Intensity, a description of the database, and more.

Museum of the City of San Francisco, California—History—Earthquakes

http://www.sfmuseum.org/hist1/index0.html#quakes

Click links to the writer Mark Twain's and the naturalist John Muir's eyewitness accounts of earthquakes, plus an "Early Work For Earthquake Research in California" (1929) by Thomas J. Maher, and other links to information on California's earthquakes.

"Origin of the Universe"
Stephen Hawking (1988)
URL: http://www.psyclops.com/hawking/resources/origin_univ.html

SITE SUMMARY: Physicist Stephen Hawking is considered one of the greatest scientific minds of our time. This essay, which first appeared in 1988 in his book *Black Holes and Baby Universes*, gives brief descriptions of various theories of the universe's origin and suggestions on the universe's evolution that describe what scientists theorized through time. Hawking notes how these theories are not quite right or have a bit of the truth to them. He then reveals his own theory as he conceived it for his doctoral dissertation, then provides his new theory, which is controversial yet irrefutable.

DISCUSSION QUESTIONS AND ACTIVITIES

1. Hawking begins his essay with the common phrase "What came first, the chicken or the egg?" How does he apply it to the essay's subject? Think of another subject, especially a science subject, to which you could apply this question. Describe why.

2. Describe one of the theories, from history, of the universe's origin and/or evolution (e.g., Steady State Theory, the Cosmological Constant, State of Infinite Density, the Big Bang). Identify who theorized it. To which of the two main "schools" does your chosen theory belong? Give Hawking's explanation of why it doesn't quite hold up or may have a bit of truth to it.

3. What question interested Hawking, which became the subject of his Ph.D. thesis? What did he aim to show? What did he suggest this meant? What happened in the scientific community because of his theory?

4. Describe Hawking's new theory, the "No Boundary State" theory. (Hint: It has something to do with one of Einstein's ideas, quantum mechanics, super strings, the Uncertainty Principle, and is related to, but different from, Richard Feynman's "Sum Over Histories" theory.) Why is Hawking's theory a good scientific theory? What profound implications does it have?

5. What does Hawking say about being able to predict, not predict, or determine the way the universe should behave?

6. Although science may solve the problem of how the universe began, what is the question it cannot answer, according to Hawking? What does he suggest? Do you agree or disagree? Support your comment.

RELATED INTERNET SITE(S)

Stephen Hawking Public Lectures Provided by Cambridge University

http://www.hawking.org.uk/text/public/public.html or *http://www.hawking.org.uk/lectures/lindex.html.html*

Links go to reproductions of Hawking's past lectures and information on his upcoming lectures. Titles of lectures online include "The Beginning Of Time," "The Nature of Space and Time," "Life in the Universe," "Space and Time Warps," and "Does God Play Dice?" One lecture is in PDF format.

Hawking's Answers to [Scientific and Other] Questions from Journalists and the Public

http://www.hawking.org.uk/text/about/qa.html

Stephen Hawking Page—Resources and Links

http://www.psyclops.com/hawking/resources (scroll to, and click, links)

Titles of lectures, essays and interviews online include "The Nature of Space and Time," "Baby Universes, Children of Black Holes," "An Interview with Stephen Hawking" conducted on June 20, 1985 by the Canadian Broadcasting Corporation's David Cherniack, and "Stephen Hawking's Universe" by Dr. Christopher Ray. Some documents are accessible only in formats that require special software.

Stephen Hawking's Universe at PBS-TV

http://www.pbs.org/wnet/hawking/html/home.html

Features an introduction by Hawking, plus links at the top of this Web page to Universes, Cosmological Stars, Strange Stuff, Unsolved Mysteries (with some answers suggested by experts), Things to Do in the Dark (a resources area), Ask the Experts, About Stephen Hawking, and a Teacher's Guide in PDF format. Annotations with the links can be found by scrolling down the page.

"The Hawking–Turok Instanton" in Quantum Cosmology—An Overview

http://www.damtp.cam.ac.uk/user/gr/public/qg_qc.html

In this non-technical overview of the astrophysics subject called quantum cosmology, and provided on a Cambridge University of England Web page, note this section on the concept of an instanton as conceived by Stephen Hawking and his colleague Neil Turok. See also the section on the instanton from the viewpoints of S. Coleman and F. DeLuccia.

"Stephen Hawking and the No Boundary Proposal" by Devin Harris

http://www.everythingforever.com/hawking.htm

Quoting Hawking's ideas, and Hawking's comments on the theories of Richard Feynman and Albert Einstein, this article's author writes about his idea on the subject, building on Hawking's theory.

"The Role of Doubt in Science"
Richard Feynman (1988)
URL: http://www.achilles.net/~jtalbot/bio/Feynman.html

SITE SUMMARY: This excerpt from the book *Why Do You Care What People Think?: Further Adventures of a Curious Character*, by noted physicist Feynman, features the author's view of science considered in relation to doubt or skepticism, or taking a closer look at and thinking again about, situations. It is also Feynman's look at other scientists, philosophers, and people in general, regarding what they think on the subject. Emphasis is on the subject and how it affects society. (Quotations on doubt by various types of thinkers are also provided.)

DISCUSSION QUESTIONS AND ACTIVITIES

1. See paragraph one. How did Feynman define "scientific knowledge"? Scientists have "a lot of experience" with which three things, according to him? Identify three types of experience that, Feynman said, scientists encounter as they work. What, did he say, is "of paramount importance"?

2. See paragraph two. What, according to Feynman, do scientists take for granted? What do people probably not realize? What should people be permitted to do?

3. See paragraph three. Feynman said that "many answers must have been given to the question of the meaning of it all" as people "have tried to fathom the meaning of life." Those answers have been "of all different sorts." How, according to Feynman, have proponents of one answer looked at the answers of others, and why? What needs to be found because of such a situation? Where might "it" be found? (For help, see paragraphs five and six.)

4. How did Feynman answer his own question: "What can we say to dispel the mystery of existence?" (Find it in paragraph four.) (Hint: Read, think about, ask yourself, then answer the following. As "science was already showing itself to be a successful venture at the end of the eighteenth century," an idea for a system arose. What is Feynman's definition of that system, and how were ideas involved? What, did he say, and conclude, are "essential to progress into the unknown"; what was clear to some people, and what, should people do to solve a problem that has never been solved? Next: How did he further define "great progress"? What should then be proclaimed, taught, and provided for "all coming generations"? Who should be responsible for doing what is referred to just above, and why?) (Tips: For help with the first group of questions/activities in the hint, see paragraph seven; and see paragraph nine for help with the hint's next second group of questions/activities.)

5. See paragraph eight. Describe what Feynman was referring to when he said: "This is it . . . !" Which part of humanity, metaphorically, did he say, is responsible for this situation, and why? Do you agree, or disagree? Explain your answer.

6. Think of a science problem, situation, or idea. (Hint: For help, visit any Web site referred to in this book.) Explain a hypothesis and suggested solution or possibility. (Note: Refer to, and apply, in your answers: Question/Activity no. 4, especially the first group in the hint and the next group's: What should then be taught? Also apply Questions/Activities no. 1, no. 2, and no. 3 [especially its Where might "it" be found?].)

7. See this book's chapter featuring the Recommended Reading: Online Articles for the Society for Scientific Exploration Young Investigators Program, and the International Crop Circle Database at the Independent Research Centre for Unexplained Phenomena Web site. Adapt the note in no. 6 above using these Web sites.

RELATED INTERNET SITE(S)

Skepticism

http://www.britannica.com/seo/s/skepticism

This site defines, and details aspects of, skepticism and skeptics from ancient through modern times, featuring references to challenges to science from philosophers (general, religious-minded, science-minded). Follow the links at the bottom of the page for more details, modern and historical, plus outline with links to particular aspects of, or views on, the subject. See the brief definition, then sign up for seventy-two hours of free access to view the article.

Skepticism Quotes

http://www.achilles.net/~jtalbot/bio/skepticism.html

Features quotations expressing skepticism on scientific theories, achievements, and inventions. See also the link to "Great Quotes From Great Skeptics."

Official Feynman Web Site

http://www.feynmanonline.com (scroll down right side to the Web Ring, click List Sites)

See links to various sites on Feynman, his work, writings, and life. Note especially: Interesting People—Richard Feynman, with quotations and links to some writings.

Science in Society: Skeptical Inquiry—Links

http://dmoz.org/Science/Science_in_Society/Skeptical_Inquiry

"Paleobiology—In the News, Highlights, Subjects, and Links"
at the National Museum of Natural History—Paleobiology Web Site
of Smithsonian Institution Online (1990–)
URL: http://www.nmnh.si.edu/paleo/index.html

SITE SUMMARY: Aiming to reveal its scientists' studies of animals and plants from the time of the dinosaurs, especially as living things in a vibrant ecosystem rather than as isolated fossil remains, the U.S. National Museum of Natural History provides this Web site on paleobiology, including paleobiology in the news that features articles or audio comments by or about staff scientists and their work, highlights including "Discover Dinosaurs" and Dinosaur FAQs, plus paleobiology links (e.g., of plants and algae, dinosaur exhibits, dinosaur extinction, global change, and evolution of terrestrial ecology [ETE]). Also included are a field calendar featuring news of current staff field studies and a Research link that goes to a page of annotated links leading to biographical information on staff paleontologists, their work, and publications. Note in addition information on a program with scientists who visit high schools, and links (e.g., to museums and institutions, organizations and societies, journals, and miscellaneous paleontology Web sites).

DISCUSSION QUESTIONS AND ACTIVITIES

1. Choose a written article or audio comments by, or about, a paleobiologist or paleontologist on the staff of the U.S. National Museum of Natural History. Provide quotations by, and facts about, the paleobiologist or paleontologist and her or his work, especially on a particular study currently being done or just completed, or work for which the paleontologist is most known. Give some biographical data that have connections to the work. (Note: Find articles or audio comments online via links under "Paleobiology in the News" via the main page of the National Museum of Natural History—Paleobiology Web Site. Note also the highlights on dinosaurs for more information on some paleontologists' work. Click the Research link to find links to paleobiologists' or paleontologists' biographical information.)

2. Write profiles of two paleobiologists or paleontologists. One may be of the present, and one of the recent past. One may be featured at the NMNH Paleobiology Web site. Aim to include quotations from and citations of the paleontologists' writings. (Tip: For more information, see the Web sites Amazing Dinosaur Scientists, Dinosaur Detectives, Paul Sereno's Dinosaur Web, and the Granger Papers Project. Their urls are cited in the Related Internet Sites section below.)

3. Click the link to Evolution of Terrestrial Ecology. Identify an ecological era. Suggest how a prehistoric plant and a prehistoric animal fit symbiotically in that era. Extra activity: Include something about a geologic feature of that era. (Hint: For extra help for any part of this question/activity, go to the magazines in the miscellaneous paleobiology links area and find article or article abstracts. You can also do a search for "prehistoric terrestrial ecology, plants, and animals" in a Web directory cited in this book's Appendix E.)

4. Identify the Burgess Scale, foraminifera, and the K/T Boundary along with its connection to dinosaur extinction theories.

5. Study various types of sources and resources, including the National Museum of Natural History Paleobiology Web site's links page with links to resources such as museums and organizations. See also Web sites with sources such as paleontological dig sites, parks and other natural areas; plus field notes, journal entries, field or lab reports, and news. (Web site urls are cited in the Related Internet Sites section below or in this book's chapters featuring the documents "Foreword by Michael Crichton to *Encyclopedia of Dinosaurs*," "Paleontology: The Window to Science Education," Paper Dinosaurs, and "Perspectives On the Past.") Choose a link for a particular resource on the NMNH Paleobiology Web site's links page. Citing examples from

that resource's Web site, identify reason(s) for the importance of this type of resource. Apply the Activity above to each type of resource or source mentioned.

6. Click the dinosaur extinction link in the National Museum of Natural History Paleobiology Web site's main links section. Identify the dinosaur extinction theory featured here, and reveal the viewpoint on the subject at this Web site. Next, go to the "Debates About Dinosaurs" Web site whose url is in the Related Internet Sites section below. Compare or show contrasts between a view here and one at the National Museum of Natural History Paleobiology Web site.

7. Choose another debate topic at the "Debates About Dinosaurs" Web site whose url is cited in the Related Internet Sites section below. Identify the main point and two or three supporting points on the topic, then tell why you agree or disagree, supporting your answer with logical claims and more data from the Web sites referred to anywhere in this book's chapter.

RELATED INTERNET SITE(S)

Amazing Dinosaur Scientists

http://www.cobb.k12.ga.us/~durham/ProjectCurrTech/DinosaurFile

Scroll to Scientist Role on this Internet WebQuest on Dinosaur Science activities page, and click links to find out about the lives and work of paleontologists, sometimes in their own words, and including Cathy Forster ("paleontologist with many hats"), a dinosaur detective, a dinosaur tracker, a dinosaur pursuer, a dinosaur veterinarian, and a Smithsonian Institution scientist. See also "Field Excavator Role," "Lab Preparator Role," and "Museum Curator Role."

Dinosaur Detectives in the Bone Zone at the *Dinosaur Interplanetary Gazette*

http://www.dinosaur.org/bonezone.htm

This site contains paleontologists' quotes, data from interviews with them, and basic facts about them.

Dinosaur Resources at Internet School Media Center

http://falcoln.jmu.edu/~ramseyil

Click the Science link, then the Paleontology link, then see the links on the Paleontology page for general sites, dinosaurs, fossils, fossil plants, paleontologists/personalities, geologic time periods, journals, museums, virtual exhibits, and more.

Paul Sereno's Dinosaur Web Site

http://dinosaur.uchicago.edu

Featuring audio highlights of this noted paleontologist's article in the June 1999 issue of *Science* magazine, this Web site provides Sereno's comments on dinosaur evolution and the evolution of continental drift with the consequences for the dinosaurs. See also the links to information on his expeditions, discoveries, documentaries, current events, biography, publications, and "Project Exploration: Using the Wonders of Science to Inspire City Kids."

Granger Papers Project

http://www.nh.ultranet.com/~granger or *http://users.rcn.com/granger.nh.ultranet*

This is an online collection of privately held expedition diaries, letters, photographs, and memorabilia by and about pioneering paleontologists Walter Granger (1872 to 1941) and Anna Granger (1871 to 1952), who explored the western United States, China, Egypt, and the Gobi Desert. The site is codirected by Vincent L. Morgan, author and contributor to the journal *Discovering Archaeology*, and Katherine R. Morgan, who teaches diary keeping and the writing process in high school. See also in PDF format a detailed Granger biography published in the 2002 *New Mexico Museum of Natural History and Science Bulletin*, noting especially the chapters "Granger's Scientific Contributions," "Singular Discoveries," and "Eocene in the American West."

Debates about Dinosaurs

http://www.dinodata.net/Discussions/dinosaurs.html

Features links to debates on dinosaur metabolism (e.g., warm blooded or cold blooded), dinosaur lifestyles, the dinosaur/bird link, and theories on what caused the dinosaurs' extinction.

"Botany for the New Millennium—The Practical"
Christine Mlot, for the Botanical Society of America (1992)
URL: http://www.botany.org/bsa/millen/mil-chp2.html

SITE SUMMARY: This document, emphasizing the practical aspects of plants, for food, fuel, fiber for clothing, and pharmaceuticals, is chapter two in *Botany for the New Millennium: A Report* (1992), edited by Karl Niklas, Liberty Hyde Bailey Professor of Plant Biology, Department of Plant Biology, Cornell University. This chapter investigates various facets of one of the main aspects of botany that the Botanical Society of America officials and members think are essential to make known at the beginning of the new millennium. (This document can also be found by clicking the report title at the Web site's index page http://www.botany.org/bsa/millen/index.html.)

DISCUSSION QUESTIONS AND ACTIVITIES

1. Read the first and last two paragraphs of chapter two of *Botany for the New Millennium: A Report*. What crisis exists at the dawn of the new millennium? What is the cause? Why is botanical knowledge crucial at this time? What is true about plants and people through history, and why will it probably be the same in the future?
2. Identify ten practical uses of plants as indicated in chapter two of the Report. Describe five, and give examples.
3. What is the effect of restoration of plants in an ecosystem? Why is it important? (See chapter two of the Report, and Ecosystem Structure and Function in the Report's chapter one which can be found via the index page cited in the Site Summary above.)
4. See the Report's Introduction, found via the index page as cited in the Site Summary above. Define botany. Explain why it is important. Name a famous botanist noted here, and describe this botanist's major botanical work and its practical aspect(s).
5. Investigate at the Web sites for the Environmental Horticulture Club at the University of California in Davis, "What Is Environmental Horticulture?" at the University of Florida Institute of Food and Agricultural Sciences, plus the EthnoBotanical Resource Directory at the University of Florida, the Society for Economic Botany, and Plants for a Future. (Their urls are cited in the Related Internet Sites section below.) Explain and give examples of other practical aspects of botany, especially with relation to the new millennium. Describe how one aspect would affect you. (Hints: plants and a particular nation or environment.)

RELATED INTERNET SITE(S)

Plants for a Future

http://www.comp.leeds.ac.uk/pfaf/index.html

This is an award-winning site by a British-based resource and information center for rare and unusual plants, particularly those with edible, medicinal, and other uses. It features links to leaflets on plants with particular uses, information on a book with suggestions involving plants and the future, a link to a plant database, and a link to its sister database in the United States.

Society for Economic Botany

http://www.econbot.org/home.html

On the main page, see links to a Brochure, and current issues of the Society's *Economic Botany* journal and *Plants and People* newsletter, all accessible in PDF format. In a pull-down menu, note links to educational resources, ethics resources, student network, and related links.

EthnoBotanical Resource Directory

http://www.cieer.org/directory.html

The Centre for International EthnoMedicinal Research provides here more than one hundred fifty links. Scroll to links under sections including "What is Ethnobotany?" articles, databases, Web directory, research projects, educational opportunities, bibliographies, publications such as *Plants and People Online Initiative/Ethnobotany Sourcebook* sponsored by the Royal Botanic Garden at Kew, UNESCO, and the World Wildlife Fund, plus professional societies, universities and institutions. See also links in the Cool Sites section, including to "Sacred Earth: An Educational Forum on Ethnobotany and Ecotourism," and links in the miscellaneous sites section, including Legendary Ethnobotanical Resources (with its own "What is Ethnobotany?" page).

What Is Environmental Horticulture?

http://hort.ifas.ufl.edu (click link)

This definition is provided by the University of Florida Institute of Food and Agricultural Sciences.

Environmental Horticulture Club at the University of California in Davis

http://envhort.ucdavis.edu/ehclub/index.htm

Links go to a Fun Horticulture Links page (which leads to sites such as EnviroPlants), and the UCD Environmental Horticulture Homepage (which leads to Growing Points publications, and more links).

Food Guide Pyramid (1992) and
Dietary Guidelines for All Americans (1995)
U.S. Department of Agriculture and U.S. Department of Health and Human Services
URL: http://www.nal.usda.gov:8001/py/pmap.htm

SITE SUMMARY: This Guide to Daily Food Choices (also known as the Food Guide Pyramid) is an outline of what to eat every day. The FGP is a general guide, not a rigid prescription, to help people choose a healthy diet that is right for them. It identifies six food types and gives recommendations for daily serving amounts. Data are provided on serving size in each food group. Each pyramid section for each food group, and words under the pyramid for each group, are clickable and take site visitors to a page with data on food in that group, and food from which to choose. (The Web site with the 1995 Dietary Guidelines for All Americans, which are geared to the Food Guide Pyramid, is at http://www.nal.usda.gov/fnic/dga/dguide95.html.)

DISCUSSION QUESTIONS AND ACTIVITIES

1. Investigate the USDA's Food Guide Pyramid and the 1995 Dietary Guidelines. What are the recommended daily allowances for people in general in each food group? State six to nine itemized dietary guidelines. Give reasons for following the second and third guidelines. See the Introduction to the 1995 Guidelines, state three things that make a diet important, and explain why. Suggest foods for one day's breakfast, lunch, and supper. Include one drink for each meal as suggested in the Web document "When Choosing Foods and Beverages, Keep These Ideas in Mind." (Its url is cited in the Related Internet Sites section below.)

2. Identify similarities or differences between the 1995 Dietary Guidelines and the 2000 Guidelines (whose url is cited in the Related Internet Sites section that follows).

3. See the Food Guide Pyramid for Kids at the Kids Health Web site. (Its url is cited in the Related Internet Sites section below.) What are the recommended daily allowances for children? Compare them to recommended daily allowances in the general USDA FGP. Suggest meals for children for one day's breakfast, lunch, supper, snack, and theme-based meal. Include something from each FGP section. Include also a drink for each meal as suggested at the Kids' Favorite Beverages and the Food Guide Pyramid Web site, being sure it coincides with the Kids Health Web site's Food Guide Pyramid for Kids. (Hints: See the Healthy Snacks and Treats for Kids of All Ages Web site for help with finding a snack. See the Recipes Database at the More Than School Meals Web site for help with finding a theme meal. See also the Building Better Health—Child Nutrition Web site. [Their urls are cited in the Related Internet Sites section below, or in this book's chapter on Nutrition and Children: A Statement for Health Care Professionals from the American Heart Association Nutrition Committee.])

4. See the USDA FGP and Adolescents at the Keep Kids Healthy: Adolescent Nutrition Web site. (Its url is cited in the Related Internet Sites section below.) How are food requirements different for adolescents and adults? Suggest a breakfast, lunch, supper, snack, and theme-based meal, all for adolescents. (Note: Adolescents are identified as average ones who are active, not athletic or less active average ones.) (Hint: Also check the Web site with A Young Person's Guide to Good Food! [whose url is cited in the Related Internet Sites section below].)

5. Imagine you are in charge of a day's school lunch and recess snack. Following the recommendations of the Web sites cited just below, suggest foods to include in a school lunch and a snack. Do you think you can provide something tasty as well as nutritious? Why or why not? (See the Web sites More Than School Meals [whose url is cited in the Related Internet Sites section below], and Healthy Snacks and Treats for Kids of All Ages [found as suggested in Question/Activity no. 3 above].)

6. See the Web sites Ethnic/Cultural and Special Audience Food Guide Pyramids, Food Guide Pyramid Links at Nutrition Central, Healthy Eating Food Pyramids and Tools, or Ethnic Diversity and Nutrition in the U.S.: Navigating the Pyramids. (Find urls in the Related Internet Sites section below.) Choose an ethnic food pyramid. If possible, choose one related to your family heritage. What are this ethnic group's recommended daily food allowances? Suggest food for a family heritage meal. Select items from each food group in the chosen ethnic pyramid.

7. Some nutrition-minded people say the USDA FGP should be turned upside down. See the Web site with "Turning the Food Pyramid Upside Down" (a Harvard Medical School Publication) and its Healthy Eating Pyramid, and the Web sites "The Four Food Groups Old and New," Dietitians of Canada—News Room, and The Doctor Will See You Now: Nutrition. (Their urls are cited in the Related Internet Sites section below.) Why has it been suggested there be an upside down FGP? Why do some nutritional and medical scientists object to the FGP as it is generally accepted? Do you agree, or disagree? Why? Support your answer with quotes from two scientists, either a nutritionist or a dietitian, and a medical doctor. (Note: The Healthy Eating [upside down] Pyramid noted in the questions above is not the same as the Upside Down Pyramid [of how Americans actually eat] found via the Food Guide Pyramid Links at the Nutrition Central Web site cited in the Related Internet Sites section below.)

8. See the Historical Food Guides Web site found via the Food Guide Pyramid Links at Nutrition Central Web site, and the Historical Food Guides Background and Development via the Dietary Guidelines for Americans—Topics Page. (Each url is cited in the Related Internet Sites section below.) See "The Four Food Groups, Old and New" Web site cited in Question/Activity no. 7 above. State the Basic Four Food Groups' and the FGP's purposes. Include how purposes have changed through time.

9. See the Web page on "Classifying Space Food into the Major Food Groups Found in the USDA FGP." (Its url is cited in the Related Internet Sites section below.) Suggest a breakfast, lunch, dinner, snack, and (optional) a theme-based meal that follow the USDA FGP or an alternative food guide at a Web site cited in this chapter and based on the food that is available to astronauts in space.

RELATED INTERNET SITE(S)

Keep Kids Healthy: Adolescent Nutrition—USDA Food Guide Pyramid and Adolescents

http://www.keepkidshealthy.com/adolescent/adolescentnutrition.html

This Web site gives selection tips recommended by a doctor and emphasizes what adolescents, especially active ones, should eat from each food group, how much, and why. Note also the Food Guide Pyramid and School Age Kids at http://www.keepkids healthy.com/schoolage/schoolagenutrition.html.

Food Guide Pyramid for Kids at Kidshealth.org

http://www.kidshealth.org/stay_healthy/food/pyramid.html

Kids' Favorite Beverages and the Food Guide Pyramid

http://applejuice.org/SmartSip.html#d

Scroll up and down this Web page to see links to, or information on, Smart Beverage Choices and more. Accessible also at http://www.applejuice.org when the Grownup Stuff link is clicked, then the Smart Sip link, then the title link or by scrolling down.

Healthy Eating Food Pyramids and Tools

http://www.oldwayspt.org

Advocating FGPs based on actual traditional diets as opposed to the USDA's "theoretical construct," the Harvard School of Public Health, Oldways Preservation and Exchange Trust and other institutions offer links to various FGPs (e.g., Vegetarian, Mediterranean, Latin American, and Asian), comparing and contrasting them to the USDA's FGP, and "showing how to follow the healthy eating patterns of cultures around the world that are scientifically proven to promote lifelong good health." See also the links to a Good Health Puzzle, and Educational Initiatives.

"Ethnic Diversity and Nutrition in the U.S.: Navigating the Pyramids"

http://food.orst.edu/kelsey/higdon.html

Originally part of an April 26, 1999 seminar at Oregon State University by Jane Higdon, this Web page document features information on "the popular but controversial" USDA FGP versus nutritional pyramids based on diets of different cultures. Introductory information, plus an outline, Internet references (e.g., Cultural Diversity: Eating in the Americas, and U.S. Ethnic Health Data) and print references, are provided.

Ethnic/Cultural and Special Audiences Food Guide Pyramids

http://www.nal.usda.gov/fnic/etext/000023.html

This page, part of the Food and Nutrition Information Center Web site, features links to FGPs in special categories, e.g., Comparison of International Food Guide Pictorial Representations (in PDF format), Bilingual Food Guide Pyramids in Over Thirty Different Languages, Cultural Food Pyramids such as a Native American Food Guide and a Russian Food Pyramid, plus, for Special Audiences such as a Vegetarian Diet Pyramid. See also links to Food Composition, FNIC Resource Lists and Databases.

Food Guide Pyramid Links at Nutrition Central

http://www.lib.vt.edu/subjects/nutr/Nutrition.Central/pyramid.htm

Links go to Cultural Pyramids (from the Southern Michigan Dietetic Association), a Northeastern Regional Food Guide, Historical Food Guides (from the USDA), What's A Serving Anyway? Ten Steps for Teaching Kids How to Eat Right at Home and at School (from the USDA Team Nutrition), and an Upside Down Pyramid (of what Americans actually eat) (not the same as the Healthy Eating Pyramid in the "Turning the Food Pyramid Upside Down" article cited below).

More Than School Meals

http://www.asfsa.org/morethanschoolmeals

On this page of the American School Food Service Association, which became the Child Nutrition Foundation in 2002, see a Recipes link which leads to a Recipe of the Month, and a searchable Recipes database that features an advanced search by ingredient, food type, theme, and more. Through a Child Nutrition link, see also the links to Research, Education, *School Food Service and Nutrition Magazine*, the electronic *Journal of Child Nutrition and Management*, Food Pyramids (especially the one for age seven and up), and Ask the Nutritionist. See also links that lead to information on Food Illness Prevention by Schools, the Nutrition Advisory Council, the Global Child Nutrition Forum, and more.

"The Four Food Groups, Old and New" by Richard H. Schwartz

http://schwartz.enviroweb.org/ffgroups.html

This page has comments on the original 1956 version of the Four Basic Food Groups and the 1992 USDA's Food Guide Pyramid. It includes a challenge to this FGP from the Physicians Committee for Responsible Medicine (a health and nutrition advocacy group). Suggestions are given by the PCRM director and fellow doctors on four new food groups, "recommended revisions to the dietary guidelines for all Americans," "shifting to a healthier lifestyle based on a plant centered diet," and helping the public "translate the scientific nutritional evidence into everyday food choices."

"Turning the Food Pyramid Upside Down" (2000–2001)

http://www.health.harvard.edu/tools/pyramid.html

In this detailed Harvard Medical School Health Publication, see and read about "a new Healthy Eating Pyramid based on carefully conducted scientific research" at the Harvard School of Public Health, and one that turns the USDA FGP upside down.

Dietitians of Canada—News Room

http://www.dietitians.ca/news/index.html

Features links to news releases on dietitians' views, public policy issues, and research, all sponsored by the Canadian Foundation for Dietetic Research, and the Dietitians of Canada. See also the links to Food and Nutrition Experts (with FAQs in PDF format), Research and Position Highlights on nutritional health, a Resource Centre, and Campaigns and Special Events with advice on foods and nutrition. In addition, see the links to Nutrition Resources, and A Career in Nutrition.

The Doctor Will See You Now: Nutrition

http://www.thedoctorwillseeyounow.com/articles/nutrition

See title links to articles under New Topics, Ongoing Topics, and Previous Topics.

Comments for the Dietary Guidelines Advisory Committee from the ADA

http://www.eatright.org/gov/lg081899.html

On August 18, 1999, these comments were offered by the American Dietetic Association, which "stands ready to assist the committee in developing scientifically based and consumer oriented guidelines."

Dietary Guidelines for Americans—Topics Page (Food and Nutrition Information Center)

http://photon.nal.usda.gov/fnic/dga

Links go to summaries and full texts of "Nutrition and Your Health: Dietary Guidelines for Americans" and "Using the Dietary Guidelines for Americans." There are also links to "How Much Are You Eating? Putting the Guidelines Into Practice," "Historical Food Guides Background and Development," "Dietary Recommendations and How They Have Changed Over Time," plus Background and Related Information, e.g., "ABCs of the Dietary Guidelines for Americans: Science and Application" (An Online Self-Study Course), "Summary Table Comparing the Five Editions of the Guidelines," "Questions and Answers on the Dietary Guidelines for Americans 2000," and more. Some documents are in PDF format.

Nutrition and Your Health—Dietary Guidelines for Americans

http://www.health.gov/dietaryguidelines

See links to a summary and the full text of the current guidelines, "Using the Dietary Guidelines" in PDF format, Release of the Guidelines, Reports of the Dietary Guidelines Advisory Committee on the Dietary Guidelines for the years 2000 and 1995, and Selected Federal Resources especially from the U.S. Department of Agriculture and the U.S. Department of Health and Human Services.

Dietary Guidelines Table of Contents (2000)

http://www.health.gov/dietaryguidelines/dga2000/document/contents.htm

See links to a summary, additional information on nutrition, and information under the topics Aim for Fitness, Build a Healthy Base, and Choose Sensibly.

Building Better Health—Child Nutrition

http://www.buildingbetterhealth.com/topic/childnutrition

Links go to Quick and Healthy breakfasts, lunches, dinners, and snacks; information on school lunches, vegetarian diets, fruits and vegetables, food safety, and more. See also links under In the News (e.g., "Texas Restricts Junk Food Sales in Schools"), Resources (e.g., Web sites, a news archive, and magazine and journal archive), and Cool Tools (e.g., quizzes).

"Classifying Space Food into the Major Food Groups Found in the USDA FGP"

http://teacher.ed.usu.edu/tlnasa/units/SpaceFoodNutrition/16.pdf

An activity from *Space Food and Nutrition: An Educators Guide with Activities in Science and Mathematics.* (An html format is available by title search at google.com.)

A Young Person's Guide to Good Food!

Http://www.cahe.nmsu.edu/pubs/_e/e-112.html

From the College of Agriculture and Home Economics at the University of New Mexico.

"When Choosing Foods and Beverages, Keep These Ideas in Mind"

http://www.ext.vt.edu/pubs/nutrition/348-710/348-710.html

A part of the Virginia State University and Virginia Cooperative Extension Publication "The Food Guide Pyramid and Dietary Guidelines—How Can You Stay Healthy?" See also information on the Milk and Cheese Group and the Fruit Group for more tips on what to drink to follow recommendations for staying healthy as provided in the Food Group Pyramid and Dietary Guidelines.

International Crop Circle Database
at Independent Research Centre For Unexplained Phenomena (1993–)
URL: http://www.cropcircleresearch.com/database/index.html

SITE SUMMARY: This site was created as a definitive database to assist in the serious study, with documents, of some mysterious phenomena which are known as crop circles, or agro-glyphs. Dismissed by many scientists, yet seen as curiosities by some scientists, these phenomena are large, complex, and mathematically precise, geometric formations, which emit temporary electrical or radioactive emissions after being formed, and are somehow etched into wheat or corn fields in ways considered beyond human capability. The database has notes on repeatable experiences involving the phenomena, using scientific and electronic equipment and done soon after a crop circle's appearance, and records of witness reports by people who have visited and experienced a crop circle soon after it was reported. Some reports on what cause the phenomena, such as unusual weather occurrences, and witnessed by people who claim to have seen crop circles being formed, are noted. The database includes reports reported before and after the time the database was set up, from the 1950s to recent times. Links lead to information on crop circles found during the current year (with chart and illustrations), months of the current year, previous years, and previous decades. Search is possible by keyword; longitude and latitude, field reports, articles, opinions, news, and research. An invitation to report a new formation is offered. Other links lead to other sites such as the award-winning Crop Circle Central and The Crop Circle Web site.

DISCUSSION QUESTIONS AND ACTIVITIES

1. Visit the International Crop Circle Database. Click the Field Reports link. Choose a listed Report (latest or from Index). Click its link. State where a circle is located. Describe its design. Reveal a reporter's science-related opinion.

2. There are many theories about the origin and creation of crop circles. State one and explain why you think it is a logical, scientific, origin/creation theory. (For help, find something at the International Crop Circle Database, or at the Web sites: Crop Circle Research: Scientific Research into Unexplained Phenomena; Crop Circles: Hoaxes or Natural Phenomena, in *Sciences Frontiers*; Crop Circle Math: Science Radio Report; "Crop Circles: Theorems in Wheat Fields" in *Science News* online; Crop Circle: Malta UFO Research Organization—Theories. [Their urls are cited in the Related Internet Sites section below.])

3. Visit the Peculiarities of Crop Circles Web site. (Its url is cited in the Related Internet Sites section below.) Choose a peculiarity said to be a crop circle's trait. Give a description based on data you find at the site. Comment on a reason given for the peculiarity. Do you agree or disagree? Support your comment in a logical, scientific way.

4. Some people claim they experience something unusual when they visit a crop circle. Find something on this subject at the International Crop Circle Database or at the Peculiarities of Crop Circles Web site. (Find as cited in Question/Activity no. 3 above.) Describe the experience. Comment on any scientific explanation for it. Does it seem logical, scientifically possible to you? Why or why not?

5. See this book's chapter featuring Recommended Reading: Online Articles for the Society for Scientific Exploration Young Investigators Program. Adapt and apply that chapter's Question/Activity no. 6 to a crop circle experience you find via the International Crop Circle Database or Web sites cited in its chapter's Related Internet Sites section.

RELATED INTERNET SITE(S)

Crop Circle Research—Serious, Scientific and Rational

http://www.cropcircleresearch.com (click link)

Note the FAQs such as "What Is Best Evidence Against Hoaxing?" (with scientific comments), and, from the pull-down menu: articles, research, and links to other sites.

"Crop Circles: Hoaxes or Natural Phenomena?"

http://www.science-frontiers.com/sf078/sf078g15.htm

This article in *Science Frontiers* magazine online cites the claim that crop circles are natural phenomena.

Peculiarities of Crop Circles

http://www.paradigmshift.com/pecs.html

Featured are comments on kinds of crops that crop circles occur in; swirl type; direction of, and change of grain in, circles; types of bending of stalks; stalks' occasional woven state; sounds; pattern change after formation; changes in underlying soil; anomalous measurements; natural features and elements under circles; alignment with natural features of the land; mathematical aspects; physical side effects of people who see phenomena; and locations of crop circles.

Crop Circle Math: Science Radio Report

http://www.aip.org/radio/scripts/crop_circle_math.txt

"Crop Circles: Theorems in Wheat Fields" at *Science News* Online, October 12, 1996

http://sciencenews.org/sn_arch/10_12_96/note1.htm

Crop Circles—Malta UFO Research Organization—Theories

http://www.mufor.org/crops.htm

"The Science of *Star Trek*"
David Allen Batchelor (1993)
URL: http://ssdoo.gsfc.nasa.gov/education/just_for_fun/startrek.html

SITE SUMMARY: NASA physicist David Batchelor describes various sciences, and the treatments of science in *Star Trek* (the television programs and the movies). In this document, reproduced online via the Space Science Data Operations Office Web site, Batchelor points out what is based on real science and pure fantasy, and what is valuable with reference to science in *Star Trek*. He also comments on critics' viewpoints on the subject.

DISCUSSION QUESTIONS AND ACTIVITIES

1. Read Batchelor's Introduction and Conclusion. Cite three of the six positive statements (in general) about the presence of science, scientists, and engineers in *Star Trek*. Identify positive comments about "the fanciful science."

2. Choose three of the twenty *Star Trek* science features Batchelor mentions. State his view on these sciences, noting if your chosen *Star Trek* sciences are probable, possible, or not likely, and if *Star Trek* presents it realistically, not realistically, or partly realistic/partly unrealistic. Check to see if you have chosen a *Star Trek* science also mentioned by Stephen Hawking in his lecture "Science in the New Millennium" and/or Lawrence Krauss in his "Excerpts from *The Physics of STAR TREK*." (Both documents are featured in other chapters of this book.) If so, cite Hawking's and/or Krauss' view(s) on the science or sciences.

3. Explain further your answers to one of the sciences you selected when doing Question/Activity no. 2 above. (Be sure, as Batchelor indicates, your choice is a present day science that could be an "ancestor" of a *Star Trek* science, but not a "fantasy science." The *Star Trek* science would then be a future or evolved version of a present day science.) Explain as suggested by Hints below, and by including data on your chosen subject, found via Web sites noted below. (Hints: Begin an essay by describing a *Star Trek* science. Find urls for Web sites on one of these *Star Trek* science subjects Batchelor mentions [e.g., Holography; Artificial Intelligence, also called Artificial Life, AI or A-Life; Healing Rays, which are therapeutic lasers, or laser-based medical treatments; Sensors and Tricorders, i.e., technical and medical instruments using sonar and magnetic resonance imaging.] Describe an evolutionary connection between today's science and the future science as used in *Star Trek*, stating the now and then connection, and supporting your claim by quoting present day scientists' research. Suggest how the *Star Trek* science indicates how Earth's civilizations will be different in the future, and how the future science would affect you or an individual living in that future time.) (Visit the Web sites StarFleet Medicine and Astrometrics, *STAR TREK* Related Science articles, Official *STAR TREK* Web site—Library—Episodes/Movies Information, *STAR TREK*: VOYAGER—Technology, Medicine, etc., Trek Tech, and *STAR TREK*—Reference Sites—Treknology, and journalist Janet Wells' article "The Science of *STAR TREK*: Fictional Technology Has Long Been the Inspiration for Real Life Scientists" [whose urls are cited in the Related Internet Sites section below; the Related Internet Sites section of this book's chapter on "Excerpts from *The Physics of STAR TREK*," or this book's Appendix B].) (For more help with what to suggest as requested above, visit the Science in Society [its Futurism area], and the World Future Society Web sites. Both sites' urls are cited in the Related Internet Sites section of this book's chapter on Hawking's document noted in Question/Activity no. 2 above.)

4. Other sciences are mentioned in *Star Trek*, including nanotechnology, genetic engineering, terraforming, and cloning. (For information, see the Foresight Institute Web site on nanotechnology [whose url is cited in the Related Internet Sites section in this book's chapter on

Richard Feynman's speech "There's Plenty of Room at the Bottom"], the International Forum for Genetic Engineering Web site [whose url is cited in the Related Internet Sites section in this book's chapter featuring Hawking's document noted in Questions/Activities nos. 2 and 3 above], and the StarFleet Medicine site [whose url is cited in the Related Internet Sites section below], plus information on terraforming and cloning at Web sites whose urls are cited in this book's Appendix B.) (For more help, see any of the other sites cited in the Related Internet Sites section below, e.g., Official *STAR TREK* Web site—Library—Episodes/Movies Information.) Apply to the *Star Trek* sciences noted above the Hints in Question/Activity no. 3 in which you are asked to describe something, then suggest something, then indicate a way each of these sciences appears in *Star Trek*.

5. Extra Optional Activity: Choose a modern science you think is a forerunner or ancestor of a *Star Trek* science not mentioned by Batchelor or in this chapter's Questions/Activities. Explain why you believe this. Support your claims with scientists' comments you find on the science at Web sites referred to anywhere in this chapter, or anywhere in this book.

6. See *Star Trek*'s "'Richter' Scale of Cultural Development" with reference to planets and civilizations in the *Star Trek* universe, found online at the *Star Trek* Federation Sim Star Fleet Web site. (Its url is cited in the Related Internet Sites section below.) State the main feature of a Class N Planet, and identify a well known planet in this category. Choose another planetary classification, then suggest what people from Earth would need to survive and establish a colony on a planet with this classification. Select one level of cultural development, then describe an Earth based culture and time similar to this level, and any type of science that is part of this cultural level. Explain a way this science is an important part of this culture.

7. Keeping Question/Activity no. 6 above in mind, read the article "Just My Type: Karashev Civilizations in Science Fiction and Beyond" at the Suite 101 Web site. (Its url is cited in the Related Internet Sites section below.) Name and identify the four types of civilizations the twentieth-century Russian astronomer Karashev proposed, and tell where he placed the civilization of the Earth of the mid-twentieth century, the time when he suggested his idea. Identify and explain the foundation on which he based his proposal. Tell how the article's author connects Karashev's scheme to the *Star Trek* Universe.

8. See the Web site featuring *STAR TREK*—News—Science Briefs, etc. (Its url is cited in the Related Internet Sites section below.) Select one Science Brief, identify its *Star Trek* connection and the real world connection. Option: Watch a *Star Trek* episode or movie on TV, in a theater or on a videotape, or read a *Star Trek* novel. Identify a science in the *Star Trek* story, connect it to a real world science, then write your own "science brief."

RELATED INTERNET SITE(S)

STAR TREK—News—Science Briefs, etc.

http://startrek.paramount.com/news/news-list.asp

Scroll to, and click, Science Brief news links that are mixed with other *Star Trek* News. Science Briefs are on subjects that have connections between real life and *Star Trek* features, or particular episodes' features. Science Brief links have included "NASA's First Science Officer Named," "The Prime Directive—First Draft" (of protecting against space germs), "Computers Inspired By Biology," "Looking For Life in All the Odd Places," and more. Note also related links at the end of each Science Brief. In addition, see the Feature Archive link to previous news, e.g., "Dispatch 5-11-00: The Science Behind the Fiction."

"The Science of *STAR TREK*: Fictional Technology Has Long Been the Inspiration for Real Life Scientists," by Janet Wells, in the *San Francisco Chronicle*, November 13, 2000

http://www.sfgate.com/science

Scroll down the left column to Resources—Search and Archive. Click the link, then, on the search page, do a search in the Archive Search area by selecting the dates November 1, 2000, to November 30, 2000, writing Janet Wells in the Byline box, then clicking the search button. The link to the article will appear.

STAR TREK—Reference Sites—Treknology

http://www.trekssearch.com/Reference_Sites/Treknology

At this in-progress site, browse for links to Web sites in the categories: Reference Sites, *Star Trek* Universe, Internet Resources, and News.

StarFleet Medicine, and Astrometrics

http://www.geocities.com/Area51/Nebula/4156/infirmary/medicine/medicine.html

Links in the right column go to Introduction, Diseases, Procedures, Equipment, and Medicine (all especially, but not exclusively, of the *Star Trek* program DEEP SPACE NINE, set in a space station in the known Galaxy's Alpha Quadrant, where Earth is located, but in an area in deep space near a planet called Bajor, and near a space phenomenon called a wormhole, that leads to the Gamma Quadrant). Note also bottom links for profile and personal logs of DEEP SPACE NINE's Dr. Julian Bashir, plus Bashir episodes at: http://www.geocities.com/Area51/Nebula/4156/ds9/logs/depisodes.html, and Medical Log: Supplemental at http://www.geocities.com/Area51/Nebula/4156/personal/links.html. See, in addition, link to Astrometrics, with information on the DEEP SPACE NINE wormhole, and the twentieth century wormhole theory, at www.geocities.com/Area51/Nebula/4156/ds9/astro/wormhole.html.

STAR TREK Related Science Articles, and Physics and Technology Encyclopedia

http://www.treknology.8m.com

Click the articles link to find links to *Star Trek* Technology and Physics articles on, for example, warp drive, and faster-than-light travel. See also links to ShipTech, and an encyclopedia with entries that are based on the official *STAR TREK*: THE NEXT GENERATION Technical Manual.

Official *STAR TREK* Web Site—Library—Episodes/Movies Information

http://startrek.paramount.com/library/episodes.asp

Note the links to Stellar Cartography, Technology, and Medical and Science. See also the links to the various *Star Trek* television series or movies.

STAR TREK: VOYAGER—Technology, Medicine, etc.

http://www.geocities.com/Hollywood/Trailer/3687/startrek.html (click Datalogs)

Choose access by the html link or the shockwave link to find information on the sciences in this version of *Star Trek* that features a star ship stranded in the Milky Way Galaxy's Delta Quadrant and striving to return to Earth in the Alpha Quadrant which is 70,000 light years away. See information on sciences including medical records, the emergency medical hologram, holographic technology, and time travel. Note also the "long distance theory" that suggests an intelligent dinosaur species in the Delta Quadrant originated on Earth, then escaped into space just as a cataclysm came and destroyed Earth's dinosaurs.

STAR TREK's "'Richter' Scale of Cultural Development"

http://www.sb254.com/fsf/guides/culture.htm

At the *Star Trek* Federation Sim (Simulation) Fleet Web site, see this document for the Star Fleet Universe, "published" by a Dr. Roeland Richter in the *Star Trek* year of 2203. This scale identifies different levels of civilization on *Star Trek* planets. On close look, parallels with various times in Earth's history can be seen. Although called a cultural scale, it also indicates any sciences existing at a particular level. Examples are given to *Star Trek* planets, with descriptions and letter designations for each level. Note, for example, Class N, and Class N+. See the Scale with links (some broken) at the nicely arranged Web site http://members.aol.com/ grewsomeco/richter.htm.

"Just My Type: Kardashev Civilizations in Science Fiction and Beyond"

http://www.suite101.com/article.cfm/sf_and_society/70188

In this article, Christopher B. Jones writes about different levels of development in civilizations on the Earth, what comments Carl Sagan and Isaac Asimov had on the subject, how science fiction (especially *Star Trek*) deals with it, what Nikolai Kardashev (a twentieth-century Russian astronomer) said about it, what concept it is based on, and where the Earth of the mid-twentieth century as well as today in the early twenty-first century may be in this scheme.

Trek Tech

http://www.geocities.com/Area51/Corridor5363/stuniverse.html

Of *Star Trek*'s twenty-fourth-century physics and technology, with quotes from writings and talks by David Batchelor (detailed), Lawrence Krauss and Stephen Hawking (both brief). Information on "The Core Computer: The Heart Of A Starship Operation," "Warp Propulsion," "Inertial Dampers," etc., plus maps of the *Star Trek* universe, a detailed *Star Trek* Timeline (in progress), and miscellaneous *Star Trek* sites.

Daystrom Institute Technical Library

http://www.ditl.org

This site is named for the Earth's greatest scientific institution in the *Star Trek* universe. It has links to personnel (e.g., *Star Trek*'s science and medical officers: Spock, Leonard McCoy, Beverly Crusher, Julian Bashir, Jadzia Dax, Tuvok, the Emergency Medical Hologram, T'Pol and Phlox). There are also many more links (e.g., to the television series' guides, and articles). In addition there is a tribute to the real life astronauts of the Columbia space shuttle where the U.S. space program's most dedicated science mission to occur in years took place in January 2003.

"International Code of Botanical Nomenclature"
International Association for Plant Taxonomy (1994)
URL: http://www.bgbm.fu-berlin.de/iapt/nomenclature/code/tokyo-e/contents.htm

SITE SUMMARY: This code (also known as the Tokyo Code) is copyrighted by the International Association for Plant Taxonomy and is the currently accepted version of the International Code, which provides science-based rules for naming plants. It was established in 1994 by an editorial committee selected by the Nomenclature Section which was part of the XV International Botanical Congress, Yokohama, Japan, August and September 1993. Finalized after discussions, decisions, and votes, at the Congress, while building on previous codes starting with Linnaeus' *Species Plantarum* (1753), this code is based on recent discoveries and scientific conclusions. The contents, with links here, are: Preface; Notes and Recommendations; Important Dates in the Code; Preamble; Principles; Rules and Recommendations; Provisions for Code Modifications; Appendixes I through VI; Subject Index; and Index to Scientific Names.

DISCUSSION QUESTIONS AND ACTIVITIES

1. Read the Code's Rules and Regulations, chapter one, article three. Name and describe principal botanical ranks in descending sequence. Give English and Latin names.
2. Define plant species, genera, families, and class. Describe how they are named according to the Code rules.
3. Read the Code's Rules and Regulations, chapter four, article twenty-nine. State how a botanical name becomes valid or does not become valid.
4. Read the Code's Rules and Regulations, chapter three, section six; and its Appendix one. See also the features of the "International Code of Nomenclature for Cultivated Plants" at the Web site: Rules for Naming Botanical Plants, at the Brooklyn Botanical Garden Online. (Its url is cited in the Related Internet Sites section below.) How should cultivated plants be named? Imagine a hybrid plant you could cultivate, and name it following the Code rules.
5. Read the article "The New Code . . . Implications for *Flora of North America*." (Its url is cited in the Related Internet Sites section below.) Cite something stated as a change in the Tokyo Code; noting how it is different from its appearance in an earlier code, and what it means for plants in North America.
6. See data on the "American Botanical Code" (1930) at Cornell University's Naming Plants—Classification of the Hierarchy of Nature Web site. (Its url is cited in the Related Internet Sites section below.) Give an example of something the American Code has contributed to the International Code.
7. Visit one of these Web sites with data that will be in the newest in-print International Code (known as the St. Louis Code): XVI International Botanical Congress—Summary Report, XVI International Botanical Congress Issues Warnings, or the XVI International Botanical Congress: "The Shroud of Turin Controversy Returns." (Their urls are cited in the Related Internet Sites section below.) Choose an unusual or an interesting problem discussed during the XVI International Botanical Congress. Briefly describe it. Suggest a solution to the problem, as stated at the Congress, or which you think of, or both.

RELATED INTERNET SITE(S)

"Naming Plants—Classification of the Hierarchy of Nature" (1998)

http://bhort.bh.cornell.edu/hort243/nomen

Click links to Linnaeus' 1753 *Species Plantarum*, and the American Code (accepted at the fifth International Botanical Congress, 1930, and added to the International Code). See also links to Rules from Linne's Time That Apply Today and Modern Principles of Nomenclature.

Rules for Naming Plants, at the Brooklyn Botanical Garden Online

http://www.bbg.org/gar2/topics/botany/names_rules.html

The rules here are clearly outlined and explained, and are based on six broad principles for the "International Code of Botanical Nomenclature" (1994), and twelve principles for the "International Code of Nomenclature for Cultivated Plants." See also http://www.bbg.org /gar2/ topics/botany/class_intro.html for a clear description of the classification of corn in seven hierarchical parts, plus reasons for each.

"The New Code—Implications for *Flora of North America*"

http://hua.huh.harvard.edu/FNA/Newsletter/Volume/V09n1.html

Scroll one third down the page for this article about the Tokyo Code; an article that appeared in *FLORA OF NORTH AMERICA News*, January–February–March 1995. The author is John McNeill, FNA Nomenclatural Advisor.

XVI International Botanical Congress—Summary Report

http://www.mobot.org/MOBOT/research/conferences/ibc99.html

This report, on the International Botanical Congress at Missouri Botanical Garden, which occurred in 1999, August first through seventh, includes the Nomenclature meeting that would establish the latest in-print International Botanical Code (also known as the St. Louis Code). Information on the unusual scientific program at the Congress is also included.

The XVI International Botanical Congress Issues Warnings

http://www.rbg.ca/cbcn/en/news/press_ibc.html

This press release, issued by the Canadian Botanical Conservation Network, reveals Botanical Congress attendees' concerns regarding humans gravely altering the Earth's physical structure and the affects it will have on plants for human survival. It cites scientists' urgings to not be "inattentive stewards" but "more fully engaged" in caring for planet Earth (i.e., do research to determine what is wrong, then strive to fix it). See also the press release at http://www.rbg.ca/ cbcn/en/news/press.ibc2.html on the "International Botanical Congress President Calls for a Seven-Point Plan to Reverse Alarming Rates of Plant Species Losses."

XVI International Botanical Congress: "The Shroud of Turin Controversy Returns"

http://www.the-scientist.com/yr1999/sept/lewis_p10_990913.html

Ricki Lewis, in *The Scientist*, September 13, 1999, provides data on talks of "ghosts of flowers past" with relation to the controversial Shroud of Turin; also a botanical curiosity. He offers details of attempts, including pollen analysis, made to determine when the shroud was made and when the impressions on it were formed. He tells of attempts that include identification and dating of the plant remnants and identification of their original habitats.

MuSICA—Music and Science Information Computer Archive (1994–)
Center for the Neurobiology of Learning and Memory,
University of California at Irvine
URL: http://www.musica.uci.edu

SITE SUMMARY: This archive, supported by the National Association of Music Merchants, features an online *Research Notes* newsletter providing music and science-related reports, brief discussions, opinions, abstracts that are summaries of upcoming discussions, and research articles. The articles are critical analyses of research on the subjects of music and behavior, including child development, perception, learning, memory, psychology, cognitive sciences, neuroscience, clinical medicine, health and related topics, music therapy, and allied fields. The newsletter's sections include a featured article, plus, occasionally, "To the Point," "Matters of Opinion," "Impact of the Arts on Learning," and "Student Music Scientists." The latest issue and back issues are available, with access by browsing a subject index, an article titles index, or a newsletter issue list arranged by year, season, and number. (MuSICA has also compiled a bibliographic database of citations and abstracts of research on music as related to behavior, the brain, and related areas. This database will be available via the International Foundation of Music Research which has a link at the MuSICA site.)

DISCUSSION QUESTIONS AND ACTIVITIES

1. Choose five documents, one each from MuSICA's newsletter's specific articles area, subject index, and the following areas in a current or back issue "Student Music Scientist," "To the Point," and "Matters of Opinion." Write descriptions of the scientific aspect of each musical subject, in fifty to one hundred words.

2. Choose a subject connected to music that is medical-related and a subject that has something to do with learning a science; selecting both from the MuSICA newsletter's subject index. In one hundred to two hundred words, write two essay descriptions of the ideas in the MuSICA articles.

3. Choose another subject from one of the sources of items in Question/Activity no. 1 above. Think of your own scientific viewpoint with regard to this music subject or a related sub-topic. Write an essay, of one hundred fifty to three hundred words, on your idea, supporting it with logical scientific analysis.

4. See *Musicae Scientiae: The Journal of the European Society for the Cognitive Sciences of Music* online. (Its url is cited in this book's Appendix D. See also a link for this journal's Web site on the Ian Cross Web page whose url is cited in the Related Internet Sites section below.) Choose an article from any of the issues, then write an essay, in seventy-five to one hundred words, describing the article's main point. Select a general subject mentioned in any article in any of the issues, and think of, then describe, in one hundred to one hundred fifty words, a particular idea related to your chosen article's general subject.

5. See Professor Ian Cross's Web document "Music and Science: Three Views." (Its url is cited in the Related Internet Sites section below.) Identify, state, and briefly define the three views that Cross wrote about. (Help hint [optional]: Think, and write about them with reference to "perception," "creation," and "production," which he mentions.) Next, identify what was important which Cross said about music with reference to the third view, as indicated at the end of the article; then think of, and describe, an example that you think illustrates what you think he states here. Next, study what Cross wrote about view three. Think on, and write of, view three, describing your understanding of it by considering one aspect of it that Cross mentions, and providing an example relating to it that you think of. (Main Note no. 1: Include in your answers information that Cross states [with citations] from one scholar or more on the subject

for Question/Activity no. 5, parts three and four; then [optional], one each for the first part. Main Note no. 2: When including music examples in your answers, use examples of music pieces mentioned anywhere at the MuSICA Web site, or in *Musicae Scientiae* [found as cited in Question/Activity no. 4 above]; or cited at, or found via, the Web sites whose urls are cited in the Related Internet Sites section below. Optional: See also the music Web sites whose urls are cited in this book's Appendix F [e.g., Pulitzer Prize in Music 1943–2000, Essentials of Music, Virtual Library: Classical Music]. If you choose as examples music pieces you know, be sure they fit the standards, and types of music, cited at sites cited in this chapter.)

6. See the section "Conceptions of Science" in Cross' document referred to in Question/Activity no. 5 above. Describe a conception of science, including relationships to all or some of the following phrases which Cross stated in connection with the scholar Lakatos: "core components" and "auxiliary hypotheses"; "the focus," "what constitutes scientific knowledge," how "science proceeds," "weight of evidence," and "weight of change" that are "in the background of . . . scientific theory"; plus "a model of scientific understanding" with relation to "societal factors" and culture. (Note: See Notes for Question/Activity no. 5 above. Apply the first part of Main Note no. 1 and Main Note no. 2 to this Question/Activity.)

RELATED INTERNET SITE(S)

"Music and Science: Three Views" (1998) by Ian Cross

http://www-ext.mus.cam.ac.uk/~ic108/RBM

This article, in English, was published in print in the *Revue Belge de Musicologie*, 52 (1998). It features a British music professor's views of music with relation to science and includes references to other scholars' viewpoints. The views are identified as physicalist or physicalism, immanentalist or immanentalism, and cognitivist or cognitivism. Note also the section "Conceptions of Science." See in addition a biography and links to a list of other publications and to the Centre for Music and Science, at Cross' page, whose url is http://www-ext.mus.cam.ac.uk/external/people/academicstaff/ic108.html.

Beyond the Pulitzer Prize: No. 5 Music and Geography

http://www.newmusicbox.org

Click the Archive link, then type Spratlan in the search box, then click search. Next, scroll to, and click, no. 5. This Web page features part of an interview with composer Lewis Spratlan, whose "Life Is a Dream" (an opera in three acts, with Act Two a concert version), won the 2000 Pulitzer Prize in Music. Included are questions and comments on place and nature with reference to Spratlan's music piece titled "When Crows Gather." Audio Clips are available.

Music and the Brain—Related Articles

http://www.educationthroughmusic.com/brainarticles.htm

The California-based Richards Institute of Education and Research Through Music online has links to various articles both at this site and at other sites. See, for example, the articles "The Brain Comes Alive to the Sound of Music" and "The Musical Brain."

The Recording Academy—GRAMMY Gateway—"Music on Their Minds"

http://www.grammy.com/gateway/flohr.html

This article, by John W. Flohr and others, is provided at this Web site which is called an "Internet nexus of reliable information about recorded sound." Sections of the article feature data on "The Brain Processing Music," "Music and Brain Research on Children," "Brain Wave Collection," and "Future Directions." Comments on music and science are included. There are also a list of references and links to more information online.

Music Education Online

http://www.childrensmusicworkshop.com/home.html

Click the Music Links link, then the Music Education Resources link. See links to articles, or Web sites with articles, such as "Music and the Brain Research," "The Natural Basis for the Do Re Me Scale," and "Music Is (and the Value of Music Education)."

"Music Therapy Makes a Difference" at the American Music Therapy Association

http://www.musictherapy.org

Links go to FAQs and data on music therapy, including Quotes About Music Therapy, Researching Music Therapy, Careers in Music Therapy, News and Events (e.g., the New York City Music Therapy Relief Project), plus links to more information, and Related Resources on the World Wide Web.

Research Links—Music—The British Library

http://www.bl.uk/collections/musicresearch.html

This Web site provides a potpourri of links to Music Resources. Note, for example, the link to "Journals Online For Musicians, Music Theorists, and Musicologists" with journals including the *Journal of New Music Research*, the *Music Research Digest*, and the *Computer Music Journal*. See also the link to the "Royal Holloway Music Department's Golden Pages: Main Index" that includes links to "Dissertation Abstracts in Music" with its keyword search area, e.g., with words including science, psychological, cognitive, technical, and other words that are science-related. Note in addition the link to the "Sibelius Academy Web site" with its Other Interesting Links to Web Sites including the World Forum for Acoustic Ecology.

"Toward a World Strategy and Utilization of Our Natural Satellite: A Report"
Chuck Meyer (1994)
URL: http://www-curator.jsc.nasa.gov/curator/lunar/lnews/lnjul94/workshop.htm

SITE SUMMARY: This report, by Chuck Meyer, a curator at NASA's Johnson Space Center, provides details about an International Lunar Workshop that was held from May 31 to June 3, 1994, in Beatenberg, Switzerland. The Workshop was hosted by the European Space Agency, and the University of Bern in Germany. Meyer reveals considerations discussed at the Workshop, especially of future plans for internationally coordinated programs for lunar exploration, including robotic and human exploration, with an emphasis on scientific aspects of exploration and their usefulness.

DISCUSSION QUESTIONS AND ACTIVITIES

1. How was "Big Science" defined, and what was said about it by the Workshop's keynote speaker? (Hint: See part of the report's paragraph two.)
2. What did Harrison Jack Schmitt, the Apollo 17 geologist-astronaut who attended the Workshop, say to recommend a return to the moon?
3. See the third statement of a declaration created at the Workshop. Which three scientific aspects were suggested for study during new lunar exploration missions?
4. Scroll three-quarters down the page. Find reproduced portions of "The Scientific Rationale for 'A Moon Programme: The European View, 1994.'" See the three sections that are titled Science of the Moon, Science on the Moon, and Science from the Moon. Choose one scientific aspect from each section, describe it, and explain its value or importance as suggested in the document and/or as you think.
5. How does this Workshop's conclusions compare with an American Space Exploration Initiative, according to Meyer? What was the status of the American Initiative at the time that Meyer wrote his Report on the Workshop?
6. Compare scientific aspects decided upon at the Workshop with aspects of the "Lunar Surface Exploration Strategy, Final Report, 1995," by the U.S. Lunar Exploration Science Working Group. Its url is cited in the Related Internet Sites section below.

RELATED INTERNET SITE(S)

"Lunar Surface Exploration Strategy: Final Report" (1995)

http://www.pgd.hawaii.edu/lexswg

This report, by the Lunar Exploration Science Working Group (LExSWG), "highlights the key elements of a strategy for the exploration of the lunar surface by robotic spacecraft" and "set[s] the stage for intense human exploration." See links to the Introduction, Science Themes and Mission Elements, Strategy for Orbital Missions, Rovers and Field Science, Sample Return Missions, Geophysical Networks, In Situ Resource Utilization, and Technology Development. The fifty page report can be downloaded in PDF format.

The Moon—A Links Page, by the NASA Space Science Data Center

http://nssdc.gsfc.nasa.gov/planetary/planets/moonpage.html

The main topics with links to information are The Moon, Missions to the Moon, Future Missions, and Other Lunar Resources. There are a moon fact sheet, FAQs, plus many links to each unmanned and manned moon probe missions. Updated in May 2002. Note especially the links to the Lunar Science Home Page, Precise Positions of LMs (Lunar Modules) and Science Experiments on the Moon, and Online Books about the Moon (including a link to Reference Books on Lunar and Planetary Science).

Exploring the Moon

http://cass.jsc.nasa.gov/expmoon/lunar_missions.html

The NASA-funded Lunar and Planetary Institute provides links to data on The Decision to Go to the Moon (as initiated by the United States President John F. Kennedy in 1961), plus the Apollo missions, and unmanned missions (e.g., Clementine, Luna, Lunar Orbiter, Lunar Prospector, Ranger, Surveyor, and Zona). Note also information about future missions.

History of Lunar Probes

http://www.permanent.com/l-probes.htm

Clementine—Return to the Moon—Deep Space Program Science Experiment

http://www.cmf.nrl.navy.mil/clementine/clementine.html

Lunar Prospector Homepage

http://lunar.arc.nasa.gov

Featured are links to information on the project, results, news, its history, and science, plus archives (with documents, plus audio and video items), resources, and an Education area.

Galileo Project Information

http://nssdc.gsfc.nasa.gov/planetary/galileo.htm

Provided are links to physical information (launch date, etc.), mission overview, science objectives, scientific firsts, scientific results, other information and data, and other sources of Galileo Project information and data (e.g., Experiment teams, education). Updated February 2002.

Future Lunar Missions

http://www.lpi.usra.edu/expmoon/future/future.html

Provided by the NASA-funded Lunar and Planetary Institute, and the Universities Space Research Association, this Web site has links to information under the categories Other Missions to the Moon, Previously Considered Missions, Private and Commercial Endeavors, Humans on the Moon, and Lunar Base Literature. Note the link to the International Lunar Exploration Working Group Web page which has links to current lunar missions, current news and events, reports and documents, a *Lunar Explorers Digest*, and www sites of interest.

Excerpts from *The Physics of STAR TREK*
Lawrence M. Krauss (1995)
URL: http://www.phys.uregina.ca/ugrad/classes/phys200/startrek_notes.html

SITE SUMMARY: Lawrence M. Krauss, the Ambrose Swasey Professor of Physics and Astronomy at Case Western Reserve University, Cleveland, Ohio, describes here various aspects of physics in relation to their treatments in *Star Trek* (the television programs and movies). This document features "*STAR TREK* Notes" adapted in 1997 from Krauss' book, revised in 1999, and reproduced online. In these excerpts, Krauss looks at "some of the most exotic concepts in physics" involved with *Star Trek*. He asks questions such as: "Is this possible? If so, how?" "What does modern science allow us to imagine about our possible future as a civilization?" "What was at the heart" of *Star Trek* creator Gene Roddenberry's vision? This document is also at http://lafite.phys.uregina.ca/ugrad/classes/phys200/startrek_notes.html.

DISCUSSION QUESTIONS AND ACTIVITIES

1. See Krauss' section fifteen: "*STAR TREK* Physics?" Identify the various ways he said *Star Trek* writers have included physics in their writings. See Krauss' Closing Remarks. What did he "argue" about, then say in a positive way (both with reference to physics and *Star Trek*)? Identify the quotation by Gene Roddenberry, *Star Trek*'s creator, that Krauss cited.

2. Choose one of the more than twenty-five *Star Trek* physics topics Krauss mentions. State his description of this field of physics, noting his view as to the *Star Trek* version of this field of physics being possible or improbable. Next, check to see if you have chosen a *Star Trek* physics subject mentioned by Stephen Hawking in his lecture: "Science in the New Millennium," or by David Batchelor in his article "The Science of *STAR TREK*." (Both are featured in other chapters of this book.) If so, cite Hawking's and/or Batchelor's view(s) on this field of physics.

3. Identify which well known physicists and their physics Krauss mentions in section one: "Inertial Dampers" (especially paragraphs two and four), and section two: "Tractor Beam" (especially paragraphs one and two). How did Krauss apply these physicists' physics to *Star Trek*, and how did he involve the Hubble telescope?

4. See one of these sections (e.g., three, nine, seven, eight, or seventeen): "Time Loops," "Warp Speed," "Black Holes," "Wormhole Time Machines," or "From Another Dimension." Describe one of Krauss' explanations of *Star Trek* and a theory in physics by Albert Einstein and Kurt Godel, Miguel Alcubierre, Stephen Hawking and Werner Karl Heisenberg, Kip Thorne, Theodor Kaluza and Oskar Klein, plus Max Planck.

5. See Krauss' section three: "Time Loops" (especially paragraphs seven, eight, and nine), and section four: "Warp Drive" (especially paragraph one). How did he connect a physics in *Star Trek*, an Einstein theory, and the Sisyphus myth?

6. See Krauss' section five: "Curvature of Space Time." Describe the "chicken and egg" dilemma. See also Hawking's "Origin of the Universe" essay (featured in another chapter of this book). Compare and/or contrast this concept's use by Krauss and by Hawking.

7. See Krauss' section fourteen: "Other Intelligent Life in the Universe." Read what he said about the "continuing mission of the starship Enterprise." What do *Star Trek* viewers "get to imagine," and why is this important, according to Krauss? Think of a problem or issue that humans must deal with. (Try to think of one that has a connection to a science in the physics field.) Describe how it was, or is, dealt with by people of a past time, and people of a foreign nation today. Imagine how people in the future might deal with it.

8. See Krauss' section ten: "Beam Me Up Scotty," especially the end of paragraph eleven. Why did Krauss compare "storage requirements for a human pattern," "information in all books ever written," and information on this site's Web page?

9. Explain further one of your answers to Questions/Activities no. 2, no. 3, or no. 4, or choose and explain another physics subject Krauss mentioned. In your explanation, feature information on your chosen subject found via these Web sites: Physics of *STAR TREK*—Links, and Jay's Physics and *STAR TREK* (whose urls are cited in the Related Internet Sites section below), or other sites cited in the Related Internet Sites section in this book's chapter on Batchelor's "The Science of *STAR TREK*"; or more Web sites in this book's Appendix B).

10. Select one physics subject you chose for Question/Activity no. 2 above, or another physics subject in *Star Trek* that Krauss mentions. Be sure, as Krauss indicates, your choice is a present-day physics subject that could be the "ancestor" of a *Star Trek* physics science; not a "fantasy science." (Note: the *Star Trek* physics subject would then be a future or evolved version of a present-day physics subject.) State the now and then connection, supporting your claim by quoting and/or citing Krauss and other present-day physicists' research. Suggest how the *Star Trek* physics subject indicates how Earth's civilizations will be different in the future, and how the future physics would affect you or an individual living in that future time. For help, see the Web sites noted in Question/Activity no. 9 above, and the Web sites: Science in Society (its Futurism area), and World Future Society. Both sites' urls are cited in the Related Internet Sites section of this book's chapter on Hawking's lecture "Science in the New Millennium."

RELATED INTERNET SITE(S)

Excerpt from Stephen Hawking's Foreword to Krauss' *The Physics of STAR TREK*

http://www.tectonicdesigns.com/sci/special/startrek.html

A brief but interesting and informative excerpt, as provided by The Science Page on a page called The Science of *Star Trek*.

Physics of *STAR TREK*—Links

http://www.phys.cwru.edu/~krauss/starlinks.html

Links are to publisher's extracts, chapter one of Krauss' book, reviews of the book, plus information on a lecture, a Web chat, and more.

"[Physicist Author Prompted to Write about *STAR TREK*]" in *The Scientist Notebook*

http://www.the-scientist.library.upenn.edu/yr1996/jan/notebook_960122.html#note2

The Scientist, January 22, 1996, featured this interesting review of Krauss' book. On this page with several books' reviews, scroll to the paragraph beginning with "Transporter rooms, warp speed, tractor beams" to see the review of Krauss' book. To see this review, free registration by an educator is required at *The Scientist* Web site.

Jay's Physics and *STAR TREK*

http://www.physicsguy.com/physandtrek/index.html

A research physicist takes a look at "what we know about physics today and applies it to some concepts used in science fiction (mainly *Star Trek*)," e.g., faster-than-light travel, relativity and subspace. Go to http://www.physicsguy.com/index.html#trek for an explanatory note about Jay's Physics and *STAR TREK* Web site.

Science Friday Archives—Lawrence Krauss and *STAR TREK*

http://www.sciencefriday.com/pages

Search by keywords (e.g., *Star Trek*, Lawrence Krauss), topic (e.g., Physics), date, and full text, for *The Star Trek Phenomenon* (July 24, 1998), and *The Physics of STAR TREK* (November 17, 1995), with an introduction and information on these National Public Radio broadcasts. Also available for the 1998 broadcast are a RealAudio version, a list of books discussed, and related links.

Science of the Future—Lawrence M. Krauss Talks about *The Physics of STAR TREK*

http://www.metroactivebooks.com/papers/metro/04.03.97/trek-physics-9714.html

A Web Exclusive interview with physicist Krauss, as conducted in April 1997 by Metroactive Books and reproduced online here.

"The Role of Planetariums in Astronomy Education"
James G. Manning (1995)
URL: http://www.griffithobs.org/IPSroleplan.html

SITE SUMMARY: This document, provided on a page at the Griffith Observatory Web site, is reproduced from the International Planetarium Society's journal *Planetarian*, 24, December 1995. It features Manning's knowledge and experience on the role and goals of planetariums, particularly with reference to education, when the first ones were built, as they are today, and what they will be in the future. Manning is president of the International Planetarium Society.

DISCUSSION QUESTIONS AND ACTIVITIES

1. Why, according to Manning, have planetariums been created for decades? Identify at least eight facts that, he says, help people appreciate the role of planetariums. Identify and specify what he says is useful to review in defining the role planetariums play. According to him, the planetarium's role has changed since the first ones were built. Tell how, then give three examples, cite the planetariums involved (one for each example), and describe in detail one example. (Hints: See paragraph three; then paragraphs four through seven, and ten; then paragraphs eleven and twelve.) (Tip: For particular ideas for the last activity, see paragraphs seventeen through twenty-five.)

2. Describe the features of planetariums' "star projectors" and theaters. What is special about the "StarLab Theater"? (Hint: See paragraph eight.)

3. See paragraph twenty-six, and indicate why planetarium educators are interested in the United States Academy of Sciences' draft proposal for national science education standards. Provide an example based on something you read in the "National Science Education Standards." (For example ideas, see planetarium Web sites noted in Question/Activity no. 5 below.) Extra Activity: Identify something of note in the "Planetarium Standards: Elevating the Profession" document, and suggest why it is important to consider in addition to the "National Science Education Standards." (Note: Both "standards" documents are found online as cited in the Related Internet Sites section below.)

4. See paragraphs forty-three through fifty-two. Identify and briefly describe one through seven of eight trends, and one hope that Manning sees or suggests for the future. Provide your own suggestions with relation to trends four through six. (Note: For something on trend five, see Question/Activity no. 7 below.)

5. See paragraph thirteen. Manning says that people who work in planetariums "strive to educate" and "strive to enlighten." Explain why he says "to enlighten . . . is not quite the same as to educate," then give your own example illustrating Manning's comment. Describe how Manning applies the phrase "you can catch more flies with honey" to people and planetariums, then illustrate this idea with your own example. Identify the fourth thing that people working in planetariums strive to do, then give Manning's example, and provide one of your own. (For help, see a planetarium Web page cited at the Planetarium Reference Library's Planetarium Web Sites and Planetarium Compendium links; via the *Sky and Telescope* Magazine—Resources—Organizations, Planetariums, etc.; or via Web directories. Their urls are cited in the Related Internet Sites section below or in this book's Appendix E.) (Note: See also paragraphs fifty-seven and fifty-eight, starting with "In the planetarium profession" and "This is the role we play.")

6. See paragraph fourteen. Manning comments that "In setting these goals, planetariums operate in all three realms of learning." Identify the three realms, and give an example for each. (Option: You may cite something that Manning cites in paragraph sixteen, then give particu-

lars of your own.) In paragraph sixteen, what does Manning suggest using, where appropriate, to attract visitors? Provide your own examples of each (i.e., identify a theme, then make something creative based on that theme).

7. See paragraph twenty-seven. How have planetariums' focus changed to feature other areas as well as astronomy? Identify four other areas, then give an example of one area stated here, and one area at a planetarium Web site (found as indicated in Question/Activity no. 5 above). Provide details for each.

8. See paragraph twenty-eight. What is a new feature at planetariums? What unusual audience does it attract? How is this feature special in a unique way, and why might it have been liked by the author of the article "June Skies" featured in another chapter of this book?

9. Manning notes some more, special, aspects to planetariums. Give his example(s) for each, where provided, then give your own examples for each. (Hints: Indoor/outdoor, night/day, and something "close to home," in paragraphs thirty-three, thirty-one, thirty, eleven, and forty-six. Unique Internet connections, in paragraphs thirty-four and thirty-eight. Special events and latest information in paragraphs thirty-five and thirty-eight. Models and exhibits in paragraphs thirty-six and thirty-seven.) (More hints: See the Web sites Space Calendar, Space—In the Spotlight, StarGazer, Skywatching Center, The Sky This Month, referred to in this book's chapter featuring the document "June Skies," specifically in that chapter's Question/Activity no. 2 and its Related Internet Sites section. In addition, study a planetarium site that you find via the Planetarium Reference Library's Planetarium Web Sites and Planetarium Compendium links; via *Sky and Telescope* Magazine—Resources—Organizations, Planetariums, etc.; or via planetarium Web directories' listings. Find their urls as stated in Question/Activity no. 5 above.)

10. See paragraphs fifty-three through fifty-six. Which words did the nineteenth-century British writer Thomas Carlisle write which Manning quotes, and what have planetariums been doing, according to Manning, to answer Carlisle's question?

11. Visit the Web sites on A Few Quotations Relevant to Astronomy and Astronomical Quotations. (Their urls are cited in the Related Internet Sites section below.) Choose words by two writers (one literary and one scientific). Explain how the words of these writers are also fulfilled in planetariums. (For help, see Question/Activity no. 5 above, searching the planetarium Web sites referred to, studying the part that starts with the word "Identify," then noting the Note.)

12. Find and explain the phrase "a sense of place" in Manning's document, paragraph three, Extra Activity: Identify the similarity of this phrase to the phrase "spirit of place" in an essay by the nineteenth-century British author Alice Meynell and online at Alice Meynell—"The Spirit of Place" and Other Essays Web site (especially in her first essay's paragraph five), cited in the Related Internet Sites section below. Describe how Meynell's similar phrase can apply to a planetarium too, even today early in the twenty-first century.

RELATED INTERNET SITE(S)

Sky and Telescope—Resources—Organizations, Planetariums, etc.

http://skyandtelescope,com/resources/organizations

On this page, part of the *Sky and Telescope* Magazine Web site, scroll down to do a search for links to Web sites of planetariums, museums, observatories, clubs, and special interest organizations, by nation, or state/province and city.

Planetarium Web Sites and Planetarium Compendium via Planetarium Reference Library

http://www.lochness.com/pltref/pltref.html (scroll to links section)

Click Planetarium Web Sites link, or Planetarium Compendium link, then choose a state or nation link for a list of links to Web sites of planetariums in that place. Note also on the main page, links to FAQs and articles.

A Few Quotations Relevant to Astronomy

http://www.seds.org/billa/psc/quotes.html

Quotations are from writers, both scientific (e.g., Richard Feynman) and literary (e.g., Antoine de St. Exupery and Shakespeare).

Astronomical Quotations

http://hone.achilles.net/~jtalbot/bio/astronomers.html

Features quotations by astronomers who have accomplished something of note in an area of astronomy (e.g., Edwin Hubble).

"National Science Education Standards"—Overview, etc. (1995)

http://www.nap.edu/readingroom/books/nses/html/overview.html

The National Academy of Sciences features twelve introductory paragraphs, then a multi-part section on "Organization of the Standards" (e.g., on science content [including earth and space sciences], science teaching, professional development for science teachers, assessment in science education, educational programs and systems), and a look at the process of standardization "Toward the Future." Note also Principles and Definitions, Perspectives and Terms at http://www.nap.edu/readingroom/books/uses/html/2.html. (See also *Science Curriculum Reform in the United States* in Appendix C in this book.)

"Planetarium Standards: Elevating the Profession"

http://www.lochness.com/pltref/standards/standards.htm

This document, by Mark C. Peterson of Loch Ness Productions, on "some thoughts about standardization," provides information gathered from a discussion panel at the July 2000 International Planetarium Society Conference.

Alice Meynell—"The Spirit of Place" and Other Essays

http://www2.cddc.vt.edu/gutenberg/etext98/sptpl10.txt

Among these literary essays by Meynell, a nineteenth-century British author, note her observations of a spirit of a place, and a horizon with the sky as an important part of it, written in a style that reveals a sharp insight similar to a scientist's perception.

"Biospheric Theory and Report on Overall Biosphere 2 Design and Performance During Mission One, 1991–1993"
John Allen (1996)
URL: http://www.biospheres.com (click Keynote Papers link, then title link)

SITE SUMMARY: Allen, an engineer with academic credentials in metallurgical-mining engineering and engineering physiology, invented and was cofounder of the Biosphere 2 facility, and was part of the team of scientists, engineers and architects who designed and operated the Biosphere Project and Experiment. Biosphere 2 was designed and built to simulate, but not duplicate, Biosphere One—Earth, and test the hypothesis that biospheres are materially closed but biologically open self-sustaining systems, and capable of long-term self-renewal. This document, first published in the *Journal of Life Support and Biosphere Science*, provides, in two parts, a detailed definition of biospheric theory, plus details on the Biosphere 2 Project, including decisions on what should be done, how decisions were made, the research team's preliminary studies, and analyses based on outcomes after the participating team's experiences in various created biomes such as a desert and a rain forest. The potential and value of biospherics in evaluating changes in Earth's biosphere and in designing planetary settlements was also discussed.

DISCUSSION QUESTIONS AND ACTIVITIES

1. Name and describe the "three major component parts" which are essential in the study of biospherics.
2. Which three things must interplay so testing and extending knowledge of biospherics can occur, as was the approach used to create Biosphere 2?
3. In addition to "fundamental scientific disciplines," which other "bodies of knowledge and sources of insight" should be considered when evaluating biospherics? Can you think of others? Explain why each type is important. How did mission participants apply these others?
4. Identify the scientists who wrote about biospheric theory in 1926, 1970, 1971, 1973, 1983, 1979, 1989, and the 1990s. What did the scientist Vladimir Vernadsky write about biospherics? Select another scientist. What did she or he determine about biospherics? How did the statements by Vernadsky and the other scientist influence the Biosphere 2 mission? Option for class: Each student should choose one of the biospheric scientists other than the one chosen to answer the questions just above, then reveal that scientist's influence on the mission, quoting if possible. (Note: Students can provide information by creating an audio- or videotape to be presented to the class or by writing a report to be read or reproduced and distributed to the class.)
5. Through history, what have theories been on biospherics and space exploration? What has been NASA's reaction to biospheric studies? Refer to Allen's paper, and to information at the Web sites Advanced Life Support at the KSC and Advanced Life Support at the JSC. Their urls are cited in the Related Internet Sites section below.
6. What is "a Biospheric Uncertainty Principle," and Vernadsky's definition of a noosphere?
7. At first, an agricultural biosphere re-creation was considered for the project. What was good about this idea? Why was it rejected? What type of biosphere was then chosen for the project, and why? What became clear from biospheric test module work by Margret Augustine, William Dempster, John Allen, Abigail Alling, and Mark Nelson, and why? What became the five basic aims and the main objective of the experiment? Name six of the sixty research project studies done during the mission. Identify four "spin-off ideas" that have come from this biosphere project. Give details for one. Suggest how one spin-off idea has an influence on you and/or the world around you.

8. What two essential things of life are needed, and in what proportions, in a biosphere re-creation, according to analyses of the mission? Make a plan to create a biosphere project, giving both scale model and actual size details. Be sure to include what is referred to in Questions/Activities nos. 1 and 3 above, and study information about the test module. (Tip: For some help, go to the Students' Corner at the Web site for Spreading Life Throughout the Solar System. Its url is cited in the Related Internet Sites section below.) Option: Make an actual mini biosphere based on your plan.

RELATED INTERNET SITE(S)

Biospherics

http://www.biospheres.com

Links go to information on the history of biospherics, definitions, keynote papers, biographies of key people, ongoing research and development, a bibliography, the *Journal of Life Support and Biosphere Science*, and related links. Note especially the Biosphere 2 Experiment, Results and Papers; Biosphere 2 Plans and Photos; "Biosphere 2: Research Past and Present" in the *Journal of Ecological Engineering*; and an in-progress area of Papers of Ongoing Work Since Biosphere 2, featuring overall assessments with quotations from noted people.

Biosphere 2 Center—Columbia University—Laboratory Research Programs

http://www.bio2.edu/Research/index.htm

Read the overview, and see the links to the B2 Laboratory, and to particular biomes such as a desert, a rain forest, and agro forestry. Note also the link to information on the Future of the Biosphere 2L Mission, and more.

Biospheric Sciences Branch of NASA's Goddard Space Flight Center

http://ltpwww.gsfc.nasa.gov/bsb

Find out about NASA's biospheric studies on this page that features information on goals and vision, plus links to an outline, highlights, programs, publications, scientists, and related Web sites.

"Spreading Life Throughout the Solar System"

http://www.nas.nasa.gov/Services/Education/SpaceSettlement

Information on the goals and basics of a strategic plan of NASA's HEDS (Human Exploration and Development of Space Enterprise) is provided. The site also features information for students to help them design a space colony or settlement biosphere structure in a space station as a class activity and as an entry for NASA's space colony student design contest. Note also links to a Students' Corner, a Teachers' Page, a Quiz, Online Space Settlement Books, Space Settlement Contest Guidelines, Other Space Settlement Web Sites (e.g., Biosphere 2 and Biosphere 2 FAQ), and Miscellaneous (such as "Isaac Asimov on Space Settlement" and Space Settlement Papers such as "A Futurist Perspective for Space" in PDF format).

"Advanced Life Support and Gravitational Biology" at NASA's Kennedy Space Center

http://bioscience.ksc.nasa.gov/oldals/index.html or *http://www.ksc.nasa.gov/index/index.html* (click link under Special Purposes Pages)

Featured are links to information on biospherics (identified as "advanced life support and gravitational biology"). Also provided are a definition of "advanced life support and gravitational biology" and links to other Web sites with useful data.

"Advanced Life Support" at NASA's Johnson Space Center

http://advlifesupport.jsc.nasa.gov

This in progress site provides data on advanced life support (ALS), plus more information and documents via links for What's New, General Information, BioPlex Documents ("Bioregenerative Planetary Life Support Systems Test Complex"), SIMA Reports ("Systems Integration, Modeling, and Analysis"), and ALS Related Sites.

Excerpts from *Science as a Candle in the Dark*
Carl Sagan (1996)
URL: http://www.uiowa.edu/~anthro/webcourse/lost/sagan.htm

SITE SUMMARY: Carl Sagan, a noted astronomer who was Cornell University's David Duncan Professor of Astronomy and Space Sciences and director of Cornell's Laboratory for Planetary Studies, was known for making the space sciences understandable to, and interesting for, average people, especially via television and in books. According to Buzz Aldrin, astronaut and National Space Society chairman, he was "beyond a doubt the most outstanding contributor to human inspiration and of thoughts of and beyond the Earth." Sagan revealed his ideas on critical thinking in one of his books, sub-titled *Science as a Candle in the Dark.* (Its main title is *The Demon-Haunted World.*) These ideas, referred to colloquially as a "Baloney Detection Kit," "The Fine Art of Baloney Detection," a kit of tools for skeptical thinking, or a critical thinking kit, are reproduced here, and feature Sagan's suggestions on how to use the kit's tools whenever new ideas are offered for consideration, to find out if each new idea can survive examination.

DISCUSSION QUESTIONS AND ACTIVITIES

1. Give an example from your life when you would "bring out" Sagan's "Detection Kit." Tell how this kit could be misused, and how it could help you. (Hint: To answer the second part of this question, see the first part, then the last part, of the "Detection Kit" document that is this chapter's main site.)
2. State how Sagan defined skeptical thinking. Identify the "tools" he suggested using when thinking skeptically. Study his examples, then give some of your own.
3. Why did Sagan distinguish between authority and expert?
4. Explain, according to Sagan, Occam's Razor, variables (including his seasickness example), and double-blind. Give an example of Occam's Razor, then think of other examples; one each for variables, and double-blind.
5. Study what Sagan said about the "spin more than one" hypothesis, and his "chain and link" concept. Give examples from your life, happenings around you, and historical or current news events.
6. Study and explain the fallacies "appeal to ignorance," "observational selection," and "it happened after, so was caused by." Develop examples following Sagan's criteria. Find and state another fallacy Sagan noted, study his example of it, then think of, and explain, another example.
7. Study Sagan's comment about space exploration and the fallacy he said is connected to his comment. Check the comments on the subject at the Web sites "Why Explore Space?" "Why We Must Explore Space," and "How Does Space Benefit You?" (See their urls cited in the Related Internet Sites section below.) Think of and explain another comment or example that supports Sagan's view.
8. Study and cite Sagan's comment about the environmental movement and the fallacy he said is connected to his comment. Find and cite a comment on this subject at the Web site featuring the Interview with Environmental Attorney Robert Kennedy Jr. (Its url is cited in the Related Internet Sites section below.) Give your own comment or example on the subject. Support Sagan's and Kennedy's views.

RELATED INTERNET SITE(S)

"Tools for Testing Arguments and Detecting Fallacious or Fraudulent Arguments"

http://www1.tpgi.com.au/users/tps-seti/baloney.html

This Web site, by the Planetary Society's Australian Volunteer Coordinators, has comments by Ann Druyan, Sagan's wife; Sagan's "Detection Kit's" main points but without his examples; plus a comment by Sagan made in 1987 on "The Exquisite Balance," and quoted here from the May 2002 issue of *Scientific American Magazine*. See also links, e.g., to Tribute to Carl Sagan, The Critical Thinking Community, Carl Sagan Productions, www.skeptic.com, and more.

Why Explore Space?

http://www.estec.esa.nl/spdwww/h2000/html/why.html

Featured are the European Space Agency's reasons for exploring space, which support Sagan's view that people who oppose space exploration are caught in a fallacy that is cited in his "Detection Kit."

"Why We Must Explore Space"

http://www.geocities.com/CapeCanaveral/Hangar/4264/nsslet.html

This undated article by Jeffrey G. Liss of the National Space Society Board of Directors includes suggested readings of books published in the mid-1990s.

"How Does Space Benefit You?" (Undated)

http://www.geocities.com/CapeCanaveral/Hangar/4264/doc1.html

An article with a "Mission Home" link preceding the title and leading to the Space Foundation Web site at www.spaceconnection.org; also at www.spacefoundation.org.

Interview with Environmental Attorney Robert Kennedy Jr.

http://www.nrdc.org/reference/qa/intkenn.asp

Kennedy, a senior attorney for the Natural Resources Defense Council, explains how environmental concerns involve both nature and people. His views support Sagan's on a fallacy involving people opposing environmentalists.

Web Sites Dedicated to Carl Sagan and Ann Druyan

http://www.carlsagan.org/revamp/links/carlsagan.html

Links go to sites featuring excerpts from Sagan's writings, speeches, talks, and interviews; information on his goals, accomplishments, and causes; his views on science and the power of thought; his biography; his involvement with NASA; plus tributes to him, including noted people's celebratory comments. Featured sites with information and quotations include *Scientific American Magazine*; "Earthwatch" and National Public Radio's "Science Friday" audio radio interviews; the *Washington Post*; CNN; the *New York Times* Science section; the Planetary Society, Cornell University, and sites that feature excerpts from Sagan's May 11, 1996 speech to students.

Biography of Carl Sagan and Excerpts from May 11, 1996 Speech to Students

http://express.howstuffworks.com/teachers/extraordinary/sagan.htm

This Web page features information about this scientist's life and work, plus excerpts from a speech he gave to students about the Earth's value and people's place with reference to it. Also available by scrolling to the Carl Sagan links area and clicking the biography link at http://express.howstuffworks.com/teachers/extraordinary.

Questions Based on "Carl Sagan: Cosmic Communicator"

http://express.howstuffworks.com/teachers/extraordinary/sagan.pdf

Six multiple choice questions help in understanding Sagan's work and views and the speech referred to. Topics of the questions include the reason for Sagan's popularity, his work's primary subject, what he compared Earth to, the value of a photograph of Earth from space, what gives the speech structure, and what the word delusion means in the speech. Requires Adobe Acrobat Reader for access. Also accessible via a Reading Comp Test link under Carl Sagan at http://express.howstuffworks.com/teachers/extraordinary, where there are also links to a Reading Comp Teachers Key, and a Writing Activity.

"Paleontology: The Window to Science Education"
Richard K. Stucky (1996)
URL: http://www.ucmp.berkeley.edu/fosrec/Stucky.html

SITE SUMMARY: This document, part of *Learning from the Fossil Record*, a hypertext book, was written for a workshop for K to 12 educators. It contains an introduction to paleontology, sets out the basic methods and goals of this science, and explains how to make paleontology relevant. The author, who studies mammal fossils and paleoecology, and was then the chief curator of the Denver Museum of Natural History, notes why and how paleontology is a good way to introduce young people to science.

DISCUSSION QUESTIONS AND ACTIVITIES

1. See paragraph two of the basic methods section. Identify what fossils are, then state two ways that fossils are discovered. In what particular manner are fossils usually found? Identify two things that a field paleontologist does, give details for the second, and tell why these things are important.

2. See paragraphs one and three of the basic methods section. Identify the four basic techniques that are part of the preparation for the scientific study of fossils. State the five, and explain four, things that happen to fossils when they are brought to a laboratory.

3. See paragraph two of the goals section. Identify paleontology's three basic goals, and give details of each. (Note: Notice the two subjects of goal three and give details of one of them.) Why is the understanding of shapes and forms important in paleontology? Choose and search one Web site that is cited in the Related Internet Sites section below. Find something you see as an example of shapes and forms with reference to what you answered for the question just above. Give details and explain your choice.

4. See paragraph one of the Relevance section. Identify five reasons why paleontology is relevant in general; then why it is relevant in particular.

5. This document's introduction suggests that "knowledge of fossils is reinforced in many aspects" in young people's lives, and reinforcement happens via the media and vacations to "some fossil Meccas." Visit the Web pages or sites referred to just below, then find and describe two interesting news items about a fossil discovery and a paleontologist's research. Next, choose and describe a fossil Mecca cited by Stucky or find and describe another one. Option: If possible, also visit a fossil mecca near you to gather data to supplement your description. (Tip: Visit the Web pages or sites on "Fossils and Ruins News," *Fossil News: Journal of Amateur Paleontology*, "Dino News," and "Top Paleontologists and Dinosaur Hunters of All Time" in Dinosaurs at the Zoom School; or magazine, newspaper, radio or TV news Web pages or sites such as *The Journal of Dinosaur Paleontology*, *National Geographic Magazine* Dinorama, *New York Times* on the Web [its Science area], Time.com—Newsfiles—Science, NPR—Science Friday, Discovery Channel News Roundup [its Dinosaurs area], also the "Bone Zone" in the *Dinosaur Interplanetary Gazette* [whose urls are cited in the Related Internet Sites section below, or in this book's Appendix B]; or Amazing Dinosaur Scientists, Dinosaur Detectives, History of Paleontology, Dinosaur Paleontology—Historical Overview, "Dinosaur Resources" at the Internet School Library Media Center Web sites [whose urls are cited in the Related Internet Sites section of this book's chapters featuring "Paleobiology—In the News, Highlights, Subjects, and Links" and "Paper Dinosaurs: A Hypertext Catalogue of Rare Documents"]. Search for descriptions and fossil meccas in the "Dino Trekking" area of the *Dinosaur Interplanetary Gazette* Web site or the Paleontology: Big Dig and Great Fossil Regions Based on North America's Physiographic Provinces Web sites [whose urls are cited in the Related Internet Sites

section below], or at the National Park Service—Nature and Science in the Park Web site [whose url is cited in this book's Appendix B].) (Hint: For a two-part definition of Mecca, search the Dictionary at http://www.infoplease.com.)

6. Describe a real science that is depicted in a movie or TV program with dinosaurs, noting if it is presented realistically, either completely or partially, then think of and describe, or write a story for, what you would provide about dinosaurs for a movie, TV program, educational Web site or CD-Rom, either fictional but realistic or a documentary. (For help, see the Web sites "Dinosaur Links—Dinosaurs As Movie Stars," plus "Behind the Scenes—*Jurassic Park*" ["the movie where science and technology came together"], and "*Jurassic Park 2*: Science [and Non-Science] of the *Lost World*" Web site. Note also "How to Create a Dinosaur Report" in the Classroom Activities area of the Dinosaurs at the Zoom School Web site. [These Web sites' urls are cited in the Related Internet Sites section below, or in that section of this book's chapter featuring Foreword by Michael Crichton to the *Encyclopedia of Dinosaurs*.])

7. See this document's Relevance section, especially the last sentence of paragraph one, and paragraph two. What are two things that, according to Stucky, paleontology can provide us with? In which three ways can paleontology help students, and how? Think beyond Stucky's document, but keep it in mind, then try to apply the basic parts of the answers you found to the questions just above to two scientific things in the world around you. Optional activity: What is a Rosetta Stone, and how does Stucky use this phrase? (Tip: For help with unusual words, search the online Dictionary cited in Question/Activity no. 5 above.)

RELATED INTERNET SITE(S)

"Fossils and Ruins News" in Science Daily

http://www.sciencedaily.com/news/fossils_ruins.htm

Click the links for "read brief news summaries" or "browse just news headlines," then choose a summary or headline link. Full documents or detailed adaptations are provided, with adapter noted, and sometimes links to more information, original sources, and related discussions.

Fossil News: Journal of Avocational Paleontology

http://fossilnews.com/fnintro.html

Read about this journal's features, targeted readers, and its writers, then click the link to see a free copy of the November 21, 2001 issue permanently online in PDF format.

Journal of Dinosaur Paleontology

http://www.dinosauria.com/jdp/jdp.htm

See links to articles under the topics Archaeopteryx, Ancient Birds, and Dinosaur—Bird Relationships; Dinosauria; Dromaeosaurids; Evolution; Fossilization; Impact Theories and Extinction Events; Legal Issues; Miscellaneous; News and New Discoveries; Oviraptorids; Society of Vertebrate Paleontologists; Stolen Fossil Alerts; and Tyrannosaurids.

National Geographic Dinorama

http://www.nationalgeographic.com/features/dinorama

See the photo links to changing features on the topics Why Feathers?, A T. Rex Called Sue, History's Nursery, Moving Monsters, Desert Discovery, Dinosaur Eggs, and Early Birds? A search for dinosaurs at http://nationalgeographic.com brings a list of sites on fossil discoveries.

Dinosaur Interplanetary Gazette: The Ultimate Online Dinosaur Magazine

http://www.dinosaur.org/frontpage.html

Recommended by the National Education Association, this site has facts presented in interesting ways (sometimes by scientists). See links to Recent Features, Recent Headlines, Top Stories—This Week, DinoGuide (e.g., The Dino News Network, and Dino Feature Stories), columns such as Geologic Timeline pop-up, Ask Dr. Fred; Dino Time Machine, Celluloid Dinosaurs, Dino-Trekking (on places where fossils can be seen), and Book of the Week. At http://www.dinosaur.org, also see the links to The Bone Zone (on paleontologists), a list of documentaries in video format, and more dino links.

Dinosaurs at the Zoom School

http://www.enchantedlearning.com/subjects/dinosaurs

This online book features links to All About Dinosaurs, Dino Info Pages, Dino Fact Sheets, a List of Dinos, Anatomy and Behavior, Classification, Extinction, Fossils, Geologic Time Charts, Mesozoic Era, Plants from the Time of the Dinosaurs, Dino News, Dino Dictionary, Top Paleontologists and Dinosaur Hunters of All Time, and Classroom Activities (e.g., "How to Create a Dinosaur Report").

Paleontology: Big Dig

http://ology.amnh.org/paleontology/stuff/findfossils_4.html

At this area of the American Museum of Natural History Web site, see an url for a Web site that provides information on fossil collecting sites that can be found in the United States and Canada. Note also links to Keeping a Field Journal, Do's and Don'ts For Fossil Hunters, Fossils You May Find, and Paleontology Web sites.

Great Fossil Regions Based on North America's Physiographic Provinces

http://www.geobop.com/paleozoo/World/NA/Regions

This Web site has information on the U.S. regions' fossil heritage, featuring indications of types of fossils and how rich or sparse each region is regarding fossils. Included are The East with the Coastal Plain and the Appalachians, The Interior with the Central Lowlands and the Great Plains, The West with the Rocky Mountains, the South West, the Far West, Alaska, and Hawaii.

Dinosaur Links—Dinosaurs as Movie Stars

http://www.acmp.berkeley.edu/diasids/dinolinks.html#movies

See links to *The BBC's "Walking with the Dinosaurs"* Series home page, the "Walking with Dinosaurs: Science of Motion" Web site, and links to other Web sites about other TV programs or movies that feature dinosaurs.

"The Science of Archaeology"
in *What Is Archaeology?* Society for American Archaeology, National Geographic Society, and the United States Department of the Interior (1996)
URL: http://www.saa.org/AtoZ.html

SITE SUMMARY: Click the link for *Archaeology and You*, then the link for Chapter Two: "The Science of Archaeology," a part of the book *What Is Archaeology?* that was first reproduced online in 2000 from a 1996 print version. Features include a definition of archaeology especially with reference to the scientific aspects of this multidisciplinary field of study, and data on the ways that archaeologists use scientific methods or enlist the assistance of other scientists to work on an archaeological site or artifacts from a "dig."

DISCUSSION QUESTIONS AND ACTIVITIES

1. Note the description of physical anthropology, and suggest its connection to the scientific aspect of archeology. Next, describe the similarities and differences between historical archeology and prehistoric archeology. (Hint: Find information in "The Science of Archaeology" document and at the Web sites with Online Companion to *Archaeology: An Introduction* by Kevin Greene [its glossary or other resources areas], Articles at the Society for Historical Archaeology and Anthropology Internet Resources whose urls are cited in the Related Internet Sites section below.)

2. See paragraph eight. Identify how each archaeological site is "a unique and fragile remnant of the past."

3. See paragraphs twelve and thirteen. Identify which two things are important for archaeologists to do at a site and with artifacts found at the site.

4. See paragraphs nineteen and twenty. How were other scientists useful to archaeologist Jeff Chapman? Which other scientists might have helped, and why?

5. See paragraphs twenty-one and twenty-three. What do archaeologists do today that may help archaeologists in the future?

6. See paragraph twenty-seven. Why is archaeology interesting to consider as a career?

7. Keeping Question/Activity no. 4 above in mind, find an online news item or an article or an article's abstract in an archaeology magazine Web site, on one of the sciences mentioned in "The Science of Archaeology." Identify the archaeological site, dig, and artifact, then the science involved and how it is useful to archaeological study in this particular situation, and to archaeology in general. (Note: Find online archaeological news items at the Anthropology in the News Web site, and in the Current Research data in the publications area of the *What Is Archaeology?* Web document. Find online magazines such as *Archaeology* and *American Archaeology*, and their articles or abstracts of articles via the Web sites for Archaeology Resources, Archaeology on the Net. Their urls are cited in the Related Internet Sites section below.)

8. Visit two of the Web areas or sites for Archaeology in the Parks—United States National Park Service—Links to the Past, Online Excavations via the WWWorld of Archaeology, Individual Archaeological Areas at Archaeology Links, Anthropology in the News, and Archaeology Resources. (Their urls are cited in the Related Internet Sites section below.) Find two archaeological "digs" (one in the United States and one in another nation). Describe each site and what is found there, then suggest how to analyze the place and its artifacts scientifically. (Hint: Use as guidelines the references to the archaeological dig sites of archaeologists Chapman and Donna Roper in "The Science of Archaeology" Web document.)

9. See the Online Companion to *Archaeology: An Introduction* by Kevin Greene. (Its url is cited in the Related Internet Sites section below.) Note especially chapter five on archeological science, then identify four main subject areas and their subtopics that are connected to archaeological study from scientific viewpoints. Visiting Web sites that are cited with the subjects, or Web sites with archaeological news or articles, then citing bibliographic information plus quotations, write about a particular example of the main topic with relation to one of its subtopics.

10. Keeping Question/Activity no. 9 above in mind, identify two methods of examination and analysis that Greene refers to with relation to raw materials and artifacts (British spelling: artefacts), then identify three types of artifact material, all as related to archaeological science. Next identify three types of conservation also with relation to archaeological science. Adapt and apply the instructions in Question/Activity no. 9 above and starting with the word visiting, to what you find with relation to artifact material, then to conservation. Optional activities: Define statistics, then experimental archaeology, both as related to archaeological science, then adapt and apply the instructions stated just above.

11. See the Web site on Anthropology Defined and the one featuring a study guide to the book *Anthropology* by Carol R. and Melvin Ember. (Their urls are cited in the Related Internet Sites section below.) Choose a subject cited in a section of the guide that is based on a chapter. Describe the subject, then select and do an online activity based on the chapter with the subject you chose. Cite and explain a question or part of an activity about your chosen subject.

RELATED INTERNET SITE(S)

What Is Archaeology?

http://www.saa.org/whatIs/arch&you/cover.html

In addition to an introductory statement and brief definition, plus the link to *Archaeology and You* and its chapters including chapter two on "The Science of Archaeology," see links to other parts of this book reproduced online. Note the links to letters from the National Geographic Society and the Society for American Archaeology, a message from the U.S. Secretary of the Interior, an introduction, chapter one on Adventures in the Depths of Time, chapter three on Archaeology as a Career or Avocation, chapter four on Preserving the Past for the Future, chapter five on Archaeology and the Law, and resources for Learning More about Archaeology. See also a link to publications that include *Archaeology and Public Education* with program and career information plus links to new Web sites, and *E-Tiquity* (an irregular online series devoted to scholarship in archaeology), and data on Current Research.

Anthropology in the News

http://www.tamu.edu/anthropology/news.html

Texas A&M University provides this site with links to anthropology news published on the Web by the Discovery Channel, *National Geographic* Magazine, *Nature* Magazine, ABC TV, CNN, *USA Today, Washington Post*, and the *New York Times*, plus university press releases, and other sources. See general list of links to Breaking News, and links to news in Archaeology, BioAnthropology, Socio/CulturalAnthropology, etc.

Archeology in the Parks—United States National Park Service—Links to the Past

http://www.cr.nps.gov/aad/SITES/Npsites.htm or *http://www.cr.nps.gov/archeology* (click link)

Click on the states on the map to find archeology and ethnography in the parks, or scroll to list of states that have parks and click title links to parks' information.

Online Companion to *Archaeology: An Introduction* (2002) by Kevin Greene

http://www.staff.ncl.ac.uk/kevin.greene/wintro/index.htm

See links to information derived from the book, plus links to related sites, especially for chapter five on Archaeological Science, and chapter two on Discovery and Investigation, then note chapter one on The Idea of the Past, chapter three on Excavation, chapter four on Dating the Past, chapter six on Making Sense of the Past, other resources, and a glossary. Note also the links on the main page to an article that introduces "Archaeology on the Web," and an article on the "Pros and Cons of Archaeology on the Net" which is based on a speech at an Oxford University Archaeological Society meeting.

Online Excavations via the WWWorld of Archaeology

http://www.he.net/~archaeol/wwwarky/wwwarky.html

Click the link to the page of links leading to information about ongoing, recently completed, or upcoming archeological digs.

Anthropology Biography Web

http://kroeber.anthro.mankato.msus.edu/information/biography/index.shtml

Scroll through the alphabetical list of name links or choose an alphabet letter link for last names starting with that letter and go to a link lists leading to information on various types of anthropologists, including archaeologists, of the past and present.

Archaeology Resources

http://www.academicinfo.net/archy.html

Links are to resources arranged under a worldwide Regions area, and a Table of Contents that includes a reference desk, digital library (with online publications), portals and general resources, and teaching resources.

Archaeology on the Net

http://www.serve.com/archaeology

See links under General and Regional categories, and the category Resources (with its field and research reports, academic journals, and more).

UCSB Department of Anthropology Links Directory: Archaeology

http://www.anth.ucsb.edu/links/pages/Archaeology

Library>Society>Social Sciences>Anthropology>Archaeology

http://www.looksmart.com

Note links to guides and directories, archaeologists, fieldwork, publications, periods and cultures, and topics.

Science>A>Archaeology

http://directory.google.com

Note links to archaeologists (with subcategories such as pioneer archaeologists), history, methodology, periods and culture, publications, sites and movements, and topics.

Archaeologists

http://www.yahoo.com (click Archaeology)

Follow links that lead to Web sites with authoritative biographies and excerpts from the writings of some noted archaeologists.

Archaeologists

http://archaeology.about.com/cs/archaeologists

Click the Biographies of Noted Archaeologists link for annotated links going to Web sites on noted archaeologists. Note authoritative biographies or information, interviews, and excerpts from archaeologists' writings. See for example, the link to the Web site for Charles Lyell (one of the first geologists) and his writings online, the link to a biography of and an interview with Mary Leakey who is known for discovering footprints of an early or prehuman species, the link to the Smithsonian Institution archaeologist William Duncan Strong Web site with some of his field notes, and the link to the Nobel prize Web site featuring Willard F. Libby who developed the radiocarbon dating method. Note also on the main page links to email interviews and archaeologist directories.

Archaeology Links

http://www.unm.edu/~jevh/archlink.html

See links to sites with basic archeological information at this occasionally updated Web site. Note links to online archeology journals; individual archeological sites, projects, or areas; archeological organizations; and general archaeology links.

Articles at the Society for Historical Archaeology Web Site

http://www.sha.org/index.html

Click title links to find information on "What Is Historical Archaeology?" and "Futures in Historical Archaeology" plus "Historical Archaeology Links."

Archaeology and Physical Anthropology at Anthropology Internet Sources

http://vax.wcsu.edu/socialsci/antres.html (click links)

Note also links listed under general and miscellaneous resources. See also the link for *What Is Anthropology?* then note its information page's references to archaeology and physical anthropology.

Reflections on Prehistory by James Q. Jacobs

http://www.jqjacobs.net/anthro/prehisty.html

More than fifteen articles on prehistoric archaeology subjects, including the titles "The Import of Archaeology," "A Timeline Assessment" (with five key events), "The First Americans," and "The First North American Civilization."

Anthropology Defined, by Carol and Melvin Ember

http://www.geneseo.edu/~anthro/anthropology_defined.php

A brief definition, including scope, approach, and questions in which anthropologists are interested, are provided here in an adaptation from the Embers' 1996 book *Anthropology.*

Study Guide to *Anthropology* (1996) by Carol R. and Melvin L. Ember

http://cw.prenhall.com/bookbind/pubbooks/ember

Via a pull-down menu see links to information and online activities based on chapters, e.g., "What Is Anthropology?" in this book on early civilization and native populations today. Each main category has subcategories including archaeology; horticulture, agriculture, and pastoralism; domestication of plants and animals; increase in food production; cognitive, psychological and emotional development; possible genetic and physiological influences; and cultural ecology, behavioral ecology, sociobiology; etc. Information links include Overview, Key Terms, Web Destinations, and Current Issues. Online activities (done after teacher arranged online registration or by printing out activity pages) include Applied Anthropology, Review and Respond, Multiple Choice, Net Search, Internet Exercises, and Message Board.

"An Inventor Never Grows Up"
George Margolin (1997)
URL: www.inventionconvention.com/americasinventor (click link)

SITE SUMMARY: Margolin is an inventor, former science teacher, and holder of multiple patents, who is best known for his involvement with background systems for the motion picture *2001: A Space Odyssey*. This article can be found in the "Exploring the Inventor's Mind: Reflections on the Creative Problem-Solving Process" section of the online magazine *America's Inventor*. In this article, Margolin reveals that there is something unique in every inventor's personality, and points out what is fascinating in the world of inventing and invention. (Other areas of *America's Inventor* include: "Profiles of Great Inventors," "Headlines and News Briefs," "Reviews" [of books, Web sites, etc.], "Mastering the Invention Process," "Critiquing the Industry," and "EarthTrends—A Look to the Future of Inventing.")

DISCUSSION QUESTIONS AND ACTIVITIES

1. What are nine words Thomas Edison said, which he believed to be "the keys to invention" and "the key to a happy and productive life"? (Hint: See paragraphs one and two.)

2. Keeping in mind that Margolin considers Edison's words to be his credo and "a nine word formula for a fun filled, fruitful life," what, briefly, according to Margolin, is an inventor, the mind of an inventor, and where does an inventor "live"? (Hint: See paragraphs three, four, and five.)

3. Identify five or six considerations involving the world of the inventor. (Hint: See paragraph four.)

4. What is so about some people (e.g., scientists, inventors, "explorers of the new and different")? How does an inventor see? What happens, and what can these people do, because of what is referred to in the two questions just above? (Hint: See paragraphs five and eleven.)

5. What does Margolin say, in positive ways, about making mistakes, and mistakes and inventors? (Hint: See paragraphs five and six.)

6. Why do some people become, or remain, inventors, explorers, etc.? (Hint: See paragraph eight.)

7. Think about, then state, as suggested by Margolin, the differences between good facts and bad facts, and being childish or childlike. (Hint: See paragraph ten, then paragraph nine.)

8. What does Margolin say about "every inventor" and "every child"? (Hint: See paragraph eleven.) These statements may be called examples of a type of syllogism (a way of thinking logically, first mentioned by Aristotle). Think of another syllogism on a science subject and explain. (Tip: Help is at the Web sites: Aristotle's Logic [especially Aristotle's Syllogism, Logic (at philosophyclass.com)], Syllogism [at bartleby.com] [especially: Categorical Syllogism]. [Full urls are cited in this book's Appendix F.])

9. Keeping in mind Margolin's comments referred to in the first part of Question/Activity no. 8 above, and in Questions/Activities nos. 1 through 7, describe a well-known invention; then think of, and describe, in two hundred words, something you could invent. (Note: Be sure to explain each choice for your descriptions in ways that show what is at work with reference to Margolin's credo or "nine-word formula"; or something related to them that he notes in his essay.) (Tip: For help, see these Web sites [with urls] cited in the Related Internet Sites section below [e.g., Smithsonian Institution—Inventors and Inventions—Selected Links, National Inventors Hall of Fame—Inventions and Inventors Search, Greatest Engineering Achievements of the Twentieth Century, Idea Finder—Contents], and other areas of the *America's Inventor* magazine site cited in the Site Summary at the beginning of this chapter.)

RELATED INTERNET SITE(S)

Thomas Edison Online

http://edison.rutgers.edu

At this site, Rutgers University, the National Park Service, the Smithsonian Institution, the New Jersey Historical Commission, and others are gradually providing online versions of the texts of fifteen to twenty print volumes of Edison's writings, ranging from 1847 through 1910. Edison's patents are now available, as are documents from 1847 through 1898. See also links to About Edison's Papers, biographies, bibliographies, and related resources on the Web.

Smithsonian Institution—Inventors and Inventions—Selected Links

http://www.si.edu/resource/faq/nmah/invent.htm

Note the links to Smithsonian's Lemelson Center for Study of Invention and Innovation (documenting, disseminating information about invention and innovation, and featuring Featured Inventors), Edison's Timeline of Invention, Edison After Forty, Women Inventors of the Twentieth Century; Science, Technology, and Invention in . . . the Southwestern United States; African American Invention and Innovation 1619 through 1930, Spotlight Biography—Inventors, and Information Sources for Inventions, plus photo links leading to information on famous inventors and inventions.

Lemelson—MIT Program Celebrating Invention and Innovation

http://web.mit.edu/invent

Click the Invention Dimension link, then the Inventor of the Week link, then its Browse Archive link. Next, click the Browse by Invention link, then click a name link beside an invention for information on the invention, invention's date and inventor.

Science and Invention News—Links to Resources

http://web.mit.edu/invent/r-archive-5.html

Components of Creativity

http://www.bemorecreative.com/fq-intro.htm

This site states and describes five steps of creativity that apply to inventing. Quotations on creativity by noted people are featured.

Abraham Lincoln's Second Lecture on Discoveries and Inventions (February 11, 1859)

http://showcase.netins.net/web/creative/lincoln/speeches/discoveries.htm

This lecture, given before Lincoln became president of the United States, was presented to the Young Men's Association of Bloomington Illinois. An introduction is provided by Abraham Lincoln Online, copyrighted 2002, and notes Lincoln's own invention.

Rear Admiral Grace Murray Hopper

http://www.imdiversity.com/villages/woman/Article_Detail.asp?Article_ID=3717

This biography is provided courtesy of The Women's Museum in Texas. It gives information about the woman who invented the computer language COBOL, and was a pioneer in the development of computer technology. It also reveals the story behind her coining the phrase "computer bug."

Quotations on the Value of Inventions

http://www.ipcreators.org/General/quote.htm

The Intellectual Property Creators Organization provides quotations on the value of inventions and patents, especially of computers, telephone and radio, airplanes and rockets, and other inventions. Other quotations are on predictions of the value of some inventions. Some featured quotations are by the Founding Fathers, U.S. presidents, lawyers and judges, among others.

National Inventors Hall of Fame—Inventions and Inventors Search

http://www.invent.org/hall_of_fame/1_1_search.asp

Choose to browse by inventor or invention by first letter of inventor's last name or name of invention. Next, choose a letter, and then an inventor's name or an invention name link to get to a page with a brief description of the invention, the inventor's biography, plus statement on the invention's impact, patent number, date of induction in the Hall of Fame, and links to sites with more data. Note: you may also choose to browse by induction date from 1973 to present, or by inventions by decade from 1790 to present. Search by subject via invention channels link is also possible. See also links to overview to the Hall of Fame and induction information.

Greatest Engineering Achievements of the Twentieth Century

http://www.greatachievements.org

See links to data on twenty great achievements, with introductions, time lines, and historical essays, from water production to laser optics.

Idea Finder—Contents

http://www.ideafinder.com/site/contents.htm

See the information and links on Idea History (e.g., Invention Facts and Myths, Inventor Profiles, Innovation Timeline, and Invention Trivia), Idea Showcase (e.g., Great Idea Award Winners, and Idea Catalog), Features (e.g., Calendar History, Idea Wish List, and Words of Wisdom), Resource Center, Guest Services (e.g., Archives), and Information (e.g., FAQs, and What's New), and Home Page.

"Ellen Is . . . Co-Inventor of Three Patents . . ." in Meet NASA Astronaut Ellen Ochoa

http://www.girlpower.gov/girlarea/gpguest/ochoa.htm (see also link to NASA biography)

"Dr. Clift and Co-Inventor Peggy Whitson . . . NASA Astronauts Have Invented a Device . . ."

http://www.universetoday.com/html/articles/2001-0115c.html (see also NASA biography at *http://www.jsc.nasa.gov/Bios/htmlbios/whitson.html*)

BirdNet—The Ornithological Information Source
The Ornithological Council (1997–)
URL: http://www.nmnh.si.edu/BIRDNET/index.html

SITE SUMMARY: This Web site, "all about ornithology—the scientific study of birds," features data provided by The Ornithological Council. It is offered online by the National Museum of Natural History at the Smithsonian Institution. Scroll to the bottom of the Web page for links to major areas of this Web site, including "What Is Ornithology?" Ornithological Issues, Birds and Birding Information, Periodicals and Magazines (with indications of what each publication's Web site has online), Research Assistance, Recent Ornithological Literature Online (not online texts, but online bibliographical citations, and special summaries called abstracts, on ornithological research), and "Guidelines to the Use of Wild Birds in Research" (a manual for the humane study of birds). See also a link to a complete index to BirdNet sources at www.nmnh.si.edu/BIRDNET/mainindex.html. Also see picture links to Ornithological Council member organizations' Web sites.

DISCUSSION QUESTIONS AND ACTIVITIES

1. Go to the BirdNet Web site. Click the "What Is Ornithology?" link in the General Information area. Define in two phrases the general meaning of ornithology. Identify eight particular aspects of ornithology that ornithologists do. Reveal what people can do to help ornithological scientists. Extra Activity: Identify two or more aspects of ornithology as provided at the Birding in the U.S.A. and Around the World Web site whose url is in the Related Internet Sites section below.

2. Go to the Learning to Birdwatch area of www.ornithology.com. Identify identification tips two through nine on what to do during birdwatching field trips. Extra Activity: Identify more bird identification tips as provided at Birding in the U.S.A. and Around the World Web site. (Full urls and Web site summaries for both Web sites are in the Related Internet Sites section below.) (Note: Go to the North American Breeding Bird Survey Web site via a link that works at the BirdNet Web site, then if the link works, identify the site's identification tips.)

3. Click the Ornithological Journals link in BirdNet's Research Assistance area or the periodicals and journals link in the General Information area. Select two periodicals or magazines that have online articles or abstracts of articles. Go to the magazines' or periodicals' Web sites, then choose three birds for which there is information in online articles. Describe the birds using as many as possible of identification tips two through eight, and (optional) other tips, found for Question/Activity no. 2 above. Identify the article's main point. Tell how it exemplifies the tips. (Option: You may also choose another online article found at www.birdwatchersdigest.com or via the Web sites for the Audubon Society and "Excerpts from the Life Histories" in *Birds of North America* whose urls are cited in the Related Internet Sites section below.)

4. Choose two other birds in the ways suggested in Question/Activity no. 3 above. Find each bird's scientific name and classify it, listing its classification aspects as indicated via the Taxonomy and Systematics links on the Scientific links page found via the BirdNet Research Assistance area and the Bird Order and Species link in the BirdNet Birds and Birding area. See also the Classification/Taxonomy or Names areas of http://www.ornithology.com or the Nutty Birdwatcher's Identification area or at one of the sites you find via its Resources page. (Its url is cited in the Related Internet Sites section below.)

5. Keeping in mind the eight particular aspects of ornithology, and (optional) other aspects, that you found for Question /Activity no. 1 above, visit two periodical or magazine Web sites found as cited in Question/Activity no. 3 above. Select two of those particular aspects of ornithology, and find articles in the chosen magazines or periodicals that refer to these aspects. Identify those articles' features, and explain how those articles are examples of those aspects.

6. Identify suggestions for attracting birds to one's backyard that you find via BirdNet's Birds and Birding links area, especially that area's Birding on the Web link and that site's links. (See also tips for attracting birds at Web sites including www.ornithology.com, Care and Concern for Animals—Roots and Shoots Activities—Jane Goodall Institute, and the Cornell Laboratory of Ornithology. [Their urls are cited in the Related Internet Sites section below. A BirdNet link goes to the Cornell Lab.]) Try one or more of these suggestions in your backyard, schoolyard garden, or community garden. Based on your observations, write a two hundred word report on how effective you find these suggestions.

7. Visit the Cornell Laboratory of Ornithology and Nutty Birdwatcher Web sites. (Their urls are cited in the Related Internet Sites section below.) Choose one bird from the Cornell Laboratory Web site's Bird of the Week feature and two birds found via the Nutty Birdwatcher's Identification page, plus four birds, one each, from Birding Databases, Online Field Guides, Specific Species, and Other Birding Sites, listed on the Nutty Birdwatcher's Resources page. Describe each bird selected using identification tips two through eight, and (optional) other tips, found at stated in Question/Activity no. 2 above. Adapt and apply Question/Activity no. 4 above to two of the birds selected.

8. Find a rare bird, an endangered bird, and an extinct bird via BirdNet's Endangered Species list link in its Research Assistance area and at Web sites cited in the note just below. Describe each bird's features, including www.ornithology.com's learning about birds tips three, four, five, seven, eight, then two, and six. Identify each bird's status. Explain why each one is endangered, rare, or extinct. (Note: Also find extinct, rare, and endangered birds via links at www.ornithology.com, in one of the articles in the magazines or journals found as indicated in Question/Activity no. 3 above, and at the Web sites: Audubon Science—Endangered Birds WatchList, the American Birding Association's Rare Bird Alert Reports, Extinct and Endangered Birds—Links to Sites, or Endangered Species—Birds—U.S. Fish and Wildlife Service. [Their urls are cited in the Related Internet Sites section below.])

9. Keeping in mind the subject and activity of Question/Activity no. 8 above, suggest how you might do something to get a rare or endangered bird off the endangered or rare birds lists. (For help, see the Web sites for Audubon Science—Endangered Birds WatchList, Audubon Society [especially its Conservation and Action area], and the Nutty Birdwatcher [via its Resources page's Conservation and Rehabilitation links]. Their urls are cited in the Related Internet Sites section below.)

10. Select a bird that lives in the area where you live, found via BirdNet's Research Assistance area's Bird Observatories in the U.S. and Canada Web page and at other sites cited just below. Identify its features from identification tips you found for Question/Activity no. 2 above. (Find checklists at the Birding in the U.S.A. and Around the World Web sites, information at the Web site with links to Spring/Fall Maps of Migrant Birds and Bird Observatories and Migration Stations in the U.S., and via the migration link at ornithology.com, plus details at the Cornell Laboratory of Ornithology Web site or the Web site featuring "Excerpts from the Life Histories" in *Birds of North America*. [Find urls for these Web sites in the Related Internet Sites section below.])

RELATED INTERNET SITE(S)

Ornithology—The Science of Birds

http://www.ornithology.com/SiteMap.html

This site, created by a university professor of biological sciences and director of an environmental institute, features many annotated links about birdwatching and the scientific study of birds.

Included are links to Learning to Birdwatch, News, Famous Early Ornithologists, FAQs, Careers in Ornithology, Question of the Month, Birds in the Backyard, Feeders and Feeding, Classification/Taxonomy, Names, Organizations and their Magazines and Journals, Aviaries and Zoos, Conservation, Ecobirding, Migration, Extinct Birds, Endangered Birds, E-mail an Ornithologist, Teacher Resources, and more.

Nutty Birdwatcher

http://nuthatch.birdnature.com/index.html

This site features a lot of information for birdwatchers and others interested in finding data about birds, especially in the Northeastern United States. Links go to an Introduction, Information on Bird Identifications (including general classification data), Gallery and Profiles, Habitats, Migration, Survival Needs, Odds and Ends, What's New (at this site), and Resources (with links to Birding Databases, Online Field Guides, Specific Species, Bird Monitoring, Conservation and Rehabilitation, Sanctuaries, Organizations, etc., Breeding Atlas, General Birding Interests, and Unique Sites with Interesting Information).

American Birding Association—Articles, FAQs, News, Young Birders, etc.

http://www.americanbirding.org/siteindex1.htm

Find the links for Birding—Features—Buiding Birding Skills—Keeping Field Notes, *A Bird's Eye View* newsletter for young people and its feature articles "What's That Bird?" and "Think Like A Bird," and Birding Links including Bird FAQs, Birding Listervs, and Ornithological Research Resources. On the index's next page, see links to Conservation, Education with "Early Birding" (an article on the ABA Education Initiative), Rare Bird Alert Reports, and Youth Birders with and Young Birders Connect (e.g., chat, webring, and penfriends), Young Birders of the Year Competition, and Young Birders News.

"Excerpts from the Life Histories" in *Birds of North America*

http://www.birdsofna.org/Excerpts.shtml

Supported by the American Ornithological Union, the Cornell Laboratory of Ornithology, and the Academy of Natural Sciences, this Web site for this book for "twenty-first-century birders" has more than thirty online profiles of birds (e.g., Clark's Nutcracker, the Ruby Throated Hummingbird, and the Nashville Warbler). See also links to Bird Facts, and What Is BNA [the Birds of North America]?

Endangered Species—Birds—U.S. Fish and Wildlife Service

http://endangered.fws.gov/wildlife.html#Species

Scroll to Species Listed in the U.S., and click Birds. On the next page, scroll down a list of birds listed alphabetically by common name, with scientific name links. Clicking a link brings basic information in a Species Profile (e.g., the bird's common and scientific names; its family, historic range, and current status; plus the date the status was reported). Links on the Profile page lead to more information on the bird (e.g., petitions for protecting the bird, press releases, government documents, and USFWS refuge reports).

Extinct and Endangered Birds—Links to Sites

http://search.msn.com (click Sciences in the Library area)

Follow links to Animals and Wildlife, Extinct Species or Endangered Species, and Birds.

Audubon Science—Endangered Birds WatchList

http://www.audubon.org/bird/watch/index.html

This Web page of the Audubon Society, with a coalition of conservationists called Partners in Flight, features a WatchList, yearly revised, of endangered birds by types, data on population decline, limited geographical range, plus breeding area, and habitat loss, with an invitation to Read About the Science Behind the WatchList. Links lead to Five Ways to Help Watchlist Birds (with emphasis on preventive action rather than last minute rescue attempts), Birds and Science—An Introduction, Kids WatchList Activities, and FAQs. Changing photos on the main page show "conservation priority" birds.

Care and Concern for Animals—Roots and Shoots Activities—Jane Goodall Institute

http://www.janegoodall.org/rs/activities (click link)

See the activities involving birds, among many nature related activities, offered for young people by this institute set up by the animal behaviorist and naturalist Jane Goodall.

Audubon Society

http://www.audubon.org

See the links to Birds and Science, Centers and Audubon News, Education, Conservation and Action, Audubon and the Internet; featured news articles, an Audubon Centers and Sanctuaries locator; and an *Audubon Magazine* index that leads to Web exclusive articles on birds and other wildlife.

Cornell Laboratory of Ornithology

http://birds.cornell.edu

Aiming to foster scientific literacy in birdwatchers through education and citizen science, this interactive site features Bird of the Week, Sound of the Week, and Slide of the Week, plus new press releases and lab news. Note also Conservation, Research, and Citizen Science, which includes Citizen Science Watch, Citizen Science in the Schoolyard, Classroom Feeder Watch, Bird Source, Birdhouse Network, and Some Bird Groups (e.g., Birds in Forested Landscapes and Great Backyard Bird Count). See, in addition, an Online Bird Guide in the Education area, More Good Stuff, such as Bird Feeding Tips, Bird FAQs, Birdhouse Tips, NestBoxCam, and a World Series of Birding, plus Multimedia and Collections, such as a Library of Natural Sounds, Audio Guides, and a Bio Acoustics Research Program. (A link at BirdNet to the Lab sometimes works.)

Birding in the U.S.A. and Around the World

http://www.birding.com

See links in box or at right to Ornithology, Checklists of Birds in Your Area (as seen in local bird observatories), Bird Records (e.g., biggest), detailed data on identifying birds (with link to USGS Bird ID Tips By Species), and more.

What Is Migration?

http://www.birdsource.org/birdcast/what_is_migration.html

On this information sheet sponsored in part by the Cornell Laboratory of Ornithology, find out about this marvelous and mysterious natural phenomenon and birds' part in it.

Spring/Fall Maps of Migrant Birds, U.S. Bird Observatories and Migration Stations, etc.

http://www.mp1-pwrc.usgs.gov/birds/othbird.html (click links)

Field Notebook Primer: How To Take Good Field Notes by Robert B. Payne

http://www.ummz.lsa.umich.edu/birds/birddivresources/fieldnotes.html

See also Resources of the University of Michigan Museum of Zoology Bird Division which provides the primer online.

Bird Song Mneumonics

http://www.1000plus.com/BirdSong

Links go to birds or birds' voices for help in discovering how particular birds' voices sound if spelled or guessed in letters (e.g., an ovenbird chirps "teacher, teacher, teacher").

"Consciousness and Neuroscience"
Francis Crick and Christof Koch (1997)
URL: http://www.klab.caltech.edu/~koch/crick-koch-cc-97.html

SITE SUMMARY: Written by Crick (a 1962 Nobel Prize winner in Chemistry for his part in the discovery of DNA, and now distinguished research professor at the Salk Institute), and Koch (of Computation and Neural Systems at the California Institute of Technology [CalTech]), this document was published in print in the *Cerebral Cortex* scientific journal (8: 97–107, 1998). It provides an account of these scientists' ongoing experimental work on consciousness. Divided into several sections, this document has section titles including: Clearing the Ground, Why Are We Conscious? Visual Consciousness, The Nature of Visual Representation, Where Is the Visual Representation? What Is Essential for Visual Consciousness? Recent Experimental Results, Action Without Seeing (with several parts), The Problems of Meaning, Philosophical Matters, and Future Experiments.

DISCUSSION QUESTIONS AND ACTIVITIES

1. What is one of the major unsolved problems of modern science, according to Crick and Koch? What do neuroscientists acknowledge, yet what do they not do, and why? What do Crick and Koch "state bluntly" on the subject, and which "tentative assumption" do they make when approaching the problem? Identify four topics they think should be stated on the subject. (Hints: See the Finale, and the section "Clearing the Ground.")
2. What do Crick and Koch say is "rather peculiar?" (Hint: See Finale.)
3. How should consciousness be approached in a scientific manner, and why, according to Crick and Koch?
4. Briefly identify the way Crick and Koch identify consciousness, then what they suggest it is better for scientists to do when thinking about it, and why.
5. Crick and Koch use an initialism and an unusual word when they refer to aspects of their work. Identify NCC. What is "qualia" and the "hard problem" about it?
6. What do Crick and Koch say the brain must do to be aware of an object or event?
7. What is essential for visual consciousness?
8. What do Crick and Koch say are two aspects that are related to the brain generating meaning? Which examples are provided? How, do they say, are these "associations derived," and which examples do they give?
9. Identify at least three experiments that should be continued, according to Crick and Koch, then identify the fascinating problem these scientists encourage young neurologists to investigate, and what they would find very gratifying. (Hints: See the Future Experiments and Finale sections.)
10. What should not be of concern with reference to philosophers, yet what should be listened to when they say something, according to Crick and Koch?

RELATED INTERNET SITE(S)

Francis H.C. Crick—Of the Salk Institute's Kieckhefer Center for Theoretical Biology

http://www.salk.edu/faculty/faculty/details.php?id=14

This Web page provides a brief overview of Crick's current position and research interests, plus past scientific accomplishments, awards, honors, and education.

Christof Koch—CalTech Professor of Cognitive and Behavioral Biology

http://www.caltech.edu (click sitemap and personnel directory links, search for Koch)

See brief description of Koch's education, expertise, and recent press releases mentioning him and his work. Follow the "more press releases" link to find a link for a November 15, 2000 press release on "The human brain employs the same neurons in seeing an object and later imagining it, CalTech/UCLA research reveals." Note also a description of scientific subjects on which he works, and a list of publications, at www.its.caltech.edu/~biology/brochures/faculty/koch.html with a "more on Koch" link that leads to a Koch Lab at www.klab.caltech.edu/index.shtml with links to research (featuring online writings by Koch with others), news, people, and places.

"Consciousness, Neurobiology of" in the *MIT Encyclopedia of Cognitive Science*

http://cognet.mit.edu/MITECS/Entry/koch

Koch and Crick as authors of this scientific encyclopedia entry provide a question, a statement, links to more online information, and lists of writings by and about Crick and Koch, and the subject.

The Electric Brain

http://www.pbs.org/wgbh/nova/mind/electric.html

Find out something about the nature of consciousness, and discover what a neuroscientist in the New York University School of Medicine says about the human brain's electric like actions that are, it is claimed, have something to do with consciousness.

Consciousness Studies

http://www.google.com (click Science>Social Sciences>Psychology>Cognitive, then Consciousness link)

See list of annotated links to Web sites on the subject (e.g., Consciousness Research Laboratory, Toward a Science of Consciousness, Metaphors of the Mind, etc.).

"Foreword" by Michael Crichton to the *Encyclopedia of Dinosaurs*
(1997)
URL: www.academicpress.com/catalog/0122268105/index.htm (click Foreword link)

SITE SUMMARY: Best known as the author of *Jurassic Park* (the 1990 book and the 1993 movie), Crichton wrote this Foreword which accompanies online samples of articles in the *Encyclopedia of Dinosaurs*, an award winning work called "the most authoritative encyclopedia ever prepared on dinosaurs and dinosaur science" and one that features current research by the top people in the field today. In this Foreword, Crichton looks at what evidence exists regarding dinosaurs and considers people's fascination with these creatures. The Foreword, in PDF format, is accessible via a page that also has links to a guide to the encyclopedia, a preface, sample images, subjects, and reviews that include one from *Prehistoric Times* which has a comment about Crichton on how his accomplishments contribute to his authoring the Foreword.

DISCUSSION QUESTIONS AND ACTIVITIES

1. See paragraph one and the first part, then the middle part of paragraph two. What happened, according to Crichton, when "the first reports of the giant bones of extinct creatures" were heard or read? How is it connected to what is happening today (a century and a half afterwards)? What is thought about "the current dinosaur mania" which happens not to be true, and what else is true in connection with this, which Crichton gradually came to realize?

2. See paragraphs two, four, and six, then the first sentence of paragraph eight. Provide an answer for Crichton's question "How do we explain the fact that dinosaurs excite the imagination of adults and children throughout the world?" Why are children "captivated by dinosaurs" according to Crichton, and to you?

3. See paragraph two and the first part of paragraph seven. Crichton points out that even small children in natural history museums screech out the complex Latin names of particular dinosaurs they see. Why do children, according to Crichton, like to pronounce those complex names, and why do you like to say the names? See the Dinosauria: Translation and Pronunciation Guide Web site or the Dinosauricon—Dinosaur Genus Web site, then choose a dinosaur's name, state and describe the name, including the scientific version and its translation, then explain why that name was given to that dinosaur. Next, see the Web site Name That Dino: What Does the Word Dinosaur Mean and How Are Dinosaurs Named? Imagine you have discovered two dinosaurs and name them using two of the ways dinosaurs are named, then tell and explain your reasons for the way you named each dinosaur. (Note: Urls for the Web sites cited above are cited in the Related Internet Sites section of this book's chapter on "Paper Dinosaurs: A Hypertext Catalog" with excerpts from papers on beginnings of dinosaur research [e.g., papers by scientists who first named dinosaurs, including Richard Owen and William Buckland].)

4. See paragraph three. Is the interest in fossils a "nationalistic thing"? Why or why not, according to Crichton, and to you? See the Web sites on Fossil Sites, Dinosaur Links (e.g., its Dinosaurs Around the World), and Paleontology—Web Sites by States and Provinces. (Their urls are cited in the Related Internet Sites section below.) Find and describe a fossil found in your state or a nation you claim as place to which you trace your family heritage.

5. See paragraph five. According to Crichton, what kind of dinosaurs do children like, perhaps the best? Elaborate on your answer, including information you find on the main subject and on related subjects at these Web sites or pages: Dinosaurs and Eggs at *National Geographic Magazine* Online, Dinosaur Embryo Discovery—Press Release—American Museum of Natural History; A Prehistoric Playground, Baby Dinosaurs, T-Rex the King of Dinosaurs, and Other

Exhibits; and "Jack Horner and Marion Brandvold: Two of the 100 Most Influential Missourians," Paleontology Field Program Message on Brandvold, Horner, Laurie and David Trexler; and in *Journal of Dinosaur Paleontology* articles (e.g., on "Egg Strategies," "Dinosaur Parenting," and "The Brooding Dinosaur" in the Dinosauria or Oviraptorids topic links areas). (Their urls are cited in the Related Internet Sites section below, or in that section in this book's chapter featuring the document "Paleontology: The Window to Science Education.")

6. What type of dinosaur do you like the best, other than the type referred to in Question/Activity no. 5 above? Explain the type's features and why you like that type. Choose a particular example of that type, then explain its features, and why you like it. (For help, see the Web sites or areas: "Specific Dinosaurs" at Dinosaur Links, "The Great Dinosaur Mystery," and Dinosauricon: Dinosaur Genus. [Their urls are cited in the Related Internet Sites section below, or in this book's chapter on "Paper Dinosaurs: A Hypertext Catalog" noted in Question/Activity no. 3 above.])

7. See paragraph eight. What do dinosaurs present for adults, according to Crichton, and also probably for other people, especially young people? What are two things that he said nobody really knows about dinosaurs? What are three things that exist that have something to do with dinosaurs? What are two things people speculate about with regard to dinosaurs? What did he say, when referring to dinosaurs, is so about "what hard evidence remains of their long vanished world," and what results from this? Choose and elaborate on something you referred to in your answers to the fourth or third questions just above. (For help check the online sample articles in the *Encyclopedia of Dinosaurs*. [Its url is cited in the Related Internet Sites section below.] See also Web sites whose urls can be found in this book's "Paper Dinosaurs: A Hypertext Catalog" and "Paleontology: The Window to Science Education" chapters noted in Questions/Activities nos. 3 through 6 above.)

8. Study the definition of Foreword in the *UBC Science Co-op: Student Handbook [Work Term Report Guidelines]*. (Its url is cited in this book's Appendix F.) How does Crichton's Foreword follow the basic definition of, or criteria for, a foreword? Choose a dinosaur related subject or another subject in paleontology, and write a foreword to a book that could be written on the subject. (For data on your subject, see any Web site in the Related Internet Sites section below or in a chapter of this book noted above in Questions/Activities nos. 3 through 7 above.)

RELATED INTERNET SITE(S)

"Jack Horner and Marion Brandvold—Two of the 100 Most Influential Montanans"

http://www.missoulian.com/specials/100montanans/list/022.html

Part of the "One Hundred Most Influential Montanans of the Twentieth Century" Web site, this page features information on dinosaur discoverer Brandvold, dinosaur expert Horner of the Museum of the Rockies, the exact location of the Montana dinosaur nest Brandvold discovered in 1978, and the type of dinosaur discovered.

Paleontology Field Program Message on Brandvold, Horner, Laurie and David Trexler

http://www.cmnh.org/dinoarch1999Apr/msg00460.html

Of the dinosaur discoveries of Marion Brandvold and Laurie Trexler (her daughter-in-law), their connection with the work of dinosaur expert Jack Horner, and paleontological research of David Trexler (Brandvold's son).

Encyclopedia of Dinosaurs—Sample Articles Online

http://www.academicpress.com/catalog/012268105/index.htm (click link)

This award-winning encyclopedia features Crichton's Foreword online and sample articles with topics including age determination of dinosaurs, definition of dinosauria, origin of dinosaurs, extinction of dinosaurs, history of dinosaur discoveries, and reconstruction and restoration of fossils.

Look Inside the *Encyclopedia of Dinosaurs* Edited by Philip Currie and Kevin Padian

http://www.amazon.com

Do a search, then, on this online bookstore's page for this book, click the links for the Look Inside pages, and see especially the inside front flap, the back cover, six pages of sample entries that include African dinosaurs, and the Age of Dinosaurs, plus a complete contents and a complete index.

Paleontology—Web Sites by States and Provinces

http://www.nearctica.com/paleo/states/states.htm

Fossil Sites

http://e.j.swearengin.home.att.net/fossils.htm

Note especially the links to U.S. States, All the U.S. State Fossils list, U.S. National Park Service Sites, Sites by Country, and Museum Sites. A *Discover Magazine* photograph leads to a Utah fossils page.

Park Geology—Tour of Fossil Parks—Paleontology

http://www.aqd.nps.gov/grd/tour/fossil.htm.

This site has links to the U.S. Park System's parks that "have a common geologic theme and links to pages about each park's geologic features."

Dinosaur Links

http://www.ucmp.berkeley.edu/diapsids/dinolinks.html

Note links to dinosaur oriented sites (e.g., Dinosaurs Around the World, Dinosaur Tracks and Traces, Dinosaur Extinctions, Classification, Special Dinosaurs, Dinosaurs for Kids, Media Coverage, basic information, and comprehensive information). Note also the links under Dinosaurs and Paleontology, and under Not Dinosaurs But Worthy of Mention.

A Prehistoric Playground, Baby Dinosaurs, T-Rex King of Dinosaurs, and Other Exhibits

http://www.wonderworksexhibits.com/traveling.html

This site features information on items in traveling exhibits such as one on various aspects of baby dinosaurs, which travel to museums such as Chicago's Sci Tech Hands-On Museum described at http://www.chicagokids.com.

Dinosaur Embryo Discovery—Press Release—American Museum of Natural History

http://www.amnh.org/welcome/press/breaking/embryo.html

This is a November 17, 1998 press release on the first discovery of a dinosaur nesting ground of a plant-eating dinosaur in the South American nation of Argentina. It reveals that many specimens discovered represent several scientific firsts.

Dinosaurs and Eggs at *National Geographic Magazine* Online

http://www.nationalgeographic.com/dinorama

Click the Dinosaur Eggs photo link, then the next page's feature link, or go directly to http://www.nationalgeographic.com/features/96/dinoeggs, for an online egg hunt that is actually a behind the scenes look at the *National Geographic* May 1996 article "The Great Dinosaur Egg Hunt" in the Gobi Desert. At the main Dinorama page, also click the History's Nursery photo link. Searches for the subjects "dinosaur eggs," "dinosaur embryos," or "dinosaur nests" via the search box at http://www.nationalgeographic.com, which also bring links to articles.

"The Great Dinosaur Mystery" by Paul S. Taylor

http://christiananswers.net/dinosaurs

To find out about dinosaurs from the viewpoint of scientists who happen to follow the Christian religion, click the links to Answers, Discovery Trail, Exploring, and For Teachers, then do searches in the search box for definitions for creation, creationism, the fossil record, dinosaurs, and ancient reptiles (not dinosaurs yet often listed with them).

Behind the Scenes—*Jurassic Park*

http://www.lost-world.com/Lost_World02/Jurassic_Park.Site

Click the link to find out about "the inside story of the making of *Jurassic Park*," the movie "where science and technology came together."

The Science (and Non-Science) of *Jurassic Park* and *Jurassic Park 2: The Lost World*

http://www.dinosaur.org/jparticles.htm

Note the links to "Dinosaurs From Amber?" by Garry Platt, "The Science of *Jurassic Park*," "Science Bloopers in *Jurassic Park 2*," "The *Lost World* Movie Junket" by Kelly Milner Halls, and book reviews. See also http://www.dinosaur.org/saurofindo.html and its *Jurassic Park* and *Lost World* links.

About Michael Crichton

http://www.crichton-official.com/aboutmc/biography.html

This page of the official Michael Crichton Web site provides details of Crichton's education, writings, and other accomplishments, including his biology and medical degrees, his work as an anthropology lecturer, his being awarded the Association of American Medical Writers award, and data on a dinosaur named after him.

"Nutrition and Children: A Statement for Health Care Professionals"
American Heart Association, Nutrition Committee (1997)
URL: http://216.185.112.5/presenter.jhtml?identifier=1779

SITE SUMMARY: The Nutrition Committee of the American Heart Association (AHA), provides in this statement straightforward recommendations for health professionals, parents and other caregivers, on a healthy diet for children, and cites surveys and research to support its conclusions. (Find also by typing the phrase "Nutrition and Children" in the search box at http://www.americanheart.org and clicking Search or your Enter key, then the title link.)

DISCUSSION QUESTIONS AND ACTIVITIES

1. See the first part of the Statement's introduction. What is the major goal of "heart healthy" diets?

2. See the second part of the Statement's introduction. What is the AHA Step One Diet? Why has it been claimed that the AHA Step One Diet is of little benefit for children and may even be hazardous? What does the AHA Nutrition Committee recommend regarding the AHA Step One Diet and children? What do Committee members claim "will ultimately result" if their recommendation is followed?

3. See the Statement's Safety section. What is a major safety issue that has been considered regarding a "heart healthy" diet and childhood? Identify another source of concern regarding dietary recommendations, and explain.

4. See the Statement's Conclusions section, paragraph one, then the first two thirds of paragraph two. What does rigorous and ongoing research show, and why is diet important? What have recent surveys of childhood nutritional intake shown, in general, and with reference to earlier surveys, and how is the AHA Step One Diet involved with both? What is recommended?

5. See the Statement's Conclusions section, the third part of paragraph two. How can a transition to a heart healthy diet be accomplished as a child's diet becomes progressively more varied after the child is age two or older? Plan a meal with specific food suggestions, and use as general guidelines the suggestions you discovered in your answer to the question just above.

RELATED INTERNET SITE(S)

U.S. Department of Agriculture—Food and Nutrition Service

http://www.fns.usda.gov/fns

Scroll to, and click, links for Child Nutrition, Team Nutrition, and Promote Healthy Eating in Schools. Click also Food, Nutrition, and Consumer Services (FNCS); then Center for Nutrition Policy and Promotion (CNPP); for more links (e.g., Nutrition Insights, Family Economics and Nutrition Review, and Symposium Proceedings).

"Children's Nutrition—Some Basic Ideas" by Karsten Alexandria, N.D., 1999

http://www.naturodoc.com/library/children/kids_nutrition.htm

"Healthy Snacks and Treats for Kids of All Ages" by Dr. Thomas Sterns Lee, 1999

http://www.naturodoc.com/library/children/snack.htm

See also links to more articles (e.g., Nutrition Ideas for Kids).

Dietary Guidelines for Healthy Children and Adolescents (1999)

http://216.185.112.5/presenter.jhtml?identifier=4575

Included are the American Heart Association's Scientific Position, and information on eating patterns for families. (Also found by searching at http://www.americanheart.org.)

Dietary Guidelines for Children (1996)

http://circ.ahajournals.org

Click the "search articles" link. Search "by citation" for vol. 95, page 1795. A citation for "Dietary Guidelines for Healthy American Adults: A Statement for Health Care Professionals" from the American Heart Association Nutrition Committee will appear. Click the "full text" link. After the text appears, scroll to the introduction. In the links box click the "Dietary Guidelines for Children" link.

Children's Nutrition Research Center

http://www.bcm.tmc.edu/cnrc

Each Consumer News area has What's New (e.g., from CNRC researchers, dietitians). Consumer News Areas include "Facts and Answers" with an index of nutrition information and FAQs by subject (e.g., nutrition for teens, vegetarians), *Nutrition and Your Child* (a newsletter for educators, parents, and health care professionals, with special issues such as "Teens and Vegetarian Diets," and "Kids and Physical Activity"), "Special Hot Topics" (e.g., teaching nutrition to children, physical activity and sports nutrition, and children's and adolescents' nutrition), "Web links" (e.g., Science4Kids—Nutrition), plus general food, nutrition, and health sites. The Research Page has annual reports, and various research areas (e.g., Determinants of Childhood Eating and Physical Activity Behavior).

National Nutrition Month

http://www.eatright.org/nnm

Read about the American Dietetic Association's National Nutrition Month, then, for more information, click links that go to Key Messages, a Fact Sheet, and Guidelines for Using the NNM Service Mark and Slogan.

Child and Adolescent Food and Nutrition Programs (1996)

http://www.eatright.org/adaposchild.html

This is a position paper from the American Dietetic Association.

"Paleontology in the Twenty-First Century"
H. Richard Lane (1997)
URL: http://www.ngdc.noaa.gov/mgg/sepm/palaios (click April 1997 and title links)

SITE SUMMARY: Written by H. Richard Lane of the Exploration and Production Technology Group at the Amoco Corporation in Houston, Texas, this article is subtitled "Which Way Ought Paleontology to Proceed from Here?" In this article, which appeared in the April 1997 issue of *Palaios*, Lane reveals what paleontologists have focused on in the past fifty years, then indicates where paleontologists are now and uses a literary metaphor to make the situation clearer. He offers a definition of paleontology, compares aspects of paleontology, and reveals what is imperative that paleontologists must do now. He also points to paleontology's connections with other sciences and uses a musical metaphor and a social metaphor to pinpoint those connections. In addition, he suggests when the laws that impact paleontological science are especially important, and lists possible positive outcomes for an international paleontology conference and workshop.

DISCUSSION QUESTIONS AND ACTIVITIES

1. See what Lane quotes at the beginning of the article, then note the article's paragraphs one through four, and eight. How does he compare aspects of paleontology? How does he compare paleontology to other sciences? Identify a literary metaphor, a musical metaphor, and a social metaphor that he uses. How, do you think, these metaphors make his viewpoints clearer?
2. What have paleontologists, according to Lane, focused on in the last fifty years? On what should they have focused? What is imperative that they do now?
3. Identify which aspects of the study of paleontology are important if a student wishes to pursue a paleontology career in a museum, and provide reasons. Identify which aspects are important if one wants to do paleontology work that is connected to industry, and suggest why.
4. See Lane's eight possible outcomes for an international paleontology conference and workshop. Choose one outcome. (Hint: See one of the outcomes numbered four, eight, five, or the second part of number one.) Write an essay offering suggestions on how to implement the chosen outcome.
5. When, according to Lane, are laws that impact paleontological science especially important, and how?
6. Read the Fossil Preservation Act of 1996, and the Antiquities Act of 1906. (Their urls can be found in the Related Internet Sites section below.) Briefly describe each law. Think of or find an example of a fossil, paleontology landmark, monument, or dig site. Including citations and quotations of specific points in the laws explain why the fossil, monument, landmark, or dig site should be saved, protected, and/or preserved. (Hint: For examples, find links to data on quarries or other real world dinosaur dig sites via the featured Web sites or the Related Internet Sites sections of this book's chapters that feature other dinosaur related documents [e.g., Michael Crichton's Foreword to the *Encyclopedia of Dinosaurs* 1997, "Paleontology: The Window to Science Education," "Paper Dinosaurs: A Hypertext Catalog of Rare Documents," "Paleobiology—In the News, Highlights, Subjects, and Links"] or the Paleontology area of the Web site Nearctica: Gateway to the Natural World of North America, whose url is cited in this book's Appendix B.)
7. Read the "Paleontological Society Code of Fossil Collecting." Find as stated in the site summary for the Web page on "What Regulations Govern Fossil Collecting?" Its url is cited in the Related Internet Sites section below. See also the "Laws, Regulations, and Conventions Related to Archeology" Web site also cited in the Related Internet Sites section below. Note in addition "Archaeology and the Law" which is chapter five in the "Archaeology and You"

section of the *What Is Archaeology?* booklet whose url can be found in the Related Internet Sites section of this book's chapter on the "The Science of Archaeology" document. Identify the parts of the laws or regulations that relate to paleontology digs and discoveries, and the scientific aspects associated with them. Next provide details from these regulations or laws to provide an explanation of the answer to Question/Activity no. 5 above, and include in your description references to professional people that Lane mentions and to avid hobbyists or dedicated fossil finders. Then adapt and apply Question/Activity no. 6 with relation to these laws.

8. Optional activity: Study Lane's possible positive outcomes numbers six and seven for the international paleontology conference and workshop. Keep in mind Questions/Activities 4, 5, and 6 above. Write an essay with suggestions on how one or both of these outcomes might be accomplished.

RELATED INTERNET SITE(S)

What Regulations Govern Fossil Collecting?

http://www.ucmp.berkeley.edu/FAQ/faq.html#Regs

See a brief explanation of basic regulations, then note a dead link to the Paleontological Society Code of Fossil Collecting that is now found at www.paleosoc.org/pscode.html, at www.prehistoricalplanet.com/features/articles/fossil_collecting.htm, and at Fossil Collecting—The Code (that features an adaptation of the Paleontological Society Code of Fossil Collecting) via www.pbs.org/wgbh/evolution/local/fossils.html with general advice on collecting, and an equipment checklist from the Rochester Academy of Science.

Laws, Regulations, and Conventions Related to Archeology

http://www.cr.nps.edu/museum/laws/lawregax.html

Has annotated links to documents on laws and regulations with relation to archeological as well as paleontological digs and specimens. Includes information about and links to the 1906 Antiquities Act, the 1916 National Park Service Organic Act, the 1935 Historic Sites Act, the 1966 National Historic Preservation Act, the 1974 Archeological and Historic Preservation Act, and the 1979 Archaeological Resources Protection Act, plus the Curation of Federally Owned and Administered Archeological Collections, the Preservation of American Antiquities, and the Protection of Archeological Resources, in addition to the 1970 UNESCO Convention on the means of prohibiting and preventing illicit import, export, and transport of ownership of cultural property.

Fossil Preservation Act of 1996

http://www.dinosauria.com/jdp/law/act.htm

Antiquities Act of 1906 (U.S. Code, Title 16, Section 433)

http://www4.law.cornell.edu/uscode/topn/2.html (click link)

Emphasizes the preservation of "prehistoric structures and other objects of historic or scientific interest."

President Theodore Roosevelt and the Antiquities Act of 1906

http://www.theodore-roosevelt.com/tr.html

Click The Presidential Years—Accomplishments link, then the link under 1906 for "Roosevelt Signs U.S. Antiquities Act."

Wilderness Society—Newsroom—Press Release—"Theodore Roosevelt IV Testifies on Behalf of the Conservation Movement Regarding the Antiquities Act" (July 17, 2001)

http://www.wilderness.org/newsroom/rls071701.htm

This press release reveals that this conservationist and great grandson of the former United States president gave a speech before the Wilderness Society to try to convince twenty-first-century lawmakers to uphold, not alter, his noted relative's accomplishment. Note also his testimony on this subject online at www.wilderness.org/newsroom/pdf/monuments_rooseveltstatement. pdf.

Fossil Expeditions Ethics, Laws, and Permits for Day Trips into Florida's Ancient Past

http://www.fossilexpeditions.com/fossil4.htm

Provides a detailed outline of rules that fossil hunters in the state of Florida must follow, and includes references to specific state laws.

"The State of Paleontological Collections in Industry"

http://jerword.nhm.ac.uk/archive/paleonet/1996/msg00205.html

Posted online on the paleonet listserv, this message, by H. Richard Lane of the Exploration and Production Technology Group at the Amoco Corporation in Houston, Texas, features a detailed request for data that will be of assistance in a research project.

"Vegetarian Diets: A Position Paper"
American Dietetic Association (1997)
URL: http://www.eatright.org/adap1197.html

SITE SUMMARY: This paper, putting vegetarianism in perspective, covers health implications of vegetarianism, nutrition considerations for vegetarianism, vegetarianism throughout the life cycle, and meal planning for vegetarian diets. It also includes a chart of food sources of nutrients of concern to vegetarians and a Food Guide Pyramid chart for vegetarian meal planning, and references.

DISCUSSION QUESTIONS AND ACTIVITIES

1. See this position paper's paragraphs one and two. What does scientific data suggest regarding a vegetarian diet? Give details. (Hint: For help with details, see also this paper's "Vegetarianism in Perspective" section [paragraph three], and its "Health Implications" section.)

2. See the "Vegetarianism in Perspective" section of this paper. Read paragraph one, then explain the differences of, and similarities between, the two types of vegetarians (e.g., lacto ovo vegetarians and vegans). Read paragraph three, then identify six considerations, other than health, that may lead or cause a person to adopt a vegetarian diet. Choose one of your answers to the activity just above, and describe with details, giving an example.

3. See this paper's "Nutrition Considerations for Vegetarians" section. Choose three points to consider. Compare and contrast these points with reference to the two types of vegetarians. Consider one point, and compare it with reference to a vegetarian and a non-vegetarian.

4. See this paper's "Vegetarianism Throughout the Life Cycle" section, paragraphs two and three. Are vegetarian diets appropriate and healthy for the general adolescent population? Is vegetarianism OK for athletes, adolescent athletes, and adolescent girls who are athletes? Identify connections between vegetarianism and adolescents with eating disorders. (Note: Include explanations in all your answers to the questions/activities just above, on how, why, or why not.) (Hint: See also the Vegetarian Kids and Teens Web site. Its url is cited in the Related Internet Sites section below.)

5. Read "What About Vegetarian Diets?" in the "Eat a Variety of Foods" section of the Dietary Guidelines featured in this book's chapter with the USDA Food Guide Pyramid. See also the Vegetarian Food Guide, the Vegetarian Food Pyramid, the Vegan Food Pyramid Web sites, and the Web sites VegSource and the International Vegetarian Union (including its Youth Pages). (Their urls are cited in the Related Internet Sites section below.) What are recommended daily food allowances for vegetarians? Suggest foods for a day's breakfast, lunch, and supper all for vegetarians. State positive and negative views on being a vegetarian, and tell why you would choose to be a vegetarian or not.

6. See the Web sites American Vegetarian Quotable Quotes, and A Unique Project to Promote Awareness of the Benefits of a Plant-Based Diet. (Their urls are cited in the Related Internet Sites section below.) Choose a well-known person or someone who has accomplished something noteworthy. Explain why this person's being a vegetarian helps define who that person is. Provide a quotation, if available.

RELATED INTERNET SITE(S)

Vegetarian Kids and Teens at the Vegetarian Resource Group Web Site

http://www.vrg.org/family/kidsindex.htm

This site provides links to nutrition information (e.g., Vegetarian Nutrition For Teens), recipes, book suggestions (e.g., a bibliography of young people's books with vegetarian or animal rights themes, and a booklist by the International Vegetarian Youth Pages), an answer to the question "How many kids are veggies?" Other links go to a poll on eating habits of youths ages eight through seventeen; information for student activists; plus details on, and a winning essay for, contests for ages nine through thirteen and fourteen through eighteen. More links go to other Web sites with information on vegetarian teens.

VegSource

http://www.vegsource.com

Featured are Latest Veg News, VegSource Sites (e.g., with doctors, EarthSave, Vegan Values, Taste of Health, Yes Youth Camps); discussion boards (e.g., VegScience, Veganism, Living Green, Get Fit, Veg Athletes, Veggie Youth); articles by professionals or in noted publications; article archives arranged by topic (e.g., health, activism, commentary, Q and A with an MD, protein and nutrients); Veg FAQs; Veggie Myths; guest essays; and a newsletter. An "our links" link leads to a Veg Central page which features with each site visit a new vegetarian-related quotation by a famous person, plus links to more news and articles. Ask an expert by posting a question on a moderated discussion board (e.g., VegScience with Dr. Campbell).

Vegan [Non-Dairy] Food Pyramid

http://www.vegsource.com/nutrition/pyramid_vegan.htm

Vegetarian Food Guide—A Conceptual Framework (1997)

http://www.llu.edu/llu/nutrition/vegguide.html
Released at the Third International Vegetarian Congress, and sponsored by the Loma Linda University Medical Center, this guide features an introduction, principles of healthful vegetarian diets, a vegetarian food guide pyramid, a detailed list of pyramid foods, and a discussion area.

Vegetarian Food Pyramid and Diet at the Healthy Eating Food Pyramids Web Site

http://www.oldwayspt.org (click the Healthy Eating Pyramids and Other Tools link)

Click the Vegetarian Pyramid icon link to go to the official traditional healthy Vegetarian Diet Pyramid, details of its contents, plus diet characteristics, and principles incorporated into this Pyramid that represents a healthy vegetarian diet. See also the links under supporting documents (e.g., vegetarianism history and culture, vegetarianism and its many forms, health and potential complications of a vegetarian diet).

Vegetarian Science at the International Vegetarian Union

http://www.ivu.org/science

See links to science articles by subject such as health and nutrition, vitamins, minerals, and nutrients. See also links to news and reports, a discussion area, FAQs, notes on the history of the Scientific Committee of the International Vegetarian Union, and a research references list. Note also the link to the IVU Youth Pages (also at www.ivu.org/youth).

Physicians Committee for Responsible Medicine (PCRM)

http://www.pcrm.org/health/index.html

Note the sections on information on vegetarian diets, recipes, preventive medicine and nutrition, advantages of vegetarian diets for children, commentary, and the Cancer Project. General links go to News, PCRM Clinical Research, Research Controversies and Issues, *Good Health Magazine*, resources, and search.

The New Four Food Groups from the Vegetarian Starter Kit by the PCRM

http://www.vegsource.com/food_groups.htm

This Web site gives details on the foods in the fruits, vegetables, whole grains, and legumes groups.

A Unique Project to Promote Awareness of the Benefits of a Plant-Based Diet

http://www.soystache.com/index.html

Note vegetarian-related links for physicians advocating a vegan diet; health facts; protein, iron, and calcium sources; recent articles in the media (e.g., teen vegetarians); interesting articles on the Web; new Web sites; vegan recipes; recent quotes; famous vegetarians' celebrity interviews; and not-so-famous vegetarians.

American Vegetarian Quotable Quotes

http://www.acorn.net/av//avquotes.html

Quotations are from noted people from the past and of the present, scientists and others, including Hippocrates, Charles Darwin, and Stephen Hawking.

"Discovering Our Selves: The Science of Emotion"
Tipper Gore (1998)
URL: http://gos.sbc.edu/g/gore2.html (or browse via G at //gos.sbc.edu/browse.html)

SITE SUMMARY: These remarks are from a keynote address at an event that was part of the Project on The Decade of the Brain. The event was sponsored by the National Institute of Mental Health and the Library of Congress. Presenting the remarks at the Library of Congress, on May 6, 1998, Mary Elizabeth Aitcheson Gore (known as Tipper Gore) was then the Mental Health Policy Advisor to President Bill Clinton, and the United States Second Lady as wife of then Vice President Al Gore. In the remarks, provided online at the Gifts of Speech Web site, Mrs. Gore spoke on definitions of, and connections between, emotions, the brain, and the mind, with reference to physical and mental health and illnesses in both present time and historical contexts. She also talked on interactions between people and between people and their environment/surroundings.

DISCUSSION QUESTIONS AND ACTIVITIES

1. See paragraph one; the first part, then the last part, then the center part. To what common greeting did Mrs. Gore refer? How did she define it? Which two science-related phrases did she mention that she thought might be discussed because of that greeting? Think of, and describe, a situation in which you might be when you might do what she defined.

2. See paragraph three. What did Mrs. Gore say the title of the conference evoked, with regard to science, and on what are they "shedding new understanding"? According to her, what are we learning more about, for example regarding the "fine lines" between which two science related conditions, and especially resulting from what interplay? What are we, according to her, also learning about the mind and the body, and especially with reference to what "linkage"? Give examples, basing them on what you discovered when you answered the questions just above.

3. See paragraph four. What did Mrs. Gore say that "this challenging conference topic" which "reminds us that who we are, the very center of what we call our selves," is "a product of"? How did she say our emotions and actions are interpreted and responded to by others? Think of, and describe, two things you have experienced or imagine you can experience, with reference to her three points from the first question above; and to what is indicated in your answer to the second question above.

4. See paragraph five. Why did Mrs. Gore say she was awestruck by knowledge in general, and neuroscience in particular?

5. See paragraphs twenty-three through twenty-seven. Describe what, according to Mrs. Gore, people of past times (e.g., the Greeks, Plato, people of the Middle Ages, and people of the seventeenth and eighteenth centuries) thought were responsible for people's good health, physical illnesses, and mental conditions. Identify, according to Mrs. Gore, what is known today, and which three things are possible "with that knowledge."

6. See the last sentence of paragraph nine, and identify which four things, including three scientific ones, have started to unveil "the mysteries of the mind," and in what amount of time.

7. Read the first sentence of paragraph ten, and identify what Mrs. Gore thought was "rather interesting." Refer to her comment and include a medical science example of the body or mind in your answer.

8. See paragraphs thirteen, twelve, and eleven, plus the list with paragraph twenty-six. Mrs. Gore mentioned "there is a chink in the walls" and "the walls are beginning to crumble." Think metaphorically as you identify the three "walls" that she referred to, and identify what, scientifically, are four things "chipping away" at these "walls." State the names, and describe,

four particular illnesses she mentioned, then identify and describe another one, and four types of it. Choose one of the illnesses referred to just above, and describe how it has been affected by the "walls" and the things "chipping away" at those "walls."

9. See paragraph eighteen. What, did Mrs. Gore say, are four things we have learned with reference to the way our "brains are 'wired' biochemically"? Give one of her examples, then think of, and describe, an example of your own. (Hints: Note her "colorful" phrases and use of the word "tapestry.")

10. See paragraph nineteen. According to Mrs. Gore, how did "the capacity for human emotions [arise]"? Give your own example of what she meant by "but it seems as if the spectrum of our emotions extends far beyond that of other species" because "our emotions give color and meaning to our environment." Think of, and describe, another example that you think explains what she meant when she added "our environment, and our interactions within it, add to our emotional lexicon." (Hints: State four basic words she cites to describe emotions. Tell what she said each word has, and what they do with reference to emotions.)

11. See paragraph twenty-two. What are four "questions that guide the search of today's researchers in the science of emotions," according to Mrs. Gore? Think of and explain your own answers to the four questions, plus examples for two of them.

12. See paragraph twenty-eight. What is something the "science of emotion" can help explain and demonstrate?

13. See paragraph twenty-nine. Read what the nineteenth-century American writer, observer of nature, and philosopher Ralph Waldo Emerson once observed with reference to meteorology (the study of weather). Make a type of Farmer's Almanac as Emerson defined it. (Hints: For help to get you started, see paragraph thirty, and identify three basic things "the masters of science" [including some conference participants] were "helping to disclose" as they aimed to "[elucidate] the science of the brain that spells the differences between health and illness of the mind" even as they aimed to "do more than enlighten us" and "explain why we feel." Refer to the third activity in Question/Activity no. 10 above.)

14. See paragraph twenty-one. Read and keep in mind what Mrs. Gore quoted from the writings of William James, the author of *The Principles of Psychology* (1890). Next, visit the Web site with James' article "What Is an Emotion?"; reading especially paragraphs one through four. Identify some emotions he referred to. Reveal what he wrote on their connections with the brain, and the body. (Option: Add more details from later paragraphs in James' article.)

15. Go to the Brain Awareness Week Web site, found as cited in the Related Internet Sites section below. Click the Science Information link, then the www.dana.org Your Brain Resource link, then the links for *BrainWork: The Neuroscience Newsletter* and *The Brain in the News*. Find summaries called abstracts of journal articles or newspaper items about the brain and an emotion and cite their titles (e.g., *The Brain in the News*, September 13, 2002, and July 31, 2002, have annotated links to articles on "How Brain, and the Spirit, Adapt to a 9/11 World"; and "Worried? Afraid? May Be Genetic"; and BrainWork, January/February 2002, and March/April 2001, have articles in PDF format on "Molecules of Emotion" and "Dogged by Emotions"). Choose one subject and write your own essay, or a summary called an abstract for an article, different from the article cited but on a similar subject.

RELATED INTERNET SITE(S)

Tipper Gore's "Discovering Our Selves: The Science of Emotion"

http://lcweb.loc.gov/loc/brain/emotion/MrsGore.html
Another version of the remarks, as found at the Library of Congress Web site.

Health Emotions Research Institute

http://www.healthemotions.org (click sitemap link)

Find details on this organization's objective (to "scientifically determine how emotions influence health") by scrolling down this page, noting especially links to Background (with mission, lead scientists, and affiliate scientists), Research (e.g., Current Projects with articles including "Effects of Stress and Mood on Disease," "Responses to Negative Emotionally Provoking Events, "The Biological Bases of Positive Affective Styles," and "Biological Effects of Meditation"), News/Events (with links to "Why Files" and *Science Magazine*'s online items on the Institute's research), Press Releases (e.g., "Getting Emotional—What Science Says about the Power of Emotions" April 16, 1998; and "Subject to Intense Scientific Scrutiny, Emotions Appear More Important Than Ever" March 13, 1998), and Special Features (e.g., "Mechanisms Underlying Coping"). A subscription to a Health Emotions Newsletter is available (in PDF format) via a Communications link. Signing a guestbook brings the latest news to site visitors.

Neuroscience for Kids

http://faculty.washington.edu/chudler/neurok.html

Informative items by various authors for young people of all ages are at this site which is supported by a Science Education Partnership Award from the National Center for Research Resources, set up and maintained by Eric H. Chudler, Ph.D. The items will help young people find out about the brain and its connection to the nervous system. Features include Internet Neuroscience Resources, Neuroscientist Network with Questions and Answers, Neuroscience in the News, Brain Awareness Week, online and off-line articles and books, free newsletter, FAQs, What Is Neuroscience for Kids? and other resources. On the search page, do searches on the Web, and at Neuroscience for Kids, both provided here. Use the phrases Emotions and the Brain and Science of Emotions to get links that go to information on these subjects.

Mental Health: A Report of the Surgeon General

http://www.surgeongeneral.gov/library/mentalhealth/toc.html

Among the eight chapters and their various parts, note Chapter One with its Introduction and Themes, plus The Science Base of the Report, and Reliance on Scientific Evidence; Chapter Two on The Fundamentals of Mental Health and Mental Illness (including the Neuroscience of Mental Health, the Integrative Science of Mental Illness and Mental Health, Theories of Psychological Development, Nature and Nurture: The Ultimate Synthesis); Chapter Three on Children and Mental Health (including adolescents); Chapter Four on Adults and Mental Health; and Chapter Eight on A Vision of the Future.

"Young People's Perceptions of the Causes of Mental Health Problems"

http://www.acys.utas.edu.au/ncys/nyars/mental/chapt-12.html

This document is chapter twelve of "Mental Health and Young People: A Report into the Nature of Mental Health Problems Experienced by Young People" (1992) for Australia's National Youth Affairs Research Scheme. It is provided online at Australia's Clearing House for Youth Studies. It includes references to emotional and behavior problems. It deals also with young people's views of mental health services.

"What Is an Emotion?" by William James (1884)

http://psychclassics.yorku.ca/James/emotion.htm

This article, first published in print in the journal *Mind*, has a detailed analysis that is related to the subject of the James quotation that Mrs. Gore quoted in her remarks.

Emotions in *Encyclopedia Britannica*

http://www.britannica.com

Select from the pull-down menu the *Britannica Student Encyclopedia*. Type the word Emotions in the search box, and click Go. Search also by choosing *Britannica Concise Encyclopedia*, Websites via britannica.com or search all of britannica.com. Lists of links to encyclopedia articles or Web sites on the subject will appear. Searches are free, but to access the articles or sites, signing up for seventy-two free hours or subscribing to britannica.com is required. A few items are freely accessible.

Brain and Mind Magazine

http://www.epub.org.br/cm

At this Web site for this magazine for average people who are interested in neuroscience, scroll to links to the current issue's and past issues' articles (e.g., "Our Feelings: Why Do We Have Them?" in the July–September 2002 issue; "Limbic System: The Center of Emotions" and "Phobias: When Fear Is a Disease" in the March–May 1996 issue; "What Is Mind?" in the December 1997–February 1998 issue; "Brain and Environment" and "Architecture of the Brain" in the March–May 1997 issue). The magazine is provided by Brazilian psychologist Silvia Helen Cardoza, Ph.D., and the Center for Biomedical Informatics. See also the link to Virtual Talks (audio and video) on Neuroscience.

"Environmental Psychology" in the *Encyclopedia of Environmental Science*

http://www.snre.umich.edu/~rdeyoung/envtpsych.html

A clearly outlined investigation, and a clear analysis, by R. DeYoung, on the interrelationship between environments (natural, educational, informational, and societal) and human behavior.

Dealing with Feelings

http://www.kidshealth.org/kid/feeling

See links to information under the topics My Emotions and Behaviors, My Thoughts and Feelings, My Home and Family, My Friends, and My School.

Mental Health Information Center

http://www.mentalhealth.org

Click the Children's Mental Health link for links to information on children's and adolescents' mental health. Do individual searches at "this site" in the search box with the words Emotions and Tipper Gore, then click Go to get a list of links that lead to information on these subjects.

Project on the Decade of the Brain, 1990–1999

http://lcweb.loc.gov/loc/brain

Featured on this home page for the Project which was sponsored by the National Institutes of Health, the National Institute of Mental Health, and the Library of Congress, are statements on the Project's initiative, and goal, a link to a presidential proclamation in 1990 by George H.W. Bush, and more links to publications, suggested activities, the Brain Web, and Brain Awareness Week.

Brain Awareness Week Home Page

http://www.dana.org/brainweek

Read about Brain Awareness Week, and when it occurs, then see the links that go to science information (a brain facts sheet), educational resources, puzzles, community outreach suggestions, an international events calendar, information for journalists, media tools, announcements, and a presidential statement (in PDF format) by George W. Bush.

Biography of Tipper Gore

http://clinton3.nara.gov/WH/EOP/VP_Wife/megbio.html

Covering Mrs. Gore's education and life accomplishments up to and including the time when she was the U.S. Second Lady, this Web page notes that she earned a B.A. degree in Psychology and an M.A. degree in Psychology, and that she has worked in prominent positions for advocacy groups whose goals are to help children and young people who participate in physical fitness or are involved with emotional, behavioral, and drug abuse.

Tipper Gore—Honorary Degree Recipient—Chicago School of Professional Psychology

http://www.csopp.edu/pages/eventsTGore.html

This site provides detailed information about Mrs. Gore's accomplishments, including her experiences with mental illness, as reasons for her being awarded this degree on November 11, 2001. It includes a link to the Web site for the National Mental Health Awareness Campaign which she is responsible for establishing and of which she is the honorary chairperson. There is also a link to a summary of the remarks that she gave during the degree ceremony.

Excerpts from "Keynote Speech at Institute of Noetic Sciences Conference on Healing Journeys" and Other Documents at IONS Online
Edgar Mitchell (1998–)
URL: http://www.ions.org
(click Events, Previous Events, *Healing Journeys* conference; scroll to Mitchell excerpts)
and (click Search, type Mitchell, click search button, select a link to an item by Mitchell)

SITE SUMMARY: Mitchell, an Apollo astronaut and the sixth man to walk on the Moon, reveals in his writings and talks an insight ("a sense of awe at the wonder of the universe and an interconnectedness beyond [his] previous experience") he acquired while on the Apollo 14 moon mission in 1971. He also reveals what that insight caused him to do, "working from the scientific point of view." He notes, in addition, what he sees for the future. The speech was presented by Mitchell as founder (in 1973) of the Institute of Noetic Sciences (IONS), whose name originates from the Greek word for intuitive knowing. This organization now aims to further Mitchell's premise "to expand knowledge of the nature and potential of the mind and spirit, and to apply that knowledge to advance health and well-being for humanity and our planet."

DISCUSSION QUESTIONS AND ACTIVITIES

1. Find and read or listen to one or more documents (in print or audio) by Mitchell that you find at the IONS Web site. Describe and explain, including quotations, Mitchell's insight which came to him during the Apollo 14 moon mission, then when exactly he experienced it, how he reacted to it, what he came to realize because of it, and the "primary issue" in his mind that involved what to discover, what to pursue, and how. Provide an example or two based on what you found out that he said as you answered the questions above. Note especially the second part of your answer to what he came to realize and to the "primary issue" in his mind.
2. Find a document by Mitchell at the IONS Web site. How did Mitchell answer his own question "What is the nature of consciousness?" Answer his question, giving a particular example based on the general topic in his answer.
3. Find a document by Mitchell at the IONS Web site. Describe how he refers to the future. Keeping any metaphoric references in mind that you discovered when answering the Question/Activity just above, note his question "Now as we go into the future, which task and which approach do we take?" Identify what he answered to this question, then answer his question giving your own example.
4. Visit the Institute of Noetic Sciences Web site. (Its url is cited in the Related Internet Sites section below.) Give a brief description to answer the question, or part of the question "What are Noetic Sciences?" (an article at the IONS site). Choose a Noetic Science or an aspect of one. Think of, provide, and describe an example of it, and what it means to you and/or society. (See also "noetic sciences" on the "What Is Noetic?" page.)
5. Select an article you find at the IONS Web site (found as noted in the IONS Web site description in the Related Internet Sites section below). Identify and describe a viewpoint in the chosen article. Apply this viewpoint to something scientific with relation to the world, and, if possible, to you.
6. Choose a quotation about an experience an astronaut other than Mitchell has had, as noted at the Web site Quotes from Astronauts. (Its url is cited in the Related Internet Sites section below.) Comment on how you think this quotation influenced or influences this astronaut, people on Earth, and you.

RELATED INTERNET SITE(S)

Edgar Mitchell, Apollo Astronaut—Biography—Astronauts Hall of Fame

http://www.astronauthalloffame.com/astronauts/mitchell.htm

Edgar Mitchell—Articles, Biography, Books, Links

http://www.edmitchellapollo14.com

Quotes from Astronauts at Earth from Space Online

http://www.planetscapes.com/solar/eng/earthsp.htm

Institute of Noetic Sciences

http://www.ions.org/index.asp (click the About link, then the What Is Noetic? link; or click Research link or Publications link, then browse; or click Search and search by last name)

Find links to articles such as "What Are Noetic Sciences?" by Willis Harman, "Toward a Noetic Model of Medicine" by Marilyn Schlitz, "Bio-Electromagnetics: Energy Medicine—A Challenge for Science" by Beverly Rubik, "Prayer: A Challenge for Science" by Rupert Shildrake, "Behavioral Links to Cancer" by Linda Temoshok, "Split Between Spirit and Nature" by Ralph Metzner, and "Mysterious Light: A Scientist's Odyssey" by Peter Russell, and "Profile of IONS Founder Edgar Mitchell" by Marilyn Schlitz. See also on a Research page links to six Research Modules areas (e.g., energy medicine, states of consciousness, emerging worldviews). See in addition Features This Week, Mission Statement, Our Vision, Inside IONS, FAQs, IONS History, awards, discussion, and community.

"First Educator Mission Specialist Astronaut Named"
National Aeronautics and Space Administration, News Release (1998)
URL: http://spacelink.nasa.gov/NASA.News/NASA.News.Releases/Previous.News. Releases/98.News.Releases/98-01.News.Releases/98-01-16.1st.Educator.Mission.Specialist

SITE SUMMARY: This news release of January 16, 1998 reveals that NASA had determined it appropriate to include educator mission specialists in the astronaut corps. It states the reasons, notes the requirements, and names science teacher Barbara Morgan as the first candidate.

DISCUSSION QUESTIONS AND ACTIVITIES

1. State two reasons why NASA decided to establish an educator mission specialist designation for another kind of astronaut. (Hint: See the News Release, paragraph two.)

2. See the News Release, paragraph two, then see the Web sites for the NASA Educator Mission Specialist Homepage, the NASA Astronaut Selection Homepage, and the NASA Astronaut Biography of Barbara Morgan. Identify the education requirements, in general, for educator mission specialist astronauts. How does Morgan fulfill these requirements? How is the educator mission specialist astronaut category similar to yet different from the mission specialist astronaut category? (The urls for the Web sites referred to are cited in the Related Internet Sites section below.)

3. How is the educator mission specialist astronaut different from the teacher in space astronaut category that was set up in the 1980s, with which Morgan was connected? What was Morgan's part then? How is the educator mission specialist astronaut different from the payload mission astronaut? (For information, see the NASA Astronaut Selection Homepage, especially its online vacancy brochure [found as stated in Question/Activity no. 2 above] plus the *Education Week* article "Educator Astronaut Trained for New Mission," and the CNN item "Barbara Morgan Looks Forward to Becoming Educator Astronaut." See also the Christa McAuliffe Biography at the Christa McAuliffe Planetarium Web site. [Web site urls are cited in the Related Internet Sites section below.])

4. Why is the educator mission specialist astronaut category different from another special kind of astronaut that has included politicians (e.g., Senator Jake Garn and Congressman Bill Nelson turned astronaut for one mission each, different from career astronaut John Glenn turned senator), millionaires, and a planned journalist in space category? (Hint: For information, see the NASA Astronaut Biographies Web site whose url is in this book's Appendix B, the First Space Tourist: Dennis Tito, and the "NASA Chose James Schefter For the Journalist in Space Program" Web sites whose urls are cited in the Related Internet Sites section below.)

5. What will the educator mission specialist astronauts be required to do, something which is not a requirement for other kinds of astronauts? How specific does NASA get when determining what educator mission specialist astronauts will do? How are NASA and teachers compatible, according to Morgan, and what, according to her, is "the best thing about all this"? (Hint: For help, see Web sites cited in the Related Internet Sites section below, e.g., the NASA Educator Mission Specialist Homepage, Educator Astronaut Program, NASA Astronaut Selection Homepage, *Education Week* Interview with Barbara Morgan, NEA Today—Interview with Barbara Morgan, and the *Education Week* article "Educator Astronaut Trained for New Mission.")

6. See the NEA Today—Interview with Barbara Morgan Web site. (Its url is cited in the Related Internet Sites section below.) Note the interview's question and comment number three, and tell why, according to Morgan, sending an educator into space is so important, then explain

why you think she made this comment. Note the interview's question and comment number two, especially the last part of the first paragraph, and tell why being a teacher can help someone be an astronaut. (For more information, see the CNN item "Barbara Morgan Looks Forward to Becoming Educator Astronaut." Its url is cited in the Related Internet Sites section below.)

7. Remembering one of Morgan's comments which you found for Question/Activity no. 6 above, apply it to a space mission situation. (Hint: Check the main Web sites and the Related Internet Sites in this book's chapters on the NASA Life Sciences Data Archive, the Apollo Lunar Surface Journal transcripts, and news from past manned space flights, or past space shuttle missions, at the NASA Human Space Flight News Web site [whose url is cited in this book's Appendix B].)

8. Imagine you would like to work toward becoming an educator mission specialist astronaut. What would you study in particular? (Hint: For general help, see your answer to Question/Activity no. 2 above.) What might be a special project, based on your particular area of study, that you would like to do while on a mission in space? (For specific help, see the Web sites in the Hint for Question/Activity no. 7 above, the Web site with "Scientific Prerequisites for the Human Exploration of Space" as cited in this book's Appendix I: Other Helpful and Interesting Science Web Sites, the featured Web site and the Related Internet Sites in this book's chapter on "Toward a World Strategy and Utilization of Our Natural Satellite," plus future or planned Space Shuttle, International Space Station, and other future [e.g., Mars, the Moon] missions, or missions involving Science, at the NASA Human Space Flight News Web site found as cited in the Hint in Question/Activity no. 7 above.)

RELATED INTERNET SITE(S)

"Teacher Turned Astronaut Assisting NASA"

www.dailynews.com/Stories/0,1413,200~20954~1152351,00.html

On February 2, 2003, this news item revealed, via the *Los Angeles Daily News* Web site, that educator astronaut Barbara Morgan, still part of the educator in space program, is focusing on what she can do to help as people struggle to cope with the Columbia shuttle tragedy, while she keeps in mind what she said in an April 2002 interview: "You do everything you can, in your training and in . . . the testing . . . ," then "you go forward."

NASA Astronaut Biographies—Barbara Morgan—Educator Mission Specialist

http://www.jsc.nasa.gov/Bios/htmlbios/morgan.html

Updated June 2000, and provided by NASA Lyndon B. Johnson Space Flight Center.

"Barbara Morgan to Be Second Teacher in Space"

http://www.spaceref.com/news/viewnews.html?id=647

This December 12, 2002 news announcement has quotations from Morgan, space shuttle commander Scott Kelly, NASA administrator Sean O'Keefe, and Senator Barbara Mukulski. It reveals in general what Morgan would have done on STS 118 in November 2003 on the Columbia space shuttle (and may still do in some way on another spacecraft), what it would mean for today's children and the future of space exploration, and how it would have carried on the legacy of Christa McAuliffe (the first teacher astronaut who died in the 1986 Challenger space shuttle tragedy).

"NASA's First Educator Astronaut Assigned First Flight"

http://www.nasajobs.nasa.gov/EducatorMissionSpecialist/ea_1st_flight.htm or *http://www.nasajobs.nasa.gov* (click link)

This feature article of December 12, 2002 has information on Morgan's background, NASA training, her planned destination in space and when she was scheduled to go before the Columbia shuttle tragedy. Links go to a biography and more information.

"Educator Astronaut Trained for New Mission" in *Education Week*, April 24, 2002

http://www.edweek.org/ew/newstory.cfm?slug=32nasa.h21

This article notes that the U.S. Department of Education is working with NASA to develop science standards with applications to the space program. It also reveals how the educator astronaut is different from the teacher astronaut of the 1980s. There are also related links (e.g., Space Shuttle Flight Launches School Activities, November 11, 1998).

Education World Interview with Barbara Morgan—May 2000

http://www.education-world.com/a_curr/curr219.shtml

NEA Today—Interview with Barbara Morgan—January 2000

http://www.nea.org/neatoday/0001/intervw.html

"Teacher Turned Astronaut Lives Dream"

http://www.acmi.canoe.ca/CNEWSSpace9912/13_morgan.html

This Canada-based news site provides an account of Morgan as the first educator astronaut, as of December 13, 1999, with information on her credentials, preparation, eagerly waiting for the mission, and silver and gold astronaut wings.

"Barbara Morgan Looks Forward to Becoming Educator Astronaut"

http://www.cnn.com/TECH/9801/20/space.teacher

On January 20, 1998 Morgan recalled Christa McAuliffe, her own work for the NASA education program, then NASA's panel reviewing her case and recommending her as an astronaut mission specialist, and why she believes in the educator in space program. See also the quicktime video of Morgan preparing for space, a video link to CNN science correspondent Ann Kellan and the Associated Press (both contributors to a report featuring Morgan), and links to related stories.

NASA Educator Mission Specialist Homepage

http://nasajobs.nasa.gov/educatormissionspecialist

Educator Astronaut Program

http://edspace.nasa.gov

NASA Astronaut Selection Homepage

http://www.nasajobs.nasa.gov/astronauts/index.htm

See requirements for, and duties of, any mission specialist astronaut, plus more information on this type of astronaut, and the payload specialist type of astronaut, via links to FAQs, application instructions and forms, selection and training, and an online vacancy announcement brochure with details on academic and other qualifications.

International Technology Education Association (ITEA)

http://www.iteawww.org

Morgan is a member of this organization for technology teachers. Note its NASA-sponsored Technology for All Americans Project at www.iteawww.org/TAA/index.htm.

"Teachers Still Eager for Trip Aboard Shuttle [After the Columbia Shuttle Tragedy]"

http://www.centredaily.com/mld/centredaily/news/5231837.htm

This February 21, 2003 news item revealed that support still exists for the astronaut educator program, with comments by teachers who still want to be astronauts, and by Leland Melvin (the astronaut manager of the continuing educator astronaut program).

Christa McAuliffe Biography at Christa McAuliffe Planetarium Web Site

http://www.starport.com/cm_bio.htm

This biography, of the teacher for whom Morgan was the backup astronaut in the 1980s temporary teacher in space program, features what led to McAuliffe becoming the program's candidate, what she planned to do while in space, and how her legacy continues although she never got to complete her mission. Also included are McAuliffe quotations, and how U.S. President Ronald Reagan was involved with the program.

First Space Tourist: Dennis Tito

http://www.space.com/dennistito

"NASA Chose James Schefter for the Journalist in Space Program"

http://www.space.com/news/schefter_obit_010126.html

A *Space Illustrated* editor tells of achievements of a veteran journalist who wrote about the space program's early days, and was chosen as a finalist for the Journalist in Space Program which was canceled after the 1986 Challenger space shuttle tragedy.

"Improving Public Understanding: Guidelines for Communicating the Emerging Science on Nutrition, Food Safety and Health"
The Harvard School of Public Health and The International Food Information Council Foundation (1998)
URL: http://www.ific.org/proactive/newsroom/release.vtml?id=17560 or via search at http://www.food-information.org/food_safety.asp

SITE SUMMARY: These guidelines, first published in the *Journal of the National Cancer Institute*, February 4, 1998, are provided to help in clearly communicating to the public, the scientific process, the evolutionary nature of research, the identity of scientific evidence, and scientists' different views, all as related to the science of nutrition, food safety, and health, from the viewpoints of scientists, journal editors, journalists, and special interest groups (i.e., for consumers). These guidelines are meant to result in communication that has effects on the public's behavior and well-being regarding the science of nutrition, food safety, and health, and for helping the public understand these subjects because people's interest in them has been growing for years.

DISCUSSION QUESTIONS AND ACTIVITIES

1. See, preceding the guidelines, comments written by Timothy Johnson, Medical Editor of the ABC TV program Good Morning America. Which four things did he urge regarding these guidelines? What, did he say, "just might make a difference," and how? Which three things did he think "the public wants"? Choose a subject on nutrition, food safety, or health-related nutrition or food, and apply to this subject the first two points of what Dr. Johnson said.
2. Briefly state the main points of the general guidelines, then those of the guidelines for scientists, for journalists, journal editors, and special interest groups.
3. Imagine you are a journalist, scientist, journal editor, then a member of a special interest group with concern for consumers. Choose four particular subjects from the items you see at any of the Web sites cited at the end of this Question/Activity or choose four particular subjects you think of after seeing the general topics of the items at any of these Web sites. Apply to the subjects you thought of, or chose, the general guidelines for all, then the particular guidelines for journalists, scientists, journal editors, and special interest groups with concern for consumers. See the Web sites Food and Nutrition Web sites, Institute of Food Science and Technology (UK)—Current Hot Topics; FAQs About Food Science, Nutrition, and Safety at the Institute for Food Science and Safety; and nutrition-related news in News Updates and Special Reports at the Center for Science in the Public Interest. (Their urls are cited in the Related Internet Sites section below, or in this book's Appendix B.)
4. See the document "Using Science to Avoid Chaos in the Food Realm," especially its question "How, exactly, do we base food safety discussions on science?" (Its url is cited in the Related Internet Sites section below.) Provide details on the answer to this question. Offer your own ideas to help answer the question, then state your reasons to support your ideas. Also support what you say by citing sources that you find (if available on your subject) at the Web sites cited in Question/Activity no. 3 above.

RELATED INTERNET SITE(S)

Institute of Food Science and Technology (UK)—Current Hot Topics

http://www.ifst.org/hottop.htm

Recent reports found via links have included titles such as "Genetic Modification and Food," "The Use of Irradiation for Food Quality and Safety," "Food Poisoning and Its Prevention,"

"Food Allergens," "Foodbourne Campylobacteria and How to Safeguard Against It," and "New Approach to Risk Assessment of Natural Toxicants in Food."

FAQs about Food Science, Nutrition and Safety—Institute of Food Science and Safety

http://www.ifst.org/ifstfaq.htm

Topics addressed are arranged in four groups that include Science and Food Fads, Food and Nutrition, Food Safety, and Additives and Packaging.

"Using Science to Avoid Chaos in the Food Safety Realm" by Thomas J. Billy

http://www.fsis.usda.gov/OA/speeches/1999/tb_chamber.htm

As the USDA Food Safety and Inspection Service Administrator, and as the chairman of the Codex Alimentarius Commission working to develop international food standards, Billy addressed the question "How, exactly, do we base food safety discussions on science?"

President's Council on Food Safety—Preliminary Food Safety Strategic Plan, and Draft

http://www.foodsafety.gov/~fsg/cstrpl-3.html

This document for public review was issued on January 7, 2000. It includes background information, an introduction, a Vision Statement, the Overarching Goal, Science and Risk Assessment, Risk Management and Risk Communication Goals, Food Safety: The Nation's Challenge, Food Safety Regulation Today, Strategic Planning, Organizational Considerations, President's Food Safety Initiative, President's Council on Food Safety, and an afterword.

Food and Nutrition Web Sites

http://www.riskworld.com/websites/webfiles/ws6aa006.htm

Under Risk World Departments, see links to Reports and Papers, News, News Archives, and Abstracts. Under Internal Web Sites, see the link to the Risk Science and Law Group.

"Learning from the Chimpanzees: A Message Humans Can Understand"
Jane Goodall (1998)
URL: http://www.sciencemag.org/feature/data/150essay.shl (click link)

SITE SUMMARY: Goodall, an ethnologist and conservationist, has studied chimpanzees in the wild for nearly fifty years at Gombe Stream Research Center, Gombe National Park, Tanzania, Africa. Now she heads the Jane Goodall Institute, set up in 1977 and dedicated to the conservation and understanding of wildlife. In this essay, Goodall reveals ways that scientists traditionally studied animals and the changes in the scientific study of animals that she and others helped to bring about. (This essay is one of a group of Essays on Science and Society written by various authors from 1848 through 1998 and represent the best *Science Magazine* articles of one hundred fifty years.)

DISCUSSION QUESTIONS AND ACTIVITIES

1. Read paragraphs one, two, and three. When Goodall began her study of wild chimpanzees, which three things about animals wouldn't ethnologists talk about because scientists did not think of them as "hard sciences"? What, did Goodall say, did one ethnologist acknowledge, yet thought should be "swept under the carpet"? What are four things Goodall didn't realize animals aren't supposed to have? What did she not realize was unscientific to discuss about animals, according to ethnologists of that time?

2. Read more of paragraphs one, two, and three. What was something that was supposed to be appropriate to do and what was something that was not appropriate to do when studying animals? If, according to Goodall, someone "in scientific circles" did _____, what was she or he guilty of? How did Goodall defy an editor when she wrote her first scientific paper, and how did this help chimpanzees?

3. Read paragraph four. (See also the Web site: Discover Chimpanzees. [Its url is cited in the Related Internet Sites section below.]) What did Goodall, in her first observations, discover chimpanzees could do? What problem did this cause, according to her mentor, Louis Leakey, in his telegram to her? How did people react to this discovery? What other observations of chimpanzee behavior by Goodall were people fascinated by? Who was David Greybeard, what did he do, and why was he important to what Goodall discovered?

4. Read paragraphs six and seven. What gradually became fashionable in animal study? How did this come about, in part, especially during the 1960s? What then became impossible, what was proven, and how? What has changed today with reference to ethnology? What is now commonplace? What has happened because of new information acquired in the 1960s?

5. While keeping Question/Activity no. 4 above in mind, read paragraph five. What special project was started in the mid-1960s? What was involved and what was it supposed to teach? Who were the two people involved? What did the scientists' discovery imply? How did the scientific community react? What did some other scientists do as a result of the discovery? What did these scientists confirm? (For some help, see the Web document "Can Chimps Talk?" [Its url is cited in the Related Internet Sites section below.])

6. Read paragraph eight. In addition to what you found by answering Question/Activity no. 3 above, what are five other facts that have emerged from Goodall's years of research involving the Gombe chimpanzees? As a result of these facts, what are now people's, both non-scientists' and scientists', attitudes and society's concern? What do you think you can do to show your concern? Explain. (For some help, see the Jane Goodall Institute Web site. Its url is cited in the Related Internet Sites section below.)

7. Visit a zoo, but before your visit, read the story about a happening at the Detroit Zoo that Goodall tells in her essay. What happened between a man and a chimpanzee there? What is

something in the story, actually the man's reason for doing something, that you may be able to do at the zoo? Prepare to take notes on a chimpanzee and on another animal that have as many of Goodall's seven facts you can include, plus, if possible, what you referred to when answering the question just above on the man's reason for doing something. Include as well, two other things Goodall did, which you discovered when answering Question/Activity no. 2 above. After your zoo visit, write two three-hundred-word essays based on your observations and notes.

RELATED INTERNET SITE(S)

Jane Goodall Institute

http://www.janegoodall.org/sitemap/index.html

Check links to Jane Goodall's Reasons for Hope and biography links (e.g., Day in the Life, Curriculum Vitae, Publications), Chimpanzees (e.g., characteristics, habitat, social organization, and communication), Jane Goodall Institute information (e.g., FAQs, links, programs, sanctuaries), Roots and Shoots (an environmental program and involvement activities for young people), and News (e.g., on the Institute's research, Chimpanzoo, and Jane's travels).

Discover Chimpanzees

http://www.discoverchimpanzees.org

At this site, created by the Science Museum of Minnesota, with the National Science Foundation, and the University of Minnesota, click links to Meet Featured Researcher, Meet Featured Chimpanzee, Gombe Update, or Try Featured Activity. In the upper left, place a mouse arrow to see a pull-down menu with links to Meet the Researchers, Meet the Chimpanzees, Tour Gombe, and links. Find out about the Jane Goodall Institute's Center for Primate Studies via a link on the Meet the Researchers page.

"Can Chimps Talk?" February 15, 1994

http://pubpages.unh.edu/~jel/nova.html

This transcript of an interview on a PBS-TV NOVA program features psychologists Allen and Beatrix Gardner of the University of Nevada and their pioneering work in the 1960s.

Chimpanzee and Human Communication Institute

http://www.cwu.edu/~cwuchci/main.html

Featured are FAQs, Enrichment, Chimpanzee Biographies, Next of Kin, and Friends, plus Teacher Information.

Excerpt from "If a Chimpanzee Could Talk" (1997), by Jerry H. Gill

http://www.uapress.arizona.edu/samples/sam1011.htm

"Overleaf Introduction" by Sylvia Earle to *Reefs at Risk*
(1998)
URL: www.dec.ctu.edu.vn/cdrom/cd5/ReefBase/HTML/RISK/html/body_intro.html

SITE SUMMARY: Earle, a groundbreaking marine scientist, looks at a part of the natural world where her career takes her. She indicates the beauty and scientific importance of reefs, what they mean to the earth's human inhabitants. She also reveals what the authors of *Reefs at Risk* have done for reefs at risk. This introduction, reproduced from the book's overleaf, is accompanied online at this site by links to the book's key findings, foreword, contents and an about page. (The World Resources Institute's Web site at http://www.wri/reefsatrisk/reefrisk.html features a link to the text of the *Reefs at Risk* book [in PDF format] with a guide to the book.)

DISCUSSION QUESTIONS AND ACTIVITIES

1. See paragraph one. Identify three types of "a fair cross-section of the major divisions of life that have ever existed on this planet" that Earle witnessed one afternoon during a dive into an ocean and its coral reef, as one of her first experiences as a marine scientist; then give one example each for two of the types from among her examples, noticing and stating, when possible, her poetic yet scientifically accurate descriptions. Give details of your chosen examples. For data see these Web site areas: NOAA's Coral Reefs; Cousteau Society's Coral Reefs, Marine Mammals and Marine Protected Areas; Missouri Botanical Garden's Marine Ecosystems in Evergreen Projects Adventures; and Oceanography in Science and Technology at the Office of Naval Research. (Their urls are cited in the Related Internet Sites section below.) Adapt the second part of the first question just above and provide details to Earle's August 16, 1999 dive's Species List. (Find url as stated just above for Web sites.)

2. See paragraphs one and two. Why does Earle say her dive of years ago and a recent dive are like journeys in time, from a scientific viewpoint?

3. See paragraph three. What does Earle mean when she says "worldwide . . . there are coral reefs and entire reef systems that appear to be as pristine today as they were in ages past"? After this comment, Earle adds: "but there is no doubt that there is an alarming global trend of decline." What does she say were, are, causes for this trend "until half a century ago" and since the 1950s? Why should what Earle says regarding the "global trend of decline" concern us when we think of what she says about pristine reefs?

4. See paragraph four. What "concern has been growing for decades . . . especially in recent years" according to Earle, and why? What have people come to realize? What are four considerations that reasons for realizations "both embrace and transcend"? Provide and explain one example each of considerations no. 2 and no. 4, including something you do, or could do. (For help with the activity stated just above, see the Web sites: Ocean Planet—Resource Room, Woods Hole Oceanographic Institute [its Research, K–12 Resources, Science School and Undergraduate Research Opportunities], Cousteau Society [its News and Expeditions] and International Year of the Ocean [its In Your Neighborhood]. [Their urls are cited in the Related Internet Sites section below, or in this book's Appendix G.])

5. See last part of paragraph four. What were three subjects of important questions asked in the year 1997, which the United Nations declared as "the International Year of the Reef"? Give details. (For help see Web sites on the International Year of the Reef 1997, NOAA's What Is the International Year of the Reef? and Earle's Ocean Planet Interview. [Their urls are cited in the Related Internet Sites section below.])

6. See parts of paragraphs five and six. According to Earle, what has not been done although coral reefs have been the subjects of many research projects in recent years? Why is it important that

what has not been done should be done? What approach have authors of the *Reefs at Risk Report* taken, and what does this make possible?

7. See other parts of paragraphs six and five. What is important about natural systems (e.g., oceans and coral reefs) with reference to people? On which three things depend the fate of natural systems, including oceans and coral reefs? What can the *Reefs at Risk* report be used as a guide for, and in which two ways? Give example of each of the two ways. Include what you can do involving way no. 2. Keep in mind your answers to the first two questions just above.

RELATED INTERNET SITE(S)

National Oceanographic and Atmospheric Association (NOAA)—Coral Reefs

http://www.coralreef.noaa.gov

See News and more links such as News Releases, the International Year of the Reef 1997, Coral Reef Initiative 2000, U.S. Coral Reef Task Force with the 1998 Executive Order 13087 on Coral Reef Protection issued by President William J. Clinton, plus definitions and locations of reefs, and other links (e.g., to Marine Sanctuaries with information on marine creatures and Northwestern Hawaiian Islands Coral Reef Ecosystem Reserve).

Missouri Botanical Garden—Evergreen Projects Adventures—Marine Ecosystems

http://mbgnet.mobot.org/salt/index.htm

Featured are detailed, interesting, and unusual data about aquatic animals, forests, and light zones, on shorelines, and in temperate oceans, and tropical oceans with coral reefs.

Oceanography in Science and Technology Area at Office of Naval Research Online

http://www.onr.navy.mil/focus/ocean/default.htm

Links go to data for students and teachers on marine mammals, ocean water, ocean in motion, ocean regions, habitats, research vessels, activities, and resources.

Ocean Planet—Resource Room—Smithsonian Institution's Traveling Exhibit

http://seawifs.gsfc.nasa.gov/OCEAN_PLANET/HTML/ocean_planet_resource_room.html

Links go to, among others, Oceanographic Resources on Internet, Q's & A's on Oceans and the Environment, Oceanography from Space, plus Other Online Exhibitions, and Ocean-Related Events and Activities at Other Institutions.

Woods Hole Oceanographic Institute (WHOI)—Research

http://www.whoi.edu/science/research_main.html

The data address ongoing ocean related research in biology, physical oceanography, applied ocean physics, marine chemistry and geochemistry, geology and geophysics, multi-disciplinary project (such as coastal briefs), and other areas.

Woods Hole Oceanographic Institute (WHOI)—K–12 Resources

http://www.whoi.edu/home/education/k12_main.html

See Daily Journal of Scientist on Research Cruise; Remarkable Careers in Oceanography such as Women Exploring the Ocean; Related Sources (e.g., marine mammals including whales, dolphins and manatees; pollution; research vessels, and miscellaneous such as life in a tide pool); plus the Join Research Expedition.

Cousteau Society

http://www.cousteausociety.org/indexmain.html

Links go to News, Expeditions, Issues (e.g., on coral reefs and marine protected areas), *Dolphin Log* in the Classroom magazine for young readers (with current issue, Creature Feature and teacher's guide), and other links (e.g., to corals, ocean and water, marine mammals, other marine creatures, and Cousteau Society Connections).

Mission Log—Species List—Dive of August 16, 1999—Florida Keys—by Sylvia Earle

http://sustainableseas.noaa.gov/missions/florida1/dailylogs/August15_16_splist.html

This list provides common and scientific names and brief information given under "titles." Titles include Among the Corals Observed; Other Obvious Invertebrates; Among Plants I Could Clearly See; Lots of Fish, But No Large Predators Other Than . . . ; and Surprising by Their Absence.

Coral Reef Alliance

http://editorial.coralreefalliance.org

Select from pull-down menu or links: Professor Polyp's Classroom, About Coral Reefs, Dive into Earth Day, etc.

What Is the International Year of the Reef 1997?

http://www.publicaffairs.noa.gov/iyorwk1.html

See also: 1997 designated IYOR page at: www.publicaffairs.noaa.gov/coral-reef.html.

International Year of the Ocean 1998—NOAA

http://www.yoto98.noaa.gov

See the links to Discussion Papers (on ocean- and shore-related research), Reporters' Resources, In Your Neighborhood, Ocean-Related Links, and Kids and Teachers Corner.

Transcript of Ocean Planet Radio Interview with Sylvia Earle, August 5, 1999

http://www.abc.net.au/rn/science/earth/stories/s24554.htm

Interviewed on Australian radio by Earthbeat's Alexandra de Blas during Science Week Oceans Forum, as part of Australia's National Maritime Museum Ocean Planet Exhibition, Earle commented on ocean scientists' warning about the state of the earth's marine ecosystems during the 1998 International Year of the Ocean. Among the questions she answered were: What Lures You Down into the Ocean? and How Has Spending So Much Time in the Deep Ocean Influenced the Way You View the World?

An Interview with Oceanographer Sylvia Earle—March 9, 1997

http://www.thetech.org/revolutionaries/earle

This interview with *San Jose Mercury News* interviewer Jill Wolfson and high school senior Mariel Haag features Earle's comments to questions on young creatures, the importance of the ocean, the consequences of human and marine life interactions, and Earle as "a Rachel Carson for the ocean."

Interview with Sylvia Earle—January 1, 1991

http://www.achievement.org/autodoc/page/ear0int-1

This interview, on six pages in the Hall of Science and Exploration at the Academy of Achievement online, features questions and answers on Earle's decision to become a marine scientist, her concern for the ocean's ecosystem, plus similarities and differences between her profession and an astronaut's profession.

Earle's Message to "Denizens of the Deep Conference on Biodiversity," June 23, 1999

http://www.gpuk.org/atlantic/what/earlelecture.html

Sylvia Earle Home Page

http://literati.net/Earle

This site reveals that Earle is the first woman to be NOAA's chief scientist, she has discovered previously unknown ocean life, and has many firsts to her credit. She helped design and build a research submarine that dives to 3,000 feet and is working on efforts to help the earth's oceans. She is also an author of ocean-related books based on her experiences, with titles including "Hello Fish"; "Wild Ocean"; "Sea Change"; and "Dive!"

"Recommended Reading: Online Articles"
for the Society for Scientific Exploration Young Investigators Program (1998–)
URL: www.scientificexploration.org/young_investigators/articles.html

SITE SUMMARY: The Society for Scientific Exploration and its Web site provide information on, and resources for, investigating mysteries that are ignored or dismissed as pseudo science by some scientists, but constantly challenge other scientists (who consider them as alternative science) to think of logical explanations for such phenomena. The Young Investigators Program (YIP) was set up, by popular request, to provide opportunities for college students to participate in these types of investigations. The YIP's "Recommended Reading: Online Articles" page and the main YIP Web page with links are aimed at YIP participants, but are also helpful in introducing high school students to the subject. Details on the YIP are provided in this book's Appendix G.

DISCUSSION QUESTIONS AND ACTIVITIES

1. Find and read the article "Curious, Creative, and Critical Thinking" by Peter Sturrock on the "Recommended Reading: Online Articles" page of the Society for Scientific Exploration Young Investigators Program Web site. See paragraphs one, three, and four, and the last part of paragraph six. State the three modes of thought which he recommends. What did the astronomers Halton Arp and William Tifft do, why did the scientific community disagree, and what, according to Sturrock, should astronomers do? What does he believe is not impossible? Give his example, then your own example that includes your support of his belief.

2. Follow links to Brian Martin's article "Strategies For Dissenting Scientists" on the "Recommended Reading: Online Articles" Web page at the Society for Scientific Exploration Young Investigators Program Web site. Note especially his Contents Page link to Strategies, and more strategies continued on the first two-thirds of the Acknowledgments page found via another link. State and briefly describe his six strategies. Do you agree or disagree with them? Think of another strategy to add to these, and describe this strategy. Choose one of Martin's strategies, and apply an "alternative science" subject example to your choice. (Note: For data on an alternative science, visit the Web sites cited in the links area of the YIP main Web page [whose url is cited in this book's Appendix G] and for which there is a link on the YIP "Recommended Reading: Online Articles" page. See also the Anomalous and Alternative Science Web sites referred to in the Related Internet Sites section below.)

3. See the "Recommended Reading: Online Articles" page at the Society for Scientific Exploration Young Investigators Program Web site. Choose an article, and describe its main point. (Note: Emphasize unusual or anomalous aspects, but also include a scientific viewpoint. Be guided by Sturrock's and Martin's suggestions provided in the articles referred to in Questions/Activities no. 1 and no. 2 above.)

4. See the *Journal of Scientific Exploration* of the Society for Scientific Exploration. (Find by clicking the Society's Home link on the YIP "Recommending Reading: Online Articles" page, then by clicking the Journal link.) (The Journal's url is also cited in this book's Appendix D.) Adapt to the Journal Web site Question/Activity no. 3 above and its Note. Choose a subject mentioned in an article in a particular Journal issue from the Journal's "Selected Articles Online" page. Find more information related to the subject as suggested in the Note for Question/Activity no. 2 above. Look for unusual or anomalous aspects, while noting a scientific viewpoint. Describe what you discover. Give your viewpoint, supporting it with logical and scientific statements, and keep in mind the Note for Question/Activity no. 3 above.

5. Adapt Question/Activity no. 4 above to an article you find by following a journal's or organization's (e.g., to *Science Frontiers*) link on the links page that is accessible via the Young

Investigators Program main Web page, which has a link on the "Recommended Reading: Online Articles" YIP page.

6. Find a "case study" story or an eyewitness story of a science-related mystery or unusual experience. (Choose from any of the publications at, or Web sites referred to on, the YIP main Web page.) Identify an eyewitness, or another particular type of person, in the case study. Describe the features of the mystery she or he experienced. Do you believe that the eyewitness, or the other person, experienced what she or he claims was experienced? Why or why not? Support your answer with logical, plausible, or believable aspects.

7. Describe what it means for a person to have an open mind and to be skeptical. Identify the type of person you think you are, and explain why you think this way. (Hints: Keep in mind mysterious or unexplained things as you answer, refer to any item you find via the links page via the YIP main Web page, see this book's chapter featuring physicist Richard Feynman's "The Role of Doubt in Science" and the Skepticism Web sites cited in that chapter's Related Internet Sites section.)

RELATED INTERNET SITE(S)

Society for Scientific Exploration

http://www.scientificexploration.org/index.html

See the message from the society's founding president, Peter Sturrock; then the links to mission statement, *Journal of Scientific Exploration*, and Young Investigators Program.

EarthFiles

http://www.earthfiles.com/headlines.cfm

Note the headlines to unusual earth-related news reports, and the links to freely accessible reports from the past one hundred twenty days, in the areas of Science, the Environment, and the Real X-Files. Links to Web sites with more information are also provided with the reports. Access to items older than four months and going back to 1998 are in the archives, and require a paid subscription for access, although headlines' key phrases can be seen without a subscription. A few special recent headlines and reports are also available only to subscribers.

Alternative Science at Scientopica

http://www.scientopica.com/b/d?n=205 or scroll to, and click, link at: *http://www.scientopica.com/index.php*

See links to regular science subjects in this area, e.g., geology, medicine, and physics, plus links to sites on alternative science, alternative science directory, and borderland sciences.

Anomalous and Alternative Science

http://directory.google.com > *Science* > *Anomalies and Alternative Science*

See links to, for example, Anomalous Sounds; Cryptozoology (e.g., living dinosaurs); Earth Lights; Medicine, Alternative; Physics, Alternative; Psychology, Alternative; Research, Alternative; and Unproven Energy Concepts.

"Science in the New Millennium"
Stephen Hawking (1998)
URL: http://clinton4.nara.gov/Initiatives/Millennium/shawking.html

SITE SUMMARY: As one of the featured participants of the Millennium Project established by President Bill Clinton and First Lady Hillary Rodham Clinton, Hawking, a foremost scientist and professor at England's Cambridge University, presented these remarks in a lecture at the White House on March 6, 1998. Looking at science as it had developed in the past and as it was at the end of the twentieth century, he suggested ways that science could develop at the beginning of the new millennium and in the coming one thousand years. He remarked on changes in, or evolution of, the human race with relation to biological evolution, mental and physical advances, and the evolution of computers and their importance to people and civilization. In addition, he spoke of his involvement with *Star Trek* and compared science with *Star Trek* science.

DISCUSSION QUESTIONS AND ACTIVITIES

1. See paragraphs eleven and twelve. What did it seem, according to Hawking, people would achieve by the end of the nineteenth century? What happened from the start of the twentieth century, however, regarding what was to be achieved?

2. What did Hawking hope will seem just common sense to children in the future although it is a paradox to people today? What does a theory by Richard Feynman have to do with it? (Hint: See paragraphs twelve and thirteen.)

3. What, according to Hawking, are two things the human race will need to do in the coming years "to deal with the increasingly complex world . . . and to meet new challenges"? (Hint: See paragraph twenty-five.) What is a challenge he mentions? Give an example of what could be done to deal with "the increasingly complex world," following one of his basic suggestions, by people in general, and by you in particular. See paragraph twenty-six, and note that Hawking says he expects "complexity to increase at a rapid rate, in the biological and electronic spheres." Give an example of each that is an indication of what could happen in the future from what is happening in today's world.

4. Hawking tends to draw analogies or comparisons between a scientific idea or something scientific and something in "everyday" life or the world. For example, to what does he compare today's computers, possible computers of the future, and what would be these future computers' importance? (Hint: See paragraph twenty-five and paragraph six.) Give another example of this tendency from Hawking's remarks. (Note: He mentioned a toy, a small life form, sports, and political references.) Think of your own comparison based on something scientific around you or in the world.

5. See paragraphs fourteen through twenty. What did Hawking say about time loops, "odd" dimensions, and supersymmetry? How are theories by the scientists Hendrick Casimir, plus Yuri Gol'fand and E. Likhtman involved? (Note also the Web site on "What Is the Casimir Effect?" [Its url is cited in the Related Internet Sites section below.])

6. See paragraph twenty-five. Explain Moore's Law with reference to computers and the human brain. (See also the Web site with Part Two of the *Scientific American Magazine*—Interview with Moore. [Its url is cited in the Related Internet Sites section below.])

7. See paragraph nineteen, then paragraph eighteen. What did Hawking mean when he said "The Holy Grail of Physics"? See paragraph twenty. How can people, according to Hawking, find "the Ultimate Theory of Everything"?

8. See paragraphs one, three, four, twenty-one, and twenty-four. Hawking referred to his involvement with *Star Trek*, then compared the *Star Trek* universe with the real universe of

modern times and the new millennium. Although he thinks *Star Trek* science is primarily fantasy, he acknowledges some real science, and something that is possible, in *Star Trek*. What did he say may come true, what does he think will not happen and why, and what importance does this have for the new millennium? Which real sciences does he mention?

9. Visit one of these Web sites: *Scientific American Magazine*—Interview with Moore (Part Four) or the International Forum for Genetic Engineering. (Their urls are cited in the Related Internet Sites section below.) Describe a present-day scientist's research on a *Star Trek* science Hawking mentions. Compare and/or contrast an aspect of one or more of the sciences as seen by Hawking and by the other scientist. Point out the science's logical evolution from the way it is today to the way it could be in the future, in reality and as *Star Trek* portrays it, which may be the same or different. (For more help, see the Science in Society—Futurism and the World Future Society Web sites, whose urls are cited in the Related Internet Sites section below; other Web sites whose urls are cited in the Related Internet Sites sections of this book's chapters featuring the documents "The Science of *Star Trek*" and "Excerpts from *The Physics of STAR TREK*.")

10. See other chapters in this book that feature Web sites with other great scientists' documents on a science that Hawking mentions; e.g., Watson and Crick's "A Structure for Deoxyribose Nucleic Acid," Einstein's "What Is the Theory of Relativity?" Compare and/or contrast an aspect of one or more of the sciences as seen by Hawking and by the other scientists.

11. Imagine you have been invited to the White House to take part in a Millennium Project sometime during the early part of the twenty-first century. Prepare by researching and writing a speech. Choose a science for your presentation. Give highlights of your chosen science's development and pioneering people in this field through time. Supporting your claims with quotations from, and citations of, primary science documents, make logical guesses how that science may develop in the next few years, as the new millennium progresses. Note how that science may effect you and society. (For ideas and data, see Web sites listed in this book's Appendix B.)

RELATED INTERNET SITE(S)

Official String Theory Web Site

http://www.superstringtheory.com

This clear and interesting site features basics of the string theory (experiments, people, history, and links), plus the theory with reference to cosmology, black holes, and mathematics. Note also a forum on the legacy of Albert Einstein and string theory, plus a String Theatre with real audio physics.

"What Is the Casimir Effect?" in *Scientific American Magazine*, June 22, 1998

http://www.sciam.com/askexpert_directory.cfm

Type "Casimir Effect" in the search box. Click go, then the link to the 6/22/1998 article.

Scientific American Magazine—Interview with Gordon Moore (1997)

http://www.sciam.com/interview_directory.cfm (select year, then links)

This interview, which took place on September 22, and October 20, 1997, with Intel Corporation's co-founder and chairman emeritus, is presented in four parts of several pages each, on "The Birth of the Microprocessor," "Moore's Law," "Pushing the Technology," and "The Future of the Computer."

Science in Society—Futurism; Science and Technology; etc.

http://dmoz.org/Science/Science_in_Society

Click the links for the topics Futurism; Science and Technology Policy; or Philosophy of Science, Technology, and Society for information on subjects related to these topics that Hawking referred to in his presentation (e.g., utopia, near and distant future). Note links to essays, general sites (including magazies, e-zines, organizations, and projects), and various subjects (e.g., millennialism), plus particular sites (e.g., Beyond 2000).

International Forum for Genetic Engineering—Articles Index Page

http://www.anth.org/ifgene/articles.htm

A forum is provided here for developing viewpoints and public awareness on genetic engineering which Hawking mentioned. There are online articles on the subject, plus social, ethical, and moral issues, spiritual implications, and underlying scientific approaches related to the subject. Articles are organized in categories that include general; The Sciences Behind the Technology: Contrasting Approaches; plants, crops, and food; animals; and human beings (e.g., gene therapy and screening). There is also a glossary. Links to sites with more information are on the main Web page: http://www. anth.org/ifgene.

Internet Resources: Quantum Physics

http://bubl.ac.uk/link/q/quantumphysics.htm

See links to sites with introductory to advanced information on Quantum Physics, one of the sciences Hawking mentioned in his "Science in the New Millennium" speech. See a list of title links, and a list of title links with site descriptions for articles, article collections, indexes, and more. Note the links, for example, to "Brief Review of Elementary Quantum Chemistry," "Do Quantum Particles Have a Structure?" "Many-Worlds Quantum Theory," "On Quantum Physics and Ordinary Consciousness," "On the Interpretation and Philosophical Foundation of Quantum Mechanics," "Particle or Wave?" and Hawking's lecture "Does God Play Dice?"

World Future Society

http://www.wfs.org

This site is for people who are interested in how technological and social developments are shaping the future. It has special features such as Interviews, Forums, Forecasts, and a Press Room, plus features from *Futurist Magazine* and *Futures Research Quarterly* (for professional futurism researchers).

Should We Return to the Moon?

http://www.ari.net/back2moon.html

Featuring a subject that Hawking mentioned in his talk, this site has a reference room, suggested topics for essays and position papers, plus the goals and concept of the National Space Society–sponsored WWW Public Policy Forum.

Questions and Answers at the Hawking Science Millennium Lecture—Transcript

http://clinton4.nara.gov/Initiatives/Millennium/19980309-227

This Q&A session after the lecture was introduced by President Clinton with comments on Hawking's remarks. Questions asked by Mrs. Clinton, an astronaut in space, and others were theirs or those sent by other people. Hawking and other scientists provided answers.

"Space—Where Now, and Why?"
Carolyn Shoemaker (1998)
URL: http://www.sciencemag.org/feature/data/150essay.shl (Scroll to 1998 articles' list, find the author and title, then click the full text link)

SITE SUMMARY: Shoemaker, an astronomer and planetary scientist now on the staffs of the Lowell Observatory and U.S. Geological Survey, discovered the comet Shoemaker Levy (in 1993), is a recipient of the NASA Exceptional Scientific Achievement Medal (1996), and is the most prolific comet discoverer alive. In this essay, first published in *Science*, November 27, 1998, and now part of the Essays on Science and Society page of the magazine's Web site, she comments on her scientific interests, the sciences with which she works, and how they are interesting in themselves and significant for the Earth now, in the past, and in the future. (Also accessible with a search by author name, essay title, and date [e.g., November 1, 1998 through November 31, 1998], in the search boxes at http://www.sciencemag.org/search.dtl.)

DISCUSSION QUESTIONS AND ACTIVITIES

1. Planetary science holds Shoemaker's interest and she has "endeavored to understand" astronomy and geology. Read paragraph one. Identify, according to her, how her main scientific interest is connected to the two other sciences she notes, then give an example. What did she say about history (the major subject of her education), and how did she connect history with the sciences with which she works? Note the poetic phrase or science fiction simile she used, give a reason why she said this, and give an example to illustrate it. (For help and more information, read and quote from the Hubble Space Telescope Page at the Space Telescope Science Institute Web site and the Web site with "Hubble Identifies Primeval Galaxies, Uncovers New Clues to the Universe's Evolution"—Press Release. [Their urls are cited in the Related Internet Sites section below.]) Compare the ways that Shoemaker and the Web sites use the phrase or simile.

2. See the last part of paragraph two. What are three unusual things about the comet that Shoemaker discovered? Suggest what she meant when she said Comet Shoemaker Levy was "everyone's comet," and identify three things she pointed out. Describe her comparison of the Comet Shoemaker Levy event with the Apollo moon exploration program. What did she say we are occasionally lucky to have? Imagine how to apply your answers to the first questions just above to another scientific occurrence, then do it.

3. Read the first two sentences of paragraph two, then paragraphs seven, eight, and the last part of nine. On what has Shoemaker concentrated her work, why, and what does this mean to her? Why does she see as important in her work astronomical phenomena close to Earth? With "the science of impact" what effect happens (which may be called a crescendoing or a type of domino effect), and what is the awareness that "the science of impact" carries? (Tip One: For help with scientific words [e.g., accretion], go to the Information Please Dictionary Web site. Its url is in cited in this book's Appendix F. Tip Two: For help with the concepts domino effect and crescendoing, in the context of the article, also search at the Information Please Dictionary Web site.)

4. Keep in mind Question/Activity no. 3 above and the paragraphs suggested there. Although comet and asteroid impacts are ongoing natural processes, what did Shoemaker believe people must do, and how would images from the Hubble Space Telescope and Earth based telescopes emphasize this fact, according to her?

5. Keeping Question/Activity no. 3 and Question/Activity no. 4 above in mind, describe Shoemaker's analogy that involves a person and a car. Note how this analogy emphasizes the

importance of Shoemaker's work and her point of view. Think of and describe another analogy example in "everyday life" that connects something astronomical with people on the Earth. (Find a definition of analogy at the Information Please Dictionary Web site, as indicated in Tip One of Question/Activity no. 3 above.)

6. See paragraph three. Why did some early humans become interested in more than physical survival? Identify five things that these early humans did that were more than surviving, then identify four more things that were more than surviving that people in cities in early times did. What did early humans imagine, which sciences began to develop then, and why did these sciences develop slowly? What are some things early humans thought and wondered that modern people still think about and wonder?

7. Read paragraphs four and five. Over time which two science-related things happened (one especially in the twentieth century) that, Shoemaker believes, caused people to see Earth in a new way and unlocked the door to our future? What is this new view of Earth? Which two things have these two sciences joined together, allowed human beings and enabled scientists to do, and in which ways? How was Shoemaker's work with Comet Shoemaker Levy connected to what is happening because of that joining? Identify which different branches of sciences have, according to Shoemaker, become integrated, and now complement Astronomy, then explain how, and give examples.

8. Read paragraph six. What have people become aware of in today's world, and why? However, why does space exploration seem frivolous and unnecessary? Identify three different ways of exploring space. What are people more concerned with? Identify and quote from her comments on and examples of what "holds many advantages," then give details, adding additional information found at the Web sites Benefits from Space Science and NASA Spinoffs—Bringing Space Down to Earth (whose urls are cited in the Related Internet Sites section below). See also the last part of paragraph nine. What else did Shoemaker think people should be aware of with reference to space exploration? Tell if you agree or disagree with space exploration, then explain why. Include in your answer if your viewpoint is because of or despite what Shoemaker said, or if what she says supports your viewpoint.

9. Read paragraph nine. Identify four natural processes on Earth; one in the biological sciences, and one in the earth sciences, that people think should be changed; then one in the biological sciences, and one in the earth sciences that people do not consider changing; according to Shoemaker. State why or why not each natural process you chose should be prevented, or its effects ameliorated, or nothing done about it. (Note: Find a definition for ameliorated at the Information Please Dictionary Web site, as indicated in Tip One of Question/Activity no. 3 above.)

10. Read paragraph ten. Why did Shoemaker say science and society are intricately entwined? What should people remember about science even if some people think it is too difficult, technical, or abstruse to apply to most people? What is pure science, and what is it "part and parcel of"? What is science likely to do? Based on your answers to the questions just above, and being sure to include them in the explanation of your choice, give an example, from the world around you, of a connection between science and society.

RELATED INTERNET SITE(S)

Benefits from Space Science

http://liftoff.msfc.nasa.gov/station/science/benefits_tech.html
This site has data that helps to answer "What has the Space Program done for me lately?"

NASA Spinoffs—Bringing Space Down to Earth

http://www.thespaceplace.com/nasa/spinoffs.html

This site covers various science subjects, plus, via the links page, NASA Spinoffs and Tech Briefs links.

"Hubble Identifies Primeval Galaxies, Uncovers New Clues to the Universe's Evolution"

http://www.ast.cam.ac.uk/HST/PR/94-52.html

A 1994 Press Release.

Hubble Space Telescope Page at the Space Telescope Science Institute Web Site

http://www.stsci.edu/hst

ASTEROID.NET

http://asteroid.net

See especially links to What's New, Papers/Research on Near Earth Asteroids and Impact Hazards, Impact Prevention and Education, Asteroid Missions, and more features coming.

Craters—Links Page

http://www.barringercrater.com/links

Links go to sites with data on meteors, meteorites and impacts; asteroid and comet impact hazards (e.g., probability of collisions with the Earth, and probability and results of various types of impacts and what we should be doing about them); ancient impacts; asteroid impact and dinosaur extinction theory; terrestrial impact craters; identification of impact sites; and help for teachers. See also the link to data on Comet Shoemaker Levy.

Asteroid Comet Impact Hazards—NASA Ames Research Center

http://impact.arc.nasa.gov/index.html

Click links to News in Brief, News Archives, Government Studies, NASA Programs, Introduction and FAQs, Related Information, and more.

Ten FAQs about Near Earth Objects

http://astrosun.tn.cornell.edu/staff/bottke/neo-faq.html

Also has link to more information at an Asteroid and Comet Impact Hazards Web site.

NEAR Earth Asteroid Rendezvous Mission—NEAR Shoemaker

http://near.jhuapl.edu

This site includes data on the probe that was named after the astronomer and planetary scientist Eugene Shoemaker (Carolyn Shoemaker's coworker and husband). This probe landed on and explored the asteroid Eros on February 12, 2001. See the links to data on this probe, including to The Descent to Eros Information, Data From Eros, a Science Updates Archive, and the NASA Science News Archive (at http://near.jhuapl.edu/news/index.html) which features menus with links to items in a News Archive, a Science Updates Archive, and APL Press Releases Archive, plus links to NEAR Weekly Status Reports, and *APL Technical Digest* articles.

"Featured Health Articles"
in the Guest Editors Column, The National Women's Health Information Center (1999–)
URL: http://www.4woman.gov/editor/index.htm

SITE SUMMARY: In cooperation with nationally recognized magazines, organizations, and Web sites, and their editors, the National Women's Health Information Center (NWHIC) features important health articles written by professionals for its online guest editor column, specifically on women's concerns, and including many of interest to girls. Examples of past articles include "Like Mom, Like Me?" (July 2002) by Catherine Cassidy of *Prevention Magazine*, "Stroke: Not Just Your Grandparents' Disease" (May 2001 by Patti Shwayder of the National Stroke Association, "Walk This Way" (March 2000 by Marlien Rentmeester of *Women's Health and Fitness Magazine*, "Genetic Counseling" (July 1999) by Laura Broadwell of *Healthy Kids Magazine*, and "The Best Vitamins for Women" (March 1999) by Miriam Arond of *American Health Magazine*. Criteria for articles chosen for the column include how the article's subject coincides with a national health observance or with a new NWHIC Web site feature.

DISCUSSION QUESTIONS AND ACTIVITIES

1. Choose an article featured in the NWHIC Guest Editors Column. Identify who wrote it, her professional status, the main point and supporting points of the article, and how the author's profession adds something important to the article. Comment on the way the article's topic, and the author's way of writing about it, may be helpful to a woman you know and to an older teen girl.

2. Visit the Web sites for the *Female Patient Journal* and the *Journal of the American Medical Women's Association*. (Their urls are cited in this book's Appendix D.) Choose two articles, one from each publication. Apply to each chosen article the parts of Question/Activity no. 1 above that start with the words identify and comment.

3. Visit the Women's Health Center at the Discovery Health Web site whose url is cited in the Related Internet Sites section below. Choose an item from the features at this Web site. Apply to this item the parts of Question/Activity no. 1 above that start with the words identify and comment.

4. Visit the Instructions to Authors in the Health Sciences Web site. (See this book's Appendix C for its url.) Pretend you can send an article that will be considered for publication to the NWHIC Guest Editors Column. Think of, or find and choose, a particular subject to write about. (Tip: For help and information, find general topics [e.g., women's health and new advances, laws, work-life, fitness] in articles at the NWHIC Guest Editor Column area or in the magazines or Web sites cited and found as noted in Question/Activity no. 2 and Question/ Activity no. 3 above, or at these Web sites or Web areas cited in the Related Internet Sites section that follow: National Women's Health Information Center, Speaking of Women's Health in the Twenty-First Century, FAQs About Women's Health, Women's Health—LifeCycle.) Following the instructions at the Instructions to Authors in the Health Sciences Web site, write something on your subject.

RELATED INTERNET SITE(S)

National Women's Health Information Center

http://www.4woman.gov/index.htm

See links to Women's Health News Today, What's New and Announcements, Press Releases, News Archives, General Health Related Hot Topics, plus Hot Topics in Congress, Featured

Sections (e.g., health articles by guest editors), and health information for special groups including Women with Disabilities, Minority Health Information, and Health Professionals. See also links to For the Media, Dictionaries and Journals, a sitemap, and Educational Campaigns (e.g., Pick Your Path to Health and Young Women's Health Summit).

FAQs About Women's Health

http://www.4woman.gov/faq/index.htm

See the links under FAQ categories such as Adolescent Health, Environmental Health, Mental Health, Nutrition and Physical Activity, Preventive Care and Screenings, and more, including particular conditions, and areas of the body affected by conditions. Note also the link to the *Women's Health Facts Daybook* (2001) in PDF format.

Women's Health Center at Discovery Health

http://www.discoveryhealth.com/centers/womens/womens.html

See a search box, plus title links or annotated links to items in the categories Get the Facts (e.g., Women A to Z, Women by the Numbers, Recent News Update), On TV, Assessments, Mental Health, and more.

Women's Health—Lifecycle

http://www.womenshealth.org/n/who.htm

Find out about women's health, bodies, minds, and activities, during the various cycles of women's lives, defined here as including adolescence, the reproductive years of adulthood, mid-life, and maturity.

Speaking of Women's Health in the Twenty-First Century

http://www.swh.net/home_middle.asp (or with frames via *www.swh.net/main.htm*)

See the welcome and introduction page, then click links to About SWH, Your Health, or In the News (current and archives). Free registration is required for access to a weekly online newsletter and to links for a health library, health brochures, quizzes, recipes, and a multimedia theater with videos of SWH "thought leaders."

"Health Information Sheets"
Young Women's Resource Center (1999–)
URL: http://www.youngwomenshealth.org/healthinfo.html

SITE SUMMARY: Written primarily by the staff of the Young Women's Resource Center which is part of the Center for Young Women's Health, these Health Information Sheets address health- and medical-related topics that are especially of interest to adolescent girls: Health and Health Care (e.g., Transitions: A Guide to Getting Older, Going to College and Staying Healthy), Nutrition (e.g., FAQs, Healthy Eating for Teens, Backpack Snacks: A Guide for Teens, How to Be a Healthy Vegetarian, Calcium and Teens, Iron and Teens, Cholesterol and Fats), health- or medical-related conditions (e.g., A Guide to Puberty and Menstrual Cycles, Sports and Menstrual Periods, Emotional Health, Eating Disorders, Scoliosis).

DISCUSSION QUESTIONS AND ACTIVITIES

1. In the "Health Information Sheets" area of the Young Women's Resource Center Web page, choose an item from the sections on Nutrition, Health Care, and a particular health related situation from other sections (e.g., sports and menstrual periods, emotional health, eating disorders, smoking, scoliosis, or a more personal/private condition or situation). Identify the article's main point and supporting points, and what the article means to you, someone you know, or someone who would find the article useful, and why. Extra Activity: Choose an item from the Adolescent Research area found via a link in the left column of the search page of the Young Women's Research Center whose url is cited in the Related Internet Sites section below. Apply the activity suggested above which starts with the word "identify." Apply to it, if possible, the last activity of Question/Activity no. 6.

2. Click the links link on the Youth Page at the Young Women's Resource Center Web site (described in the Related Internet Sites section below). Select a Health-Related, Nutrition, or Exercise/Sports link, and choose a link on the links page of one of these topics. At the site whose link you chose, search for an item on a particular subject of the topic you selected. Adapt and apply to it the instructions that start with the word "identify" in Question/Activity no. 1 above.

3. Visit the Adolescent Health Transition Project, found via a link you discover by following the Health-Related Sites link on the Health Links page of the Youth Page that is part of the Young Women's Resource Center Web site. Find as stated in Question/Activity no. 2 above. Choose a health-related item from this Web page. Identify, in general, the transition that the item refers to. Adapt and apply to the item the instructions that start with the word "identify" in Question/Activity no. 1 above.

4. Keeping Question/Activity no. 3 above in mind, and then another type of transition referred to below, visit other Web sites or pages cited just below and apply the activities in Question/Activity no. 3 to two of them. Find the Web sites or pages as follows: At the www.girlpower.gov Web site, do a search for its "Health Science Curriculum" area via a search box, and note its links. See also the "Information for Teens and Young Adults: Adolescent Health Transition Project" Web site. (Each site has a link on the Center for Young Women's Health Web site's Youth Page's Health-Related links area.) See in addition the "Girls and Chronic Disease and Disability" area of www.4girls.gov and the "U.S. Department of Health and Human Services—Specific Populations"; both cited and described in the Related Internet Site section below. Option: You may also do site searches at the Web sites for "Children with Disabilities—Research Links" with A Youth to Youth Index Page, the "National Information Center for Children and Youth with Disabilities," "National Organization on Disability—Sitemap Page" with links, and "Disability Related Resources" at the International Center for Disability Information," whose Web pages' urls are found in this book's Appendix I.

5. Visit one of these Web sites or areas: "Exploring Adolescence" at Women's Health Online, "Girls Health" at HealthDiscovery.com, "Health Issues" at SmartGirl.com, "FAQs About Adolescent Health" in FAQs About Women's Health, or "Adolescents and Teens" in Health Topics A-Z. (Their urls are cited in the Related Internet Sites section below, or in this book's Appendix B.) Select an item from one of these Web sites or areas. Adapt and apply to them the instructions that start with the word "identify" in Question/Activity no. 1 above. Next, find a similar item at the "Ethics and Moral Issues—Health" Web site area whose url is cited in the Related Internet Sites section below, and explain both items' viewpoints on the subject. Option: Choose another item from the above cited Web sites or areas and one on a similar subject in the "Ethics and Moral Issues—Health Web" site area, and explain both items' viewpoints on the subject.

6. Visit the Web site for the *Journal of Adolescent Health* whose url is cited in this book's Appendix D. Choose an article, one that interest girls, from this journal's Selected Full-Text Articles Online or Special Issue Online areas. Adapt and apply to it the instructions that start with the word "identify" in Question/Activity no. 1 above. Next, tell who wrote the article and her or his professional status (if available), where the article was published (if it was), how the author's profession and/or the person who did research (as the author notes in the item) adds something important to the article's point, the people (or types of people) featured in a research project noted in the item.

7. Think of something you would like to write about a health-related subject of interest to young women in general, and/or to you in particular. Look at the Your Stuff area of the Youth Page at the Young Women's Resource Center site (found as stated in Question/Activity no. 2 above). Write something that could be posted here. Next, click the Youth Page's Health Links link, then the next page's Health-Related Links link, and then check these Web sites whose links are listed here: "Teen Growth"; "Our Health, Our Futures"; and "Kidshealth.org for Teens." Study what can be contributed to these Web sites (e.g., questions, notes), and write something that could be posted at these sites.

8. Visit the "Instructions to Authors of the Health Sciences" Web site or the "Improving Public Understanding: Guidelines for Communicating the Emerging Science of Nutrition, Food Safety and Health" Web document, especially the General Guidelines, and Guidelines for Journalists or Special Interest Groups (e.g., for Consumers). Imagine you are a journalist, or think of yourself as a member of a special interest group that has concerns for consumers. Write something on a subject you choose and in one of the formats suggested. (Tip: For the main topic or particular subject ideas and information, to help you get started, you can look for general topics in items at or via the Young Women's Resource Center Web site or check the other Web sites cited in the Related Internet Sites section below or referred to anywhere in this chapter.) (Note: The Instructions' Web site url is cited in this book's Appendix C. The Guidelines' Web site url is cited in another chapter of this book which features that document.)

RELATED INTERNET SITE(S)

Young Women's Resource Center—Center for Young Women's Health

http://www.youngwomenshealth.org/resourcecenter.html

Besides the link to the Health Information Sheets via a Health Information link, this Web page features an online tour of the center, plus links to a Youth Page and a Parent's Page. Health links (accessible via the Youth Page) feature links to chats, publications, and organizations, plus particular subjects, including Puberty, and Exercise/Sports, plus particular medical or medical related conditions (e.g., acne, osteoporosis, substance abuse), and are primarily written by professionals associated with other health-related Web sites. The Parent's Page features links to advice for talking with teens on tough issues. A search page, requiring JavaScript to use, includes a keyword search box and pull-down menu of topic articles that include the Health Information Sheets. A Clinician Education link leads to a manual ("How to Start a Youth Web Advisory Program," available in PDF format), links to sites with more information, and a booklist. An Adolescent Research link leads to brief looks at research being done at the Center for Young Women's Health.

"Exploring Adolescence" at Women's Health Online

http://www.estronaut.com/n/adolescence.htm

Note especially Puberty, Nutrition for Female Athletes, Archives, Facts and Tips, plus Ask the Women's Health Specialist Dr. Karen Sarpolis. See also the links for mind, body, looks, eat, and move, with information for women, including some of interest to girls.

"Girls' Health" at HealthDiscovery

http://health.discovery.com

Type Girls in the search box, click Go, and see a list of annotated links featuring news or research items on girls from infants to young adults and some items on women's health.

"FAQs About Adolescent Health" in "FAQs About Women's Health"

http://www.4woman.gov/faq (click Adolescent link, then particular subject links)

See the links to Adolescent Health—An Overview, plus subjects including Puberty, Menstruation, Calcium Intake, Acne, Attention Deficit Hyperactivity Disorder, and more. Note also other links to FAQs About Women's Health in categories such as Nutrition and Physical Activity, Environmental Health, Mental Health, Preventive Care, and Screening.

"Health Issues" at SmartGirl.com

http://www.smartgirl.com/pages/issues/index.html (click Archives link)

Scroll down and click the link to a subject under the topics: body image, health and body, or individual health concerns that include acne, menstruation, learning disability, and depression. Issues are answers to questions sent by young site visitors, and are from the past ten months. (Educators or parents may want to look first at some items before students see them. Some subjects may be considered harsh or objectionable.)

Girls and Chronic Disease and Disability

http://www.4girls.gov/chronic

See especially the links for Body Basics and Go Surfing.

U.S. Department of Health and Human Services—Specific Populations

http://www.hhs.gov/specicificpopulations/index.shtml

On this index page, click the link to "Adolescents/Teens/Youth." On the next page, click the "Girl and Adolescent Health" link (found in the General section), or the "Girls Health Information" link (under the Pages Designed for Teens section). Also on the index page, click the link for "Birth Defects, Developmental Disabilities, Kids with Chronic Illness," then the next page's link to "For Kids with Disabilities (Centers for Disease Control and Prevention)," and the link for "About Developmental Disabilities (Center on Birth Defects and Developmental Disabilities)."

Ethics and Morality Issues—Health

http://re-xs.ucsm.ac.uk/ethics/health_and_body

Provided by the Britain-based Religious Education Exchange Service for schools, this Web site has links to information for young people ages eleven to sixteen, including some especially for girls and their teachers, on physical health, mental health, healthy eating, health conditions involving alcohol, drugs, smoking, and personal relationships, all considered from an ethical viewpoint.

"Perspectives on the Past"
Meave Leakey (1999)
URL: http://www.archaeology.org/9907/etc/past.html

SITE SUMMARY: Leakey, a world famous paleoarchaeologist, is the head of the Division of Palaeontology at the National Museum of Kenya in Nairobi, Africa. In this article, published in the July/August 1999 issue of *Archaeology*, a journal of the Archaeological Institute of America, Leakey reveals her first, and, as she says, unusually interesting, discoveries. She also provides her observation of women in science through time and her look at the future with reference to the past from her perspective as a scientist in general and as a scientist in the fields of archeology and paleoarchaeology.

DISCUSSION QUESTIONS AND ACTIVITIES

1. How does Leakey compare and contrast evolution regarding fossils (as shown in the fossil record) and technology? What does she conclude from this?

2. Leakey says that women through time have had to strive to prove their value in science and to show their significant contributions in scientific research. Go to any of the Web sites or areas cited just below and choose information on four women paleoarchaeologists, archaeologists, paleontologists, or physical anthropologists. Find, choose, and comment on what a woman in one of these sciences from the past, of the present, of a North American nation in the past or present and of another nation in the past or present has accomplished in a particular field and how the scientific community has viewed or interpreted each one's accomplishments. (Note the Web sites or pages on FemArc—Women's Network in Archaeology, Women in Paleontology via the Biographies links page at Strange Science: The Rocky Road to Paleontology, and Celebrating Women in Anthropology. Find these Web sites or pages cited in the Related Internet Sites section below or in that section of this book's chapters featuring the documents "The Science of Archaeology," "Paleobiology—In the News, Highlights, Subjects, and Links," "Paper Dinosaurs," and Foreword by Michael Crichton to the *Encyclopedia of Dinosaurs* [1997]. You can also find a women in science Web site cited in this book's Appendix B, or at women in paleontology, women in paleoanthropology, women in archaeology or women in anthropology Web sites found via Web directories cited in this book's Appendix E, and like the yahoo.com and google.com examples referred to in the Related Internet Sites section below.)

3. Leakey's experiences with archeological finds involved discoveries revealing the human brain's evolutionary expansion. What was a thrilling discovery in 1972, and why? What did a "three dimensional jigsaw puzzle" have to do with it and how was she involved with the puzzle? What was surprising and what was it compared or contrasted with? How was the discovery placed in time? What are two other discoveries that were compared or contrasted to the first one, and in which ways? What did all the discoveries demonstrate about the human brain's evolution?

4. What does Leakey say scientific research is primarily focused on? Why? What does she hope for the future? Study a document on recent research at the Web sites listed just below and whose urls are cited in the Related Internet Sites section at the end of this chapter. See the Leakey Foundation—News, Discoveries, Mission, Educational Resources, etc. and *Current Archaeology* Online Web sites. Evaluate the research with reference to what Leakey claims.

5. Which advances in technology, according to Leakey, in addition to the computer, are revolutionizing the way the past is studied? Extra Activity: Choose an archeological subject from one of the Web sites cited just below, whose urls are cited in the Related Internet Sites section at

the end of this chapter. Tell how that subject was studied in the past and how a new technology Leakey mentions has changed the way that subject has been studied recently. (Hint: Two technologies helping research today are common in your world.) (See the Web sites on Technology in Archaeology, Photogrammetry and Archaeology, or Computing in Archaeology, Leakey Foundation—News, Discoveries, Mission, Educational Resources, etc., and *Current Archaeology* Online.) (Note also related items at the following Web sites whose urls are cited in the Related Internet Sites section of this book's chapter that features "The Science of Archaeology" [e.g., Archaeology Resources, Online Excavations via the WWWorld of Archaeology, Archeology in the Parks—United States National Park Service—Links to the Past, and Anthropology in the News].)

RELATED INTERNET SITE(S)

Leakey Foundation News, Discoveries, Mission, Educational Resources, etc.

http://www.leakeyfoundation.org (click links)

See the links to News and Events, Discoveries and Projects, Educational Resources, audio archives of scientific pioneers recounting discoveries, and The Foundation (with information on the Foundation's mission and history and the Leakey Family story featuring patriarch Louis Leakey, matriarch Mary Leakey, the next generation of Richard Leakey and his wife Meave, and the third generation represented by Louise Leakey, plus other noted scientists whom the Foundation helps, such as Dian Fossey and Jane Goodall). Recent archeological discoveries are highlighted.

Meave Leakey

http://www.suite101.com/article.cfm/biographies_scientists/77855

This article by Jackie DiGiovanni (an adjunct community college instructor and technical writer) was posted online August 20, 2001, and features a look at Leakey's life along with quotations by her, and links to more Web sites with information by or about her.

Current Archaeology Online

http://www.archaeology.co.uk (click links)

At this Web site for this Britain-based print magazine, find the links for "What's New in Archaeology?" and "The Best of Science Diary: An Introduction to the World of Archaeological Science," plus About *Current Archaeology*, Our Favorite Web Sites This Month, Walk the Timeline, Current Issue, Next Issue, and search for items by subject in a database that ranges from 1967 to the present (issues one through one hundred eighty, and more) and features bibliographical data on the journal's articles and books from all issues, and from letters and a science diary from issue 96 to the present.

FemArc—Women's Network in Archaeology

http://www.uni-koeln.de/al008/naafwebl.html or *http://www.femarch.de/Netzwerk/text/naafwebl.html*

Click the link to "Archaeology and Gender: What Does It Mean?" (If trouble accessing this site, do a search for "Women's Network in Archaeology" via www.google.com.)

Paleoanthropologists and Women Paleoanthropologists

http://www.yahoo.com

Click links for Science>Anthropology and Archaeology>Anthropologists>Archaeologists or Paleoanthropologists, then look for links to Web sites on women in those fields, or search in the search box for paleoanthropologists or women paleoanthropologists.

Archaeologists and Women Archaeologists

http://www.google.com

After clicking the links for Science>Social Sciences>Archaeology, look for links to particular types of archaeologists such as bioarchaeologists, geoarchaeologists, zooarchaeologists, plus archaeobotanists, ecoarchaeologists, astroarchaeologists, and pioneers in archeology, then look for name links to Web sites on women archaeologists. Note also archaeologists by regions.

Celebrating Women Anthropologists

http://www.cas.usf.edu/anthropology/women

Click name links for highlights of the lives and accomplishments of well-known and lesser-known women anthropologists of the past and who worked in particular anthropology fields including physical anthropology and archaeology.

Computer Applications in Archaeology—Links to Sites

http://www.gla.ac.uk/Archaeology/resources/index.html (click links)

Click the link for Computer Applications in Archaeology (also called Computers in Archaeology), then click the Projects link for a links page to Web sites on, for example, Archaeological Data Archive Project, Archaeological Data Service, Archaeoguide, DigIT, Knowlton Henge Complex, and the Visualization of Landscapes Project. Also on the Computer Applications in Archaeology page, see links to a database, online publications, other collections of links, other materials, plus Geographical Information Systems, Visualisation and Reconstructions, and more. Note in addition on the index page, the link to the *Archaeological Computer Newsletter* (with Tables of Contents online).

Photogrammetry and Archaeology

http://www.univie.ac.at/Luftbildarchiv/wgv.phoarc.htm

Click the links for an "Introduction to Photogrammetry for Non-Photogrammetrists," "a list of Photogrammetrical Applications to Archaeology with examples," and "a list of Literature Documenting Photogrammetry and Its Archaeological Applications," for data on a particular way to use photography in archaeology.

Technology in Archaeology

http://kroeber.anthro.mankato.msus.edu/archaeology/archtechnology/index.shtml

See links to an explanation, history and uses on topics such as "Determining Ages of Sites and Artifacts," "3D Scanning of Artifacts," "Aerial Photography," and more.

Comparative Mammalian Brain Collections

http://www.brainmuseum.org

This easily accessible and understandable site looks at the evolution, development, circuitry, function, and sections, plus atlases, of the human brain and animal brains. Also included are a list of specimens and related Web sites. The site, offering national sources for the study of brain anatomy, is provided by the University of Wisconsin, Michigan State University, and the National Museum of Health and Medicine.

"Physical Activity and Health—Adolescents and Young Adults: A Report"

Surgeon General of the United States (1999)
URL: http://www.cdc.gov/nccdphp/sgr/adoles.htm

SITE SUMMARY: Part of the *Report of the U.S. Surgeon General on Physical Activity and Health*, this document is provided by the Centers for Disease Control and Prevention and the National Center for Chronic Disease Prevention and Health Promotion, Division of Nutrition and Physical Activity. It emphasizes young people ages twelve through twenty-one, with reference to physical activity and health concerns unique to them. Its sections include Key Messages, Facts, Benefits of Physical Activity, and What Communities Can Do.

DISCUSSION QUESTIONS AND ACTIVITIES

1. Read the Report's "Key Messages." Identify suggested moderate physical activity, and moderately intense activity, both referring to time spent and type of activity.
2. Look again at the Report's "Key Messages." What might excessive amounts of physical activity do negatively?
3. Read the Report's "Benefits of Physical Activity," and identify three.
4. Read the Report's "What Communities Can Do." Identify three suggestions. Reveal some health benefits for all three. Select one suggestion and give details of what could be done. (Note: Find details at one or more of these Web sites whose urls are cited in the Related Internet Sites section below: How to Celebrate National Physical Fitness and Sports Month, Education World: Special Theme: Physical Fitness Month, Kids Walk to School, National Coalition for Promoting Physical Activity—Key Resources, and Healthy People 2010.)
5. Read the "CDC Physical Activity and Health Initiative" at the Centers for Disease Control and Prevention Web site. (Its url is cited in the Related Internet Sites section below.) To what does the Initiative's Focus Statement refer when it states that the Center for Disease Control and Prevention provides something scientific and technical? Identify the Initiative's seven key components. See Examples of the Centers for Disease Control Activities and state how one example follows the Focus Statement. Choose something at the Web sites cited just below and state why your choice would initiate or influence you to do physical activity. (Visit the Web sites Health Windows, FitTeen, and Kids Walk; also [optional] "Physical Activity in the Life of Girls" and Girl Power. [Their urls are cited in the Related Internet Sites section below, or in this book's Appendix B.])

RELATED INTERNET SITE(S)

How to Celebrate National Physical Fitness and Sports Month

http://clinton3.nara.gov/WH/PCPFS/html/pfp.html

Features include when this celebration occurs, when it started, what it promotes, and tips on how to celebrate (e.g., how to get started, a plan, suggested events, promotion and publicity, and a sample proclamation). There is also a note on the President's Council on Physical Fitness and Sports and the celebration in 1994.

Education World: Special Theme: Physical Fitness Month

http://www.education-world.com/a_special/physical_fitness.shtml

See links for "Fitness Fun Times Five," "The Web Puts Fizz into Physical Fitness," "Let's Get Physical," and more.

CDC Physical Activity and Health Initiative

http://www.cdc.gov/nccdphp/sgr/npai.htm

See information under The Challenge, The Focus, and Examples of CDC Activities on this Web page that is part of the Web site for the Centers for Disease Control and Prevention, National Center for Chronic Disease Prevention and Health Promotion, Division of Nutrition and Physical Activity.

National Coalition for Promoting Physical Activity—Key Resources

http://www.ncppa.org/resources_index.asp

See links to a Resource Guide; Tools to Promote Physical Activity; Landmark Reports, Statistics, and Research; Physical Activity Information and Fact Sheets. See also links to Public Affairs and Policy (e.g., Physical Activity Policy), and a New News page with information on, for example, the Physical Activity for Youth Policy Initiative that was started in the Winter and Spring of the years 2000 and 2001, with a related document in PDF format.

Health Windows: Your Window to Good Health

http://www.healthwindows.com/healthwindows/index.asp

This site features an Up Front article, Health Headlines titles, Press Releases, a Did You Know statement with a link to more information, and a Daily Tip. More links, which require an educator's registration, are to a Health Library, Family Health, Kids Health, Food and Nutrition, Mental Health, Travel Healthy, Sports and Health, Music and Wellness, and the Brave New World of Twenty-First-Century Medicine.

FitTeen: Fitness for Teens of All Ages

http://www.fitteen.com

Featured links go to News on current interest subjects, Exercise (on specific routines, sports workouts, and writing a Fitness Log), and Diet/Food (on a healthy eating lifestyle that feeds the body and the mind, with recipes, a food diary, shopping list, fitness tests for calculating calories and more, plus information on eating disorders, and what is in fast foods. See also the links to FAQs database, About Fit Teen (for the site's goal), take a mini poll, post comments, and go to a chat. On the home page, read about a plan for eating healthy, and about other subjects of interest (e.g., being a vegetarian). See links to sites on related subjects, and note the Fit Tips pop-up window.

Kids Walk to School—A CDC Program

http://www.cdc.gov/nccdphp/dnpa/kidswalk/index.htm

Part of the Centers for Disease Control and Prevention Web site, this page features goals and anticipated benefits of the program, plus links to Resource Materials (e.g., in PDF format: a guide, a fact sheet, Ideas to Generate Enthusiasm, Working With the Media and Government Officials), Health Benefits, and related links, e.g., to the American Medical Association's "Scientific Position on Exercise (Physical Activity) and Children."

"Physical Activity and Sport in the Lives of Girls: A Report" (1997)

http://education.umn.edu/tuckercenter/pcpfs/default.html

Under the direction of the Center for Research on Girls and Women in Sports at the University of Minnesota, with the President's Council on Physical Fitness, and sponsored by the Center for Mental Health Services at the U.S. Department of Health and Human Services, a detailed investigation of the physiological, mental health, and sociological dimensions of the subject are provided here. There are also messages from the President's Council on Physical Fitness and Sport and the Secretary of Health and Human Services.

Healthy People 2010

http://www.health.gov/healthypeople/Document/tableofcontents.htm

This page is part of a Web site that provides "a statement of national health objectives designed to identify the most significant preventable threats to health and to establish national goals to reduce these threats." The Healthy People 2010 Information Access Project, helped by the National Library of Medicine and the Public Health Foundation, aims to make it easy to find information and evidence-based strategies related to the Project's objectives. See links to full texts of information of publications published in the year 2000 and featuring the main topics Understanding and Improving Health, and Objectives for Improving Health. Under these topics see sub-topics including Health Communication, Leading Health Indicators such as physical activity and environmental quality, Educational and Community Based Programs, Environmental Health, Nutrition, and Physical Activity and Fitness such as physical activity in adults and physical activity in children and adolescents.

Physical Activity in Young People

http://www.hersheynutrition.com/physical/index.asp

Read this document's abstract (a type of summary), then click links to read more, including the introduction, Physical Activity Levels of American Children and Youth, Correlates of Physical Activity, Physical Activity Intervention for Children and Youth, Conclusion, more link, a brochure with a definition of physical activity, factors influencing physical activity, what experts recommend, plus activities at home, school, and in the community (including links to Web sites on biking and walking).

Physical Activity and Health—A Report of the U.S. Surgeon General

http://www.cdc.gov/nccdphp/sgr/sgr.htm

Part of the site for the National Center of Chronic Diseases and Health Promotion, this page has links to At-A-Glance, Report Contents, Executive Summary, Facts Sheets, Nutrition and Physical Activity, and Related Information. The first link leads to links on A New View of Physical Activity, The Benefits of Regular Physical Activity, A Major Public Health Concern, What Is a Moderate Amount of Physical Activity? Examples of A Moderate Amount of Physical Activity, Precautions for a Healthy Start, Status of the Nation—A Need for Change (e.g., for adolescents and young adults), A Special Message for Special Populations, e.g., teenagers, and Ideas for Improvement. The second link goes to links with information on Physiologic Response and Long-Term Adaptations to Exercise, The Effects of Physical Activity on Health and Disease, Patterns and Trends in Physical Activity, Understanding and Promoting Physical Activity. The third link goes to a link leading to a Message from the Health and Human Services Secretary. The fourth link leads to information on women, people with disabilities, the CDC's National Physical Activity Initiative, and more. The fifth link leads to links on Highlights, Press Releases, information on physical activity, nutrition, and public health programs. The sixth link leads to items such as "Ready, Set, Its Everywhere You Go: The CDC's Guide to Promoting Moderate Physical Activity."

Establishing the President's Council on Physical Fitness—Executive Order 11074

http://www.lib.umich.edu/govdocs/jfkeo/eo/11074.htm

Issued January 8, 1963, by President John F. Kennedy.

Physical Fitness and Sports—Executive Order 12345

http://envirotext.eh.doe.gov/data/eos/reagan/19820202.html

Issued February 2, 1982, by President Ronald Reagan, this order was made to continue the President's Council on Physical Fitness and to expand the program.

WebElements
Mark Winter (1999–)
URL: http://www.webelements.com (click the student/scholar version link)

SITE SUMMARY: This interactive version of the Periodic Table of Chemical Elements (especially for students in upper high school and college) is an adaptation of the first Periodic Table (by Dmitri Mendeleev in 1869). Provided online by Mark Winter of the University of Sheffield in England, WebElements features the Periodic Table with new discoveries and 118 elements (with elements 113, 115, and 117 assumed; and 114, 116, and 118 recently reported). New names in the table were given according to rules by the International Union of Pure and Applied Chemistry (IUPAC), sometimes in conjunction or competition with the American Chemical Society, during the 1990s. Winter provides access to information by causing an element name to appear when a site visitor places the mouse arrow over each element symbol box, then by bringing a page of an element's basic information (e.g., physical properties) after a click of an element's letter symbol and number box on the table. Clicking on a topic brings data on that topic for the element.

DISCUSSION QUESTIONS AND ACTIVITIES

1. There are scientific features and formulas unique to, and identifying, well-known natural and man-made elements (e.g., calcium, CA; zinc, ZN; oxygen, O; uranium, U); and for elements not well-known. Find and describe the elements noted above and four other well-known elements; one each that is in the groups to which belong the elements referred to above. Find, and describe, from each group, four elements not well-known or ones new to you; then a fifth one from a fifth group in the table. (Hint: For descriptions, cite an element's letter[s] symbol, atomic number, atomic weight, structure, physical properties or physical data, the name of the group to which element belongs, and the element's history, plus uses in general, and in particular, with relation to a science; then note if the element is man-made or found in nature. Cite any other interesting data for an element.)

2. What are the different groups, families, or types of elements in the Periodic Table? (Hint: Note the colors and the rows or columns.) Explain the unique features of each type. (For help, see the following Web sites: Interactive Periodic Table of Elements, 1996–2002; General Chemistry Online—Companion Notes—Periodic Table; Periodic Table of Elements—A Resource for Students—Los Alamos National Laboratory; Periodic Table of Elements—Meet and Learn; and Periodic Table [Detailed Description]. [Find their urls in the Related Internet Sites section below.]) Give an example of each which is not noted in Question/Activity no. 1. Identify who discovered these different groups or types of elements. (For help, visit the Web sites: History of Chemistry—Classic Papers, Biographies, and Related Links; Selected Classic Papers from the History of Chemistry; or the ChemTeam's Classic Papers Menu. See their urls in the Related Internet Sites section below.) (Hint: See, for example, Dmitri Mendeleev, Antoine Lavoisier, John Alexander Newlands, and Sir William Ramsay.)

3. Identify the discoverers and features of their research for the first three, plus a fourth, of the following things which have become "basic information" for elements in the Periodic Table: element, atomic weight number, atomic mass number, structure, electron, neutron, and proton. (For help, visit the Web sites cited in Question/Activity no. 2 above and see documents by scientists including, for example: J.J. Thomson, Baron Kelvin [also known as William Thomson], and Daniel Rutherford. See also the History of the Periodic Table Web site found via the ChemDex—The Periodic Table Web site whose url is cited in the Related Internet Sites section below.)

4. Visit the Selected Classic Papers from the History of Chemistry Web site (its Nomenclature, Periodic Table, and Periodic Law, areas); plus the ChemTeam's Classic Papers Menu; the History of Chemistry—Classic Papers, Biographies, and related links; or Athena—Authors and Texts

Related to Science Web sites. (Find as noted in Question/Activity no. 2 above, or in this book's Appendix B.) Find and read writings by scientists who were influential in the creation of the Periodic Table or who provided an important adaptation or addition to it, e.g., Dmitri Mendeleev, Henry Moseley, Niels Bohr, Lorenzo Avogadro, Jons Jacob Berzelius, Stanislao Cannizzaro, Johann Dobereiner, Irving Langmuir, Daniel Rutherford, and John Alexander Newlands. (Hints: Find data on and explain the relationship of elements' properties to their atomic weight; chemical symbols and formulas; the "law of triads"; the "law of octaves"; the "law of definite proportions"; the law involving gases with relation to molecules, temperature, and pressure; and the philosophy of chemistry.)

5. Visit the Web sites, and their areas, noted in Question/Activities no. 2 and no. 4 above (e.g., Elements: Nature, Number and Discovery; and Gases; at the Selected Classic Papers from the History of Chemistry Web site). Find and read a chemist's paper, then describe, including quotations, a discovery that is related to the Periodic Table and its elements (e.g., papers by Joseph Priestley, Sir Humphrey Davy, Louis Jacques Thenard, Sir William Ramsay, Sir James Chadwick, and J.J. Thomson). For some help, see the History of the Periodic Table Web site, found via the ChemDex—The Periodic Table Web site. (Its url is cited in the Related Internet Sites section below.)

6. Find Antoine Lavoisier's "Preface to Elements of Chemistry" via the Nomenclature section of the Selected Classic Papers from the History of Chemistry Web site. Read paragraphs seven and nineteen, then other paragraphs. Describe his comments on how the study of science is like a child learning, and what chemistry has to do with it.

7. Read the biography and the autobiography at The Seaborg Center—The Life of Glenn Seaborg, 1912–1999 Web site. (Its url is cited in the Related Internet Sites section below.) Quoting from his autobiography, identify Seaborg's contributions to the Periodic Table and why they are especially important. Describe, with quotations, what he thought about the discovery process.

8. Many unusual types of "periodic tables" have been created. For examples, see the links at the Web sites: Martindale's Reference Desk: Chemistry Center, and the ChemDex—The Periodic Table, whose urls are cited in the Related Internet Sites section below. Choose a science topic. Create your own unusual "periodic table" and explain it.

RELATED INTERNET SITE(S)

Dmitri Mendeleev Online

http://www.chem.msu.su/eng/misc/mendeleev/welcome.html

See links under the categories: Overviews, Writings, Periodic Law, Periodic Tables, and Miscellaneous.

ChemTeam—Classic Papers Menu

http://dbhs.wvusd.k12.ca.us/Chem-History/Classic-Papers-Menu.html

This site has title links to papers important in the history of chemistry. Papers are arranged by years, from ancient times to the mid-twentieth century. See also links to some biographical articles, secondary articles, and miscellaneous articles.

History of Chemistry—Classic Papers, Biographies, and Related Links

http://www.chemistrycoach.com/history_of_chemistry.htm

This site has title links alphabetically arranged by a chemist's last name, with important years noted.

Selected Classic Papers from the History of Chemistry

http://webserver.lemoyne.edu/faculty/giunta/papers.html

See links to papers under the following subjects: Periodical Table and Periodic Law; Elements: Nature, Number; Discovery; Atomic Hypotheses and Discrete Nature of Matter; the Electron and the Electronic Structure of Matter; Nomenclature; Gases; and more. A link to papers arranged alphabetically by author name is also provided.

General Chemistry Online—Companion Notes—Periodic Table

http://antoine.frostburg.edu/chem/senese/101/notes.shtml (click Periodic Table link)

Find out about Learning Objectives, Prerequisite Skills, Lecture Notes, Concepts to Review, FAQs, Glossary, and links.

Periodic Table of the Elements—Meet and Learn

www.periodictable.com

Click the Teachers, Students, Biologists, or Chemists link.

Periodic Table (Detailed Description)

http://www.bartleby.com/65/pe/periodtbl.html

Interactive Periodic Table of Elements, 1996–2002

http://www.chemicalelements.com

This is a user-friendly, multiple-access version of the Periodic Table, with links to information on the element groups or families. Access is available to table versions featuring especially elements' names, symbols, years of discovery, and indications of structure.

Periodic Table of Elements—A Resource for Students—Los Alamos National Laboratory

http://pearl1.lanl.gov/periodic/elements/default.html

This version of the Periodic Table for elementary school and middle and high school students features one hundred nine elements and places for assumed elements with higher numbers. There are links to "What Is the Periodic Table?" "How to Use the Periodic Table," "Naming New Elements," "Chemistry in a Nutshell," "Mendeleev's Original Periodic Table," and a list of alphabetic elements with their symbols and numbers. Click an element in the table to find more data. The site also has areas for asking a question and for giving comments or suggestions.

The Seaborg Center—The Life of Glenn Seaborg, 1912–1999

http://seaborg.nmu.edu/gts

This Web site is for the noted twentieth-century U.S.-born Swedish-American chemist known for identifying several elements now in the Periodic Table, including one named for him; and for sharing a Nobel Prize with E.M. McMillan for their work on transuranium elements. He is also known as the only person to obtain a patent for an element, for working with U.S. presidents, then for promoting peaceful uses of nuclear power. Features of the site include "Glenn T. Seaborg, Citizen-Scientist" (a biography by Peggy House); links to an autobiography; a list of his accomplishments; and reviews of, and an excerpt from, *Adventures in the Atomic Age* (a book completed by his son Eric Seaborg, from notes the scientist was preparing for publication). A links page is in progress.

"It's Element-ary!" in *Odyssey Magazine* Online, November 2000

http://www.cobblestonepub.com/pages/odysmain.htm

Click the Teachers Guides link, then scroll and search the links for this activity for ages 10–16, based on the print issue for that month and year.

Explore the Periodic Table and Families of Elements—Some Important Facts

http://www.ruf.rice.edu/~sandyb/Lessons/chem.html

What Is the Periodic Law and How Was It Formulated?

http://members.aol.com/profchm/periodic.html

Note the links to "Dmitri Mendeleev" and "Glen Seaborg." Note also the Periodic Table References link at http://members.aol.com/profchm/bm_chmed.html.

ChemDex—The Periodic Table

http://www.chemdex.org/index.php

Click the Periodic Table link under the Top Level Categories at the far right of the page, for links to the Table made by various sources, as provided at this Web site by the University of Sheffield in England. Note Periodic Tables in various languages from many nations, Special Periodic Tables, Periodic Tables for Children (including some for and by high school students), General Purpose Sites (with a wide range of data), Minor Sites with more information (including unusual ways of seeing the Table), and the History of the Periodic Table (with notes on early versions and changes reflecting discoveries regarding how the Periodic Table should be and where elements should be in it).

The Schemata of the Elements

http://www.the-periodic-table.com/sys-tmpl/theschemata

This Web site provides an unusual unnoticed way of arranging the Periodic Table. It is a way that produces "astounding patterns of symmetry" and shows additional data on the elements.

"Periodic Tables" at Martindale's Reference Desk: Chemistry Center

http://www-sci.lib.uci.edu/HCS/GradChemistry.html#TABLES-GEN

See links to various types of the Periodic Table of Elements, including those in different languages, a Table Database, Tables for Fun, and an interesting site with a Pictorial Table and alternative Tables. Tables have been made by universities, organizations, and people who work in the chemistry field.

"The Naming of New Elements"

http://www.iupac.org/reports/provisional/archives/index.html

On this page of "Links for the Provisional Recommendations for Naming Elements," at the Web site for the organization which has the final authoritative word on the names and naming of elements, scroll to, and click, the article title link under the "Published" category. Information found via this page has been approved for publication in the IUPAC journal: *Pure and Applied Chemistry*. See also on the bottom of the archives' index page, a link to the part of the *IUPAC Handbook* that provides the "Procedure For Comment and Approval of Recommendations on Nomenclature and Symbols."

IUPAC Generic Naming Convention for the Chemical Elements

http://www.sweethaven.com/chemele/chemele.html (click the Periodic Table link)

Adapted from David L. Heiserman's *Exploring Chemical Elements and Compounds* (1992), this Web site features a description of how an element's name and symbol are devised by rules set up by the International Union of Pure and Applied Chemists (IUPAC). A Periodic Table with elements up to no. 168 is also provided. See also, on the main page, a link for excerpts from the book that has brief but interesting information on one hundred seven elements, plus part of that book's introduction that has an anecdote about the author's discovery of chemistry when he was a junior high school student. (If trouble accessing, do site title search at google.com.)

Modeling the Periodic Table

http://www.genesismission.org/educate/scimodule/cosmic/ptable.html

This Web site is for students and teachers who want to create their own unique Periodic Tables. A teachers guide and tips are included. Special software, downloadable here, is required to access all of the Web site's features.

Flora of North America
Editorial Committee (2000–)
URL: http://www.fna.org/FNA/index.html (click The Project link)

SITE SUMMARY: *Flora of North America* is a multi-national project in progress that will culminate in a multi-volume print publication published by Oxford University Press and featuring an online counterpart which is represented on this Web site especially by the Project Introduction, Scope and Rationale, Content, History and Volume One, plus the FNA Newsletter, and Editorial Centers. Endorsed by the American Society of Plant Taxonomists, the Canadian Botanical Association and the Botanical Society of America; and sponsored by the U.S. National Science Foundation and other organizations, the FNA Project (the only one of its kind), and the criteria (or basic aspects), have been set up for botanical researchers to make standard identification records ("authoritative, up to date information" of about 21,000 species) of all known plants in North America, especially the U.S. and Canada.

DISCUSSION QUESTIONS AND ACTIVITIES

1. See Introduction to the Project, paragraph six, part one. Identify how North American non-cultivated plant species descriptions are determined to be authoritative, in general and also for this Project.

2. Identify the basic aspects (also known as treatments) for a botanical specimen, as noted in part two of the sixth paragraph of the Introduction to the Project.

3. Study Volume One, Chapter Fourteen, at the FNA Volumes Online area. (Its url is cited in the Related Internet Sites section below.) Cite four aspects of classic botanical historical note related to the basic aspects for Flora of North America. Cite similarities and differences between the historical aspects and the basic aspects (which you found when answering Question/Activity no. 1 above). (Hint: See A.P. de Candolle, G. Bentham and J.D. Hooker, H.G.A. Engler and K. Prantl, and C.E. Bessey.)

4. Study further Volume One, Chapter Fourteen, at the FNA Volumes Online area (found as found as cited in Question/Activity no. 3 above). What have "major schemes of classification of flowering plants . . . attempted to portray" in the past century? Choose one botanist or botanist team from the past, then describe the botanist's or botanists' theory and how it influenced, or does not hold up, with reference to the theory through time and present-day viewpoints. (Note also Chapter Fifteen for second item just above.)

5. See the beginning and the conclusion of Volume One, Chapter Fifteen, at the FNA Volumes Online area (found as cited in the Related Internet Sites section below). What can be said of the validity of taxonomic schemes in general, and regarding particular ones (e.g., the Linnaean one)?

6. Read Volume One, Chapter Eleven, at the FNA Volumes Online area (found as cited in the Related Internet Sites section below). Read especially the sections Defining and Delimiting Species, Toward a Broader Biological Species Concept (paragraph thirteen), and New Ideas on the Treatment of Genera. Briefly define species and genera. Describe the problem of defining and delimiting species.

7. See Volume One, Chapter Ten, at the FNA Volumes Online area (found online as cited in the Related Internet Sites section below). See first paragraphs. When did the American conservation movement start to gain momentum? Describe one early conservation effort by a person and by a government. How is each effort still important today? Read the section Importance of Conserving Biodiversity, state the "four main lines of reasoning" regarding plant conservation, then give details of one, and describe how your chosen "line" would affect you and the

world around you. Read the section Contributions of Plant Conservation Efforts, then cite an organization, national agency or law, and describe its conservation effort(s). Read the section Present and Future Challenges, then give one example of what needs to be done, and explain why it is important. Option: For the first and third activities just above, see also the writings at the Web sites: Evolution of American Conservation Movement and U.S. EPA Laws and Regulations. (Their urls are cited in the Related Internet Sites section below.)

8. See the area for the FNA Volumes Online, or the area for the FNA Editorial Centers. (Their urls are cited in the Related Internet Sites section below.) Find a volume, then chapter, or center. Follow links to plant information, choose a plant, and describe the plant's features following the basic aspects (which you found when answering Question/Activity no. 1 above). Next, describe that plant in the different ways botanists described plants in past times (which you found when answering Question/Activity no. 3 above).

RELATED INTERNET SITE(S)

Flora of North America—Published Volumes Online

http://www.fna.org/FNA/volumes.html

Click Volume One Contents link, then link to Introduction by Nancy Morin and Richard Spellenberg, noting especially Historical Background, FNA Project, and Resources. Note also links to fifteen chapters sub-divided by topics, including Arthur Conquist's A Commentary on the General System of Classification of Flowering Plants (Chapter Fourteen); James L. Reveal's Flowering Plant Families—An Overview (Chapter Fifteen); G. Ledyard Stebbins' Concepts of Species and Genera (Chapter Eleven); and George Yatskievych and Richard Spellenberg's Plant Conservation in the Flora of North America Region (Chapter Ten). (Volume Two on Pteridophytes and Gymnosperms, Volume Three on Magnolisphyta, and Volume Twenty-Two on Magnoliophyta, will soon be online.)

FNA Newsletter

http://www.fna.org/FNA/newsletter.html

Links go to the current issue, and archive of past issues for updates on the FNA Project.

Flora of North America—Editorial Centers

http://www.fna.org/FNA/administration.html

Scroll to, then click, the link to the Editorial Centers. Links go to particular editorial centers where botanical scientists are providing information for the FNA Project. Note these institutions' noted botanical scientists in charge of their institutions' FNA affiliation.

American Society of Plant Taxonomists—Newsletter

http://www.sysbot.org (click newsletter link)

Evolution of American Conservation Movement, 1850–1920

http://lcweb2.loc.gov/ammem/amrvhtml/conshome.html

EPA (U.S. Environmental Protection Agency) Laws and Regulations

http://www.epa.gov/epahome/rules.html

Olympic Sports Technical Performance Rules and Glossary of Techniques
United States Olympic Committee (USOC) (2000)
URL: http://www.usoc.org/home/top.html (scroll to pull-down menu at top right)

SITE SUMMARY: Selected Olympic sports for the Summer and Winter Games are featured in this area of the Official Web site of the United States Olympic Committee. Click on the menu, choose a season, then select a sport from those listed alphabetically. Next, click the sport's name to go to a page of general information on the sport and to links that go to pages with technical rules, a glossary of performance techniques, history, and athletes related to this sport. Note the basic rules and requirements for athletes' performance in each sport. Via an athletes link, see current athletes to note and particular sports' athlete legends. Each sport's page also has a link that goes to a sport's official U.S. organization's Web site, with news, and a link to the site of the sport's official international organization. The rules follow the International Olympic Committee's recommendations, which state that a sport's national and international organizations are responsible for setting and maintaining rules.

DISCUSSION QUESTIONS AND ACTIVITIES

1. For a list of Olympic sports, click the USOC Web site's menu. Choose a Winter Olympic sport and a Summer Olympic sport that you like. For each one identify and describe three to six technical performance rules that United States Olympic athletes must follow in these sports. If there are different requirements for women and men, state both. (Note: If a sport has more than one area, choose one such as figure skating singles, rhythmic gymnastics, or synchronized swimming.)

2. Find data on four United States Olympic athletes who are sports legends. Search for and choose four Olympic athletes of the past (e.g., two women and two men). State the accomplishment(s) in each athlete's Olympic participation, including which medal was won (if any), for which sport, when, and, if possible, which technical moves they did well in their sports or which they are remembered in connection with. Tell what they became after their Olympic career, if their post-Olympic occupations are connected somehow to their sports, the Olympics, or scientific aspects of these sports. (Note: In your answers include athletes' quotations, if found online.) Extra Activity: Choose a particular sport you like. Imagine, then explain, something you could do in that field, with a science connection, after your "Olympic accomplishment." (Tip: To answer the questions just above, find information by visiting the Official USOC Web Site—Main Page whose url and site summary are in the Related Internet Sites section below. There, click the Bios link, or do a search in the search box for Where Are They Now? and Hall of Fame [also found by checking the Programs area for the Hall of Fame icon link]. Look there too for athlete legends for a particular sport on the sport page. Find as noted in this chapter's featured site's Site Summary above, for this site's sports areas.)

3. Find data on two Olympic athletes who are sports legends in a nation other than the United States. Choose athletes of a nation from which your family claims its heritage or another foreign nation. Apply to this activity the three parts of Question/Activity no. 2 above, particularly the sentences that start with the words search, state, and tell. Find information on sports legends of nations other than the United States in the Athletes area of the International Olympic Committee Official Web site, via individual sports' Olympic committee Web sites or searches of Internet search directories. Their urls are cited in the Related Internet Sites section below or in this book's Appendix E.

4. Find an article's citation on a science-related Olympic sports topic. Think about the subject

in the title, and write a two hundred word essay on the title's subject. Aim to include a fact on a recent and maybe well-known Olympic sport and athletes as applied to the subject. U.S. and other nations' athletes may be mentioned. (To find article citations, go to the Web pages for Proceedings—International Symposium for Olympic Research and *Olympika: International Journal of Olympic Studies*, both in the Publications area of the Ontario Canada's International Centre for Olympic Studies Web site. Also visit the ICOS related links page [noting especially its section on Research Sites and Documentation Centres with links leading to their sites, then each site's Publications Areas], see data at the IOC Medical Commission Web site, and search the Sport Science Meets the Olympics Web site. In addition, note the Official USOC Web site—Main Page, clicking the News link or doing a search for the News Archives or Sports Medicine, or choosing a sport from the menu, then, on that sport's page, choosing the History link. [Urls for all Web sites mentioned above are in the Related Internet Sites section below.])

5. Visit the Amateur Athletic Association of Los Angeles—Search Page and the Sport Science Meets the Olympics Web sites. (Their urls are cited in the Related Internet Sites section below.) Think of three science-related Olympic sports subjects. Find an article on each subject, one from each site. Read the articles or their summaries, then write one hundred word essays on the facts in each article. Aim to include a fact on a recent, maybe well-known, Olympic sport and athletes as applied to the subject, if possible. U.S. or other nations' athletes may be noted.

6. Animals have been chosen as Olympic mascots that serve as symbols representing Olympic athletes' characteristics and skills. Each mascot also has a connection to the host nation where an Olympics takes place. Visit the Web site areas including Mascots at the International Olympic Memorabilia Federation and Olympic Mascots in the AAFLA Olympic Primer. Also try a Mascots search in the Official USOC Web site—Main Page search box. Choose two wild animals that have been represented by mascots, one from the United States and one from another nation. Describe each animal and its natural features, including type of animal, particular kind of animal, distinguishing marks, behavior traits, habitat, and geographic area where it lives. Why do you think these animals were chosen as mascots or as bases for cartoon character mascots? (Tip: For help identifying the animals' features, see the All About Animals Web site.) (Each url for the Web sites or Web site areas suggested above is cited in the Related Internet Sites section below.)

7. Keeping Question/Activity no. 6 above in mind, and the Web sites cited in it, think of or pick two wild animals you would choose as mascots for two Olympics, one in the United States and one in another nation. Describe each chosen animal's particular features that are referred to in general terms in Question/Activity no. 6 above, and explain why you chose that animal. (Note: You may choose mascot animals for actual past or upcoming Olympics and host nations, but choose animals not yet chosen as mascots. You may also choose mascots for an Olympics in a nation and a nation's city [which includes that city's surrounding region] which have not yet been selected as a host nation or a host city.)

8. Go to the Web page on "The Environment—The Third Dimension of Olympism." Identify basic features of the guidelines that guide the Olympic movement where the environment is concerned. Identify one or two documents that have been selected as guides. Cite two examples of an Olympics where those guidelines and the guide document(s) have been followed, one example from a United States Olympics and the other example from another nation's Olympics. Include references to athletes where possible. Extra Activity: Think of, or find via the Olympic Studies Directory Search Page or by searching an Internet search directory, something else that may be done at an Olympics, or has been done, where the guidelines and guide documents regarding the environment have been followed. Cite guide documents and

guidelines, and provide quotations when possible. This example may be from a U.S. or other nation's Olympics. (Urls for Web sites or Web pages referred to in this question/activity can be found in the Related Internet Sites section below. Find urls for Internet search directories in this book's Appendix E.)

9. Go to the Web page about the Olympic Prize in Sport Science. (Find via link on the IOC Medical Commission Web site whose url is cited in the Related Internet Sites section below.) Identify the goals that the commission aims for when deciding who should be awarded this prize. Do a search for a winner of the IOC Sport Sciences prize via an Internet search directory or search at these Web sites or Web pages whose urls are cited in the Related Internet Sites section below: the International Centre for Olympic Studies, the Olympic Studies International Directory, keyword search of the database at the Sport Wissenschaft im Internet, the Amateur Athletic Association of Los Angeles—Search Page, and the Official USOC Web site—Main Page. (Find urls for Internet search directories in this book's Appendix E.) Explain how the winner's work is a particular example of the basic goals the commission adheres to when awarding the prize.

RELATED INTERNET SITE(S)

Sport Science Meets the Olympics

http://whyfiles.news.wisc.edu/019olympic/index.html

At this site funded by the National Science Foundation featured articles include "How are science and technology changing the games?" and "Why your mind might help you jump higher." See also the Glossary and the Bibliography with links and the numbered links that lead to information on sports psychology, biomechanics, mechanics, and more.

"Athletes" at the International Olympic Committee Official Web Site

http://www.olympic.org/uk/athletes/index.uk.asp

Click a famous or medal winning athlete's photo link to read a biographical note on the athlete's Olympic accomplishment, click an alphabetic letter to find biographical notes for athletes whose names start with that letter, or, after clicking the link for Medal Winners Search, do a search by selecting all of the following: an individual or a team; women, men, or mixed; gold, silver, and bronze medals; continent; nation; Olympic sport; event (e.g., singles, team); Olympic Games edition (e.g., Winter Games, Summer Games, or a particular city and year). Next click Search.

International Centre for Olympic Studies, Ontario, Canada—Publications, Lectures, Links

http://www.uwo.ca/olympic

Links go to Proceedings—International Symposium for Olympic Research and *The Olympika: International Journal of Olympic Studies*, with menus leading to citations of proceeding speeches and journal articles. There is also a link to a Lecture Series with a biography of the current lecturer, and there are links to Related Sites including other Research and Documentation Centres and their publication areas.

Amateur Athletic Association of Los Angeles—Search Page

http://www.aafla.org/search/search.html

Click boxes next to listed online publications with Olympics, sports, or international in their titles (e.g., *Olympic Official Reports, Olympic Review, Revue Olympique, Olympika, Olympic*

Research Symposia, the audio *Olympic Oral Histories*, and *Journal of Olympic History*, plus *International Sports Studies, Sporting Traditions*, and *Journal of Sport History*). Next, enter a key word or key phrase (e.g., sports science, physiology, medicine, psychology). Type a year or range of years (optional). Click Search Now. A list of article title links to articles on the keyword subject from these publications will appear.

Official United States Olympic Committee (USOC) Web Site—Main Page

http://www.usoc.org

See search box under menu, links to FAQs, News/Features, The Week in Review, and Quick Picks (e.g., For Kids, Bios). At page's bottom, see the link to Education (with links to data in PDF format, e.g., Supplemental Dietary Information 2001), and see a link to About the USOC, that goes to a page of links to Programs (e.g., a Hall of Fame icon link), plus Documents and Public Notices, What Is the USOC?, What We Do, and Mission.

All About Animals at the Friends of the National Zoo Web Site

http://fonz.org/animals.htm

See the Animal Index link and the Library of Animal Facts link.

Olympic Mascots at the International Olympic Memorabilia Federation

http://www.collectors.olympic.org/e/fimo/fimo_mascots_e.html

Click a Summer or Winter Olympic Game year and host city on the timeline to get to a colorful mascot picture, name, details or features, animal (or something else) it is based on, why it was chosen as mascot, its designer, and sometimes how a mascot was chosen.

Olympic Mascots in the Amateur Athletic Foundation of Los Angeles Olympic Primer

http://www.aafla.org

Click the Olympic Information Center link, then the Olympic Primer link. Select Winter Olympic Mascots, Summer Olympics Mascots from the pull-down menu, then scroll to see a color picture and interesting tidbits of information on each mascot.

The Education Site for the 2002 Olympics and Paralympics

http://www.uen.org/2002

This prolific site has links to an educator's guide in PDF format (featuring menus that go to articles on many subjects, e.g., fitness and health; Olympic heroes; mascots; countries: Welcome the World, and Your Family Is from Where?), sports (with links to information that includes science concepts), and more.

2002 Olympics Education Site—Curriculum—Science

http://www.lightwithing.org/curriculum/content_areas/science/science.html

Scroll to links to lesson plans for older students (e.g., Earth—Our Greatest Resource, Chemistry and Sport, Biology: Ecosystems and the 2002 Games, Physics: Newton's Laws and Winter Sports). Note also younger students' lessons' subjects and think of how they may be adapted for older students (e.g., Geology and the Wasatch Mountains; Biodiversity of Plant and Animal Life in Northern Utah; Higher, Swifter, Stronger, Animals; and Heat and Insulation). In addition, at www.lightwithin.org/curriculum/content_areas/physed/physed.html, see links to scientific aspects of physical education, such as cardiovascular training and conditioning or pacing for particular sports.

International Sports Federations—Links Page

http://www.olympic.org/uk/organization/index_uk.asp

Two pull-down menus have links that go to Web sites for individual winter and summer sports' international federations that aim to keep their technical performance rules for athletes in agreement with Olympic Sport Performance Rules as outlined in the *International Olympic Committee (IOC) Charter.*

National Sport Organizations—Links, at Sport Wissenschaft im Internet

http://www.sponet.de (click British flag icon link for English version)

At this Germany-based sport science database, choose English Language, All Countries, and Basic Level from pull-down menus, then "Technical Sports" from the Topical Areas menu, and "Organisation Info" from the Type of Source" menu. Click Search. See links to Web sites for individual winter and summer sports' national organizations, including those that aim to keep their athletes' technical performance rules in agreement with sport performance rules as stated in the *IOC Charter.* (Note: for searches of other subjects, subject word(s) can be typed in a textstring box.)

National Olympic Committees—Links Page

http://directory.google.com/Top/Sports/Events/Olympics/National_Olympic_Committees

IOC Charter via the Olympic Documents Page

http://www.olympic.org/uk/utilities/reports/index_uk.asp

Click the "complete text" link under *IOC Charter* to go to a page about it, then click the link to it in PDF format.

International Olympic Committee (IOC) Medical Commission

http://http://www.olympic.org/uk/organization/commissions/medical/index_uk.asp

This area of the official Olympic Movement Web site features data on the commission's history and mission, nutritional supplements and the anti-doping stance the commission advocate. Featured links go to more information on nutrition and anti-doping, plus data on the IOC World Congresses on Sport Sciences, and the IOC Olympic Prize in Sport Science (e.g., in the medical, biological, psychological, and physiological sciences).

"The Environment—The Third Dimension of Olympism"

http://www.olympic.org/uk/organization/missions/environment_uk.asp

On this page of the Official IOC Web site, data on the protection and wise use of the environment with relation to the Olympics are featured, along with international organizations' and United Nations' environmental directives all Olympics must follow.

Olympic Studies International Directory

http://olympicstudies.uab.es/scripts/main.asp

On this search page, click the circle beside institutions; leave ALL in the country, subject, and index, menus; type the word Science in the "by name" box; then click Search. Links will appear to the Web sites for the Centre for Sports Science and History (with useful links), Library of Human Movement Sciences and Sports, and Research Institute for Sport and Exercise Science. The search page subject menu lists medicine, psychology, environment, information science, information technology, new technologies, and more.

Centre for Olympic Studies—University of New South Wales—Resources, Publications

http://www.arts.unsw.edu.au/olympic (click Resources link or Publications link)

On the Resources page, click the link for links to Olympic News sites, Yahoo Olympic sites, Great Olympians, and more sites on Olympic Studies. On the Publications page, title links go to abstracts of articles on Olympic studies subjects with relation to the 2000 Summer Olympics in Sydney, Australia.

"Remarks on the Completion of the First Survey of the Entire Human Genome Project"
Bill Clinton, Tony Blair, Francis Collins, and Craig Venter (2000)
URL: http://www.ornl.gov/TechResources/Human_Genome/project/clinton2.html

SITE SUMMARY: These remarks, online via the Human Genome Information Web site, and presented at the White House on June 26, 2000, feature comments defining the Human Genome Project and its First Survey, plus what they meant at the time the remarks were given, and what they mean for the future. Featured remarks are by Dr. Francis Collins, co-head of the publicly funded project at the National Institutes of Health, Dr. Craig Venter of the Celera Corporation, U.S. President Bill Clinton, and Britain's Prime Minister Tony Blair.

DISCUSSION QUESTIONS AND ACTIVITIES

1. Venter identified the date of the occasion when these remarks were given as "an historic point in the one hundred thousand year record of humanity." See his remarks, paragraph two, and Collins' remarks, paragraphs four, five, and fourteen. Referring to the reason why Venter made that comment, according to Collins, what milestone and revelation did they celebrate that day? What did eighteenth-century British writer Alexander Pope write that fits the occasion, and in what way? What have we "caught the first glimpse of" that "was previously known only to God"? What did President Clinton say to further describe Collins' statement about catching a glimpse? (Tip: See Clinton's first remarks, paragraph eight, and the first part of paragraph nine.) What did Venter announce, which he saw as marking that "historic point"?

2. See Clinton's first remarks, paragraphs four and five. Identify the historic happening, U.S. President, explorer, and product the explorer made that Clinton mentioned. Describe what he said the "product" defined (generally) and the connection he made between what happened at that past time and what happened the day of the remarks. What did Prime Minister Blair contemplate and comment on regarding this subject? (Hint: See Blair's first remarks, paragraph one.) What did Clinton say in his first remarks, paragraph nine, the last part, that agrees "even more" with Blair's comment?

3. See Collins' remarks, paragraph nine, and the first sentence of paragraph ten. He mentioned the "sequencing of the human genome." What does this mean? What has an international consortium of scientists done involving it? (Tip: For help, see the Web sites for the Human Genome Project Information, Introduction to the Human Genome Project, the National Human Genome Research Institute—Research, and the National Human Genome Research Institute—In the News. Their urls are cited in the Related Internet Sites section below.) What is the "EST approach" or "expressed sequence tag" that Venter used, according to Collins in his remarks, paragraph eighteen?

4. What will researchers in a few years have trouble imagining, according to Collins? (Hint: See his remarks, paragraph fourteen.)

5. See Venter's remarks, paragraphs ten, eleven, and seventeen. In paragraph ten, what did he say he learned when he was a young man in the medical corps in Vietnam, what did that experience inspire, what did he realize, and why? In paragraph eleven, what did he say our physiology is based on? In paragraph seventeen, what did he say "the complexities and wonder of how the inanimate chemicals that are our genetic code" "give rise to" and what does this mean for which types of people?

6. Keeping Question/Activity no. 5 above in mind, what comparison did Venter draw to make the comment in paragraph eleven clearer? By making this comparison, he used a writing method that is called analogy. (For a definition of analogy, search at the Information Please

Dictionary Web site whose url and directions for use are in this book's Appendix F. Search for Comparison or Analogy.) Think of your own analogy or comparison with reference to Venter's comment, and be sure to feature something scientific as your first statement.

7. Still keeping Question/Activity no. 5. above in mind, and after finding out what Venter meant in his comment in paragraph seventeen, write something in the way a writer he refers to would write. (Optional help: Check out the Web sites with "Science in the Poetry of Emily Dickinson"; "A Science" (poem no. 100) and "The Brain is" (poem no. 632) by Emily Dickinson; William Blake's "To see a world in a grain of sand"; Walt Whitman's "A Noiseless Patient Spider"; or Marianne Moore's "The Jellyfish." Their urls are cited in this book's Appendix C.)

8. Again keeping Question/Activity no. 5 above in mind, identify the comparisons Clinton draws between the discovery announced that day of the remarks and the discoveries of the scientists Galileo, Watson, and Crick (with others). (Hint: See Clinton's first remarks, paragraphs eight, nine, and six.)

9. See Venter's remarks, paragraphs four, five, and eleven. He and his team "determined the genetic code" of how many species of living things and human beings? Identify the different human beings he worked with, tell why he choose them, then reveal what he discovered, and give illustrations or examples of all. Which four types of other species did he work with?

10. See Collins' remarks, paragraph thirteen, and Venter's remarks, paragraph thirteen (the second part), paragraphs fourteen and fifteen. What, according to Collins, must now be learned, developed, provided, and why? What, according to Venter, is the potential the "genome sequence" represents, will be catalyzed, will be newly developed, may the new knowledge be the basis of, and must be done together? How did Clinton and Blair comment on these subjects? (Hint: See Clinton's first remarks, paragraphs nine, ten, thirteen, and fourteen; his second remarks, paragraph two; Blair's first remarks, paragraph five on a revolution, paragraphs seven through ten, and his second remarks, paragraph two.) Think of and describe examples of two major points mentioned above (i.e., beneficial use, and misuse versus protection).

11. See Collins' remarks, paragraph four, and Venter's remarks, paragraph seven. How did Collins define science? What did Venter comment about "The beauty of science"? Think of and tell of your own examples to illustrate each one's comment.

12. Referring to "this stunning and humbling achievement" (the reason for the meeting featuring the remarks), what did Clinton say on what has been pooled, tapped, by whom, and where, then what has been revealed? (For help, see his first remarks, paragraph seven.) How did Blair refer to it? (See his first remarks, paragraph six.)

RELATED INTERNET SITE(S)

National Human Genome Research Institute—Human Genome Project—Research

http://www.genome.gov/page.cfm?pageID=10001694

See an overview of the Human Genome Project, then note links to Genome Technology, Functional Analysis of the Genome, Genome Informatics and Computation Biology, Sequences and Maps, plus to educational resources, Newsroom, HGP Reports, Genome Hub of online resources, another overview including HGP history and goals, and more.

Introduction to the Human Genome Project

http://www.genome.gov/page.cfm?pageID=10001772

See introductory information, plus information on What Is the Human Genome Project? A Brief History of the Human Genome Project, Remaining Goals of the HGP, and How the National

Human Genome Research Institute Manages the HGP. See also links to HGP Information for Researchers, Online Educational Resources, Fact Sheets on genetic research and background on the NHGRI.

National Human Genome Research Institute—In the News

http://www.nhgri.nih.gov/NEWS/Finish_sequencing_early

Featured links are to What Is DNA and Why Is the HGP Studying It? The Book of Life: Reading the Sequence of Human DNA, Media Release, and Twenty Questions About DNA Sequencing (with answers), including What is DNA? What's a genome? How many bases, or letters, are in the human genome? Why do scientists want to sequence the human genome? What is the Human Genome Project's plan for DNA sequencing? What else does the Human Genome Project do? How will scientists benefit from the sequence provided by the Human Genome Project? What does "finishing" the sequence mean? What areas of the sequence will be finished first? What is "quality" sequence? What happens after the genome is sequenced?

NHGRI—Smithsonian Institute—Campus on the Mall Lecture Series

http://www.nhgri.nih.gov/DIR/VIP/SI/Collins/links.html

At this Web site, called "A Users Guide to Genetics: Medicine of the Future," sponsored by the National Human Genome Research Institute, the National Institute of Health, and the Smithsonian Institute, see the link to the Dr. Francis Collins Home Page, plus links to Web sites on What Is the Human Genome Project? A New Gene Map of the Human Genome, information about the National Human Genome Research Institute (NHGRI), and Internet Resources.

Human Genome Project Information

http://www.ornl.gov/hgmis

Featured are the "Science Behind the Human Genome Project"; News Sources; Project Information; About the Human Genome Project; Research (including Research in Progress); Publications (e.g., *Human Genome News, A Primer On Molecular Genomics*); Medicine and the New Genetics; Ethical, Legal, and Social Issues; Educational Resources; Publications; Topical Fact Sheets; the U.S. Department of Energy Genomics Research Programs; Meetings and Reports; Sitemap; Search; and more. Placing a mouse arrow on a main topic causes a description to appear.

Genetic Science Learning Center at the Eccles Institute of Human Genetics

http://gslc.genetics.utah.edu

This center at the University of Utah offers this Web site to "help people understand how genetics affects our lives and society." There are links to controversial features (e.g., on stem cell research and "Pharming for Farmaceuticals"). Other links lead to information on The Basics and Beyond, Genetic Testing of Newborn Infants, Genetic Disorder Center, Bringing RNA into View, and Hands-On Activities for the Classroom and Home.

The Institute for Genomic Research

http://www.tigr.org

See links to press releases and articles with titles and summaries under News and Genome News Network. See also links for Genomic Databases, What's New, FAQ, About TIGR, Careers, Education and Training (e.g., a mobile lab designed to enhance high school bioscience curricula), plus to a list of scientific publications, a sitemap, and many related links.

PBS Interview with Francis Collins (2000), conducted by Bob Abernathy

http://www.pbs.org/wnet/religionandethics/transcripts/collins.html

Collins succinctly defines the Human Genome Project; reveals its promise, realistic possibilities, greatest hope; and suggests analogies to describe it. He also notes his great fear about the project, debates on where the project should go, concerns for individuals' genetic profiles, and what might be said about the project one hundred years from now.

"Cooperation Key to Mapping Human Genome" in the *Scientist*, July 24, 2000

http://www.the-scientist.com/yr2000/jul/hot_000724.html

This article by Jennifer Fisher Wilson is based on an interview with the group leader of the Human Genetics Department of Cambridge England's Sanger Centre Wellcome Trust Genome Campus. Details of a Human Genome Map are given, as is a link to more data at http://www.ncbi.nlm.nih.gov, where clicking the sitemap link leads to links under "Genomes and Maps," "Education" (e.g., a *Science Primer*), and more.

An Animated Primer on the Basics of DNA, Genes and Heredity

http://vector.cshl.org/dnaftb (click Enter at center, or main subject boxes at right) or *www.cshl.org* (click DNA Learning Center link, then DNA from the Beginning link)

This detailed and interestingly presented primer, by the Cold Spring Harbor Laboratory's Dolan DNA Learning Center, has links to data that explain "the science behind key concepts" with main subjects and their particular subjects, such as Classical Genetics (and e.g., Children Resemble Their Parents), Molecules of Genetics (and e.g., A Gene Is Made of DNA, The DNA Molecule Is Shaped Like a Twisted Ladder), and Genetic Organization and Control (and e.g., Master Genes Control Basic Body Plans, A Genome Is an Entire Set of Genes, Living Things Share Common Genes, DNA Is Only the Beginning for Understanding the Human Genome). Special links are provided to concept; "narrated" animation and biographies featuring the scientists Collins, Venter, and James Watson; problems, gallery, audio video interviews, and links to more information. Note a DNA shaped animated lady presenting factoids. See links to contents pages, an index of people responsible for providing information, and a keyword index.

"The Ultimate Field Trip: An Astronaut's View of Earth"
Kathryn D. Sullivan (2001)
URL: http://www.jsc.nasa.gov/people/astronotes.html (click link)

SITE SUMMARY: Sullivan, a mission specialist astronaut in the U.S. Space Program, was a veteran of two space flights at the time she wrote this document. In this document, she gives her reasons for becoming an astronaut, then describes what astronauts (especially mission specialists) do, what is marvelous about her profession, and what astronauts can see when they are in outer space.

DISCUSSION QUESTIONS AND ACTIVITIES

1. Sullivan said "my role as a Mission Specialist aboard the Space Shuttle gives me two exciting avenues for exploration on each mission." Identify what she said she does with reference to the first avenue, then the second avenue, and then how she compares both avenues.
2. Why did Sullivan say, "There's also great responsibility here?" What must be done, when, how, and why? What do astronauts also train themselves to do and why? Explain why and how her statement and explanations are good ways to approach and do any profession, especially a science profession, and its various aspects.
3. Sullivan left her profession as a marine geologist to become an astronaut. Why did she say she did that? (Hints: See your answer that refers to the second avenue in Question/Activity no. 1 above; then note Sullivan's comments, including the words "In my case," and "In my mind.") Choose a science profession you might like to pursue or find out about. Apply Sullivan's comments with reference to the ways you would work in this profession. (Note: If possible, suggest applications of her comments with reference to your "chosen profession" in connection with your being an astronaut. For help, keep Sullivan's essay in mind, and see the Web site for the NASA Astronaut Selection Home Page whose Web site summary and url are in the Related Internet Sites section of this book's chapter on "First Educator Mission Specialist Astronaut Named.")
4. Read the descriptions titled "Kathryn Sullivan's Hometown," "Well-Known Peninsula," and "Namib Desert." Visit the Web sites Earth from Space—Astronauts' Views of the Home Planet—A Database of Selected Imagery, and NASA Biography—Kathryn D. Sullivan. (Their urls are cited in the Related Internet Sites section below.) Find, then describe, as if you are seeing them from space, some natural geographical features. (Be sure to choose some things that were photographed from a shuttle in which Sullivan worked, including, for example, something in the region where you live, in a region that your family claims as its ethnic heritage area, and two features or places, including one well known and one that is interesting.) (Tip: Include the names, numbers, and flight dates of the space shuttles whose astronauts took photographs.) (Hint: To find out on which shuttles Sullivan was a crew member, visit the Web page with the NASA Astronaut Biography—Kathryn D. Sullivan. Its url is cited in the Related Internet Sites section below.)

RELATED INTERNET SITE(S)

NASA Astronaut Biography—Kathryn D. Sullivan, Ph.D., 1992

http://www.ksc.nasa.gov/persons/astronauts/q-to-t/SullivanKD.txt

Earth from Space—Astronauts' Views of the Home Planet—A Database of Imagery

http://earth.jsc.nasa.gov

The Johnson Space Center provides here "a database of selected astronaut acquired imagery of Earth." Searches can be by earth landscapes (e.g., reef, island, mountains), water habitats, weather, distinctive features (e.g., Assateague Island, Amazon River, Baja Peninsula), and geographic regions (e.g., a nation, large body of water, or specific areas such as USA-NY), among others. Choose the topic, select Thumbnail [small photo] + Text, then click search. Read the caption and then select Technical Information to read data on natural features, noting the shuttle whose astronauts photographed it and when.

FAQs and Fact Sheets at the Gateway to Astronaut Photography of Earth

http://eol.jsc.nasa.gov (scroll to, and click, the links in the left column)

NASA's Johnson Space Center, Office of Earth Sciences, provides technical questions and answers on these special photographs and how to interpret them, plus fact sheets on research and photography in space. The FAQs area provides links to questions and answers on these photographs in specific topic categories such as resolution and remote sensing, research and development, a descriptive database, and other topics. The fact sheets area provides links to information on the Space Shuttle and the International Space Station Earth Observation Photography, Crew Earth Observations, and Earth Science Research from the Space Shuttle and the International Space Station.

Remote Sensing Data and Information—Table of Contents

http://rsd.gsfc.nasa.gov/rsd/RemoteSensing.html

This Web site provides links to a remote sensing archives, plus remote sensing data involving earth images from space, space and astronomy, weather and climate, specific instruments such as the Geostationary Operational Environment Satellite (GOES) and Landsat, plus organizations and projects, and miscellaneous (e.g., a Satellite Situation Center and Employment Opportunities).

The Remote Sensing Core Curriculum

http://www.research.umbc.edu/~tbenja1

This Web site provides five volumes, including an introduction, to Photo Interpretation and Photogrammetry, Overview of Remote Sensing of the Environment, Introductory Digital Image Processing, Applications in Remote Sensing, and K–12 Education. Note also the links listed under Remote Sensing Resources and the curriculum goal via the link for Educating Tomorrow's Technology Leaders.

Land Remote Sensing Policy Act (1992)—U.S. Code, Title 15, Chapter 82

http://www4.law.cornell.edu/uscode/15/ch82.html

See links to twenty-six sections including findings, definitions, archiving of data, Landsat Program management, data policy, conditions for operation, technology demonstration program, future considerations, and notes. Also accessible at http://www4.law.cornell.edu/uscode by clicking the link for Title 15, then the link for Chapter 82.

"[NASA's First Science Officer] Writes Home about Life in Space"
Peggy Whitson (2002)
URL: http://www.mtayrnews.com/archives/20021031nw.htm

SITE SUMMARY: In October 2002, NASA's first Science Officer astronaut wrote letters to earth from the International Space Station. Two letters, numbered ten and eleven, with selections reproduced on this Web site, were first published on October 31, 2002 by the *Mount Ayr Record News*, a newspaper in the Iowa town where she was born and where she went to high school. In these letters, Whitson wrote about her work on the International Space Station and of her being chosen as the U.S. Space Program's first science officer.

DISCUSSION QUESTIONS AND ACTIVITIES

1. What is something that happens to people in space physiologically and why, according to Whitson?
2. Why does Whitson think she and fellow astronauts will not gain weight although there is concern that they might?
3. Why does Whitson compare a space capsule with a car?
4. What is the Inventory Management System? Why is it useful? How might you adapt it and use it?
5. What, to Whitson, is one of the most striking things about the structure of the international space station (ISS)? What happens to these things during the sunrises and sunsets that the ISS experiences, and what happened to them when the Progress supply ship was coming to the ISS?
6. How does Whitson describe the arrival of the Progress supply ship as the unmanned spacecraft approaches the ISS? Optional Activity: Consider how, then write an essay about, some scientific principles that may be seen in the approach of the Progress ship. (Hint: Think physics, and study the online documents and Web sites on Isaac Newton and his works, whose urls can be found in this book's Appendix J.)
7. What was one thing that Whitson and fellow ISS inhabitants were concerned about receiving from the Progress supply ship? What do you think this situation suggests for living in space? (Option: For hints, see the Web site for the Space Island Project whose url is cited in this book's Appendix I.)
8. What does Whitson say is "a key element to success" in space? Which example did she give? Can you think of another?
9. Which tasks does Whitson say are interesting and fun to do?
10. With which well-known science fiction media franchise, and particular aspects of it, did Whitson compare her situation? How and why? Tell why you think these comparisons are both interesting and significant. (Hint: For help, see Web sites referred to in this book's chapters that feature documents by David Batchelor and Lawrence Krauss.)
11. See other excerpts from one of the letters referred to above, as provided in the Web document "Expedition Five Letters Home" whose url is provided in the Related Internet Sites section below. First, what did Whitson do "on the payloads front" and why was it important that she did things exactly as she did them? Next, what did she photograph and what did she observe about them? What did she and fellow cosmonaut command the ISS computer to do, which metaphor did she use and to what was she referring? What are FOD and what did they have to do with this? How were a robotic arm and a camera involved?

RELATED INTERNET SITE(S)

NASA Names First ISS Science Officer, September 16, 2002—Press Release

http://www.spaceref.com/news/viewpr.html?pid=9269

On Peggy Whitson, an astronaut and a biochemist, being named the first Science Officer of the International Space Station, her qualifications and experiences, viewpoint, plus immediate and follow-up duties, that support her being given this designation. What she is doing and what future science officers may do on the space station (even in a similar way when the space program continues after probes into the Columbia shuttle tragedy) are also indicated.

NASA Biographies—Astronauts—Peggy Whitson—January 2003

http://www.jsc.nasa.gov/Bios/htmlbios/whitson.html

"Expedition Five Letters Home"—Number Ten Excerpts—by Peggy Whitson

http://www.spaceref.com/news/viewsr.html?pid=6594

In these excerpts from the letter that was written on September 20, 2002, note paragraphs not given in the selections provided by the *Mount Ayr Record News.*

Philly Youngsters Meet Astronaut Peggy Whitson Via Ham Radio

http://www.w4cn.org/Nov/letter.htm

In this reproduction of the November 1, 2002 newsletter of the Amateur Radio Transmitting Society (ARRL), information is provided on NASA's first Science Officer speaking via ham radio to students of the Spruce Hill Christian School of Philadelphia and telling students about life in space and of living in a microgravity environment.

STS–113 Crew Post-Landing Press Conference on 8 December 2002 (audio file)

http://insideksc.cjb.net:8081/wwwroot_45/PICS/KSC/sts-113/STS-113.Pos (or link at *http://insideksc.cjb.net:8081/wwwroot_45/PICS/KSC/sts-113/STS-113.PostLandingPC.mps*)

Scientists' Answers to the Hypothetical Question: "What Are the Pressing Scientific Issues for the Nation and the World, and What Is Your Advice on How I Can Begin to Deal with Them?"
Twenty-First Century U.S. President (2003)
URL: http://www.edge.org/q2003/question03_index.html

SITE SUMMARY: Scientists were asked this question January 4, 2003 at this Web site for the Edge Foundation's World Question Center. The question is one that the Web site's editor imagined, as people may imagine, that a United States president in the first years of a new century and millennium would ask someone who is being considered for the position of presidential science advisor. Answers to this question, including some first published in the *New York Times*, are offered at this site, of which the *New Scientist* magazine has said: "Big, deep and ambitious questions . . . breathtaking in scope. Keep watching . . . ." The site was started, and is edited and published, by the author of *The Next Fifty Years: Science in the First Half of the Twenty-First Century*, John Brockman.

DISCUSSION QUESTIONS AND ACTIVITIES

1. Find, read, and identify the main points of some answers to the Center's editor's question, as provided by the well-known scientists J. Craig Venter (of the Human Genome Project), Freeman Dyson (who thought of the concept of a space-based artificial biosphere now called a Dyson Sphere), Eric R. Kandel (a 2000 winner of the Nobel Prize in medicine), and Mary Catherine Bateson (anthropologist), in addition to a well-known person involved with science (e.g., PBS-TV *Scientific Frontiers* host Alan Alda). Comment on why you think these scientists' or science thinkers' ideas are good ones for the new millennium and century. (Note: Find Web sites with information on these scientists or science thinkers and their work in this book's chapter: "Remarks on the Completion of the First Survey of the Human Genome Project" (2000), in this book's Appendix J, or by following links found with the scientists' or thinkers' thoughts at the Question Center's Web site.)

2. Find, read, and identify the main points of answers to the Center's editor's question, as provided by four other lesser-known yet prominent scientists or science thinkers, including two women and two men. Adapt and apply the comment activity of Question/Activity no. 1 above to this Question/Activity. Additional Optional Activity: Comment on why these ideas may be good yet not what you would think of as the most important ideas for a new millennium and century, or what you might consider in addition to these ideas.

3. Think of a scientific idea that you would suggest as an answer to the Center's editor's question. Identify the idea's main point(s), then comment on why you think this idea is important for the new millennium and century. (Option: If you are not sure of an idea to choose, note the following suggestions to get some help: visit and search the Web sites cited in the Related Internet Sites section below or any Web site cited in this book's Appendix B [Science News from Media Sources], references in this book's chapter on "Science in the New Millennium" by Stephen Hawking, as well as any other Web sites on news subjects and futuristic science cited anywhere in this book.)

RELATED INTERNET SITE(S)

"Science and Humanity in the Twenty-First Century" (1999)

http://www.nobel.se/peace/articles/rotblat

An article by Joseph Rotblat (physicist and 1995 Nobel Peace Prize winner), published September 6, 1999.

Twenty-First-Century Science

http://www.21stcenturyscience.org

Click links to News Headlines, Newsletter, Curriculum Issues, A Flexible Model, and A Partnership at this Web site which has been set up by the Neuffield Curriculum Centre and University of York, both in England, with the aim of guiding educators of students of ages fourteen through sixteen as they teach the sciences that will be prevalent and relevant in the new century.

Twenty-First-Century Science and Technology Home Page

http://www.21stcenturysciencetech.com

A magazine with scientist consultants that "challenges assumptions of scientific dogma" while aiming toward a "science based on constructible (intelligible) representation of concepts" and shunning methods associated with Newton and Galileo. See links to current issue contents page, back issues contents pages, news, and a page of links to sample articles online (to which new articles are periodically added). Some items provide interesting unusual insights, while other items' views might be considered highly unusual.

Edge Foundation and Its World Question Center

http://www.edge.org and *http://www.edge.org/questioncenter.html*

This Web site aims to "promote inquiry into and discussion of intellectual, philosophical, [and other] issues" and "to work for the intellectual and social achievement of society." It also aims "to arrive at the edge of the world's knowledge, seek out the most complex and sophisticated minds" and "put them in a room together" to ask and provide answers to questions. Note links to questions that the Center's editor has asked in the past (e.g., "What Now?" on scientists' and other thinkers' thoughts related to September 11, 2001, including the Editors of *Nature Magazine*, and scientists ranging from Julian Brown to Margaret Wertheim). See also articles of note by or about scientists (e.g., "Seven Scientists: An *Edge* Obsequy for the Astronauts of Space Shuttle *Columbia*" by Nicholas Humphrey and others, February 10, 2003). A Features link leads to a links page of archived previously featured questions and articles.

VIII
Appendixes

APPENDIXES—LIST OF SECTIONS
Recommended Internet Primary Sources Databases and Web Directories in the Sciences, Plus Other Online Areas with Important Science Connections

A. Subject Guide to Primary Science Documents Online and Featured in This Book's Chapters

B. Selected Internet Science Databases and Web Sites with Authoritative Data and Important Science Resources in the Sciences
   - Science Biographies and Career Sources
   - Science Databases with Primary Documents and Web Sites with Authoritative Data and Important Resources in the Sciences
   - Science News from Media Sources

C. Other Special Online Science Resources (Ready Reference Sources Featuring Science Subjects and Web Sites that Include Pages on Science Connections with Other Subjects)

D. Web Sites with Selected Resources from Magazines, Journals, and Newspapers

E. Specific Science Web Directories and Selected Special Search Engines with Science Areas
   - Specific Science Web Directories and Search Engines
   - Special Web Directories and Web Sites with Science Links
   - General Web Directories and Search Engines with Science Areas

F. Web Sites and Particular Web Directories with Science Connections

G. Web Sites of Organizations with Special Opportunities for Students (Online and Offline)

H. Web Sites with "Ask a Scientist"; "Ask a Science Question"; Frequently Asked Questions and Previously Asked Questions; Plus Facts and Tips on Science Subjects

I. Other Helpful and Interesting Science Web Sites

J. Additional Web Sites Featuring Primary Science Documents and Authoritative Data of Note

APPENDIX A
Subject Guide to Primary Science Documents Online and
Featured in This Book's Chapters

Archeology

(See also: *Paleontology*)
"Perspectives on the Past" (1999)
"The Science of Archaeology" (1996)

Astronomy and Space Sciences

(See also: *Earth and Planetary Sciences, Geology, Paleontology*)
Alfred Russel Wallace Web Site (1842–1913)
Apollo Lunar Surface Journal (1969–72)
"Biospheric Theory and Report on Overall Biosphere 2 Design and Performance During Mission
    One, 1991–1993" (1996)
"Dedication" to *The Revolutions of the Heavenly Bodies* (1543)
"First Educator Mission Specialist Astronaut Named" (1998)
"June Skies" (1932)
NASA Life Sciences Data Archive (1961–)
"[NASA's First Science Officer] Writes Home about Life in Space" (2002)
"Origin of the Universe" (1988)
"The Role of Planetariums in Astronomy Education" (1995)
"Space—Where Now, and Why?" (1998)
Star Spectral Classification Chart (1918–)
"Toward a World Strategy and Utilization of Our Natural Satellite: A Report" (1994)
"The Ultimate Field Trip: An Astronaut's View of Earth" (2001)

Beginnings of Scientific Thinking

"Dedication" to *The Revolutions of the Heavenly Bodies* (1543)
The Linnean Correspondence (1735–78)
Manuscripts of Leonardo da Vinci (1469–1518)
"On Experimental Science" (1268)
"On the Rise and Progress of the Arts and Sciences" (1742)
"Preface" to *Novum Organum* (1620)
"Travels Through North and South Carolina, Georgia, East and West Florida . . . Containing An
    Account of the Soil and Natural Productions of Those Regions . . ." (1791)

Biology

Alfred Russel Wallace Web Site (1842–1913)
BirdNet—The Ornithological Information Source (1997–)
"Consciousness and Neuroscience" (1997)
NASA Life Science Data Archive (1961–)
"[NASA's First Science Officer] Writes Home about Life in Space" (2002)
"Paleobiology—In the News, Highlights, Subjects, and Links" (1990–)
"Remarks on the Completion of the First Survey of the Entire Human Genome Project" (2000)
"A Structure for Deoxyribose Nucleic Acid" (1953)
"Travels Through North and South Carolina, Georgia, East and West Florida . . . Containing An
    Account of the Soil and Natural Productions of Those Regions . . ." (1791)

Botany, Gardening, Horticulture, and Plant Science

Alfred Russel Wallace Web Site (1842–1913)
"Botany in the New Millennium—The Practical" (1992)
Excerpts from *On the Growth of Plants in Closely Glazed Cases* (1852)
Flora of North America (1999–)
"International Code of Botanical Nomenclature" (1994)
Journals of Meriwether Lewis and William Clark (1804–6)
The Linnean Correspondence (1735–78)
"Paleobiology—In the News, Highlights, Subjects, and Links" (1990–)

Chemistry

"The Chemical History of a Candle: Lecture One" (1827)
"On a New Radioactive Substance Contained in Pitchblende" (1898)
"On the Discovery of Radium" (1921)
"Rays Emitted from Compounds of Uranium and of Thorium" (1898)
"A Structure for Deoxyribose Nucleic Acid" (1953)
WebElements (1999)

Computer Science

"As We May Think" (1945)
"Science in the New Millennium" (1998)
"There's Plenty of Room at the Bottom" (1959)

Critical Thinking

Excerpts from *Science as a Candle in the Dark* (1996)
"Perspectives on the Past" (1999)
"The Role of Doubt in Science" (1988)
Scientists' Answers to the Hypothetical Question: "What Are the Pressing Scientific Issues for the Nation and the World, and What Is Your Advice on How I Can Begin to Deal with Them?" (2003)

Earth and Planetary Sciences

(See also: *Geology, Paleontology*)
Alfred Russel Wallace Web Site (1842–1913)
Apollo Lunar Surface Journals (1969–72)
"Interview with Charles F. Richter" (1980)
"Overleaf Introduction" by Sylvia Earle to *Reefs at Risk* (1998)
"Safir–Simpson Hurricane Damage Intensity Scale" (1971)
"Space—Where Now, and Why?" (1998)
"The Ultimate Field Trip: An Astronaut's View of Earth" (2001)

Ecology and Environmental Sciences

Alfred Russel Wallace Web Site (1842–1913)
"Biospheric Theory and Report on Overall Biosphere 2 Design and Performance During Mission One, 1991–1993" (1996)
"Botany in the New Millennium: The Practical" (1992)
"Overleaf Introduction" by Sylvia Earle to *Reefs at Risk* (1998)
"Paleobiology—In the News, Highlights, Subjects, and Links" (1990–)

Ethics and Science

"As We May Think" (1945)
Excerpts from *Science as a Candle in the Dark* (1996)
"Hippocratic Oath" and "The Law of Hippocrates" (Fifth Century B.C.)
"Paleontology in the Twenty-First Century" (1997)
Scientists' Answers to the Hypothetical Question: "What Are the Pressing Scientific Issues for the Nation and the World, and What is Your Advice on How I Can Begin to Deal with Them?" (2003)
"The Social Responsibilities of Scientists and Science" (1966)
"What Is the Theory of Relativity?" (1919)

Exercise and Physical Activity

(See also: *Health, Medical, and Psychological Sciences, Nutrition Science, Sport Sciences*)
"Physical Activity and Health—Adolescents and Young Adults: A Report" (1999)

Geology

(See also: *Astronomy and Space Sciences, Earth and Planetary Sciences, Paleontology*)
Alfred Russel Wallace Web Site (1842–1913)
Apollo Lunar Surface Journal (1969–72)
Journals of Meriwether Lewis and William Clark (1804–6)
"Paleobiology—In the News, Highlights, Subjects, and Links" (1990–)
"Space—Where Now, and Why?" (1998)

Health, Medical, and Psychological Sciences

"Consciousness and Neuroscience" (1997)
"Discovering Our Selves: The Science of Emotion" (1998)
Excerpts from "Letter Concerning the Education of Women Physicians" (1851)
"Featured Health Articles" (1999–)
"Health Information Sheets" (1999–)
"Hippocratic Oath" and "The Law of Hippocrates" (Fifth Century B.C.)
"Improving Public Understanding: Guidelines for Communication the Emerging Science on Nutrition, Food Safety and Health" (1998)
NASA Life Sciences Data Archive (1961–)
"[NASA's First Science Officer] Writes Home about Life in Space" (2003)
"Nutrition and Children: A Statement for Health Care Professionals" (1997)
"Physical Activity and Health—Adolescents and Young Adults: A Report" (1999)
"A Proposal for a New Method of Evaluation of the Newborn Infant" (1953)

Inventors and Inventing

Alexander Graham Bell Notebooks Project (1875–)
"An Inventor Never Grows Up" (1997)

Music and Science

MuSICA—Music and Science Information Computer Archive (1994–)

Mysteries of Science

Excerpts from "Keynote Speech at Institute of Noetic Sciences Conference on Healing Journeys" and Other Documents at IONS Online (1998–)

International Crop Circle Database (1993–)
"Recommended Reading: Online Articles" (1998–)
"Scientific Anomalies" (1976–99)

Natural History

Alfred Russel Wallace Web Site (1842–1913)
Journals of Meriwether Lewis and William Clark (1804–6)
"Travels Through North and South Carolina, Georgia, East and West Florida . . . Containing An Account of the Soil and Natural Productions of those Regions . . ." (1791)

Nutrition Science

Food Guide Pyramid (1992) and Dietary Guidelines for All Americans (1995)
Improving Public Understanding: Guidelines for Communicating the Emerging Science on Nutrition, Food Safety, and Health (1998)
"Nutrition and Children—A Statement for Health Care Professionals" (1997)
"Vegetarian Diets: A Position Paper" (1997)

Ornithology

Alfred Russel Wallace Web Site (1842–1913)
BirdNet—The Ornithological Information Source (1997–)
The Journals of Meriwether Lewis and William Clark (1804–6)
"June Skies" (1932)
"Travels Through North and South Carolina, Georgia, East and West Florida . . . Containing An Account of the Soil and Natural Productions of Those Regions . . ." (1791)

Paleontology

(See also: *Archeology, Earth and Planetary Sciences, Geology*)
"Foreword" by Michael Crichton to the *Encyclopedia of Dinosaurs* (1997)
"Paleobiology—In the News, Highlights, Subjects, and Links" (1990–)
"Paleontology in the Twenty-First Century" (1997)
"Paleontology: The Window to Science Education" (1996)
Paper Dinosaurs: A Hypertext Catalog of Rare Documents (1824–1969)

Physics

Excerpts from *The Physics of STAR TREK* (1995)
"On a New Radioactive Substance Contained in Pitchblende" (1898)
"On the Discovery of Radium" (1921)
"Rays Emitted by Compounds of Radium and of Thorium" (1898)
"What Is the Theory of Relativity?" (1919)

Popular Culture and Science

Excerpts from *The Physics of STAR TREK* (1995)
"An Inventor Never Grows Up" (1997)
"Science in the New Millennium" (1998)
"The Science of *Star Trek*" (1993)
Scientists' Answers to the Hypothetical Question: "What Are the Pressing Scientific Issues for the Nation and the World, and What Is Your Advice on How I Can Begin to Deal with Them?" (2003)

Religion and Science

Alfred Russel Wallace Web Site (1842–1913)
The Bible and Science (1889)
"Dedication" to *The Revolutions of the Heavenly Bodies* (1543)
Excerpts from "Keynote Speech at Institute of Noetic Sciences Conference on Healing Journeys" and Other Documents at IONS Online (1998–)
Leonardo da Vinci Manuscripts (l469–1518)

Society and Science

"As We May Think" (1945)
"Botany in the New Millennium—The Practical" (1992)
Excerpts from "Keynote Speech at Institute of Noetic Sciences Conference on Healing Journeys" and other documents at IONS Online (1998–)
Excerpts from *Science as a Candle in the Dark* (1996)
"First Educator Mission Specialist Astronaut Named" (1998)
NASA Life Sciences Data Archive (1961–)
"Science in the New Millennium" (1998)
Scientists' Answers to the Hypothetical Question: "What Are the Pressing Scientific Issues for the Nation and the World, and What Is Your Advice on How I Can Begin to Deal with Them?" (2003)
"The Social Responsibilities of Scientists and Science" (1966)
"Toward a World Strategy and Utilization of Our Natural Satellite: A Report" (1994)

Sport Sciences

(See also: *Exercise and Physical Activity*)
Olympic Sports: Technical Performance Rules and Glossary of Techniques (2000)
Sport Science Resources (1971–)

Technology

"As We May Think" (1945)
"Science in the New Millennium" (1998)
"There's Plenty of Room at the Bottom" (1959)

Women and Science

"Botany for the New Millennium—The Practical" (1992)
"Discovering Ourselves: The Science of Emotion" (1998)
Excerpts from "Letter Concerning the Education of Women Physicians" (1851)
"Featured Health Articles" (1999–)
"First Educator Mission Specialist Astronaut Named" (1998)
Flora of North America (2000)
"Health Information Sheets" (1999–)
"June Skies" (1932)
"Learning from the Chimpanzees: A Message Humans Can Understand" (1998)
"My Acquaintance with Zoological Park Animals" (1923)
"[NASA's First Science Officer] Writes Home about Life in Space" (2002)
"Overleaf Introduction" by Sylvia Earle to *Reefs at Risk* (1998)
"Perspectives on the Past" (1999)
"A Proposal for a New Method of Evaluation of the Newborn Infant" (1953)

Scientists' Answers to the Hypothetical Question: "What Are the Pressing Scientific Issues for the Nation and the World, and What Is Your Advice on How I Can Begin to Deal with Them?" (2003)
"Space—Where Now, and Why?" (1998)
Star Spectral Classification Chart (1918–)
"The Ultimate Field Trip: An Astronaut's View of Earth" (2001)

Young People and Science, Young Scientists, and Young Inventors

"Consciousness and Neuroscience" (1997)
"Foreword" by Michael Crichton to *Encyclopedia of Dinosaurs* (1997)
"Health Information Sheets" (1999–)
"An Inventor Never Grows Up" (1997)
"June Skies" (1932)
"Learning from the Chimpanzees: A Message Humans Can Understand" (1998)
"My Acquaintance with Zoological Park Animals" (1923)
"Nutrition and Children—A Statement for Health Care Professionals" (1997)
"Overleaf Introduction" by Sylvia Earle to *Reefs at Risk* (1998)
"Perspectives on the Past" (1999)
"Physical Activity and Health—Adolescents and Young Adults: A Report" (1999)
"Recommended Reading: Online Articles" (1998)

Zoology

Alfred Russel Wallace Web Site (1842–1913)
BirdNet—The Ornithological Information Source (1997–)
Journals of Meriwether Lewis and William Clark (1804–6)
"June Skies" (1932)
"Learning from the Chimpanzees: A Message Humans Can Understand" (1998)
"My Acquaintance with Zoological Park Animals" (1923)
"Paleobiology—In the News, Highlights, Subjects, and Links" (1990–)
"Travels Through North and South Carolina, Georgia, East and West Florida . . . Containing An Account of the Soil and Natural Productions of Those Regions . . ." (1791)

APPENDIX B
Selected Internet Science Databases and Web Sites with Authoritative Data and Important Resources in the Sciences

SCIENCE BIOGRAPHIES AND SCIENCE CAREER SOURCES

America's Career Infonet—Reading Room—Online Articles and Web Sites—Science

http://www.careertools.org/rlib

Use the keyword "science" to do a search in the search box.

Archaeologist to Zoologist at What Do They Do?

http://www.whatdotheydo.com

Click a link for a science career to find out basic information on what a scientist in this science does, then see a fictional story with a realistic situation that involves such a scientist and makes clear what a job in that science is about.

Archaeology, Futures in

http://www.sha.org/sha_kbro.htm

The Society for Historical Archaeology provides information about a career in this field. Information is divided into sections that include Looking at Historical Archaeology, Becoming an Archaeologist, What Kinds of Jobs Do Archaeologists Do? and What Are Rewards of Being an Archaeologist?

Astronaut Biographies at the NASA Lyndon B. Johnson Space Center

http://jsc.nasa.gov/Bios/index.html

To find out about different types of astronauts, click links to career astronauts, payload specialist astronauts, astronaut candidates, and cosmonauts, plus astronaut information, provided by the Flight Crew Operations Directorate at the Johnson Space Center. Follow the links for active astronauts, management astronauts, former astronauts, and international astronauts to find name links to biographies, including some annotated links with astronaut names and their titles such as "Leading Astronaut for Medical Issues," "Manager of Environmental Physiology Laboratory," "Earth and Planetary Scientist," and "Chief Scientist of NASA."

Careers in Botany: A Guide to Working with Plants

http://www.botany.org/bsa/careers/index.html

Careers in Earth Science

http://kids.earth.nasa.gov/archive/career/index.html

Click a link for a particular type of earth scientist to find out basic information on what earth scientists do. Careers featured range from atmospheric scientist to oceanographer.

Careers in Health and Medicine Theme Page

http://www.cln.org/themes/careers_health.html

At this site provided by the Community Learning Network of British Columbia, Canada, see links for general and special health career sites.

Careers in Science

http://www.aas.org/careers

At this page which is provided by the American Association for the Advancement of Science, career information is offered by links to *Science's Next Wave* (a weekly online publication on career development), a Science Careers Web site, and Web sites about internships and fellowships in the mass media, and for students with disabilities, and in national and international science-related governmental areas.

Environmental Career Opportunities

http://ecojobs.com

Find out about various types of jobs that involve the natural environment. See links including one to a page with data on actual Environmental Science and Engineering Jobs and one to a page of information on The Number One Source for Environmental Jobs (which includes a Science and Engineering link). Note also links to environmental college degree programs and internships.

Eric Weisstein's World of Scientific Biography

http://scienceworld.wolfram.com/biography

A physicist provides a scientific biography site with searches by name using a search box, or links to an alphabetical letters index, branches of science, historical periods, nationality, gender or minority status, and prize winners. There are also links to what's new and FAQs.

Faces of Science: African-Americans in the Sciences

http://www.princeton.edu/~mcbrown/display/faces.html

Click a link to Index by Profession or Index of People, or Women Scientists; or scroll to a links list of names under types of scientist from biochemists to zoologists. At the top of the page, click link to The Past, The Present, or The Future. Scroll to the bottom of the page for a bibliography for research and information on instructional opportunities.

4000 Years of Women in Science

http://www.astr.ua.edu/4000WS/4000WS.html

See links to biographies, references, photographs, and an introduction.

How to Learn about Careers in Astronomy and Space Science

http://adc.gsfc.nasa.gov/adc/how_to/learn_about.html

At this site for NASA's Astronomical Data Center, note links to A New Universe to Explore: Careers to Explore (with the American Astronomical Society's Education Office Reports), NASA's Careers in Aerospace, and Young People's Forum, plus links beside NASA's Space Science Work. For more information on the subjects related to these careers, see links for Astronomy and Space Science News, Answers to Astronomy Questions, Resources for Amateur Astronomy, and Other Astronomical Web Sites.

Important Figures in the Health Sciences—Their Lives and Works

http://www.mla-hhss.org/histlink.htm (scroll to, and click, link)

Amid alphabetically arranged links, find and click links to Profiles in Science; Famous Geneticists; People and Discoveries: Medicine and Health; Women in Health History; Distinguished

Women of the Past and Present; Real Women in Health Care; American Nurses Association Hall of Fame; and individuals (e.g., Dr. Elizabeth Blackwell, Florence Nightingale, Louis Pasteur, Jean Piaget, Jonas Salk, etc.).

Medical and Health Career Descriptions—Links Page

http://www.furman.edu/~snyder/careers/medical.html

Medical Doctor Occupational Profile

http://www.alis.gov.ab.ca/career/main.asp (click Occupational Profiles link)

Click Occupations by Title Search, then click M, then scroll to and click link for medical doctor. Provided by the Alberta Learning Information Service of Center, Canada.

Physician Authors

http://endeavor.med.nyu.edu/llit-med/lit-med-db/physicianindex.html

See the alphabetical list of physicians with title links to detailed summaries of, and commentaries on, the works they have written. For brief biographical information on these physician authors, click Authors link in the left column, then find a name in the alphabetical name link list that was listed in the Physician Authors list (e.g., Albert Schweitzer, Oliver Sachs). See the title links list of writings on a biographical page or in the title links on the physician authors page, and note especially the writings in the genres such as autobiography, biography, case study, essay, investigative journalism, journal, memoir, and treatise.

Physicians and Surgeons and Related Occupations in Occupational Outlook Handbook

http://www.bls.gov/oco (do search)

Physics and Astronomy People and Discoveries

http://www.pbs.org/wgbh/aso/databank/physastro.html

At this site for PBS-TV's A Science Odyssey program, see links under People for biographies with quotations for names ranging from Jocelyn Bell to Erwin Schrodinger. See also links under Discoveries with dates beside name and/or discovery links or both in links that lead to more information.

Science Careers: Future Trends and Current Realities

http://www.hhmi.org/grants/undergraduate/meetings/1997

Career outlook information is provided at this site for the first Howard Hughes Medical Institute meeting on undergraduate and precollege science education and careers. A pull-down menu features links to an overview of the meeting, keynote address, preface, introduction, summaries on undergraduate and informal science education, employment of scientists, and conclusion, plus resources for career planning.

Science Careers—Science Magazine

This magazine's job source page includes some career information via an Advice link that leads to an Advice and Perspectives page featuring links to more information and an archive. See also the links to New This Week (e.g., Hot Topics, Diversity in the Scientific Workplace), Employer Profiles, Career Fairs, and *Science's Next Wave* (an online career development publication).

Scientists and Science at the HyperHistory Timeline

http://www.hyperhistory.com/online_n2/History_n2/a.html

Click the green science box link. Find scientists' names in green-coded name boxes, and note the Science Web Links link. Click People, then select Special Lifelines, then Famous Women, to find names of women in science in green-coded name boxes, and to see a www link for Women in Science. Click name links to find brief biographies, plus links to other sites about the scientists or online texts of their writings. See also an index link that leads to an alphabetical links list of names with, for example, a green S for Science, beside each scientist's name, or an asterisk that indicates a name link leads to Web links.

Scientists at the Best Source for Canadian Science

http://www.science.ca/scientists/scientists.html

See photographs of, and quotations from, three of the Most Popular Scientists, then click details link for each for more information. See also Major Profiles area featuring name links with science specialty icon, specific category, and distinction or discovery noted. In addition, see name links under Nobel Laureates and Biographies at Other Science Web Sites. Searches are possible by subject category, gender, and region. There are also links to Ask a Scientist, Reference, Quiz, and Activities.

Super Scientists

http://www.energyquest.ca.gov/scientists

Click on a photo link above a name in an alphabetically arranged list to find a biography page and links to more information for scientists ranging from Marie Curie, Albert Einstein, and Michael Faraday to Isaac Newton and Rosalyn Yalow.

Women in Astronomy—History

http://cannon.sfsu.edu/~gmarcy/cswa/history/history.html

Provided by the Astronomical Society of the Pacific, this History of Women in Science Web site has links to information (including data on primary writings) on women as astronomers, or as primary workers on astronomical projects. Women of the past and women making history today are featured, ranging from Caroline Herschel, Maria Mitchell, and Annie Jump Cannon to comet discoverer Carolyn Shoemaker and astronaut Sally Ride.

Women in Physics

http://www.physics.purdue.edu/wip/index.html

Providing this Web site the Department of Physics at Purdue University has a Spotlight Scientist area with biographies and Web links on women physicists. After clicking the main Spotlight link, find links to the current, and past, spotlight scientists, then note the links for WIP Links and "Herstory" of Women in Science.

Women in Science

http://www.fi.edu/qu98/me3

At this Web page that is part of the Franklin Institute Online, find annotated links to sites in categories such as Heroes, Women Programmers of ENIAC (the first electronic digital computer), More Admirable Scientists, More Women and Science Sites, and Women in Science and History Hotlists. There are also Treasure Hunts featuring questions using online databases with links here. An introduction invites girls to do something scientific when they grow up.

Women in Science, Math, and Technology

http://www.ericse.org/whm2000.html

This site features links to resources highlighting women's contributions to science, technology, engineering, and mathematics, in our society. There are links under the categories Biographies, Databases, and Gateways to Extensive Collections, Other Related Web Sites, Educational Resources, and Information for Educators.

Women in the Sciences, and Women in Medical Fields

http://frank.mtsu.edu/~kmiddlet/history/women/wh-sci.html

http://frank.mtsu.edu/~kmiddlet/history/women/wh-med.html

At these connected Web pages, parts of the Web site for the American Women's History: A Research Guide, links go to databases, bibliographies, biographical resources, historical overviews, journals in the field, and primary sources in digital collections and archival collection guides.

SCIENCE DATABASES WITH LINKS TO PRIMARY DOCUMENTS, AND WEB SITES WITH AUTHORITATIVE DATA AND IMPORTANT RESOURCES IN THE SCIENCES

The Ada Project: Tapping Internet Resources for Women in Computer Science

http://tap.mills.edu (click TAP Junior link, or About TAP link)

In this area of the Mills College Web site, see links to Computer Girl: A Bridge from High School to the Computer World, and other Web sites for girls and computers, via the TAP Junior link. See also the Publications link that leads to a links page of articles and reports from *Computing Research News* and others magazines. Search for Ada Lovelace in the search box to find links to sites with information that reveals why The Ada Project was named to honor her.

Advocates for Women in Science, Engineering, and Math

http://www.awsem.com

This Web site for a group that aims to encourage girls' interest in science, engineering, and mathematics provides links to a message board, a page of links to Web sites with more information, news on meetings and classes, science opportunities for students, and women's accomplishments in science. Online and real world activities for girls, educators, science professionals, and parents, are provided on individual Web pages. Click also the link for "Gender Equity" to see articles (in PDF format) and Facts in Brief.

AgNic Plant Science Homepage

http://deal.unl.edu/CYT_agnic/SiteForUser/index.html

At this search page provided by the Agricultural Network Information Center of the University of Nebraska Library, type these three words: plant, science, and kids; one each in the three search boxes, then select the word Teacher under the subject Education in the list of subjects below the search boxes. Click the search button. A page of links to Web pages or sites on plant science that will be useful to students will appear.

American Heart Association (AHA) Scientific Statements

http://www.americanheart.org

In the search box, do a search for the scientific statements topic list, then follow links and see links to various statements on health- and medical-related subjects including Women, Children,

Athletes, Behavior, Diet and Nutrition, Critical Pathways, Prevention, Risk Factors, Genetic Testing, Exercise, and particular conditions.

Association for Women in Science

http://www.serve.com/awis

At this site for this organization which aims to encourage women's interest and participation in science and technology, click links to Outstanding Scientist of the Month, an essay contest for high school students and undergraduate college students, and Press Releases. Note also a Resources area with links to publications, mentoring, internships, and more; plus a Voice area with links to the AWIS magazine, book reviews, and what's new. See, in addition, via a links link, links to sites with more information and documents (e.g., to Organizations, Resources for Kids, Education, and Electronic Publications).

Astrobiology Web—Terraforming

http://www2.astrobiology.com/astro/terraforming.html

See annotated links to scientific magazine articles and Web sites under the topics Opinion and Scientific Extrapolation and Technical and Scientific References. See links to articles or sites with subjects such as "Terraforming Information" and "Terraforming Mars?"

Astronomical History, Documents of

http://condor.stcloudstate.edu/~physcrse/astr106/doc.html

This site features excerpts from the writings of early astronomers, other scientists, and philosophers with scientific viewpoints (e.g., Plato, Aristotle, Ptolemy, Copernicus, and Galileo).

Athena—Authors and Texts Related to Science

http://un2sg4.unige.ch/athena/html/sc_txt.html

Links at this site go to historical scientific writings that were written in, or have been translated into, English, although there are some writings in other languages. The writings are by well-known and lesser-known science writers from the ancient and recent past, and range from Aristotle and Archimedes to Babbage, Volta, and Zeeman.

Botanical Links and Other Major Link Sites of Botanical Interest

http://www.inform.umd.edu/PBIO/FINDIT/malk.html and *http://www.inform.umd.edu/PBIO/FINDIT/sear.html*

On these pages at this Web site by the Norton-Brown Herbarium, the University of Maryland, there are links to Web sites, special search engines, and special areas of Web directories, on topics such as agriculture, botany, horticulture, gardening, and plants.

Botany Online—Internet Hypertextbook

http://www.biologie.uni-hamburg.de/b_online/index.html

At this site for an ongoing botany project, click the link to Botany Online—Contents, and see the links under subjects such as Introduction; The Plant Kingdom: An Overview; Ecology; Classic Genetics; Intercellular Communication; Anatomy of Cells and Tissues; Interactions Between Plants and Fungi, Bacteria, and Viruses; Molecules and Molecular Reactions in Plant Cells; Evolution; Essays and Related Projects. Click also other links for pages of annotated links that lead to interesting botanical sources.

Catalogue of Internet Resources—Science and Scientists

http://www.bubl.ac.uk/link/s/scientists.htm

This page at the Web site of the BUBL Information Service, Centre for Digital Research, Strathclyde University, Glasgow, Scotland, has links to sites with scientific documents, and articles (e.g., "On Being a Scientist: Responsible Conduct in Research"), and magazines (e.g., *Science's Next Wave*). There are also links to sites with information on people of science and science organizations (e.g., Union of Concerned Scientists and Scientists for Global Responsibility). Note also the link to the Catalogue of Internet Resources' main page's subject menu page at http://www.bubl.ac.uk/link/menus.html with links to sites that have information and documents on more than fifty science subjects ranging from aeronautics to zoology.

Center for Science in the Public Interest—Documents Library

http://www.cspinet.org/reports/index.html

See links to documents under topics including Reports, Petitions, Statements/Testimony, Fact Sheets/Charts/Case Studies, and click the CSPI U.S. link at the bottom of the page for the main index of the CSPI Web site which features links to Special Reports, News Updates, and a Nutrition Health Newsletter.

Community of Science Inc.—U.S. Manual of Patent Classification

http://www.cos.com (click sitemap link, then U.S. Patents link)

Search by classification, state, country, or main search. The classification area features Electronics, Physics, Chemistry, Biology, Engineering, Transportation, Electricity, Mechanical, and Design. Each main classification area has a sub-group (e.g., computing, electricity, electronics, optics, biochemistry, agriculture, heating/cooling, office devices, vehicles, and tools).

Contexts—Science

http://www.english.upenn.edu/~jlynch/FrankenDemo/Contexts/science.html

At this temporary Web page for a Web project that the University of Pennsylvania will make permanent, read about science in a historical context from its beginnings through the late nineteenth century. See also the links to particular sciences, plus themes and biographies of people of science.

Eighteenth Century Resources—Science

http://www.c18.org/li/science.html

Links go to sites on general science, medicine, scientists, and scientific instruments.

Elsevier Science: Your Gateway to Science

http://www.elsevier.nl

This noted science publisher provides a "search our full text articles" box and links for readers (e.g., journal issues, tables of contents), librarians (e.g., new and forthcoming titles), and others. See also the News links and the More News link.

Health Topics A to Z at the Centers for Disease Control and Prevention

http://www.cdc.gov/health

Has links by health topics (e.g., Environmental, Occupational, Travelers, Adolescents and Teens, Infants and Children, Women, and Men, plus Injuries and Foodbourne Illnesses, as well as In the News and Other Sites) and subjects found via alphabet letter links. Some documents are in PDF format.

History of Astronomy

http://www.astro.uni-bonn.de/~pbrosche/hist_astr

This site provides links to general texts, persons, historians of astronomy, observatories and other places, publications, and topics (e.g., Ancient Astronomy, Astrometry, Astrophysics, Celestial Mechanics, Cosmology, Geodetic Astronomy, Extragalactic Astronomy, Eclipses, Nebulae and Star Clusters, Radio Astronomy, Solar Astronomy, Stellar Astronomy, Space Exploration, and more).

History of Horticulture Index

http://www.hcs.ohio-state.edu/hort/history.html

An ongoing index using information from a course on The History and Literature of Horticulture: From Earliest Times to the Present, first taught at Ohio State University. It features search archives and browse archives via links from the twelfth century B.C. to recent times.

History of Science in the Modern Age

http://www.ksu.edu/history/faculty/Holt/histsyllabus.htm

Kansas State University provides a syllabus online, with plans for articles, assignments, study guides, listservs, and links on the History of Science in the Modern Age. Topics in this syllabus include Classical Astronomy, Classical Biology, Classical Chemistry, Classical Physics, Natural History, The Atomic Age, and A New Understanding of Life.

History of Science Society—Resources for Teaching and Research

http://www.hssonline.org (click the sitemap link)

On the sitemap page, see, under Profession, links to The Guide to the History of Science, Recent News, and Archived News Items. See also, under Teaching and Research, links to Resources for Teaching and Research, bibliographies, and essays (e.g., "Historians of Science and the 'Real World' " and "Science and Technology in the Twentieth Century"). Note also links to lists of winning award entries, including those by graduate college students, teachers, and women in the sciences. Access is also by a text-only link and an Enter link (for computers with the required technology).

Holography—Introductory and Historical Information

http://www.eio.com/holghist.htm

Electronics Information Online has here up to date and historical information on holography. See the links to A Guide to Practical Holography and History and Development of Holography. Note also the link to the Holography Hyper E-mail Discussion Group.

Human Space Flight at NASA Spacelink

http://spacelink.nasa.gov/NASA.Projects/Human.Exploration.and.Development.of.Space/Human.Space.Flight

At this aeronautics and space resource for education there are many links to information under subjects such as Spaceflight Questions and Answers, NASA Human Spaceflight Program History, Mercury Missions, Gemini Missions, Apollo Missions, Apollo-Soyuz, Skylab, the Space Shuttle, Shuttle-Mir, and the International Space Station. See also Related Materials at spacelink.com and Related NASA Internet sites.

Instant Photography and Edwin Herbert Land in the Invention Dimension

http://web.mit.edu/invent/archive.html (click the L link)

Find the name link for this inventor of instant photography, then click it to read about him and his invention.

International Federation of Invention Associations—Links to Articles, etc.

http://www.invention-ifia.ch

See the link to a page which features articles, speeches, and guidelines related to the Internet and of interest to inventors and friends of inventors (e.g., Computer Age and the Inventor).

See also the links to International Patent Law and Patent Uses, Other Useful Sites on Inventors and Inventions, and Sites Linked to the IFIA site (e.g., sites on patents from various nations). Note also the link to a youth page with links to information on Policies to Promote Creativeness, Unique Invention Contests, inspiring quotations including four main dimension of creative thinking, plus more sites, including some especially for girls.

International Society for Artificial Life—Publications, and Links to More Information

http://www.alife.org

At this in-progress site, click the publications link and follow the links to downloadable *ALife Journal* articles by issue or to see annotations of journal articles. Other features include a links link that leads to a page of links leading to articles or sites with more information. There is also a Topics link that leads to a search box and clickable topics such as science, technology, the Internet, news, announcements, book reviews, education, quick links, and more leading to information on artificial life and a topic as provided by message senders.

Internet Biological Sciences Resources

http://arnica.csustan.edu

The California State University Biological Sciences Web Server provides these resources via links to information on basic biological sciences ranging from Agricultural Science, Botany, and Environmental Science to Human Biology, Behavioral Biology, Marine Biology, and Zoology, plus Biodiversity, Biotechnology, Genetics, and more subjects and special sites such as for instructional resources, multimedia materials, the U.S. Government, and "other valuable servers."

Internet Reference Sources—Science and Medicine Topics

http://www.lib.virginia.edu/reference/science/scindex.html

The University of Virginia provides this page of links to sites with information on science topics including Astronomy, Biology, Botany and Horticulture, Chemistry, Climatology, Environmental Sciences, Geology, Physics, Psychology, and Medicine, Health, and Pharmacy, plus Biography.

Invention of the Fax Machine

http://www.ideafinder.com/history/inventions/story051.htm

Find out about the fax machine's history, how it works, fun facts, and links to other sites.

Laser Therapy Internet Guide

http://www.laser.nu

See the link to the Latest News and Updates: New Editorial, and their page with a link to Science. See also on the main page, the links to news, reports, and articles on subjects such as laser therapy as treatment for conditions of the eyes, mouth, wounds, and more, via links such as Laser Therapy Science—Abstracts, FAQs about LLLT (Low Level Laser Therapy), Laser Therapy Literature Search Sites, FDA Approves Laser Therapy, Internet Discussion about Treatment with LED versus Laser Light, and more.

Living and Working in Space at NASA Spacelink

http://spacelink.nasa.gov/NASA.Projects/Human.Exploration.and.Development.of.Space

At this aeronautics and space resource for education site, scroll to and click the link for Living and Working in Space. There are many links to information, including About the Space Shuttle, the International Space Station, the Advanced Life Support Program (on growing plants for food and oxygen regeneration), Space Flight Questions and Answers, and Space Biology FAQs, in addition to a link for Living and Working in Space. See also Related Materials at spacelink.com and Related NASA Internet Links

Magnetic Resonance Sites on the World Wide Web

http://www.ismrm.org/mr_sites.htm

The International Society for Magnetic Resonance in Medicine offers this page of links to resources and articles in the subject areas Education—Technical and Education—MRI for the Public. In these areas, see the links to the articles "An Introduction to MRI"; "All You Really Need to Know about MRI Physics"; "MRI Tutor"; "The Basics of MRI"; plus "Intro to MRI Scans" and "Patient Information Sheets—FAQs." See also the links under other subject areas such as Links to NMR/MRI Sites, Other Sites of Possible Interest, Journals, Organizations, Research Laboratories, and Spotlight on MRI Safety.

The National Academies: Advisors to the Nation on Science, Engineering and Medicine

http://www.nas.edu

At this Web site the National Academy of Sciences, the Institute of Medicine, the National Research Council, and the National Academy of Engineering feature Top News, Science in the Headlines, Site Highlights, Subject Index, Events, New Online Books, and Quick Search of more than 1,500 books and more than 2,500 reports online.

NASA Quest

http://quest.arc.nasa.gov

Dedicated to bringing NASA people, space, and science to classrooms through the Internet, this site provides Late Breaking News, a Bio of the Week, a Question of the Week, and a Journal Entry of the Week, plus a What NASA People Do search page, Questions and Answers, Facts, News, an AstroVenture online activity, live online events and how to participate, and an area for educators and parents.

National Park Service—Nature and Science in the Parks

http://www.nps.gov (click the NatureNet link)

In this area for the U.S. National Park Service, see links to information on Air Quality in Protected Areas of the Parks, plus Biology (e.g., wildlife and plants), Geologic Resources, and Water Resources in the Parks. See also the Science link, the pull-down menu of Related Links (e.g., to National Natural Landmarks), and a link to past features at this site. On the main NPS page, click the News link to see press releases, park tips of newsworthy items, morning reports, and resources, with subjects such as NPS Natural Resources Honors Award and NPS Science Scholars. Click, in addition, the main page's search link and search for science subjects such as "fossils in the national parks."

Nearctica: Gateway to the Natural World of North America

http://www.nearctica.com

This site for students, educators, parents, and scientists provides original materials and links to many Web sites. See sections including Popular Topics, Table of Contents, Search by Keywords, Instant Gratification site links list, and links to subjects including the environment, ecology, conservation, geophysics, natural history, paleontology, education, and more.

NewScientist.com—Hot Topics

http://www.newscientist.com/hottopics

See links to in-depth reports on science topics in the news (e.g., artificial life and intelligence, astrobiology, climate change, cloning, dinosaurs, genetically modified food, the environment, a quantum world, technology, and science debates). See also links to bizarre science, disasters, and bioterrorism, plus Science and the September 11 attacks.

Patent Café's Space for Young Inventors

http://www.patentcafe.com/index.asp

This "number one guide for elementary to high school young inventors" has links to Explore Science, How to Invent, Famous Inventors and Inventions, a Patent-O-Pedia, an *Invention Magazine*, an Inventioneers Club for Young Inventors, and a page with links to Resources for K–12 Teachers and Parents.

Science Resources in Education Resources at the Internet Education Resources Index

http://cl.k12.md.us/EducationResources.html

In this Index which is provided by the Caroline County Public Schools in Maryland, choose Science from the "Search by Content Area" pull-down menu, then click the "start search" button. Page one of many pages with more than eight hundred descriptions with site links will appear. A search can be narrowed by also choosing an alphabet letter from another pull-down menu and by typing a keyword in a keyword search box, before clicking the "start search" button.

Sciences in the Scout Report Archives

http://sout.cs.wisc.edu/archives

Scroll to the area for browsing subjects in the format known as Library of Congress subject headings. Click the S link, or a letter link for a particular science, to get to links that lead to reports. Searches by keyword, title, or advanced search are also possible.

Scientific Milestones by Generations of CalTech Faculty, Alumni, and Students

http://www.admissions.caltech.edu/history/milestone.htm

See subject statement links to information, such as "The Birth of Modern Earthquake Science"; "The Dawn of the Aerospace Age"; "Left Brain/Right Brain"; "Recommended Daily Adult Requirement"; "The Foundations of Molecular Biology"; and more.

SONAR at the World Wide Web Virtual Library

http://www.dai.ed.ac.uk/students/ashley/Sonar/sonar.html

Some "pointers to information on SONAR" that are available on the Web can be found here via links to sites on Artificial SONAR/Ultrasonic Imaging Systems (e.g., airborne, underwater, and medical), Biological SONAR (e.g., for land and marine animals), and online databases, e-letters and mailing lists, URL libraries, societies, and publications.

Space Science in the Goddard Space Flight Center Library

http://library.gsfc.nasa.gov (click the Subject Channels link, then the Space Science link)

Features links to documents and reports, databases, data collections, journals, and guides to information resources including Web Resources, Ask a Librarian, and Discussion Lists. Note also the links to library catalogs, resource organizations, and the Space Science Directorate. See, in addition, the links in the right column for the Goddard Projects Directory and article/paper search engines.

Sport Science Center at Gatorade Sport Science Institute

http://www.gssiweb.com/sportsciencecenter

See topic links for articles, e.g., sport science research findings and practical applications for sports science professionals and athletes, sports-specific information, sports science exchange and roundtable review articles, scientific journals' articles on research studies conducted by the Gatorade Sports Science Institute, and Educational Tools in PDF format, plus an invitation to personalize your view of the GSSI.

Terraforming Information Pages

http://www.users.globalnet.co.uk/~mfogg/index.htm

Features definitions and links to articles and references, e.g., to "The Terraforming Simulator Project"; and papers including "Terraforming: A Review of Research" and "Technological Requirements for Terraforming Mars"; NASA Student Projects and Theme Reports such as "Developing Ecosystems on Mars"; plus press releases, book reviews, essays, bibliographies, correspondence, and more links to other sites.

Untimely Inventions

http://www.didyouknow.cd/firstfax.htm

Of some well-known and popular products that took a long time to be accepted, and even one hundred years to get to the marketplace.

USDA for Kids

http://www.usda.gov/news/usdakids/index.html

This area of the Web site for the U.S. Department of Agriculture includes icon links to the features Agriculture for Kids, Backyard Conservation, Food for Thought, Food Guide Pyramid, Preventing Foodborne Illnesses, Gardening, Nature Watch, Natural Resource Conservation Education, Kids' Science Page, Science for Kids, Team Nutrition, Weather, Facts about Agriculture, History of Agriculture, the USDA Hall of Fame, and "more cool links."

Virtual A-Life Library

http://www.cs.brandeis.edu/~zippy/alife-library.html

This site provides a list of links to online papers on artificial life as provided by individual authors, institutions, and miscellaneous sources. Subjects included in the papers range from robotics and autonomous agents to genetic programming, learning, and evolution. There is also a link to other A-life resources.

Virtual Library: Science

http://vlib.org/Science.html

This site provides links to information on science subjects including Biosciences, Computer Science, Medicine and Health, Technology and Medicine, Microscopy, Chemistry, Earth Science,

Physics, Science Fairs, and the History of Science. There are also links to Agriculture, Engineering, Forensic Toxicology, Complex Systems, and Social Sciences (e.g., Anthropology, Archaeology, Psychology, and Urban Environment Management).

Virtual Nutrition Center—Health Science Guide

http://www-sci.lib.uci.edu/HSG/Nutrition.html

See the Nutrition Overview box with links to Web sites on Nutrition Online Journals and featuring information on Food Science and Nutrition; Clinical Nutrition; Nutrition Literature and Patent Searches; plus Nutrition, Food and Health Dictionaries; and Online Nutrition Calculators. See also the Nutrition Interactive Databases and Tutorials box with links to more resources.

Voice of the Shuttle: Anthropology

http://vos.ucsb.edu (click the Anthropology link)

See links that lead to Web sites with information that treat anthropology in historical, cultural, and societal contexts, as well as from these points of view.

Voice of the Shuttle: Archaeology

http://vos.ucsb.edu (click the Archaeology link)

See links that lead to Web sites with information that treat archaeology in historical, cultural, and societal contexts, as well as from these viewpoints.

Voice of the Shuttle: Science, Technology, and Culture

http://vos.ucsb.edu (click the Science, Technology, and Culture link)

This area of this Web site provides resources on science, medicine, and technology, within historical, societal, and cultural contexts. See the links to the History of Sci-Tech, Major Sci-Tech Projects, Philosophy of Science, Sci-Tech and Cultural Studies, Sci-Tech and Ethics, Science and Religion, and Cyberculture. See also links to particular sciences including Space, Medicine, Artificial Life, Alternate Sci-Tech, Sci-Tech journals, and general resources.

SCIENCE NEWS FROM MEDIA SOURCES

ABCNews.com—SciTech Index

http://abc.news.go.com/sections/scitech

See annotated links to featured news items, more news, and Today at SciTech. Click also the Health link in the left column to get to the Health page with Today on Health, annotated links to featured news and more news, plus a health topic search menu.

BBC News: Science/Nature

http://news.bbc.co.uk/hi/english/sci/tech

See annotations with links to featured science and nature news items. See also links to science news in the realmedia column and links to technology, health, and other related news items at this site provided by the British Broadcasting Company.

CBSNews.com—Sci/Tech

http://cbsnews.cbs.com/sections/tech/main205.shtml

See annotated links to featured stories, plus Space Place, Interactive, and Gizmorama columns. See also the link to HealthWatch at the top of the page.

CNN.com—Sci/Tech

www.cnn.com/TECH or *www.cnn.com/TECH/space* or *www.cnn.com/TECH/health*

See annotated links to top news stories, more news, Cool Science, and Next@CNN, in Technology, Science, Nature and the Environment. Click links to Space news and Health news pages in the left column.

DEP News Clippings from the Pennsylvania Department of Environmental Protection

http://www.dep.state.pa.us/newsclippings

See annotated links to Daily Internet News Clips, plus links to news releases, CNN Earth News, the EnviroLink News Service, EPP Internet News Briefs, Internet Resources for Environmental Journalists, Earth Minute, and more. There is also a link to an archives of previous daily news clips by month for the past four years.

Discovery Channel News Roundup

http://dsc.discovery.com/news/news.html

See the current science or nature news story, top science or nature news stories, and Explore More via the archives' pull-down menu with topics such as Animal Alert, Ocean Alert, Dinosaurs, Go Deeper: Space, and Planet Earth.

Earthfiles.com—Headlines

http://www.earthfiles.com/headlines.cfm

This site, awarded the Britannica Internet Site Award, provides photographs with annotations about, and links to news reports on, various anomalous unexplained natural phenomena. See also the link at left to Science phenomena headlines. Earth phenomena, plus Outer Space phenomena with relation to the Earth, are covered. Note recent headlines and dates, plus archive headlines and dates on each page. A headline report is free to see for one hundred twenty days after headline date. Headlines in archive area and items searched for in archives after this time require a subscription payment for access, although looking at archive headline sentences and dates is free.

Environmental News Network

http://www.enn.com

Read Today's News Story, Headlines, Press Releases, Radio EarthNews, Environmental Update audio and video reports, special topics reports (e.g., on global warming, alternative energy), and an online quiz.

EurekAlert! A Service of the American Association for the Advancement of Science

http://www.eurekalert.org

This site features links to Breaking Science News and Science News by Subject (e.g., Agriculture, Archaeology, Atmospheric Science, Biology, Chemistry and Physics, Earth Science, Medicine and Health, Space and Planetary, Technology and Engineering).

Faith-Science News

http://asa3.calvin.org/ASA/topics/Faith-ScienceNews/index.html

This site has a list of annotated links to scientific reports and opinions with a religious slant. Items from the current month from various sources including space.com, the magazine *Nature*, and the *New York Times*, are featured. The site is provided by the American Scientific Affiliation, an organization of scientists with religious interests.

Girl Power! In the News Index

http://www.girlpower.gov/press/news/index.htm

Sponsored by the U.S. Department of Health and Human Services, this site, whose purpose is "targeting health messages to the unique needs, interests, and challenges of girls" of ages nine to fourteen, features in this news area links to News Room, Press Releases, and Research Studies and News.

Latest News at Site for Research and Scientific Interpretation into Unexplained Sciences

http://www.cropcircle.com/index2.html (click Latest News link)

See links to press releases and field reports, plus articles on unexplained phenomena, especially on crop circles, with attempts to provide scientific analyses.

MacDonald Observatory, University of Texas at Austin—Press Releases and Archive

http://stardate.utexas.edu/pr/pr.html

NASA Human Space Flight News

http://spaceflight.nasa.gov/spacenews/index.html

Find out, on the space news page, about Current NASA News (e.g., Status Reports and News Releases that are current press releases and documents from the archives). See also Today@NASA and Center News (on happenings at NASA facilities), plus News Resources (e.g., Fact Sheets with historical information, first flights, research and science facilities; press kit of press releases and background information on a given mission; and the Johnson Space Center JSC up-to-date status reports e-mail).

NASA Human Space Flight Index—News, etc.

http://spaceflight.nasa.gov/index.html

See links to space station news, current shuttle mission information or preparation for an upcoming one, and a menu at the top of the page. Touch this top menu and click links for Space Shuttle data, Space Station data, and "Beyond" (e.g., Mars missions) data; plus History, Outreach, Realtime Data, and Gallery. The top menu links lead to information such as science, future and past missions, benefits, status, virtual tour, why explore, crew or advance scouts, and basic reference information; plus history of NASA and space flight programs; educational resources and programs; career data; and sighting opportunities. A Web Launch Pad has ISS status reports, Q's and A's, and more.

NASA Kennedy Space Center—Newsroom Headlines

http://www-pao.ksc.nasa.gov/kscpao/release/newsroom.htm

Read Headline News Items' first paragraphs, then click links to read more. See also the link to other NASA Centers and their news. Note, in addition, more links (e.g., to news releases, headquarters' news releases, shuttle status, Today@NASA, and to updates on the space station, the Hubble Telescope, and space probes).

NASA News

http://spacelink.nasa.gov/NASA.News/.index.html

Links go to current and past news releases; launch dates and payloads; status reports on NASA projects and events; NASA online newspapers, and the NASA TV Schedule. Other links go to related NASA Internet sites, related material on Spacelink, and more.

National Optical Astronomy Observatory—News Releases

http://www.noao.edu/news

Provided by NOAO, which is operated by the Association of Universities for Research in Astronomy under agreement with the National Science Foundation, this site has annotated links to current news at NOAO for the current year, plus link to news from the previous year. See also links to Science Highlights, a NOAO newsletter, an image gallery, and a search current news box.

New York Daily News

http://www.nydailynews.com

In the right column, see a pull-down menu with links to Health and Medical Information topics (e.g., teen health).

New York Times on the Web

http://www.nytimes.com

At this Web page based on the newspaper click the Science, Health, Technology, or Education link in the News column at the left or scroll down to title headline links under Science, Technology, or Health. See also some title links to reviews of science-related books in the Books area. Also search the archives for items from the past thirty days. If the Education link is clicked, note that page's Learning Network link, and note the Network's page with a Science Q and A link; plus links to Explore the Learning Network by Subject (e.g., Technology, Science, and Health). See also the links to pages for Ask a Reporter, Conversation Starters, and Web Tours with science-related items.

News and Events at the National Women's Health Information Center

http://www.4woman.gov/sitemap/index.htm

Scroll to and click links under this topic (e.g., to Women's Health News Today, Press Releases, and Hot Topics in Congress).

News Updates and Special Reports at the Center for Science in the Public Interest Online

http://www.cspinet.org

At this site for the publisher of the *Nutrition Action Healthletter*, see links to information under News Updates and Special Reports. Click also links for the Healthletter (e.g., to a Newsroom page with title links to more nutrition-related news and a Featured Articles page that includes nutrition-related News from CSPI links with items in PDF format).

NPR—Fresh Air—Science Topics

http://freshair.npr.org/aboutFA.cfm (click Archived Shows link)

At this site for the National Public Radio's Fresh Air Program, scroll to the far right, then down, to the "search by topic' search box. Search with the word Science. Next, click links by date and subject or guest to see a show's science information, a show's guest who talks on a science subject, or to hear the show that features something about science.

NPR—Science Friday

http://www.sciencefriday.com

This site, for the National Public Radio program Science Friday, has descriptions of, and links to more on, the current week's show, plus an audio version of that show. There are also archives of audio reproductions of the weekly science topics for the past five years. Note also book title links to audio versions of the show on which the book was discussed. Click the link to a lounge area where, after free registration, lounge visitors can discuss science news or comment on the topics of the weekly programs.

NPR's Environmental News Show—Living on Earth

http://www.loe.org/index.php

Every weekday, the Living on Earth Network News is provided in audio format online here by the host of National Public Radio's Sound Journalism for the Planet program. See links to "this week's shows," plus the series archives, a Living on Earth Today feature, and more related links.

PBS Online—News and Views

http://www.pbs.org/neighborhoods/news

In this area at this site for PBS-TV stations and their programs, click links to NPR News (with headlines, including live dispatches) and Explore PBS subjects (at right). Click Explore links such as Science and Technology, Nature and Wildlife, or Health and Religion that lead to links for feature stories and data on General Science, Archaeology and Anthropology, DigiTechnology, Earth and Space, Life Science, Physics, Inventions, and Mysteries, as presented on PBS programs. Note also the links to TeacherSource Science and Teaching with Technology.

Planetary Science Research Discoveries

http://www.psrd.hawaii.edu

Of latest research on ideas and discoveries that planetary scientists are sharing.

Research Matters at Harvard University

http://www.researchmatters.harvard.edu

At this site that provides "public entry to the latest news" about basic science, medical treatments, technological advances, earth and space exploration, and societal research, click links to news on these subjects for the non-specialist: Mind, Body, Earth, Space, Technology, and Society. See also annotated links to Recent News and a Feature Story, plus a search/browse area.

SciCentral: The Award Winning Portal to Breaking Scientific Research News

http://www.scicentral.com or *http://www.sciquest.com/index.html* (click scicentral link)

In the center of this Web page, see annotated links to data from news sources and research journals under the science subjects Biology or Biological, Earth and Space, Engineering, Health, Physical and Chemical Sciences. Find more data on these subjects via pull-down menus. On the left of this Web page, see links to Science Databases, Women and Minorities in Science, K–12 Science, Institutions and People, a Career Center, Science Policy and Ethics, Journals, a Media Room, U.S. Government Agencies, and more resources. Find also links to Science Literature or Science Articles Search, Listen to a Two Minute Science Log, the Week in Review, and a

SciCentral e-newsletter. Find the SciCentral Index via a link after clicking the link to the sitemap page.

ScienceDaily Magazine: Your Link to the Latest Science Research News

http://www.sciencedaily.com

This site features title links to Today's Headlines and title links under News by Topic (e.g., Life Sciences, Physical Sciences, Science and Society). See also More News via links to Today's Summaries, Yesterday's Summaries, and This Week's Headlines. Note, in addition, a search ScienceDaily box and a free e-mail newsletter.

Technology and Science Front Page at MSNBC

http://www.msnbc.com/news/Tech_Front.asp

See list of title links to top stories on technology and science subjects, plus links under Science, Space News, Tech Talk, and more. See also headline news at top right of the page, and, in the left column, a link to a Health page with a Front Page, headlines at the top right, and WebMD Health Resource, Health Watch, Health Beat, Health Library, Nutrition Notes, Smart Fitness, Your Environment, On the Cutting Edge, Breaking BioEthics, and Birthing for a New Millennium.

Time.com—Newsfiles—Science

http://www.time.com/time/newsfile

At this site for the print magazine Time, see featured, among various news topics, a column with annotated links to the latest research on science subjects (e.g., the Future of Medicine, the Genetics Revolution, Human Behavior and Biology, Space, Astronomy/Cosmology, Weather, and Dinosaurs. See also, in the left column, a link to a Sci-Health page with links to health-related science news, such as the State of the Planet, special features (e.g., Young and Bipolar), more stories, and a "search the archives" box.

Yahoo News—Science, Health, Technology

http://story.news.yahoo

In the left column, click the Science, Health, or Technology link. On each page, see links at the center to main stories and links at the right to sites with news on the subject. On the Science page, see also links at the left, under Full Coverage, to news in particular sciences such as Animal News, Environment and Nature, Astronomy and Space, Biotechnology and Genetics. On the Health page, see also links to particular health news topics, such as food safety, diet and nutrition, and the West Nile Virus.

Your Health—Dr. Frank Field's Health Reports

http://www.upn9.com/news/medica./index.asp

At this site for a New Jersey–based network news program, see links to information on new health-related happenings (e.g., a video pill), plus news on long-time health problems and possible solutions (e.g., teen drug abuse). See also links to a medical stories archive.

APPENDIX C
Other Special Online Science Resources
Ready Reference Sources Featuring Science Subjects and Web Sites That Include Pages on Science Connections with Other Subjects

Aristotle's Logic and Philosophical Query into Method

http://www.csudh.edu/phenom_studies/methods_phil/lect_3.htm

Notes Aristotle's ideas about science (e.g., its being theoretical, practical, and productive).

Astronomy 101 Glossary

http://www.wpo.net/glossary.html

Benchmarks for Science Literacy

http://www.project2061.org/bsl/default.htm

This Web page provides a detailed overview of a book that was published by Oxford University Press in 1993. It gives tips on what students should know and be able to do in the sciences by the end of the twelfth grade. Note also the links to designs, resources, and relational education Web sites.

Biodiversity Crossword Puzzle

http://www.nytimes.com/learning/students/xwords/september98_image.html

See also links to science, technology, health, and geography puzzles at the *New York Times* archive links page http://www.nytimes.com/learning/teachers/xwords/archive.html.

Emily Dickinson's "A science, so the Savants say"

http://www.americanpoems.com/poets/emilydickinson/100.shtml

Emily Dickinson's "The Brain is" and "The Brain within"

http://www.bartleby.com/113.html (click Index of First Lines link)

Search alphabetically, then click the first lines links to see these 1924 versions (the first publications) of these poems by Emily Dickinson: "The Brain is wider than the sky" and "The Brain within its groove." (Each one is also known, in slightly different versions, as poem no. 632 and poem no. 556, respectively, in the 1955 authoritative edition edited by Thomas H. Johnson). (See also an entry below for an article titled "Science in the Poetry of Emily Dickinson.")

Exploring the Relationship of Medicine and Literature

http://www.medicalprose.com/index.shtml

Famous Quotes by Subject—Science, Technology, Health, and Medicine

http://www.quotationspage.com/subjects (click each subject's link)

Field Techniques Used by the Missouri Botanical Garden—Compiled by R. Liesner

http://www.mobot.org/MOBOT/research/library/Fieldtechbook/tpage.html

"How a Research Paper in Astronomy Is Written"

http://itss.ratheon.com/café/cafe.html (café with or without the diacritical mark)

At the Web site for the Astronomy Café, click the link for "Inside a Research Paper."

"How Can the Study of Creation Be Scientific?" and "How Can Origins Be Taught in High School and College?"

http://www.creationscience.com/onlinebook

Scroll to the links for the questions numbered 254 and 315, then click to find these questions which Walt Brown, director of the Center for Scientific Creation, provides. An answer is given through a detailed Origins Research Project link, and a questions and answers link, under number 315. The aim here is to help high school and college students think logically and scientifically to analyze evidence and describe a theory of the earth's origin or creation. The project guidelines do not take Darwin's evolution theory nor religious viewpoints as absolute truth. Note also other question links or chapter title links, or subjects links via an alphabet links list, for the rest of Dr. Brown's book *In the Beginning: Compelling Evidence for Creation and the Flood* (1995–2002) (seventh edition, online and in print) to which the featured parts noted above belong.

Instructions to Authors in the Health Sciences

http://www.mco.edu/lib/instr/libinsta.html

This Web site, by the Raymond H. Mulford Library of the Medical College of Ohio, has links in alphabetical order to other Web sites of scientific organizations and journals that have instructions for writers who write on health and life science subjects.

Introduction to the Scientific Method

http://teacher.nsrl.rochester.edu/phy_labs/AppendixE/AppendixE.html

Note the links for, or scroll to, information on "The scientific method is"; "The scientific method has four steps"; "Hypotheses, models, theories, and laws"; "Testing hypotheses"; "Are there circumstances in which the scientific method is not applicable?"; "Common mistakes in applying the scientific method"; plus Conclusion and References.

Learning Guides to Movies—Subject Matter Index—Science and Technology

http://www.teachwithmovies.org/heritage-list.htm

In addition to the link to guides for Science and Technology movies, note the links to guides for other movies with science subjects, including Aviation, The Environment, Medicine (including Psychiatry), Space Exploration, and science people through the Biography link leading to guides to movies featuring lives of noted people.

Literature, Arts, and Medicine Database

http://endeavor.med.nyu.edu/lit-med-db/about.html

Features links to keywords, annotations, and many full texts of literary writings containing medical subjects and data on their authors.

Marianne Moore's "The Jellyfish"

http://www.clas.ufl.edu/users/pcraddoc/manywor.htm

At this Web site which features excerpts adapted from the *Many Worlds of Poetry*, a book by Jacob Drachler and Virginia B. Terris (1969), scroll to the last quarter of the Web page to find Moore's poem and a brief analysis of it.

Medicine in Quotations Online

http://acponline.org/medquotes/index.html

The American College of Physicians and the American Society of Internal Medicine offer more than three thousand quotations. Find a quote by typing an author's last name and a one word subject, then click Search, or do a subject search via alphabet letters.

"The Methods of Science and Journalism" by Bruce Murray

http://www.facsnet.org/tools/sci_tech/methods.php3

Note the sections "Defining and Contrasting the Methods"; "Good Science, Bad Science, and Fraud"; and others. See also the links to "Understanding Biotech Stories" and "Covering the High-Tech Story."

National Association of Science Writers—Important Documents

http://nasw.org

Features, under Important Documents, links to "A Field Guide for Science Writers," including the Contents Page and a sample page on "Using the Internet for Reporting"; "Communicating Science News"; "Advice for Beginning Science Writers"; "The End of Science Writing"; and "How to Keep Readers Interested." Note also, under Important Links, the link to the Evert Clark/Seth Payne Award for Young Science Journalists.

"Nurturing Scientific Literacy Among Youth Through Experientially Based Curriculum Materials" by Robert L. Horton, Ph.D., and Suzanne Hutchinson, Ph.D.

http://www.ag.ohio-state.edu/~youth4h/expedu

This document, developed for the National Network for Science and Technology Cooperative Extension Service—Children, Youth, and Family Network, is based on, and expands upon, D.A. Kolb's 1984 definition of experiential education. Note the abstract, introduction, five chapters, conclusions and recommendations, five appendixes, references, and contributors.

Online Science Dictionaries at MedBioWorld: Online Scientific and Medical Dictionaries

http://www.sciencekomm.at/advice/dict.html

See the links to Online Medical Dictionaries and Online Dictionaries for the Life Sciences, Chemistry, Computers, plus Other Online Science Dictionaries and Dictionary Collections (e.g., Zoological Glossaries, Dictionaries, and Acronyms).

Reflections—Medical College of Wisconsin—HealthLinks

http://healthlink.mcw.edu/reflections

Features poems, stories, and essays by students and physicians and other professionals. See also the links to Health News, Dear Dr. Becky, The Doctor Is In, and Health Topics.

Resources for Students Interested in Science Journalism, Museums, and Related Fields

http://web.mit.edu/career/www/GraduateStudent/science_journalism_museums_etc.html

See links to Science and Journalism Web sites, Articles, Books; Organizations (e.g., the National Association for Science Writers [NASW] and its "Advice to Beginning Science Writers"); Other Related Fields; and more.

Roster of Physician Writers

http://hometown.aol.com/dbryantmd/index.html

This site contains entries on literary people who are or were also in the medical profession or wrote on medical subjects (e.g., Erasmus Darwin to Michael Crichton). It features short biographies plus titles of writings and links to actual writings or brief information on them and to author Web sites. Access is via alphabet letter links at left to links by writers' last names. People solely in the medical profession are not included.

Science and Technology, Health and Fitness, at www.buzzle.com

http://www.buzzle.com/chapters/science-and-technology.asp

http://www.buzzle.com/chapters/health-and-fitness.asp

In these areas of a site called "The Intelligent Side of the Web" see annotated links to articles and Web sites with more information on various aspects of the featured subjects.

"Science Curriculum Reform in the United States" (1995) by Rodger W. Bybee

http://www.nationalacademies.org/rise/backg3a.htm

A reprint from *Redesigning the Science Curriculum* (1995), edited by Rodger W. Bybee and Joseph D. McInerney.

Science Dictionary, Science Glossary, and Science Terms Directory

http://www.glossarist.com/glossaries/science (click links)

Note especially the links for Definitions of Key Terms, General Science Glossary, Applied Science, Science Glossary, Computer Science, Earth Sciences, Life Sciences, and Physical Sciences.

"Science in the Poetry of Emily Dickinson" by Fred D. White

http://www.cswnet.com/~erin/ed13.htm

This article, which appeared in print in *College Literature* (February 1992), is online with an abstract, full text with Dickinson quotations, an appendix, notes, works cited, and Dickinson's science poems listed by subject.

"Science, Technology and Society"—A Social Studies Curriculum Standard

http://www.ncss.org/standards/2.8.html

This Web page features a description of number eight, one of Ten Thematic Strands in the Social Studies Curriculum Standards recommended by the National Council for Social Studies Curriculum Standards, and one of a few that include other subjects in combination with the primary concerns of Social Studies. See also the "People, Places, and Environments" Standard at http://www.ncss.org/standards/2.3.html. In addition, note the Standards' Table of Contents at http://www.ncss.org/standards/toc.html.

"Science Terms" in the American Heritage Book of English Usage

http://www.bartleby.com/64/4.html

The Scientific Method Quiz

http://antoine.frostburg.edu/chem/senese/101/intro/scimethod-quiz.shtml

General Chemistry Online provides this multiple choice quiz featuring four basic questions, with the easiest to difficult being from number four to number one. See also links to other Web pages including FAQs, Glossary, Exam Guide, Resources, and a Tutorial Index.

Scientific Quotations, A Short Dictionary of

http://naturalscience.com/dsqhome.html

This site features quotations that span known history, e.g., from 235 B.C. to the present. There are quotations by well-known and lesser-known scientists and writers writing on science subjects, e.g., Archimedes and Lucretius to Mark Twain and Stephen Hawking, with brief quotations and their sources.

Sherlock Holmes and the Scientific Method, by Professor Larry Meinert

http://www.wsu.edu:8080/~meinert/SH.html

A university seminar outline by a physical science professor investigating geological and general scientific aspects of Sherlock Holmes. Note the seminar descriptions, the list of session activities and reading assignments, and the writing assignments, especially numbers three, four, and five. In the Reference list, see *Diagnosis and Detecting: The Medical Iconography of Sherlock Holmes.*

Space Botany and Space Biology Curriculum Outlines

http://www.pc.cc.va.us/Patterson/Science/Projects/CHROME/CHROME.htm

Click the subject links to go to the course outlines with descriptions of what will be studied (e.g., Human Biology in Microgravity and Plant Growth and Development in Microgravity). On the main page, click the WWW Links link for a page of links to Web sites on aspects of the subjects of study (e.g., NASA Space Biology). Click also the Topics link and the Introduction link, and follow the links to more information. The outlines were developed by community college assistant professor John M. Patterson.

Strategian: A Strategic Guide to Quality Information in [the Sciences]

http://www.strategian.com

The Windsor Science Library at Grinnell College in Iowa provides this strategic guide to help in "tracking down high quality information useful when writing a paper, preparing for oral presentation, seeking more depth on a news report, answering a question, supporting the results of a lab experiment, etc." It provides a search the database option and browsing links such as Core Reference Materials, Core Indexes and Abstracts, and Hot Topics, plus "Critically Evaluate the Information You Gather," free full text documents, and listen to or view the Information Strategy. See also the links for contents, students, and teachers. In addition, note the related site at http://www.lib.grin.edu/places/scilib/index.html, with links to Subject Guides, Databases, Reference Sources, FAQs, Bibliographies, Online Journals, and How to Evaluate What Is Found for biology, chemistry, computer science, energy, general science, medicine, physics, psychology, and weather and climate.

"Toward an Understanding of Scientific Literacy" by Rodger W. Bybee

http://ehrweb.aaas.org/ehr/forum/bybee.html

Walt Whitman's "A Noiseless Patient Spider"

http://www.bartleby.com/142/208.html

"What Scientists Have to Learn" (1993) by Robert M. Young

http://www.human-nature.com/rmyoung/papers/paper31.html

A revised version of a talk given at the Conference on the Changing Image of Science: The Role of the Media and Education. See also links to Young's other writings, many science-related, at http://human-nature.com/rmyoung/papers.

William Blake's "To See a World"

http://www.library.utoronto.edu.ca/utel/rp/authors/blake.html

Click the "Auguries of Innocence" link at this Web site for Representative Poetry Online, provided by Canada's University of Toronto. See especially lines one through four.

Writing Center—Lab Reports for Biology

http://www.hamilton.edu/academics/resource/wc/bio_lab.html

Find out what lab reports in biology should contain, noting information under format, style, introduction, presentation, writing, audience, materials and methods, results, discussion, acknowledgments, references, and literature cited.

Writing Guidelines for Scientific and Engineering Students

http://filebox.vt.edu:10021/eng/mech/writing

Links go to information on writing Formal Reports (e.g., Lab Reports, Design Reports, Progress Reports, Theses, and Dissertations), Other Documents (e.g., Proposals, Instructions, Journal Articles, and Presentation Slides), Introduction (e.g., Assessing the Audience, Selecting the Format, and Crafting the Style), Correspondence (e.g., Memo Format and Sample, Letter Format and Sample, Job Letters and Resumes), and Conclusion, plus Appendixes on Sample Formats and Documenting Resources, glossary, references, and acknowledgments. Note also links to writing exercises, teacher resources, writing courses, and supporting books.

Writing Lab Reports in Psychology

http://www.hamilton.edu/academics/resource/wc/WritingPsychPapers.html

Find out what lab reports in psychology should contain. Note information under title, abstract, introduction, method (including subjects, procedure, and materials/apparatus), plus results and discussion.

APPENDIX D
Web Sites with Selected Resources from Magazines, Journals, and Newspapers

AdAstra Online Digest

http://www.nss.org/adastra

This online version of the National Space Society's magazine has an annotated contents page of the current issue with links to selected features. There is a featured article, plus departments including Launch Pad, Lifting Off, Mission Control (e.g., with space medicine articles and What's Up data on shuttle flights), and Space Community (on space activism). Features have included The Future of Space Transportation, A Day in the Life of the Space Shuttle, The Need to Colonize, and Space Standards.

Archaeological Institute of America—Publications—Overview

http://www.archaeological.org (click Publications link)

Click links to *Archaeology* and *AJA* (the *American Journal of Archaeology*); then follow the links to these magazines' Web sites that have online articles, news reports, a contents page of the current issue with some links to features online (including some in PDF format), past issues, and search areas. Click also the link to *Dig*, the archaeology magazine for ages eight to thirteen. Follow links to summaries of the current issue's features, and some back issues' features, an online teachers' guide for each issue, plus Fantastic Factoids, a Glossary, a Quiz, an Ask Dr. Dig page, and a state by state guide to archaeology and paleontology events for schools and families.

Artifax

http://www.msn.fullfeed.com/~scribe/artifax.htm

This quarterly newsletter is published in conjunction with the Institute for Biblical Archaeology and the Near East Archaeology Society. It contains a digest of information on the latest discoveries and developments in Biblical archaeology and related subjects. Issues for the past seven years are online.

Astronomy Magazine, Star Chart, Space News

http://www.astronomy.com/home.asp

This site features Today's News and Featured Story for hobbyists and science-minded readers, plus Tonight's Sky, Hobby Tip, The Sky Online for Beginners, Astronomy Quiz, Calendar of Astronomical Events coming up or just past, Fun Fact, and Glossary. A Site Map has, for parents and teachers, links to sky charts and more on the subjects of Today's News and Featured Stories. Contents of the current issue and the next issue, plus links to selected special online features related to the articles in those issues, are provided. Indexes in PDF format are provided for back issues.

Astronomy Now Online

http://www.astronomynow.com/index.html

Features Breaking News Stories (with links to more information), plus links to Past Breaking News stories, Spaceflight Now, The Night Sky, Resources, and Index, and a News Alert e-mail newsletter.

BioMedNet Magazine

http://www.biomednet.com/magazine

Full access is provided only to subscribers, but access to articles published in the last fourteen days and available on the main page of this magazine, which is published every two weeks, will be given after free registration by a teacher.

Brain and Mind—[An] Electronic Magazine On Neuroscience

http://www.epub.org/br/cm/home_i.htm

The award-winning magazine for students, non-specialists, and average people includes online features from the current issue and six years of back issues. It also has virtual online talks and links to other features such as news, biographies, resources, an index, and links to more sites on the brain and the mind.

Brain Power Magazine

http://www.mso.com/brain/mag/index.html

This magazine, provided by the Mind Sports Organization Worldwide, provides articles, news, and archives with items from past issues, on the topics of thinking, intelligence, memory, and life. Items have included subjects such as Animal Intelligence, Mind Mapping Explained, Intelligence about Intelligence (e.g., Can the Human Brain Detect Natural Disasters?), Mind Exercises May Help (e.g., Alzheimer's Disease, Dyslexia). See also links to Mental Skills News, Creative Thinking, and IQ Puzzles.

British Archaeology Magazine

http://www.britarch.ac.uk/ba/ba.html

To find online features, click the link for the contents page of the current issue or the links to the contents pages for any issue from the past seven years.

Career Journal

http://www.careerjournal.com

Do a search for scientists in the "search for articles" box, or do a search for a particular kind of scientist in the "search for a job" box.

Cobblestone: The Magazine That Makes History Come Alive

http://cobblestonepub.com/pages/cobbmain.htm

See a teacher's guide and find out something on each occasional science-related issue's basic facts on people, things, or happenings, with some published on special anniversary dates, and including special anniversary subject articles, at this Web site for this history magazine for ages eight to fourteen. Find a guide by clicking the link for Reading Comprehension Questions. Next, choose and click the link for a particular science subject issue found by the year of publication. See, for example, Our Voyage to the Moon, July 1981; Environmentalism, August 1989; Mt. St. Helens, May 1981; Natural Disasters, April 1986; Lewis and Clark, September 1980; Meet Albert Einstein, October 1987; John Audubon, April 1980; Thomas Edison, February 1980; Helen Keller, May 1983; People with Disabilities, 1989; and Elizabeth Blackwell, 2003.

Discover Magazine

http://www.discover.com

See Web Exclusives, plus Feature Story, News Flash, Web Pick, NeuroQuest, Ask Discover, and Departments (e.g., Letters, Research and Development, Breaking News, Science Travel, Vital Signs, Sky Lights, Future Tech, and Works in Progress), plus Current Issue, Recent Issues, Archives, [This Month's] Highlights, Science News, and Education Guide.

EEK! Environmental Education for Kids

http://www.dnr.state.wi.us/org/caer/ce/eek/index.htm

The Wisconsin Department of Natural Resources provides this electronic magazine for young readers aged nine to thirteen. The magazine features Nature Notes, Our Earth, In the Outdoors, Cool Stuff (e.g., Things to Do), Monthly Riddler to answer online, What's New, Get a Job (Careers in Natural Resources areas), and a Teachers Page (with a search box, resources, activities, and what's new at this site). An active Monthly Spotlight box invites visitors to Click Here to Find Out More About [a featured subject stated here].

Elementary Science This Month

http://www.lme.mankato.msus.edu/ci/elem.sci.html (click Back Issues link)

This in-progress site has items starting from 1996. Features include This Month's Science Activities, Animal of the Month, Scientist of the Month, [a month's] Night Sky, Constellation of the Month, and Tell Me Why.

Female Patient Journal

http://www.femalepatient.com

Note links to special editions, patient editions, primary care editions, and archives (with selected articles, patient handouts, and a signature series on special subjects) on medical concerns especially for women and other medical conditions as they involve women.

HMS Beagle: The BioMedNet Magazine—Archives

http://www.biomednet.com/hmsbeagle

Issues of this magazine, which was published between 1998 and March 2002, are available here. Features include Today's Quote from a Scientist, Interview, Profile, Meeting Brief, Trends Previews, Press Box, Opinion, Book Reviews, Essays, and Poems. Replaced by BioMedNet Magazine.

International Wildlife

http://www.nwf/internationalwildlife

This Website for the print magazine is provided by the National Wildlife Federation. It has plain text articles of special features, plus links to past issues and selected articles from the past year, and an index of previous issues' articles with links to some that are online. Features online include Department items such as Action Report, Nature's Voice, and NWF View. Note also a link to Education and a link to a Sneak Preview of the upcoming issue, with selected items online.

Internet Scout Project's NSDL Reports

http://scout.cs.wisc.edu/nsdl-reports

These bi-weekly reports are part of the National Science, Technology, Engineering and Mathematics Education Digital Library Project and the Internet Scout Project of the Computer Sciences Department at the University of Wisconsin-Madison, with sponsorship from the National Science Foundation. These reports feature, in the life sciences, physical sciences, engineering, and technology areas, "the most valuable and authoritative resources available online" for librarians, educators and students at the K–12 and higher levels, and others. Report sections include Research, Education, Topic in Depth, and General. For the last Scout Report in the category Science and Engineering, one of several subject-specific publications provided formerly by the Internet Scout Report Project, go to http://scout.cs.wisc.edu/report/sci/current/ index.html, or click the Scout Archive link and look for links to reports by searching for science subjects via alphabet links. Note also the NSDL Reports archive.

Issues in Science and Technology Online

http://www.nap.edu/issues/index.html

This publication, from the National Academy of Sciences, National Academy of Engineering, and the University of Texas in Dallas, features a recent issue online and online back issues for the past six years. Sections include Forum Editor's Journal, From the Hill [Capitol Hill], Perspectives, articles, book reviews, and archives.

Journal of Adolescent Health

http://www.medicaldirect.com/journal/journal?sdid=5072

In this multidisciplinary publication of the Society for Adolescent Medicine, note links to the current issue, previous issues, search this journal, and author information. See also Related Links (e.g., to journals, associations such as the Society for Adolescent Medicine, and resource sites such as the Adolescence Directory Online). Visitors can view issue contents, but only Society members have access to the articles.

Journal of Scientific Exploration—Selected Articles

http://www.scientificexploration.org/jse/articles.html

This journal is published by the Society of Scientific Exploration, which investigates "important areas that remain almost unexplored." It provides a titles page with links to tables of contents of issues from the past six years and features links to full-text articles, or abstracts of them, in PDF or plain text formats. A link at the bottom of the page leads to a Young Investigators bulletin board with commentaries on, or questions about, the articles at this site. Articles have included, in plain text, Curious, Creative, and Critical Thinking; Anomalies in the History of Relativity; and The Subject of Science; and, in PDF format, What Can Elementary Particles Tell Us about the World in Which We Live? Significance Levels for the Assessment of Anomalous Phenomena; What Has Science Come To? and Twentieth and Twenty-First Century Science: Reflections and Projections.

Journal of the American Medical Women's Association

http://www.jamwa.org

See links to past and upcoming issues, the contents page of the current issue, and the women's health links library, plus featured Back Issue (e.g., Health and Adolescent Girls, Summer 1999, including Exercise and Female Adolescents; and Addressing Health Needs of Adolescent Girls in Modernizing Countries). See also the Question of Month by clicking the current question's link, which leads to a page with a links list to past questions such as those on the health of adolescent girls. Also see the link to information for contributors.

Kids Ark—A Cyber Space Station

http//web.ukonline.co.uk/conker/contents.htm

This interactive magazine, with a British slant, includes links to information on, and links to more sites about, Fossil Collecting, Pond Dipping (with plants and animals), and Weird Beasts (some real). There are also a link to an archive of previous articles, a search the Ark box, and links to more sites.

"The Last Word Science Questions and Answers" in the *New Scientist* Magazine

http://www.newscientist.com/lastword or *http://www.last-word.com*

This area of the *New Scientist* magazine features answers to more than five hundred questions sent by *New Scientist* readers about "the small mysteries in life" on topics including Planet Earth, the Seaside, Plants, Animals, Weather, Light, the Universe, Your Body, Energy and Forces, Liquids, Solids, Gases, Gadgets, Communication, Sound and Music, Sports and Leisure. Note also Ask a Question, News, Hot Topics, Opinion, and Web links.

Mercury Magazine

http://www.astrosociety.org/pubs/mercury/mercury.htm

This online version of this bimonthly publication, of the Astronomical Society of the Pacific, features items "from the latest science developments to history, education, observing, archaeoastronomy, and culture," plus sky maps and events. It has the current issue's contents and some featured articles. Archives of the contents of the issues from the past eight years are provided and also include selected articles online. Click the link to a *Mercury E-zine* which features items that were sent to *Mercury Magazine* but were not chosen for publication in the print publication. Reproduced here, these items include book reviews, articles, and sidebars.

Musicae Scientiae

http://musicweb.hmt-hannover.de/escom/english/index.htm (click link)

This journal of the European Society for the Cognitive Sciences of Music has links to issues by date, or by special subject issues, from the first issue of Spring 1997 to the present issue, with selected online articles. See, for example, *A Psychological Investigation of Meaning in Music* (Spring 1998), and *Temporal Mechanisms of the Brain as Fundamentals of Communication with Special References to Music Perception and Performance* (special issue 1999–2000). Note also an ESCOM Newsletter, Other Interesting Servers (e.g., the Foundation for BioMusicology, and the Society for British Music Therapy), and Other Events.

Musings

http://www.amnh.org/learn/musings/index.html

This newsletter, from the American Museum of Natural History, provided especially for educators, has online features that include Stories and Perspectives from educators and scientists, Practical Suggestions That Promote Inquiry-Based Investigations of Science and Culture, Ideas for Schools, Homes, and Communities to Connect with Local Resources, and other educational resources. Theme issues have included Environmental Stewardship, Genetic Literacy, Scientific Observation, Student-Directed Research Projects, Field Trips, Museum Exhibitions, Research, and Discoveries. Highlights of each issue often include a profile of a scientist, an examination of a scientist's writings, In the Classroom, In the Museum, In the Community, Teacher Feature, and Mind Boggler.

Nanotechnology Magazine

http://nanozine.com

See links to articles on subjects such as What is nanotechnology? Why is nanotechology happening? NanoPioneer, NanoInterview, NanoMedicine, NanoEcology, NanoLaw, and Atoms . . . How Small, How Strong?

National Geographic for Kids

http://magma.nationalgeographic.com/ngforkids

This online edition of a classroom magazine has online adventures, articles, cool links, a "worldwise" glossary, contests, This Month's Game, an archive, and a teacher's area.

National Geographic Online

http://www.nationalgeographic.com

This online edition of the print magazine has Today's Features, Guides (e.g., for Teachers, of Animals and Nature), Kids Creature Feature, Today's News, Extra, Multimedia, On TV, Search, and More to Explore.

National Geographic World Magazine for Kids

http://www.nationalgeographic.com/world/index.html

This magazine's Web site features include Amazing Animals, World Stories, Kids' Guide, Today's Fun Fact, Try This, Surprise, Poll, Archive, Hot Links, and Send Us Ideas.

National Science Teachers Association—Teacher Resources—Journals

http://www.nsta.org (click link)

Links to Web versions of print publications are provided, e.g., *The Science Teacher*, for high school educators; *Science Scope*, for middle and junior high school teachers; *Journal of Science College Teaching*; and *Science and Children*, for elementary school teachers.

National Wildlife Federation—In Print and on Film

http://www.nwf.org/printandfilm

Scroll to the link for the Web page that has the Federation's *National Wildlife* magazine with features including NW Features This Issue, NWF View, News of the Wild, Backyard Habitat, Environment, Your Health, Action Report, and e-mail newsletter. Free teacher registration is required for access.

Natural History Magazine

http://www.amnh.org/naturalhistory

This online version of this magazine, which is published by the American Museum of Natural History, features a current issue's Feature Story; Online Extras; Special Feature; The Natural Moment; Natural Selections; Biomechanics; Picks from the Past; Web Site Archive; NH Interactive; Online Media Kit; and a table of contents for the print version of the magazine, with links to some articles that are online.

Nutrition and Your Child—Index

http://www.bcm.tmc.edu/cnrc/nyc.htm

The U.S. Department of Agriculture and the Agricultural Research Service (USDA/ARS), and their Children's Nutrition Research Center at the Baylor College of Medicine in Houston, Texas, with the motto "Studying Nutrition Today for the Health of Future Generations," provides this free newsletter online for parents, educators, and health care professionals, although its topics will interest students. The current issue is online in plain text format. Recent past issues are online in PDF format, with subjects including *Tips for Vegetarian Teens* and *What Vegetarian Teens Need Every Day* (Winter 2000); *Proper Nutrition Should Be Part of Training Young Athletes* and *The USDA Offers School Program to Help Adolescents* (Summer 1998); and *High Fiber, Low Fat, Means Better Nutrition for Teens* (Summer 2000). See also the link to the A–Z Nutrition Information Archive. Note also, at the top of the page, the link to the Consumer News link and see that page's features including Facts and Answers: An Index to Nutrition Information and FAQs by Subject, and Web links to articles under Hot Topics, Just for Kids, Government Resources, General Food, Nutrition, and Health Sites.

Odyssey: The Science Magazine for Ages Ten Through Sixteen

http://cobblestonepub.com/pages/odysmain.htm and *http://www.odysseymagazine.com*

On the first cited page, see the link to a sample article. Next, click the link for Teachers' Guides for online teaching and learning tips geared to issues on particular topics (e.g., Cosmic Showers, Science or Hoax? When the Sparks Fly: Science Feuds, Brain Matters, What Is a Dinosaur? and Life in Motion). On the second cited page, see the current issue, Virtual Classroom (with links to subject sites), Special Science Features (e.g., scripts of the PBS-TV program Stargazing with Jack Horkheimer; Ask a Scientist; live webcams), plus All about Science, Fun Stuff, Just for Teachers, and a link to Science NetLinks.

Outdoor Photographer

http://www.outdoorphotographer.com

See links to a list of subjects for feature articles on wildlife photography, scenic photography, digital outdoors, and how to, plus an Eco Concerns articles column and a free e-mail newsletter. Some features of the current print issue are online. In the search box do a search with the word science for more online articles.

Planetarian—Journal of the International Planetarium Society

http://www.griffithobservatory.org/IPSPlanetarian.html (scroll to selected articles links)

See articles such as *Astronomy Education: A Global Perspective, Lessons from a Total Eclipse*, and *Grade Appropriate Concepts*, plus articles on subjects that aim to make science popular. See also a link to a subject index.

Popular Science: Fuel for the Curious Mind—Contents

http://www.popsci.com/popsci/contents

Features links to articles under News, Special Report, Tech, and Departments that include FYI and Looking Back. Links at the top of the page go to items on Science, Aviation and Space Technology, Medicine and Biotechnology, Computers and Consumer Electronics, and Home Tech. There is also a link to View the Table of Contents from Previous Issues.

Science Made Simple

http://www.sciencemadesimple.com/index.html

This site for a monthly newsletter features links to Science in the News, Science Subjects, Science Projects, and What Is Science Made Simple?

Science Magazine

http://www.sciencemag.org

This online version of a science magazine provided by the American Association for the Advancement of Science, and part of the Science Online Web site, has Special Features that include Essays on Science and Society, Enhanced Perspectives: Links to Web Resources, Supplemental Data to Augment Reports, and NetWatch. There are also links to the current issue's contents (with summaries and full texts), archives, subject collections, and a Guide to Science Online. Other magazines which are part of the Science Online Web site and have links here include *Science Now* and *Science's Next Wave*. Access to features is available after applying for a free subscription.

Science News Online: The Weekly Newsmagazine of Science

http://www.sciencenews.org

See links under This Week's Featured Articles; Online Features, including the Timeline: Seventy Years Ago in Science News; Last Week's Featured Articles; Archives; and From the Archives: Focus. Registered subscribers have access to full texts of all articles and their reference and sources links.

Scientific American

http://www.sciam.com

At this Web site based on the print magazine, see headlines and links to more information in the sections Today's News, Feature Articles, Explore, Perspectives, Skeptic, Voyages, Puzzling Adventures, Reviews, Today's Trivia Question and Answer, and Ask the Experts' Question and Answer. Issues for the current year and past two years are online. Click archive link to do a free browse or search and to see citations of articles from the print magazine from 1993 through the present. Payment is required before articles or issues, which are in PDF format, can be downloaded and read.

Scientific American Frontiers

http://www.sciam.com/sciam_frontiers.cfm

This Web site provides links to information that is related to subjects in the episodes of the PBS-TV program provided by Scientific American magazine. Recent subjects include The Gene Hunters, Beneath the Sea, The Bionic Body, and Different Ways to Heal. Some episodes can be seen online in the video archive. Note also the links to Special Features, Previous Shows, Upcoming Shows, and For Educators.

Sky and Telescope

http://www.skyandtelescope.com

See the News and News Archives links and a searchable magazine archive with some articles in PDF format. Click resources links for an event calendar with a searchable "find an upcoming astronomy-related event in your area"; plus organizations, planetariums, observatories, and museums. See also Internet sites, special subjects such as SETI and Saving Dark Skies. In the pull-down menu at the top of the page, click "search online articles" and type a subject word such as stars or spaceflight. In an observing area, note also links to This Week's Sky at a Glance, observing highlights, sky chart, celestial objects, and almanac.

Smithsonian Magazine

http://www.smithsonianmag.si.edu

This online version of the print magazine, inviting visitors to explore science, history, and art, features In This Month's Smithsonian, keyword search; reader panel; and a free e-mail newsletter.

Smithsonian Magazine Presents Kids Castle

http://www.kidscastle.si.edu/home.html

See links by title under Here's What's New, and click icons or their words to go to particular areas including those that are on science subjects (e.g., Animals, Air and Space, and Science). Note also Cool Link of the Day and within each area see What's New? Feature Articles, Facts and Photos, and Message Topics.

SpaceLink—NASA Online Newsletters

http://spacelink.nasa.gov/NASA.News/NASA.Online.Newspapers/.index.html

This site includes links to many newsletters published or recommended by NASA. See, for example, Discovery Dispatch, Insights Magazine, SISN (the Science Information Systems Newsletter on outreach activities), NASA Spinoff Online, Spaceport News, Today@NASA, and Microgravity News.

Time for Kids (Specials)

http://www.timeforkids.com/TFK/heroes/index.html

Time Magazine Online includes special issues for young readers, with subjects such as Heroes of the Planet and Environmental Challenge (e.g., Let the River Run Wild, Can You Save a Precious Place? Fighting for the Gray Whale). See also the link to a page with information for teachers.

Universe in the Classroom

http://www.astrosociety.org/education/publications/tnl/tnl.html

This newsletter is designed for teachers who have some interest in, and knowledge of, astronomy. Each issue features a topic of current astronomical interest along with a hands-on classroom activity to make the topic come alive for students. There is an archive of past issues. Subjects have included Biography of a Star, Take a Virtual Voyage in the Milky Way, Comet Shoemaker-Levy, Archaeoastronomy, and Astrobiology: The Frontier of Astronomy Education. There are also links to educational resources.

What on Earth: A Newsletter for the Earth Sciences

http://www.whatonearth.org

This new version of a ten-year-old newsletter is for educators and students who are interested in the geo-sciences, especially in North America, at the junior high school through college levels. As the new site begins, there are links to features in the old newsletter's issues, when the newsletter was named *What on Earth*, after its affiliation with the University of Waterloo in Ontario, Canada. These past issues feature sections titled Be Informed, Earth Connections, Fossils, Choosing a Career In, and Web Sites. Articles have included "The Three Mary Annings"

(Spring 2000); "Rocks with a Roll," "Tips for Amateur Fossil Hunters," and "Munchkin Meets Mastadon" (Fall 1998); "Women in the Earth Sciences," and "Earth Sciences in Everyday Life" (Fall 1996); "Choosing a Career in the Earth Sciences" (Spring 1999); "The Rise and Fall of the Great Lakes Revisited," and "Excavating the Internet" (Fall 1999).

APPENDIX E
Specific Science Web Directories and Selected Special Search Engines with Science Areas

AgNic

http://www.agnic.org

This site, for the Agricultural Network Information Center, features a search box option and browsing by subject, including Plant Sciences, Medical and Biological Sciences, Earth and Environmental Sciences, Forestry, Food and Human Nutrition, Animal and Veterinary Sciences, Aquaculture and Fisheries, and Science and Technology.

AstroWeb: Astronomical Internet Resources

http://www.stsci.edu/science/net-resources.html

The Space Telescope Science Institute, NASA, and the AstroWeb Consortium provide this site of "pointers to potentially relevant resources" on the Internet, with options to find information by searching or by clicking links to browse topics, an index, or categories.

BioTech

http://biotech.icmb.utexas.edu

This site of life sciences resources and reference tools aims to "serve everyone from high school students to professional researchers" by providing links to sites with information on biology and chemistry. See links to Bioinformatics (on biology and computer science), Cyberbotanica (on medicinal botany), BioMedLink, Glycolysis (on human biochemistry), plus Science Resources, a dictionary, chemical acronym database, a search area, and a guided tour of the site.

Earth Sciences—GeoGuide—Browse or Search

http://www.sub.uni-goettingen.de/ssgfi/geo/index.html

http://www.sub.uni-goettingen.de/ssgfi/search/search_geo.html

On the index page, see the Subject catalog and choose an Earth Science subject to browse for links to Web sites on those subjects. Subjects to browse include Geology, Mineralogy, Petrology, Geography, Oceanography, GeoPhysics, GeoChemistry, Soil Science, Meteorology and Climatology, Interdisciplinary, and more. On the search page, type a word, choose a category (e.g., keyword, description, title, links), or do an advanced search in an Earth Science subject. The Web site is provided by the Goettingen State and University Library in Germany.

GeoIndex

http://www.geoindex.com/geoindex

This geo-environmental search engine provides links to news and allows one-word searches in environmental, geology, geotechnology, and energy subjects.

GeoSearcher

http://www.serve.com/garden/geosearcher

This Net resource for geology and earth science provides a link to popular categories, plus subjects including paleontology, ecology, environmental science, global environmental change, meteorology, atmospheric chemistry and physics, and more Internet directories.

Scientopica

http://www.scientopica.com/sci/index.php

Browse categories from Aeronautics to Zoology. See also links to Science News, Science Calendar, and Resources. Also search by keyword, choosing from pull-down menu to search in the Scientopica Directory or in Science on the Web. Note the poll question and discussion area.

SELECTED SPECIAL WEB DIRECTORIES AND WEB SITES WITH LINKS TO SCIENCE SUBJECTS

http://www.academicinfo.net

Scroll to the Subject Gateways and click Sciences, Health and Medicine, or Social Sciences. See also the links for Reference Desk, Browse by Subject, and Search by Keyword. A free newsletter for updates and new site listings is also available.

http://www.edinformatics.com

Click Science in the Directory of Databases or Science Project, or go to http://www.edinformatics.com/msdirect/msdirect.htm.

Encyclopedia Britannica

http://www.britannica.com/browse/subject

Click links under Science or Technology and the Social Science link under Society. Subscribers have access to articles, as do visitors who sign up for seventy-two free hours.

Hunting with Spiders, Indexes and Search Engines

http://matrixmagic.com/tools/hunt.html

See links to subject guides and special subject indexes. Follow links to find science subjects.

Resource Discovery Network

http://www.rdn.ac.uk

Search via the search box or browse the links for Geography and Environment, Health and Medicine, Life Sciences, Physical Sciences, and Social Sciences. See also Behind the Headlines (e.g., to Space Sciences news).

Science Directories via Special Subjects at Search Engine Watch

http://www.searchenginewatch.com

Click link for Search Engine Listings, then Specialty Search Engines, then Science Search Engines or Medical Search Engines. See links to some current and new science and medical search engines or Web directories.

Science Topics in the Librarians' Index to the Internet

http://lii.org/search/file/science

At this site, provided by the Library of California, see links to several general resources in the sciences, from Agriculture to Zoology. Note also links to special subjects including cloning, optical illusions, molecules, micro-organisms, pearls, expeditions, science projects, scientists, and periodicals, plus a link to science, computers, and technology.

Selection of Ready Reference Web Sites

http://www.lkwdpl.org/readref2.htm

This site, with selections by the staff of the Lakewood Public Library in Ohio, features links to sites on particular subjects arranged by the numerical (Dewey Decimal) method often used to organize materials in public libraries. See links for the Natural Sciences, Technology and Applied Sciences, Social Sciences, and Philosophy and Psychology.

SCIENCE AREAS OF SELECTED GENERAL WEB DIRECTORIES AND SEARCH ENGINES

http://www.accessplace.com/science.htm

http://www.altavista.com

Scroll down left column to Directory, click More links. On the next page, find the Sciences link under the Library links area. Surf the links or do a search in the search box.

http://www.ask.com

Click the Browse by Subject link, then choose the Science link or the Health link. Next, choose a particular topic and follow links until a links page of Web sites appears.

http://www.beaucoup.com/1scieng.html

http://dmoz.org

Click the links for Science, Health, or Kids and Teens > SchoolTime > Science.

http://www.einet.net/galaxy or *http://www.galaxy.com* (click the Science link)

http://www.excite.com

Choose the Directory or the Web, then type Science, and click Search.

http://www.go2.com

Click the Directory, then the Health and Wellness link.

http://directory.google.com

See the search box and note the links for the directory subjects: Health, Science, Kids and Teens > School Time > Science

http://www.looksmart.com

Choose Library, then click the Sciences link or the Education link. If the Education link is clicked, follow the links to K–12 Education > For Educators > Teaching Resources > By Subject > Science; or K–12 Education > For Students > High School > Science.

http://learn.msn.com/reference

Scroll to the Library and choose Sciences. Also go to http://search.msn.com, click Guides link under Inside Encarta and note Today's Highlights links.

http://dir.lycos.com

Click the link for Health or Science and Technology, or follow the links for Kids and Teens > School Time > Science.

http://www.maximumedge.com/dir

See the search box and links for Science and Health or follow the links for Kids and Teens > School Time > Science

http://search.netscape.com

Do a search in the search box with the word Science or with a science-related word.

http://www.webcrawler.com

Click the Health link, then see links to particular health topics, e.g., Teen Health.

http://www.yahoo.com

Choose the link for Science, Health, or Social Science.

OTHER SELECTED WEB DIRECTORIES AND SEARCH ENGINES WHERE SEARCHES FOR SCIENCE SUBJECTS CAN BE DONE

http://www.allsearchengines.com

Click the Science and Technology SEs link, or the Health and Medicine SEs link.

http://www.dogpile.com

Do a search via the search box.

http://www.findwhat.com

Do a search via the search box or choose a subject link for Computer or Health.

http://www.locate.com

Do a search via the search box or choose a link under the subject Health.

http://www.profusion.com or *http://www.intellisearch.com*

Do a search via the search box or choose subject links under Science or Health.

http://www.savvysearch.com or *http://www.search.com*

Do a search via the search box or choose links in the Directory under Health or Medicine.

http://www.search321.com

http://www.seek123.com/site-map/default.htm

See the Computing, Gardening, and Health links, plus the Search Other Categories link.

SOME SPECIAL SCIENCE–RELATED SEARCHES VIA WEB ENGINES AND DIRECTORIES

Special Search—Example One

For: Photography—Advice and Techniques—[Scientific Techniques and Science Subjects]

- Go to http://www.looksmart.com.
- Click the Library link, then follow the links for Humanities > Visual Arts > Photography >Advice and Techniques, then > Technique > Astrophotography, or > Nature and Landscape.
- Investigate listed sites in Techniques area (e.g., bird phtography), or

- Select the "search this area only."
- Then type a particular kind of photography (e.g., color photography) in search box and click Search.

Special Search—Example Two

For: Photography—Advice and Techniques—[Scientific Techniques and Science Subjects]

- Go to http://www.msn.com.
- Click the Search link at top (not the search box search button).
- Next, click the Library link, then follow, step by step, the following links: Humanities > Visual Arts > Photography > Advice and Techniques > then > Techniques, then > Astrophotography, or Nature and Landscape.

APPENDIX F
Web Sites and Particular Subject Web Directories with Science Connections

Aristotle—Science and Human Values

http://www.rit.edu/~flwstv/aristotle1.html

An article by Fred L. Wilson of the Rochester Institute of Technology, New York.

Asian Studies WWW Virtual Library

http://coombs.anu.edu.au/WWWVL0AsianStudies.html

Scroll to link to search the Asian Studies Virtual Library, or scroll to Regional Resources links or links for individual countries. Click and follow links, or type search words when possible, to find sites on a particular nation's sciences, scientists or science news. Note also the link to Asia: Public Health and links to e-lists, e-journals, bibliographies by subject, and more.

Euroseek

http://www.euroseek.com

At this directory and news site featuring links to information about Europe, choose links in the directory area to Science or Health, and in the News section, click links under Science and Technology.

Flowcharting Help Page (Tutorial)

http://home.att.net/~dexter.a.hansen/flowchart/flowchart.htm

See definition, uses, basic types, analyzing, and tips.

Gifts of Speech

http://gos.sbc.edu

This site, provided by Sweet Briar College for Women and the Sweet Briar College Libraries, features print reproductions of speeches presented by influential women from around the world since the nineteenth century. Access is by a search box on the main page, the Nobel Prize Speeches page (via link on main page), and the Featured Speakers browse page (with search by alphabetic letters of last names or by year) (via a link on the main page). Typing a subject (e.g., science), a profession (e.g., astronaut), or a name in the search box, then clicking search, brings results.

GirlPower! In the News Index (with Research Studies and News)

http://www.girlpower.gov/press/news/index.htm (click Research and News)

This site is provided by the U.S. Department of Health and Human Services.

Glossary of Rhetorical Terms with Examples

http://www.uky.edu/ArtsSciences/Classics/rhetoric.html

Click links to terms, or scroll through glossary.

Great Norwegians

http://www.mnc.net/norway

Features information on Norwegians and Norwegian-Americans in various professions, including the sciences. Scroll down to find links to information on people in the exploration and science categories. Links page has links to Famous Norwegians and Norwegian-American Hall of Fame sites.

Information Please Dictionary

http://infoplease.com/dictionary.html

At this site provided by the Family Education Network, scroll down to the search box, type in a word or phrase, and click Go! See also links to Encyclopedia, Biography, and Health and Science.

Internet History Sourcebooks Project

http://www.fordham.edu/halsall

This site includes links to, for example, The Internet Science History Sourcebook, plus Ancient History Sourcebook, Medieval Studies Sourcebook, and Modern History Sourcebook, with documents that contain some references to science or the beginnings of scientific thinking.

ISO Glossary of Terms and Definitions

http://www.nlc-bnc.ca/iso/tc46sc9/standard/glossary.htm

A glossary of terms and definitions that follow rules set up by the International Organization of Standardization for standard terms or special words to be used in official and professional documents. Provided by the National Library of Canada.

Learn Photography

http://www.photo.net/learn

Note under Taking Pictures links to primers on, for example, astrophotography, nature photography, underwater photography, infrared and ultraviolet photography, then note links under Making Photographs, Background links (e.g., history of photography), and Related Links (e.g., to a bird photography site). In a search box, using the word science or a word for a particular science, do a search of the Web site's content.

Logic—Science-Humanities Education Service

http://www.philosophyclass.com/logic.htm

Scroll to Categorical Syllogisms. See also Philosophy of Science at www.philosophyclass.com.

Logic in the Works of Aristotle

http://libertyonline.hypermall.com/Aristotle/Default.htm

Scroll to the logic area, then click links for translations of *Prior Analytics* and *Posterior Analytics* to find out what Aristotle wrote about the syllogism, a method of logical thinking and analysis.

Music Hall: Music Education Resources for Teachers and Students

http://www.edgate.com/musichall/educator

The Copernicus Education Gateway features links to information on music appreciation, music composition, music theory, music history, instrumental music and its instruments, vocal music, world music, and music styles. Some links in each category feature science-related aspects of music.

Music Research Links—British Library

http://www.bl.uk/collections/musicresearch.html

Links go to sources on British, American, and other nations' music. Links to note lead to the British Music Information Centre, Bibliography of Dissertations on Musicology (including those on music and computers or electronics), Classical Net, Music Libraries Online Project, and Music Resources, Mechanical Copyright and Protection Society.

New Music Box: Covering New American Music on the Web

http://www.newmusicbox.org

This Web magazine of the American Music Center was founded by noted American composer Aaron Copland. Notice especially the Archive link, and click. See links to issues including Technology and the Future of Music (October 1999); Orchestra Tech (October 2001); and You've Got to Be Carefully Taught (May 2002), which includes information on computer music. See also links to News, Hear and Now, Interview (e.g., first person), In Print, Sound Tracks, and Lead Sheet.

Peace's Internet Reference Pages

http://www.gis.net/~peacewp/home.htm

This site, by William Peace, aims to provide students with an organized group of Web sites so that they don't get bogged down sifting through the Internet. Links are included for a variety of subjects, including many sciences (e.g., Health and Fitness, Science News, Space/Astronomy, Biotechnology, Chemistry, Physics, Earth Sciences, Environment, Medicine, Zoology, and More Science).

Photographic Resource

http://www.photostart.com

This site, for teachers, students, and others who are interested in photography, has main links to Interesting Sites, Resources, and Historical; then links, to, for example, Kodak Publications (Techniques/Technical Info), Astrophotography, *National Geographic* Photographers, Photo Tips, and Albumen Photograph: History, Science and Preservation.

Pulitzer Prize in Music, 1943–2000

http://www.american.edu/heintze/Pul1.htm

Note descriptions of the technical precision in each music piece and some titles revealing works meant to express aspects of nature.

Syllogism

http://www.bartleby.com/65/sy/syllogis.html

Note the three aspects of a syllogism and the three basic types of syllogism and their parts: conditional, hypothesis, and categorical syllogism. Read also of the Venn Diagram.

Technical Writing Guidelines

http://www.ent.ohiou.edu/~valy/techwrite.htm

These clear, in-progress guidelines include, or will include, tips on writing style, informational reports, lab reports, and memos. See also the introduction and links to sites with more guidelines.

UBC Science Co-op: Student Handbook [*Work Term Report Guidelines*]

http://www.sciencecoop.ubc.ca/info/technical.html

The University of British Columbia, Canada, offers explanations of a report's parts for students in a cooperative school/work program, but information is useful to any students writing science reports. Parts featured include a topic statement, general format, and a specific format showing the pattern a report writer should use (e.g., foreword, summary, introduction, body, methods and materials, conclusions, and references).

U.S. Patent and Trademark Office Homepage

http://www.uspto.org

See links to Activities and Education, News and Notices, Patents, Trademarks, How To, and Check Status and Emergency Alerts. Touching before clicking mouse arrow on last five topics brings a menu of features found on that topic's page. To access printable patent forms in PDF form, choose Sitemap from the pull-down menu, then click alphabet letter f, then link for: Forms, USPTO.

Virtual Library—Classical Music

http://www.gprep.org/classical

Georgetown Preparatory School provides an alphabetical list, and seven sections, of links to information on classical music Biographies of Composers and Artists; Organizations; Online Periodicals; Reference (on works and compositions, theory, composition, performance, instruments); Miscellaneous (e.g., music sites, libraries), reviews, announcements, broadcast information (including British); Discussion Forums; and software. Note, in the alphabetical list, science and music links, including *Computer Music Journal*, Medical Matters of Interest to Performers, Medical Waiting Room Music Videos, Music Technology Tutorials and Articles, Musicians and Injuries, and Texas, University of, at San Antonio, Institute for Music Research.

Written Document Analysis Worksheet, by U.S. National Archives

http://www.archives.gov/digital_classroom/lessons/analysis_worksheets/document.html

This worksheet has six multipart questions to answer. Some questions request data on a document's basic parts, e.g., type of document, such as a patent, report, or memorandum; its unique physical qualities, such as having notations or being handwritten; the audience for whom it was written; its date(s), creator or author, and the author's position title. Other questions request document information such as important things in it, why it was written, evidence from it that suggests why it was written (i.e., quotations), things it tells about life in the United States at the time it was written, and a note to the author about something left unanswered in the document.

APPENDIX G
Web Sites of Science Organizations with Special Opportunities for Students
(Online and Offline)

Association for Women in Science—Essay Contest for High School and College Students

http://www.serve.com/awis (click the Essay Contest link)

Click the link for Essay Contest Winners, then links to the six winning essays for AWIS's thirtieth anniversary essay contest for high school and undergraduate college students on the subjects Science in the Twenty-First Century and Women in the Sciences. See "Women: Taking a Positive Role in the Twenty-First Century," the first prize essay by a high school student, and "Make a Difference," the first prize essay by an undergraduate college student. Other winners include "A New Beginning"; "Motivation for Twenty-First Century Growth"; "The Little Differences"; and "Weaving Our Own Baskets."

Astronomical League—National Young Astronomer Award

http://www.astroleague.org/al/awards/nyaa/noya.html

Aiming to encourage an interest in astronomy in students of ages fourteen to nineteen, although schools rarely teach it and urban skies' light pollution limits opportunities, this Web site, for "the world's largest federation of amateur astronomy," features rules for the competition, plus biographies of winners for the past few years and data on their projects. See the link to the Jack Horkheimer Award, also for young contestants, and note the links to more information about the federation and Astronomy Day.

Astronomical Society of the Pacific—Project ASTRO

http://www.astrosociet.org/education/astro/project_astro.html

With its primary aim being to link professional or amateur astronomers with students to help these young people, especially in grades four to nine, to act like scientists, this site provides online sample activities, guides, and resources, while promoting astronomer-teacher partnerships and astronomers adopt-a-class visits that help students have hands-on, inquiry-based astronomy and science activities and planetarium visits.

Astronomy Classes for Students

http://www.kidsastronomy.com/academy/index.htm

At this site for the Online Astronomy Academy's self-guided, teacher-supervised, six to ten week free course, scroll to the page's bottom and click the Take a Tour link, then, from the main page, select astronomy packets for course two (for ages thirteen to eighteen) and find printable forms that go with the course lessons. There is also a course one (for ages seven to twelve).

Bayer/NSF Award

http://www.nsf.gov/od/lpa/events/bayernsf/start.htm

Inviting middle grade students to participate in a free science- and community-based competition involving "an issue that three or four members of a team care about" and attempt to "use science and technology to develop an innovative solution," this Web site provides links to an introduction, guidelines, news, an entry form, standards, sample entries, a virtual trip to finals week, plus ambassadors and team names, for this competition with sponsors that include the National Science Foundation, the Bayer Corporation, and the Christopher Columbus Fellowship Foundation. New York City's *Queens Parents Paper*, November 2000, stated that it "incorporates recommendations of the National Science Education Standards emphasizing teamwork, inquiry and real-world settings to attract students to science, technology and community." For grades eight, seven, and six.

CERES Project Educational Activities

http://btc.montana.edu/ceres/html/EdActivities.html

Using current NASA science data, and following the National Science Standards, this Web site offers SpaceQuests and Student Inquiries/Extension lessons in astronomy and astrobiology for K–12 students. Activities for high school students are on subjects that include The Drake Equation, Remote Sensing, the Sun's Impact on Earth's Temperature, and The Habitable Zone. Note also NASA Themes and Classroom Resources. Find out about the Center for Educational Resources (CERES) Project at http://btc.montana/ceres.

Children's School of Science—Woods Hole, MA

http://www.childrensschoolofscience.org

Links lead to information about the school; a brochure in PDF format with general information, schedules, class descriptions, registration information, and applications; plus FAQs on practical concerns related to class requirements, and field activities; and links of interest (e.g., to OceanQuest, the Woods Hole Oceanographic Institution, and the Marine Biological Laboratory); all on ocean-related summer classes with field trips, direct observation, hands-on classroom and field activities, for students of ages seven to sixteen, with parent participation, for three to six weeks, ninety minutes daily.

"Earth Tomorrow," "Teen Adventure," and "Earth Savers" in Ranger Rick's Kid's Zone

http://www.nwf.org/kids

On this young people's page provided by the National Wildlife Federation, scroll to the Kids Clubs area near the bottom right of the page and click the links to these online clubs for "kids who care about the environment and want to learn more about nature and the environment." "Earth Tomorrow" is for high school students and features information on developing community projects, gaining work experience, and exploring environmental careers. "Teen Adventure" is for middle school students. "Earth Savers" is for younger students. Newsletters for each club are also available.

Global Solar Partners

http://www.solarpartners.org

Students worldwide, through this Web site, share their ideas on solar energy and their solar energy projects. See links to Solar Partners school projects, Solar Youth Expo, Solar Data Exchange, Classroom Resources, Solar Links and to organizations sponsoring the Web site (e.g., Association for Science Education, BP Solar). See also a keyword search.

Green Room—Kids Club House—Greenpeace USA

http://www.greenpeaceusa.org/green/clubhouse.htm

Encouraging young people to "make a difference in protecting our planet," this Web site has links to Greenpeace Living: Tips for Living a Greener Life, Earth Alert Game, Quick Quiz, Send a Postcard, and What's Your View? See also the links to Save the Whales and Amazing Earth Facts. Also note the links to information at the main Greenpeace USA Web page (e.g., current features, oceans, forests, global warming, nuclear, and toxics). Via the Greenpeace International Web site at http://www.greenpeace.org, do a search for "young people and

Greenpeace" in the search box, and follow the links to various sites such as FAQs, Kids for Forests, and Earth Summit 2002.

Intel International Science and Engineering Fair

http://www.sciserv.org/isef

At this site for an "Olympics of Science Fairs" for students in grades nine to twelve, see the links to a Documents Library, a Science Project Primer, Rules, Press Releases on recent winners, plus pages for students and teachers and more.

Intel Science Talent Search

http://www.sciserv.org/sts

At this site for a science research contest for high school seniors, see the links to a Documents Library, pages for students and teachers, and more.

International Federation of Inventors Associations—Youth Page

http://www.invention-ifia.ch/ifiayouth.htm#top

Features links to Unique Invention Contests, such as the International Invention Olympiad, and Experiences of IFIA Members (e.g., as members of science clubs and associations of young inventors). See also the links to inspiring quotations, Policies to Promote Creativeness in Youngsters, an article on girls and invention, and more links.

International Science Olympiads

http://olympiads.win.tue.nl/index.html

This unofficial but informative Web site has links to information on international olympiads in astronomy, biology, chemistry, physics, and informatics (computing science). There are also links to regional science olympiads, and national science olympiads, plus science on the WWW, FAQs, recommended reading, and a mailing list. Individual science pages include links to regulations, subject sites, olympiad Web site, national olympiad Web sites, recommended reading, and magazines and journals. The United States has participated in the chemistry, physics, and informatics olympiads. Some olympiads are for all high school students; others for high school seniors. (See also the U.S. Physics Olympiad listing and site summary below.)

International Vegetarian Union—Youth Pages

http://www.ivu.org/youth

See the links to news on activities, articles by and about teenagers, books, Green Teens for vegetarianism and conservation, penpals, and more.

Invention Competition—National Gallery for America's Young Inventors

http://www.pafinc.com/about.htm

At this site for Partnership for America's Future, Inc., which specializes in educational inventions, click the link to the home page and see links to invention news, then click the links link for a links page to competition sites. Click also the Students link for a links page to a Challenge List, Student Ideas for a Better America, and a Young Entrepreneur Award. In addition, see the links for teachers and the MarineQuest program.

Junior Paleontologists Program

http://www.projectexploration.org/junior_paleontologists.htm

Discover how to explore for dinosaurs through this program set up by the organization founded by noted paleontologist Paul Sereno and educator Gabrielle Lyon. See the archive with the course syllabus, plus links to mission statements, mission responsibilities, a Digging for Dinosaurs Web site, and excerpts from students' field notes. For ages twelve to seventeen.

Leonardo da Vinci Competition

http://www.ecf.toronto.edu/apsc/davinci

Since 1997 the faculty of Canada's University of Toronto, Applied Science and Engineering Department, has offered this competition for twelfth grade students with an interest in engineering and science, including chemistry and physics. It provides this site with data on the competition, including Why da Vinci? Why Participate? How to Participate, the Exam, and Previous Years' Exams and Solutions. See also an inspiring quotation by da Vinci.

MIT Undergraduate Research Opportunities

http://web.mit.edu/urop/index.html

The Massachusetts Institute of Technology (MIT) offers a variety of research opportunities, many science-related, to its students and to students in an exchange program with its neighbors: Cambridge University and Wellesley College. Opportunities are available on campus and in cooperation with other places including NASA and the Woods Hole Oceanographic Institute. See the link to Explore, which leads to the links for Project Openings, Research Descriptions, and Other Areas to Explore. See also the links to UROP Guidelines, Resources, Paperwork, Getting Started, Participate, Awards, and Special Funds.

NASA EarthKam

http://www.earthkam.ucsd.edu

NASA gives students an opportunity to take part in U.S. space missions by allowing them to remotely operate a camera for particular purposes in the international space station or in a space shuttle. This site provides a brief introduction and a sample photograph, plus more information via links including Get Involved, About the ISS Earthkam, Image Library, News, Students, and Educators. A search box is also provided.

NASA Human Spaceflight—Outreach for Students and Teachers

http://spaceflight.nasa.gov/outreach

Find out here about programs for high school students, undergraduate and graduate college and university students, and teachers for various grades. Note programs including the Summer High School Apprentice Research Program and the NASA Student Involvement Program, plus the Undergraduate Student Research Program, the Lunar and Planetary Institute Summer Intern Program, the Graduate Student Aerospace Medicine Clerkship, and summer workshops for teachers at NASA facilities.

NASA Student Flight Opportunity

http://www.wff.nasa.gov/~nasaed/flightops

NASA gives high school and college students, as well as younger students, opportunities to take part in the U.S. Space Program by contributing experiments for astronauts to carry out. Note the link to the Competition Profile, then see the Mission Statement. On the Profile page, see the links to Designing an Experiment, Research Project Components, Entry Categories, Judging Criteria, and Learning Goals. Note also, on the main page and on this page, the links to the Teacher Guide, History, Launch Schedule, Application, and Directory. See also the links to the education programs, Space Experiment Module, and Suborbital Student Experiment Module. The Directory link goes to a page of links leading to the competition's Web pages (e.g., the NASA Student Involvement Program, NSIP; the Shuttle Small Payload Project, SSPP; the Space Experiment Module, SEM; and the Getaway Special Program, also known as the Small Self-Contained Payload Program, SSCP, for educational institutions and others). Projects are for students in teams of two to four. There is also a link to information on the NASA Wallops Flight Facility which is responsible for these student opportunity programs.

National Marine Educators Association—Student Opportunities

http://www.vims.edu/bridge/student_opp.html

The Virginia Institute of Marine Science, with the National Marine Educators Association and the National Oceanographic Partnership Program, provides this site with links to information on a variety of opportunities in the field, such as the Young Naturalists Award for grades seven to twelve, the ExploraVision Awards Competitions for grades K–12, the National Ocean Sciences Bowl for grades nine to twelve; F.I.R.S.T. (Female Initiation into Research in Science and Technology) for high school girls, the Mote Marine Laboratory High School Intern Program, and more.

NSTA Student Competitions

http://www.nsta.org/highschool

Scroll down and to the far right to get to the link for Student Competitions on this Web page, then click the link to find out about the National Science Teachers Association and businesses teaming up to sponsor competitions for high school students, which include the ExploraVision Awards for grades K–12. See also awards and competitions for younger students and teachers, at http://www.nsta.org/276.

Office of Transportation Technologies—Student Vehicle Competitions

http://www.ott.doe.gov/student.shtml

Part of the U.S. Department of Energy, this office has information on competitions for high school, college, and elementary students, that are meant to encourage young engineering talent by helping them to take part in competitions which use students' hands-on experience to tackle problems, especially for designing more efficient and environmentally friendly vehicles (e.g., solar-powered, electric, and intelligent). See the links for high school competitions including the EV Challenge. See also the links for Open Competitions which high school students can enter (e.g., the American Solar Challenge). See more links for the "Student Vehicles Competition" document in PDF format and Other Student Competitions.

Physical Activity and Fitness Program Awards—School Recognition Programs

http://www.indiana.edu/~preschal/recognition/school_recog.shtml

Find out about opportunities for students and schools that are part of a program called the U.S. President's Physical Activity and Fitness Challenge and include the Physical Fitness State Champion, the Active Lifestyle Model School, and the Physical Activity and Fitness Demonstration Center. See also the links to the programs for Active Lifestyle, Physical Fitness, and Health Fitness, plus PC Resources. In addition, note the Program Overview page which also has information for special young people (e.g., homeschoolers and young people with disabilities).

Programs for College Inventors at the Invention Place

http://www.invent.org/iplinks.shtml

Note the links for Invention Sites, then click the Invention Competitions and Awards link, and click in this area the link for the National Inventors Hall of Fame's Collegiate Inventors, then the link for Collegiate Inventors, which is a program of National Collegiate Inventors and Innovators Alliance.

Rachel Carson Homestead—Education Programs and Resources

http://www.rachelcarsonhomestead.org/educate.html

This Web site for the birthplace of the naturalist and environmental activist provides information and details about what school groups, scout troops, and homeschoolers of all ages can discover on guided field trips at the homestead, through outreach visits from homestead people, via a traveling exhibit provided by the homestead organization, or from events at the homestead. Guiding principles for all activities come from Rachel Carson's book *The Sense of Wonder* and an emphasis on critical inquiry.

Roger Tory Peterson Institute of Natural History

http://www.rtpi.org

Note especially the mission statement with reference to children at the bottom of the page, then see the links to General Information and Educational Programs (e.g., My Place, a nature-related activity program for families and educators involved with children ages eight to twelve; Teaming with Nature, an interdisciplinary program for middle school and upper elementary students; and a teacher workshop).

Roots and Shoots Environmental Program for Young People—The Jane Goodall Institute

http://www.janegoodall.org/rs/activities

Note the information on three areas that program participants focus on (e.g., the care and concern for the environment, animals, and the community), and click links to sample activities (e.g., adopt a place, save an animal, build a birdhouse, start recycling, do a planting project, or grow native plants).

Science Fair Central: Creative Investigations into the Real World

http://www.school.discovery.com/sciencefaircentral

This Discovery Channel Web site has a Soup to Nuts Handbook with everything you need to know about creating a science fair project, a Project Ideas list, questions and answers, Books and Links for Research, Teachers Get Ready, Parents Get Involved, and tip sheets for astronomy, biology, chemistry, earth science, and physical science projects. See also the Discovery Channel Young Scientists Challenge Contest for students in grades five to eight.

Smithsonian Institution—Seeds of Change Garden

http://nmnhwww.si.edu/garden/welcome.html

See the link at the bottom of the page for What Is a Seeds of Change Garden? Note also the history and learning links. See especially the Activities for All Season link that goes to a page that features a Parent/Teacher Overview link that leads to A Practical Guide for Implementing an Educational Garden. There are steps for starting and keeping up a garden, with activities for each season.

Society for Scientific Exploration—Young Investigators Program

http://www.scientificexploration.org/younginvest.html

YIP is for undergraduate and graduate college and university students interested in opportunities for "studies of anomalous phenomena and other frontier areas of science not presently addressed by traditional academic program and professional forums." Note recommended reading (e.g., online articles, book lists, videos), links to useful online resources, and a bulletin board, plus society-sponsored internships and independent research projects, online courses of study, institutions with relevant courses or degree programs, events, and chat rooms. The first three sources and some events are especially adaptable for high school students' assignments.

Space Sciences Activities for Students

http://ssdoo.gsfc.nasa.gov/education/kids.html

This site includes links to an Interactive NASA Space Physics Ionospheric Research Experiment (INSPIRE) on observing natural and man-made radio waves, for high school students, the Shuttle Amateur Radio Experiment (SAREX) for talking to astronauts on a space shuttle, and Just for Kids space life sciences activities especially for K–6 students. Note also the link to LIFTOFF to Space Education with activities by NASA for young students. Go to http://ssdoo.gsfc.nasa.gov/education/education_home.html, or click its link here, and see information on more projects, including the Radio Jove Project which allows students to use a radio telescope to listen for radio sounds from Jupiter and the sun, a project allowing students to track satellites, and a project allowing students to see what NASA's Cosmic Background Explorer satellite is seeing now.

Students for the Exploration and Development of Space

http://www.seds.org

At this site for the SEDS organization, hosted by the University of Arizona chapter at the Lunar and Planetary Laboratory, see links to information on Space, Astronomy, Aerospace and Aeronautics, Rocketry and Planetary Science, resource guides, other resources, publications, What Is SEDS? More about SEDS (e.g., How to Start a Local SEDS Chapter, SEDS Bylaws, Ideas for Activities, a search box, and Visions of the Future on upcoming missions or mission ideas being studied for possible missions).

Think Earth

http://www.thinkearth.org

This California-based site features tips to help students start an environmental club and suggested club, community, or school projects or activities to learn about and help the environment. See also a teachers' area, a students speak area, news, Did You Know? (of facts and figures and ask an expert), What's New, and information on the environment, issues, events, and opportunities for local high school students to help their communities.

Try Science

http://www.tryscience.org

Provided by the New York Hall of Science in the New York City borough of Queens, this Web site helps local students connect with students around the nation and the world to learn science together via educational simulation games.

U.S. Physics Olympiad

http://www.aapt.org/olympiad

The American Association of Physics Teachers provides this site with information on the history and accomplishments of the U.S. Physics Olympiad teams. See links to Web sites on the most recent physics olympiad, some past physics olympiads, screening exams, and sites with related information on physics and competitions.

Vegetarian Kids and Teens

http://www.vrg.org/family/kidsindex.htm

The Vegetarian Resource Group provides this Web page which features links to information on an annual essay contest, its rules, a lesson plan, and past winners; for student activists; and about an intern position. See also the links for the National Association for Humane and Environmental Education (NAHEE) TeenScene and other similar organizations; Books for Young Vegetarians; Nutrition Information; Vegetarian Family; an e-mail list for parents; and more.

Young Astronaut Council—Young Astronaut Program

http://www.yac.org/yac

The aim of this council, which was formed at the White House in 1984, is to help young people ages three to fifteen, including a thirteen to fifteen age group, experience the fun and adventure of learning about space. See links to Web site features including Mission: Science, Space School TV, Young Astronauts Online, the Kids House, a Kids Page, an Adults Page, and a Members Page. See also links on these pages (e.g., to online lessons, contests, online chats with astronauts, AstroNews, a What's Hot newsletter, How to Join, a CD-ROM: Space Station Alpha: Encounter, and more).

Young Birder of the Year Competition

http://www.americanbirding.org/programs/ygbcom.htm

Young people ages ten to eighteen who are interested in birds and bird watching, and especially in the related activities of taking field notes, writing about birds, or drawing birds, will be interested in this competition. Find out how to take part in this competition via information on this page and via links on the index page whose link is on the bottom of this page. A field ornithology camp scholarship is the top prize.

Young Environmentalists Action—Environmental Action and Education Network

http://www.globalresponse.org/yea

This site features a link to a page that invites young people of all ages to write letters about their ideas for protecting the environment. There are also links to newsletters for younger and older participants, with current issues online; an Ideas Page with information on current environmental problems; and suggestions on how young people can try to help solve environmental problems. More links lead to a page of links to organizations that are cooperating in the environmental movement, letter-writing tips, successes, current action, past actions index, about the Network's Global Response Mission (including FAQs and the Eco-Club Actions for high school students), and pages for teens, kids, and teachers.

Young Women's Health Summit

http://www.4woman.gov

On this Web site for the U.S. Department of Health and Human Services, Office on Women's Health, also known as the Nation Women's Health Information Center site, scroll to and click the link for information on the most recent National Young Women's Health Summit. Find information on this summit for girls ages twelve to fourteen and fifteen to seventeen, including the summit's goals, objectives, day-by-day format, and sponsored attendees, mentors, and parents. See also on the NWHIC's main page the Young Women's Health Summits link under Educational Campaigns. Near the time of a summit, registration information and FAQs are provided.

APPENDIX H
Web Sites with "Ask a Scientist"; "Ask a Science Question"; Frequently Asked Questions and Previously Asked Questions, Plus Facts and Tips on Science Subjects

Ask a Biologist

http://ls.la.edu/askabiologist

At this Arizona State University site for K–12 teachers and their students, click the "submit a question" link to ask a biology question. See also the links for articles and profiles, experiments and stuff, and Web sites to more information on biology subjects.

Ask a Dinosaur Expert (David Trexler) at Dinosaur Treks

http://library.thinkquest.org/C005824/extinction.html (click the Dinosaur Treks link)

Read about dinosaur extinction theories, take a poll, and click a link to send your extinction theory. Scroll to the bottom of the page and click the Dino FAQs link. If you do not find your question or answer here, click the e-mail an expert link and ask.

Ask a Geologist

http://walrus.wr.usgs.gov/docs/ask-a-ge.html

In this area of the United States Geological Survey Web site, click the USGS FAQs link and search the FAQs for questions and answers on earthquakes, volcanoes, rocks, mountains, lakes, rivers, and ground water. If your question is not here, read the instructions for asking a geologist, then click the Ask-a-Geologist e-mail link. See also sample questions.

Ask a Geologist at EarthNet's Geology in the Classroom

http://agc.bio.ns.ca/schools/EarthNet/english/start_geology.html

Click links to questions and answers just posted, question a geologist about Canadian geology, and Ask a Geologist about U.S. Geology.

Ask a High Energy Astronomer

http://imagine.gsfc.nasa.gov/docs/ask_astro/ask_an_astronomer.html

At this site for NASA's Laboratory for High Energy Astrophysics, search for questions and answers on topics such as quasars, black holes, and gamma rays. See twenty-one topics, and links to questions and answers on many of them, or click to use a search engine. Note also the guidelines for teachers. If you do not find an answer to your question, follow the instructions for asking a high energy astronomer.

Ask a Question at the Neuroscientist Network

http://faculty.washington.edu/chudler/questions.html

At this site with information on the brain, scroll to links to Questions and Answers on File or click the link for Previous Questions. If you do not see your question, click the link for "ask a question" and ask. See also this site's pages for FAQs about the Neuroscience for Kids Web site at http://faculty.washington.edu/chudler/nfkfaq.html and questions with answers on the brain at http://faculty.washington.edu/chudler/split.html.

Ask a Scientist at Odyssey Magazine

http://www.odysseymagazine.com/pages/level2.html

Scroll to Ask a Scientist and Ask a Scientist Archives links to see recent and past questions and answers at this site for a science magazine for ages ten to sixteen. If questions or answers you have are not here, go to the Ask a Scientist page, click an e-mail link, and ask.

Ask about Science Fair Projects

http://www.school.discovery.com/sciencefaircentral/scifairstudio/askjvc.html

At this site with Janice Van Cleave's Science for Fun Questions and Answers, students, teachers, and parents can type a word or phrase and search for previously asked questions and their answers about science fair projects or see a list of Van Cleave's books.

Ask about Science, Health/Fitness, and Jobs/Careers in Science

http://allexperts.com

Click a link to Science, Health/Fitness, or Jobs/Careers, then links under Careers: Science/Technology for links to experts in these topics' specific subject areas.

Ask an Archeologist: Dr. Dig

http://digonsite.com/drdig/archive.html

First browse the FAQs and questions on particular subjects, then e-mail her and ask if you do not see your question and an answer.

Ask an Earth Scientist

http://www.soest.hawaii.edu/GG/ASK/askanerd.html

At this site, the Department of Geophysics at the University of Hawaii provides questions and answers on rocks, earthquakes, volcanoes, the environment, and related subjects. An invitation to ask questions not yet answered here, and links to other sites, are also given.

Ask an Ecologist in Kids Do Ecology at the National Center for Ecological Analysis

http://www.nceas.ucsb.edu/nceas-web/kids/main_pages/ask.htm

At this site by the National Center for Ecological Analysis and Synthesis, see link to What Is Ecology? Next, scroll to annotated links on FAQ, ecology, and biomes. Look for questions and answers. If your question is not here, click Ask an Ecologist link, and ask.

Ask an Expert Sources—Science, Fitness/Health/Medicine, etc.

http://www.cln.org/int_experts.html (scroll to subject links)

Ask an Oceanographer or Marine Scientist

http://www.vims.edu/bridge/ask.html

The Virginia Institute of Marine Sciences provides this page of links to Web sites that have questions and answers on marine animals and ocean-related subjects, plus an invitation to ask a question not yet asked. Questions are answered by experts including an oceanography professor and a U.S. Navy oceanographer.

Ask Jack Weather Questions

http://www.usatoday.com/weather/askjack/wjack3.htm

Scroll to see questions and answers or click a link to the index to past questions, the FAQs index, or the FAQs on past weather. If your question and answer are not here, click "submit questions here" and ask Jack.

Ask the NASA Experts about a Current Mission

http://spaceflight.nasa.gov/index.html

To ask a question during a current mission involving a space shuttle, the international space station, or ground control click Feedback, then Ask the Experts link, then choose from pull-down menus: the shuttle crew, the station crew, or the Mission Control Center. Ask your question, then fill in other requested information, and click the send button. On the Feedback page, see also links to previous questions and answers via each crew's menu. Note also links to Yesterday's Space Facts searchable by date or keyword, a search box for searching archives, and a chat schedule for talking with NASA experts online.

Ask the Naturalist about Animals and Plants in the Eastern United States

http://www.explorenature.org/about/ask.htm

Ask the Naturalist about Birds and Other Natural History Topics

http://www.nhaudubon.org/naturalist.htm

See question links to answers and a definition of natural history. If your question is not here, follow the directions for asking the naturalist at this site for the New Hampshire Audubon Society.

"Ask the Space Scientist" Archive and "Ask the Astronomer" Archive

http://itss.raytheon.com/café (click title links)

The Astronomy Café, providing both Web pages, with periodically updated questions and answers, is produced by the NASA Satellite Image Project and the ITSS Raytheon Information Technology and Information Services/NASA Goddard Space Flight Center. Each area shares features with the other or has its own features (e.g., questions and answers on the Moon, Solar System, Cosmos, and Everything Else). See also links to a career guide, astronomy articles, inside a research paper, and Web resources. The site no longer accepts new questions.

Ask the Wildlife Doctor in Australia

http://www.earthgarden.com.au/bj.html

See a few letters by people with questions about the wildlife where they live in Australia and sent to the wildlife doctor via Earth Garden, an organization devoted to planet care. All questions are of interest, and some are of use, to anyone anywhere. Click the e-mail link to send the wildlife doctor a question.

AskMe.com—Science

http://www1.askme.com/ShowCategory.asp?cid=767

Choose a subcategory of science (e.g., agriculture, archeology, astronomy, aviation, biology, botany, chemistry, ecology and the environment, energy, entomology, geology, inventors and inventions, medical science, meteorology, natural history and anthropology, oceanography, paleontology, physics, zoology, science careers, science for kids, and social science [e.g., psychology]). In each subcategory, click links to see what is on a question board or to see the questions scientists have already been asked. See also a box of changing questions. Ask questions by typing a topic in a search box and clicking go, by clicking "ask a question on the message board," or clicking "find an expert."

Frequently Asked Questions about Paleontology

http://www.ucmp.berkeley.edu/FAQ/faq.html

Find answers to questions such as "What is paleontology?" "What training is necessary to become a paleontologist?" "What are the practical uses of paleontology?" "What should I do with fossils I pick up?" and "Where are some other WWW servers dealing with paleontology?"

Gardening Questions and Answers

http://www.garden.org/qanda

See the Q and A Library for question links to answers on topics including Gardening for Kids; Garden Care and Pests; Home and Hearth; Fruits, Veggies, and Herbs; and Flowers and Bulbs. If your question is not here, use the search box.

General Chemistry Online: Just Ask Antoine

http://antoine.frostburg.edu/chem/senese/101/just-ask-antoine.shtml

See a list of recent answers to questions. Browse via links to answered questions (e.g., an introduction to chemistry), or click question links under Most Asked Questions and Favorite Questions. See also a list of recent answers. If your question is not here, click the "ask a question" link.

Mad Scientists Network

http://www.madsci.org/submit.html

Via links, search the archives, FAQs, and the Library. If your question is not here, read the instructions about sending a question, then click the "ask a question" link.

NASA Goddard Space Flight Center Science Question of the Week

http://www.gsfc.nasa.gov/gsfc/educ/science.html

Every week a question is posted and the answer by a new scientist each week (as of 2002) appears the following week. Links to questions and answers by one scientist from the past six years are also provided.

Scientific American.com: Ask the Experts

http://www.sciam.com/askexpert_directory.cfm

Click links under Current Questions or Questions by Subject (e.g., Astronomy, Biology, Chemistry, Computers, Environment, Geology, Medicine, or Physics). If your question and an answer are not there, click the link for "Have a Question? Send It In."

Where Can I Find Questions and Answers on [This Science Subject]?

http://www.ask.com

In the search box at this Internet directory, type the first part of this question, add a science subject you think of, then click the ask button, and see a links page to sites with answers and questions on your subject.

Appendix I
Other Helpful and Interesting Science Web Sites

American Chemical Society—Educators and Students—K–12 Links

http://www.acs.org (click the Educators and Students link) (scroll to the K–12 category)

Links go to a variety of chemistry-related Web sites, lessons, and activities for students. Note for example the links to *ChemMatters* (a magazine), Chemagination (an essay contest), ChemCom (Chemistry in the Community), and a Chemistry Olympiad, all for high school students.

"Aspects of One Century and Prospects for the Next" (2000)

http://home.earthlink.net/!jsgaravelli/MYTALK.HTML

An article by John S. Garavelli of the Philosophical Society of Washington.

Bandaids and Blackboards: Chronic Illness, Health Education, and Children

http://www.faculty.fairfield.edu/fleitas/healthed.html

Professor Joan Fleitas, R.N., Ed.D., of the nursing program at University of Fairfield, Connecticut, provides links to "resources for teachers and school nurses so they might better help students who come to school with significant medical problems." General data on disabilities, and data on particular abilities, are included. Click the link at the bottom of the page to get to a sitemap with links to more information under the categories Teen Content (e.g., with What's It All About? Finding Support, etc.); Child Content; Adult Content for teachers, parents, health professionals (e.g., with "Teacher Talk" Adolescent Mental Health); and Content for Everybody (e.g., Do You Know about Disabilities? and Dictionary about Disabilities).

Beyond 2000—Your Window on the Future

http://www.beyond2000.com/news/index.html

Brain Explorer

http://www.brainexplorer.org/sitemap/sitemap.html

See links to a human brain atlas (with quotes by Hippocrates and Aristotle), parts of the human brain, an introduction, neurological control, brain disorders, glossary, and more.

"A Century of Science" (2000) by Jim Wilson

http://www.popularmechanics.com/science/research/2000/century_of_science/print.phtml

American Chemical Society—Educators and Students—K–12 Links http://www.acs.org (click the Educators and Students link) (scroll to the K–12 category).

Chemist's Message to Young People

http://www.iupac.org/publications/index.html

Scroll to, and click, the link for *Chemical Education International*. Follow the link to the current issue's interview with a chemist who answers questions and provides comments on subjects that will interest young people. The interview is meant to encourage young people to pursue a career in chemistry. For young people already interested in a chemistry career, the interview is meant to reveal various interesting aspects of the field.

Children with Disabilities—Research Links, with Youth to Youth Index Page

http://www.childrenwithdisabilities.ncjrs.org/research.html and *http://www.childrenwithdisabilites.ncjrs.org/kids.html*

Research pages feature links to publications, other resources, definitions, and a search area. The Youth to Youth page features What to Read, Fun Things to Do, Let's Talk, and Lots of Different

Stuff. A Highlights page has links to information for families in the categories Areas of Concern, In the News, and New Links.

Children, Youth, and Families at the ACF Programs Web Site

http://www.acf.hhs.gov/programs.html#cyfa

At this site for the Administration for Children, Youth, and Families, provided by the U.S. Department of Health and Human Services, see links to e.g., Youth Information, Child Outcomes Research and Evaluation, Family and Youth Services Bureau, National Clearinghouse on Families and Youth.

Creation Versus Evolution, Part II

http://library.thinkquest.org/29178 (click the image link)

This discussion debate Web site for and by teens provides links to Debate Creation Versus Evolution, Take the Site Quiz, Learn about Creation, Learn about Evolution, What's New, Bibliography, and a Teacher Area that invites "plan lessons and activities."

"Disability Related Resources" at the International Center for Disability Information

http://www.icdi.wvu.edu

Click the West Virginia Research and Training Center link. On the next page, scroll to Services, then click the "Untangling the Web" link to find a list of links.

Division of Adolescent and School Health, the NCCDPHP

http://www.cdc.gov/nccdphp/dash/index.htm

This site for this division of the National Center for Chronic Disease Prevention and Promotion of the Centers for Disease Control has links to publications (e.g., guidelines for school health programs that involve healthy eating, physical activity, and deal with health problems such as injuries, violence, cancer, tobacco use, and AIDS), health topics (e.g., asthma, drug abuse, personal behavior), and about the program (e.g., for healthy youth, school health defined, four strategies for national school health).

Global Issues of the Twenty-First Century—United Nations Challenges (1997–)

http://www.globalchallenges.org/index.html

Note links to Science Trends, Prospects, Ethics, and Cultural Issues; Environment: Related Scientific, Economic, and Energy Trends; and Health, Global Trends, Policies, Issues, Advances, and Threats.

History of Inventions—A Timeline

http://www.cbc4kids.ca/general/the_lab/history_of_inventions/default.html

History of Science—Links to Sites

http://directory.google.com/Top/Society/History/By_Topic/Science

See for example a link to a timeline Web site with links to information on science through history, from before 1650 to the present.

Inventor Ed's Inventor Resource Internet Pages

http://www.inventored.org/site-index

James Webb Space Telescope Home Page

http://ngst.gsfc.nasa.gov

Find out about the next generation telescope that was named on September 10, 2002 for the second administrator of NASA. Note the link to Question of the Week with an answer about Webb's accomplishments, including his being responsible for setting up and having carried out more than seventy-five science experiments as part of the U.S. space program and his writing an article advocating that a space telescope be a major part of the space program. Note also the links to the JWST Science Information and Science Goals pages, the Educator Resources page of links, and papers by teams that represent the JWST/NGST and were presented at a Society of Photo-Optical Instrumentation Engineers (SPIE) Astronomical Telescopes and Instrumentation Conference in Hawaii.

Living History Museums and Outdoor Areas

http://dir.yahoo.com/Arts/Humanities/History/LivingHistory (click links, e.g., to U.S. Living History, then Museums and Memorials)

Manned Versus Unmanned Spaceflight

http://rso.cornell.edu/scitech/archive/97sun/man.html

This document provides a viewpoint by an electrical engineer.

Moon Trees

http://nssdc.gsfc.nasa.gov/planetary/lunar/moon_tree.htm

Of trees grown from seeds that traveled to the moon on Apollo 14 as part of a joint NASA/USDA project, with former park service employee turned astronaut Stuart Roosa in charge. Includes lists of locations where the seeds were planted, the types of trees, and when the trees were planted, including on the White House grounds, at the Forestry Commission Headquarters, several space facilities, and a girls' camp grounds.

NASA Cites 2002 Accomplishments in Space and on Earth

http://usembassy.state.gov/tokyo/wwwh200123a4.htm

Among the accomplishments: first science officer of the U.S. Space Program and for the international space station is chosen, educator astronauts program activated, space technology on the earth, and new directions for the U.S. space program (which may still happen although somewhat changed because of the Columbia space shuttle tragedy).

NASA Office of Biological and Physical Research—Updates

http://spaceresearch.nasa.gov/research_projects/researchupdate.html

Has links to articles describing significant results from OBPR technical areas and specific projects on the ground, on the international space stations, on space shuttles, and on other spacecraft, for the current and past four years, including some data retrieved from the Columbia shuttle crew during January 2003 while in space before shuttle's destruction.

National Information Center for Children and Youth with Disabilities

http://www.nichcy.org

Has links to What's New, About NICHCY, FAQs, Our Publications, and Zigawhat. Our Publications include general information, disability information fact sheets, news digests, parent and student guides, transition guides to help youth from high school into the adult world, research briefs, resource lists, and state resources, plus IDEA publications with data on the 1997 Individuals with Disabilities Education Act. The Zigawhat Page, for young people, has an index of links to Tips, Learn, Connect, Games, and Tell Your Story.

National Organization on Disability—Sitemap Page

http://www.nod.org/dsp_sitemap.cfm

See links under Education (e.g., to articles and resources), Information and Resources, Health Care, Technology, Community, News, and more.

Nature Debates

http://www.nature.com/nature/debates

At this site which aims to "define the landscape of international scientific controversy," note the link to More about Debates, plus links to debates including "Why Are There So Few Women in Science?" "Is the Reliable Prediction of Individual Earthquakes a Realistic Goal?" "Is the Fossil Record Adequate?" "Benefits and Risks of Genetic Modification in Agriculture," and "Future E-Access to the Primary Literature." Date, moderator, and contributors are noted, and an invitation to e-mail comments is given.

New Scientist and Greenpeace Debates

http://www.newscientist.com/hottopics/sciencedebates

Being between a magazine and an activist organization, which are two sources with opposing positions, the debates are on the subject "Science, Technology, and the Future: The Big Questions."

"The New U.S. Space Transportation Initiative—Statement—June 20, 2001"

http://www.spacetransportation.org/TFRstatement.htm

"Submitted in testimony before the Space and Aeronautics Subcommittee of the United States House of Representatives Science Committee," by T.H. Rogers, Chief Scientist, Space Transportation Association, this statement advocates space-based civilian activities so scientist astronauts can be free to pursue space exploration. Suggested activities for civilians on the earth and in space include constructing and sending into space: artificial satellites, low gravity space laboratories, and orbiting solar power devices, plus setting up businesses such as cargo runs, working while living in space, and tourism.

Nobel Prize Internet Archive

http://www.nobelprizes.com/nobel/nobel.html

See links to information on Nobel Prize winners in the areas of chemistry, medicine, and physics, as well as female Nobel Prize winners.

NOVA—The Science Behind the News—Australian Academy of Science

http://www.science.org.au/nova

See the link to basic science concepts and icon links to news in biology, the environment, health, physical sciences, and technology, plus particular headline subjects and an e-mail announcements offer.

PBS-TV—Science

http://www.pbs.org/neighborhoods/science

Find information via links under categories (e.g., Editor's Picks, For Educators, For Kids, and a Science Index with Archeology and Anthropology, Earth and Space, Health and Medicine, Life Sciences, Physics, Digitechnology, Inventions, General Science, and Science Mysteries).

PBS-TV—Secrets of the Brain

http://www.pbs.org/wnet/brain

Links go to information on the human brain's history (with a detailed outline and notes on writings about the brain), scanning, 3D anatomy, and mind illusions.

Religious Philosophical Scientific Debates

http://members.tripod.com/BenBrown/home.html

Introductory information, plus links to documents on Science Versus Religion (e.g., Evolution Versus Creation, The Big Bang Versus Creation) and others.

Science Ministries via the Christianity.com Network

http://www.christianity.com/scienceministries

At this site which "addresses issues in science and biotechnology from a Christian World View," see the links on the left side of this Web page for news and information on subjects including Bible Science, BioEthics, Creation Science, Archaeology, DNA Technology, Apologetics, Beyond Science, and Truth for Youth. See also the links on the right side of this Web page for Science News, and Hot Links. (If the url does not work, go to http://www.christianity.com, do a search via the search box for science ministries, then look for and click the link for the Science Ministries homepage.)

Science Portal with Breaking News from the USA, Europe, and Asia

http://www.101-sci.com

Scientific Debate on Global Climate Change and U.S. Policy

http://cnie.org/NLE/CRSreports/Climate/clim-24.html

Via this site for a survey of scientific research and policy reports on global change, April 13, 2000, scroll to the Contents links. Click the link for the debate. See also the main page's abstract and summary on the survey, of which the debate is a part. Note also the link to the survey's introduction.

"Scientific Prerequisites for the Human Exploration of Space"

http://www.nas.edu/ssb/chx1bib.htm

See the links to Executive Summary, Introduction, Critical Research Requirements, Research for Mission Optimization, Conclusions, Bibliography, and Appendix.

Space Exploration via the NASA Advanced Programs Office

http://hedadvprograms.nasa.gov/speceexploration.html

Note the New Strategy Driven by Science and Discovery as set up before the Columbia shuttle tragedy. See the Introduction, Stepping Stones, Strategic Technical Challenges, Technological Hurdles, Places We Could Go, and NASA Exploration Team. See also the colorful diagrams.

Space Island Project

http://www.spaceislandgroup.com

Of an organization starting to implement practical plans for the next generation of space exploration, including a group of space stations dedicated to particular tasks (e.g., a medical research and treatment station, an agricultural station, etc.). Note the Education area with a science contest. See also comments by science fiction writer Arthur C. Clarke and U.S. senator John McCain.

Sport Wissenschaft im Internet

http://www.sponet.de (click the British flag icon link)

In this sport science database, searches are possible by choosing from the topical areas pull-down menu: training science, technical sports, technical and natural sciences, biological and medical sciences, or social sciences, then by choosing from the type of source menu: electronic publication or article, electronic journal, information page, research paper, tech report, dissertation, diploma work/thesis, multimedia document, newspaper, organization information, congressional proceedings, actual news, miscellaneous, or links. Also choose from pull-down menus: Basic Level, particular country, and English language. Keyword (called textstring) searches are also possible.

UNESCO—World Conference on Science for the Twenty-First Century—An Overview

http://www.unesco.org/science/wcs/eng/overview.htm

Of a conference that took place in Budapest, Hungary from June 26 to July 1, 1999. See also the document "World Conference on Science for the Twenty-First Century" at http://unesdoc.unesco.org/images/0012/001207/120706e.pdf.

"What Is the Relationship Between Nature and Nurture in Acquisition of Knowledge?"

http://accessexcellence.org/21st/SER/BE/whata.html

In this article, part of the "Classroom in the Twenty-First Century" area of the Access Excellence Web site, the author Carolyn Csongradi takes "a new look at an old debate."

What Space Needs: The Human Touch

http://science.nasa.gov/headlines/y2001/ast20may-1.htm

Science@NASA provides this document in text, and in audio via an MP3 Player, with a look at manned versus unmanned spaceflight.

Why Do We Explore Space?

http://adc.gsfc.nasa.gov/adc/education/space_ex/issues.html or *http://adc.gsfc.nasa.gov/adc/education/space_ex/essay1.html*

Why Explore Space? In Why NASA FAQs Part I

http://www.nasa.gov/qanda/why_nasa.html

APPENDIX J
Additional Web Sites Featuring Primary Science Documents and Authoritative Data of Note

Barbara McClintock Papers at the National Library of Medicine's Profiles in Science

http://profiles.nlm.nih.edu/LL/Views/Exhibit

This Web site features writings by McClintock, a genetics scientist who lived from 1902 to 1992. Her lectures, science magazine articles, and letters on her work in genetics especially in connection with a type of corn known as zea maize are featured. Each section includes a narrative, sometimes with quotations, describing her work at particular times in her life and a link to a page of links to her writings in PDF format. Note the sections on Biographical Information, Education and Research at Cornell University, Breakthrough Fusion Bridge: The University of Missouri, From Ithaca to Berlin and Back Again, Controlling Elements: Cold Spring Harbor, On the Road Lectures, Searching for the Origins of Maize in South America, The McClintock Renaissance, and the Nobel Prize in Physiology/Medicine in 1983 for her work on "mobile genetic elements."

Ben Franklin's Lighting Bells (1753) and (1772)

http://sln.fi.edu/franklin/bells.html

Excerpts from a letter to a scientist friend: Peter Collinson, and a paper read at a meeting during which lightning rods were discussed as safety devices for buildings. See also the article "Benjamin Franklin as a Scientist" at http://sln.fi.edu/franklin/scientst/scientst.html. (Note in addition Franklin's 1774 letter on marsh gas to fellow scientist Joseph Priestly at http://webserver.lemoyne.edu/faculty/giunta/franklin.html.)

Collected Works of Florence Nightingale Project

www.sociology.uoguelph.ca/fnightingale (or do search at www.uoguelph.ca/wstudies)

See links to Celebrate One Hundred Years of Nightingale's Work, Introduction to the Project, Themes, Nightingale and Public Health, Equality Statement, etc. See "A Selection of Letters" via Clendening History of Medicine Library link on Other Web Sites page and www.sociology.uoguelph.ca/online_papers (e.g., with her "Rural Hygiene").

"[Columbia Astronaut] Laurel Clark's Final E-mail to Family, Friends"

http://www.msnbc.com/news/860812.asp?0cl=cR

Sent via the Columbia space shuttle from orbit on January 31, 2003 by this astronaut doctor, the day before she died in the shuttle's explosion, this e-mail reveals Clark's feelings about awe-inspiring views, about the science projects she was doing, and about representing the United States, scientists, and science in outer space. A photo of Clark is featured, along with a photo taken by the Columbia crew on January 26, 2003 of a sliver of the moon hovering above the earth's atmosphere which appears as a powder blue haze above clouds. (Text is also at www.channeloklahoma.com/news/1951903/detail.html.)

Environmental History

http://www.oah.org/pubs/magazine/environment/norwood.pdf (or via html link at google.com)

From Vera Norwood's "Women's Roles in Nature Study and Environmental Protection" which appeared in the Spring 1996 issue of the Organization of American Historians' *OAH Magazine of History*. See also the Web site "On American Women and Nature" cited below.

Eric R. Kandel—A 2000 Winner of the Nobel Prize in Medicine

http://www.nobel.se/medicine/laureates/2000/index.html

Click links to his Nobel Lecture, Banquet Speech, Interview, Autobiography, Curriculum Vitae, and Other Resources.

"The Evolving Gaia Theory"

http://www.unu.edu/unupress/lecture1.html

This paper, presented at the UN University in Tokyo in September 1992, features detailed information about the Gaia Theory as viewed by James Lovelock. (See also "Gaia Hypothesis Proposed by James Lovelock in Collaboration with Lynn Margolis" below.)

"[First U.S. Woman Astronaut] Sally Ride, Tells Girls to 'Reach for the Stars'"

http://www.news.ucf.edu/FY2002-03/030202.html

This item tells of physicist Ride keeping a scheduled appearance at a University of Central Florida science fair on February 2, 2003, the day after the Columbia space shuttle tragedy. It notes her giving the keynote speech to which she added comments about the space program after the Columbia shuttle tragedy (i.e., that "the torch" of the Columbia astronauts would be taken up and carried).

Freeman Dyson 1993—1990s Laureates—Enrico Fermi Award

http://www.sc.doe.gov/fermi/html/Laureates/1990s/freemanj.htm

Freeman Dyson Page

http://www.a-ten.com/alz/dyson.htm (scroll to Dyson links).

Find links to *Dyson's Brain* (1998 *Wired* Magazine Interview), *Omni* Magazine Interview (1978), "Time Without End: Physics and Biology in an Open Universe" (of 1978 conferences reproduced in the 1979 *Reviews of Modern Physics* and online). See also "An Evening with Freeman Dyson" by Greg Beatty at http://www.strangehorizons.com/2001/20011231/freeman_dyson.shtml, and "Dyson Sphere FAQs" at http://www.d.kth.se/!nv91-asa/dysonFAQ.html.

"Gaia Hypothesis Proposed by James Lovelock in Collaboration With Lynn Margolis"

http://www.magna.com.au/~prfbrown/gaia.html

This online document has detailed information on the concept known as the Gaia Theory or Gaia Hypothesis which refers to scientists' belief in a living earth. Chapters online include the 1979 view of James Lovelock (a British atmospheric scientist), the view of his contemporary Lynn Margolis (an American microbiologist), historical background that includes the 1790 view of James Hutton (a geologist who is thought of as the "father of the Gaia theory"), the view of Gregory Bateson (an early twentieth-century naturalist and anthropologist), and late twentieth-century views. On the Lovelock page note the Lovelock quotation cited from Elizabeth Sahtouris' *Earth Dance: Living Systems in Evolution*. (See also "The Evolving Gaia Theory" Web document cited above.)

Great Debates in Astronomy

http://antwrp.gsfc.nasa.gov/diamond_jubilee/debate.html

See the link to the famous 1920 "The Scale of the Universe" debate between Heber Curtis and Harlow Shapely. Note also the links to 1990s debates on "major quests in astronomy and astrophysics" as the new millennium approached. All debates were first presented in the Baird Auditorium at the Smithsonian Institution's Museum of Natural History. (See also cited on page 316 a Web site featuring "Woman Puts Great Astronomy Debate to Rest.")

Isaac Newton—Excerpts from *Mathematical Principles of Natural Philosophy*

http://www.fordham.edu/halsall/mod/newton-princ.html

Excerpts from Newton's writings, translated into English, of his philosophical rules of reasoning with relation to the natural world.

Isaac Newton—Excerpts from *Scholium* (Translated into English)

http://www.spirasolaris.ca/scholium1c.html

These excerpts from the end of Newton's *Mathematical Principles of Natural Philosophy* provide the scientist's discussion of the actions of the solar system's natural objects and possibly suggestions of the intelligent design theory of creation and scientific activities. See also other translated excerpts from the *Scholium* on space, time, motion, and rest, with quoted comments from the works of philosophical thinker Immanuel Kant, at http://www.philosopy.ucdavis.edu/kant/NEWTON.HTM.

Isaac Newton—Laws of Motion

http://ffden-2.phys.uaf.edu/211_fall2002.veb.dir/anca_bertus/Newton's Laws.htm

At this site provided by the Physics Department in the University of Alaska at Fairbanks, see Newton's three laws of motion succinctly stated. See also links to data and references from Newton's works on his Law of Gravitation, his book: *Principia*, and his life.

Isaac Newton—*Opticks* (1704)—Excerpts from "Query Thirty-One"

http://webserver.lemoyne.edu/faculty/giunta/newton.html

The Selected Classic Papers from the History of Chemistry Web site provides these excerpts, translated into English, from this document by Newton in which he discusses a scientific method of analysis now identified as the induction method. See also his discussion of the theory of atomic particles.

Isaac Newton—Top Biography

http://top-biography.com/0016-Isaac Newton/index1.htm

Click his words link, then links to information on his life, achievements, chronology, works, quotations in English, comments by other people of note, and features such as Newton as a wonder child of science and as a philosophical scientist.

Margaret Mead: Human Nature and the Power of Culture

http://www.loc.gov/exhibits/mead/field-samoa.html

This area of the Library of Congress Web site provides information on, and excerpts from, letters about the American anthropologist Margaret Mead's in the field study of Native people in Samoa, especially with reference to the study of nature versus nurture (i.e., biological aspects versus societal or cultural aspects), particularly as a reason for rebellious adolescent behavior. Data and comments by and about the Australian anthropologist Derek Freeman's studies with reference to his questioning Mead's conclusions are also presented.

"On American Women and Nature"—Notes from Vera Norwood's *Made from This Earth: American Women and Nature* (1993)

http://www.vcu.edu/engweb/eng384/norwood.htm

See also the related Web site on Environmental History above.

"Rachel Carson and the Awakening of Environmental Consciousness"

http://www.nhc.rtp.nc.us:8080/tserve/nattrans/ntwilderness/essay/carson.htm

A six-page article by Linda Lear of George Washington University, a biographer of the naturalist and writer, online at the National Humanities Center Web site.

Rachel Carson, Biologist, Ecologist—Life and Legacies—Resources, Links and Legacies

http://www.rachelcarson.org (click links)

At this Web site that provides information about Carson and her work, note, on the Resources page, links under Online Commentary (e.g., "A Scientist Alerts the Public to the Dangers of Pesticides" at the Online Ethics Center of Case Western University), Current Interest Features, and Printed Sources (e.g., reviews of her books). On the Links and Legacies page, note links to sites featuring "people of the millennium," including Carson (e.g., *Time Magazine*'s Most Influential People of the Century, the National Women's Hall of Fame), and organizations that carry on movements that were of interest to her or provide information on subjects that interested her (e.g., Society for Environmental Journalists and American Society for Literature and the Environment).

Scientists at the National Women's Hall of Fame, Seneca Falls, New York

http://www.greatwomen.org/women.php

Do a search in the search box using the word: scientists.

"U.S. Tries to Move on from Space Tragedy"

http://www.twincities.com/mld/twincities/5090798.htm

This February 2, 2003 news item issued by the Associated Press features quotations by physicist astronaut Sally Ride (the first American woman in space) and Jack Lousma (a former Columbia space shuttle commander) on the need to go on with the space program to honor the memories and goals of the lost Columbia shuttle astronauts.

Woman Puts Great Astronomy Debate to Rest

http://www.space.com/news/milan_debate_000331.html

This site provides information on an insight that Henrietta Leavitt of the Harvard College Observatory had while cataloging stars just before and at the beginning of the twentieth century. This insight led to a "yardstick" now identified with her: a "yardstick" for measuring "cosmic distances." She thereby solved one of the great debates of the early twentieth century: a debate over an astronomical puzzle on what became known as spiral nebulae. Her insight also inspired Harlow Shapely as he undertook his "Scale of the Universe" debate with Heber Curtis in 1920 (found at the "Great Debates in Astronomy" Web site cited above).

Index

The author has used italics to highlight items throughout the text on which particular emphasis has been placed.

Mysteries, Scientific (*continued*)
113; logical explanations considered for, 199, 200; *Loch Ness*, 106; mathematical connections with, 105, 106, 107; national monuments and, 106; *Nazca Lines*, 106; new headlines and, 105, 200; of the mind, 181; people's experiences of, 125, 126, 185; real life *Doctor Doolittle* (animal communicator), 107; religious viewpoints of, 50, 106; research and, 199, 200; scientists and, 107, 112; skepticism and, 199, 200; *Stonehenge*, 106; *Vortices*, 106

Naming Birds, 161, 162
Naming Chemical Elements: 221, 223; after discoverers, 223; American Chemical Society and, 221, 225; Curie, Marie and Pierre and, 81; *Exploring Chemical Elements and Compounds* (Heiserman) and, 225; International Union of Pure and Applied Chemistry (IUPAC) and, 221, 224, 225; *IUPAC Handbook* and, 223; naming new elements and, 223, 224; Seaborg, Glenn and, 223
Naming Dinosaurs: 31, 32, 33, 168
Naming Plants, 45; cultivated, rules for, 131, 132; *Naming Plants—Classification of the Hierarchy of Nature*, 131, 132; science based rules for, 131, 132
Nanotechnology, 85–86; ants and, 85; Feynman, Richard and, 85, 86; history of, 86; in the news, 85, 86; projected applications of, 85, 86; scientists' information on, 85, 86; size and, 85; *Star Trek* and, 86; suggested uses of, 85
NASA: Ames Research Center, 206; Goddard Space Flight Center, 88, 90, 91, 145; *Human Exploration and Development of Space Enterprise* (HEDS), 145; *Human Space Flight News*, 188; Jet Propulsion Laboratory, 71; Johnson Space Center, 87, 136, 144, 146, 188, 239; Kennedy Space Center, 144, 145; *Life Sciences Data Archive*, 87–89, 188; Office of Earth Sciences, Johnson Space Center, 239; *Small Shuttle Payload Project*, 88; *Shuttle Student Involvement Program*, 88; Space Science Data Center, 136; Space Science Data Operations Office, 127; *Student Involvement Program*, 71, 88–89; *Technology For All Americans Project* (NASA sponsored), 190. (*See also* National Aeronautics and Space Administration)
NASA Life Sciences Data Archive, 4, 87–89, 188
[*NASA's First Science Officer*] *Writes Home About Life in Space* (Whitson), 4–5, 240
National Aeronautics and Space Administration: *Apollo* moon missions, 97; biospheric studies, 144, 145, 146; education program, 189; educator astronauts, 187, 188, 189, 190; Expedition of Lewis and Clark and, 28, 29; futuristic perspective on space exploration, 145; *Life Sciences Data Archive*, 87–89; nanotechnology, 86; physicist of, on *Star Trek* science, 127, 128; press release, 187; Sagan, Carl and, 148; science officers on ISS, 4–5, 241; space colony student design contest, 145; spin-offs from space exploration, 205, 206. (*See also* NASA)
National Hurricane Center of the National Weather Service: *Saffir-Simpson Hurricane Damage Potential Scale* and, 98, 100
National Mental Health Awareness Campaign, 184; Tipper Gore and, 184
National Museum of Science and Technology (Milan, Italy): da Vinci papers and, 12
National Park Service, U.S.: archeology and, 153, 154; Expedition of Lewis and Clark and, 28; nature and science and, 151; Thomas Edison Online and, 159

National Parks: archeology in, 153, 154, 215; as fossil sites, 170; ethnography in, 154; geology in, 170; Gombe National Park, Tanzania, Africa, 193; nature and science in 151; unusual scientific aspects or phenomena in, 106. (*See also* National Park Service, U.S.)
National Science Education Standards, 270, 272, 273, 274; astronomy in planetariums and, 141, 143; earth sciences and, 143; space program and, 189
National Women's Health Information Center (NWHIC), 43, 207, 208; Web site with articles of interest to women and girls, 207, 208; *Young Women's Health Summit* and, 208
Nations and Science: Africa, 170, 193, 213, 214; Australia, 148, 197, 233; Britain, 212; Canada, 123, 132, 226, 227; China: paleontology, 116; Copernicus and, 15; Curie, Marie and, 51, 54; diet and nutrition, 123; Egypt: paleontology, 116; flora, 226, 227; Germany, 136, 232; issues in science in twenty first century and, 242; Japan: botany, 131; Leakey, Meave and, 213; Linne, Carl Von and, 20, 21; *Nobel Prize* speakers and, 51–53, 84, 93; Olympics and, 229, 230, 231; Poland, 15, 51, 54; photography from outer space and, 239; scientists of Canada, 255; scientists of Norway, 291; South American, 170; sports and, 230; Sweden, 20, 21, 51–52, 84, 93; Switzerland, 136; terms or special words for official documents from, 292; Ukraine, 72; warning in press release from Canadian Botanical Conservation Network, 132. (*See also* United States)
Natural History: Expedition of Lewis and Clark and, 27–30; *Natural History* (Pliny), 10; religious viewpoints and, 49–50; the *Bible* and, 49–50
Natural Phenomena: religious viewpoints of, 49; unusual, 105, 106, 107, 125
Natural Selection, Theories of, 38–40
Naturalists: Attenborough, David, 26; Audubon, John James, 24, 25; Bartram, William, 24, 25; Burroughs, John, 24, 26; Carson, Rachel, 300, 315, 316; Custis, Peter, as naturalist of Expedition of Lewis and Clark, 30; helpful to Lewis and Clark, 30; instructors of Meriwether Lewis, 30; Miller, Olive Thorne, 24, 26; Muir, John, as eyewitness to earthquakes, 110; Peterson, Roger Tory, 24, 26, 300; women as, 24, 25, 26, 300, 313, 315; Wright, Mabel Osgood, 24, 25
Nature, Study of: women and, 313, 315, 316. (*See also* Naturalists)
Neuroscience: consciousness and, 166, 167; Crick, Francis and, 166, 167; emotions and, 180; explanations of, by scientists, for children, 182; future experiments and, 166; human brain activity and, 167; Koch, Cristof and, 166, 167; music and, 133, 134, 135; *What is Neuroscience for Kids?* (Chudler), 182
Neuroscientists: on human brain activity, 167; what they acknowledge, 166; what they do not acknowledge, 166; what those starting in profession are encouraged to investigate and will find gratifying, 166
Newspapers and Newsletters, General and General Special, 40, 60, 88, 90, 98, 100, 129, 133, 148, 154, 188, 197, 240, 241, 242; *Amateur Radio Transmitting Society Newsletter*, 241; *Bird's Eye View, A* (a newsletter for young people), 163; *Young Birders News*, 163. (*See also* Magazines, General and General Special)
Newspapers and Newsletters, Scientific, 79, 109, 116, 118,

134; noetic, 185, 186; of astronomical objects' impact on earth, 204, 205, 206; of interest to average people, 1, 3, 4, 5; of interest to young people, 1, 3, 4, 6; of, on, and from, moon, 136, 137; of the future (*see* Futurism); on learning about, via documents available online, 1, 2, 3, 4, 5, 6; people and, 113, 205; photography and, 74, 75, 76, 238, 239, 313; practical aspects of, 36–37; problem solving in, 113, 166; progress in, 22, 23, 113; similes as aids to expressing experiences in, 66, 69, 96; skepticism in, 113, 114, 147, 200, 243; society and, 22, 60, 73, 74, 75, 92, 94, 114, 193, 201, 202, 203, 204, 236, 242, 243; space exploration and, 87–91, 136, 137, 144, 145, 146, 205; sports and, 102–104, 228, 229, 230, 231, 232; study of, compared to child's learning, 222; unusual aspects of, 105, 106, 107

Science, Alternative, 199, 200. (*See also* Mysteries, Scientific)

Science, Applied, 5

Science, Controversies in, 5, 343. (*See also* Debates, Scientific; Mysteries, Scientific; Science, Alternative; Science: Skepticism in; Theories, Scientific)

Science Fairs: creating projects for, 300; Olympics of, 297; photography and, 75; questions and answers about, 304

Science Frontiers Digest Online, 105

Science in the New Millennium (Hawking), 5, 127, 128, 138, 201, 202, 203, 242

Science, Modern: as precursor to sciences of the future, 85–86, 127, 128, 138, 139, 201, 202, 203; compared with sciences of the past, 53, 54, 73, 74, 75, 76, 201, 202, 203; genetics as, 234, 235, 236, 237; high school students and, 243; in twenty first century, 5, 242, 243; influential and seminal texts of, 93; issues in, as main concerns of twenty first century, 242; *Life Sciences in the Twentieth Century* (Allen), 84; major unsolved problem in, 166; scientists challenging assumptions in, 243; *Star Trek* and, 127, 128, 138, 139, 201, 202; stimulated by the *Bible*, 49; study of human consciousness as, 166, 167; thoughts about God and, 234

Science of Archaeology, The (Society for American Archaeology, and others), 153–154, 175; 213

Science of Emotion, The (Gore), 180–181

Science of STAR TREK, The (Batchelor), 127, 128, 138, 202

Science of the Future (*see* Futurism; Science, Modern)

Science, Pure, 5

Scientific Anomalies, 4, 105

Scientific Creationism, 49, 50

Scientific Discoveries: 92, 93, 95, 96, 97. (*See also* Scientific Research)

Scientific Discovery, 2, 6

Scientific Evidence: food safety and, 191; health and, 191; nutrition and, 191

Scientific Experience, 10–11, 113, 125, 126

Scientific Experiments, 10–11, 51, 52, 87–88, 89, 90, 91, 95, 96, 97, 125

Scientific Frontiers Digest Online: 4, 105

Scientific Instruments and Items: electron microscopes, 85; fax machines, 260; flow charts, 47, 291; maps, 29, 234; microfilm, 85; terrariums, 44, 45, 46. (*See also Apgar Score; Apgar Score Chart; Food Guide Pyramids; International Code of Botanical Nomenclature;* Inventors and Inventing; *Periodic Table of Chemical Elements; Richter Earthquake Damage Intensity Scale; Saffir-Simpson Hurricane Damage Potential Scale; Star Spectral Classification Chart*)

Scientific Knowledge, 134; defined, 113

Scientific Laws (*see* Laws, Scientific)

Scientific Method: introduction to, 271 quiz on, 274; Sherlock Holmes and, 274

Scientific Profiles of: animals, 28, 193, 231; birds, 24–26; fossil finder Mary Anning, 31, 35; inventor, 158; Olympic mascot animals, 229, 231

Scientific Research, 51–52, 53–55, 63–65, 75, 81–82, 83, 84, 87–91, 92, 93, 95, 213, 234, 235, 236, 237; focus of, 213; hope for future of, 213; noetic sciences and, 186; on Crop Circles, 125, 126; on emotions, 181; on food safety, 191; on health, 191; on nutrition, 191. (*See also* Scientific Discoveries)

Scientific Revolution: sparked by biologist Rosalind Franklin, 83. (*See also Copernican Revolution*)

Scientific Theory (*see* Theories, Scientific)

Scientific Thinking, 10–11, 14–16, 17–18, 22–23, 36–37, 47, 51–52, 53–55, 60–62, 63, 73, 74, 75, 77–78, 81–82, 83, 84, 111, 112, 113, 114, 116, 117, 147, 148, 149, 166, 167, 174, 175, 199, 200, 234, 235, 236, 237, 242, 243, 291, 292, 293; authors and, 10; average people and, 10, 113, 147; beginnings of, 10–11, 14–16, 17–18, 22–23; invention process and, 47, 158; music and, 133, 134, 135; neuroscience and, 166, 167; paleontology and, 175, 176; religious viewpoints and, 234; scientific community and, 10, 14, 17, 60, 113, 67, 199, 200, 234, 242, 243; scientific mysteries and, 125, 126, 199, 200, 243; skepticism and, 147, 148, 199, 200; unusual phenomena and, 125, 126, 199, 200, 243; young people and, 22, 70, 77, 78, 79, 113, 133, 166. (*See also* Critical Thinking)

Scientists and Scientific Thinkers, 113, 114, 242; Alling, Abigail, 144; Archimedes, 257, 274; Augustine, Margret, 144; Bacon, Francis, 3, 5, 17, 18; Bacon, Roger, 3, 5, 10, 11; Billy, Thomas J., 192; Braun, Werner Von, 40; Brown, Julian, 243; Casimir, Hendrick, 201, 202; Chudler, Eric H., 182; Coleman, S., 112; connecting people and science, 7, 8, 36, 37, 63, 147, 148, 149; Curtis, Heber, 314, 316; DeLuccia, F., 112; Dempster, William, 144; ethnic heritage and, 15, 54; ethical standards and, 7, 8, 9, 60, 94, 236; Euclid, 60; Fossi, Dian, 214; Franklin, Benjamin, 313; Galileo,15, 235, 243; Gol'fand, Yuri, 201; Gutenberg, Beno, 108; Hoyle, Fred, 40; Hume, David, 3, 5, 22, 23; Hutton, James, 314; in times of peace and war, 5, 73, 92, 94; Kanamori, Hiroo, 108; Lakatos, Imre, 134; Leibnitz, Gottfried Wilhelm Von, 73; Likhtman, E., 201; Lovelock, James, 314; Lucretius, 274; Margolis, Lynn, 314; Moore, Gordon, 201, 202; Nelson, Mark, 144; Newton, Isaac, 23, 60, 61, 71, 76, 231, 240, 243, 255, 315; on answer to hypothetical question on important science concerns in twenty first century, 242; philosophers and, 10, 11, 14, 15, 16, 22, 23, 40, 166; Paley, William, 40; Pliny, 10; Ptolemy, 10; quotations by, about vegetarianism, 177, 178, 179; religion and, 7, 8, 11, 49, 234; responsibilities of, 63, 92, 94; Rogers, T.H. (chief scientist, Space Transportation Association), 310; Shapely, Harlow, 315, 316; society and, 63, 92, 94, 147, 148, 149, 201, 202, 203, 236, 242, 243; study of emotions and, 181; various views of the science of food safety, health, and nutrition, 191; Vernadsky, Vladimir, 144; Volta, Alessandro, 257;